Translational Criminology in Policing

With contributions from international policing experts, this book is the first of its kind to bring together a broad range of scholarship on translational criminology and policing. Translational criminology aims to understand the obstacles and facilitators to implementing research by decisionmakers to improve effectiveness, fairness, and efficiency in the criminal justice system. Although the emergence of the translation of knowledge from research to policy and practice has gained momentum in policing in recent years, it is imperative to understand the specific mechanisms required to create collaborative structures to produce and disseminate information. This progressive and cutting-edge collection of articles addresses the growing interest in creating and advancing evidence-based policing through translational mechanisms. It describes a varied, dynamic, and iterative decision-making process in which researchers and practitioners work simultaneously to generate and implement evidence-based research. Not only does this book incorporate a process for translating criminological information, it offers varying perspectives on researcher-practitioner partnerships around the world.

Translational Criminology in Policing provides practical principles to help research, practitioner, and policymaker audiences facilitate evidence translation and research-practitioner partnerships. It is essential reading for policing scholars and policymakers, and may serve as a reference and textbook for courses and further research in translational criminology in policing.

Muneeba Azam is a doctoral student in the Department of Criminology, Law and Society at George Mason University.

Jordan Kenyon (née Nichols) is a senior lead scientist at Booz Allen Hamilton. She received her Ph.D. in Criminology from George Mason University in 2021.

Kiseong Kuen is a doctoral student in the Department of Criminology, Law and Society at George Mason University and a graduate research assistant for the Center for Evidence-Based Crime Policy.

Yi-Fang Lu is a doctoral student and a graduate research assistant in the Department of Criminology, Law and Society at George Mason University.

Kevin Petersen is a doctoral student in the Department of Criminology, Law and Society at George Mason University and a graduate research assistant for the Center for Evidence-Based Crime Policy.

Sean Wire is a doctoral student in the Department of Criminology, Law and Society at George Mason University and a graduate research assistant for the Center for Evidence-Based Crime Policy.

Xiaoyun Wu is a senior research associate at the National Police Foundation. She received her Ph.D. in Criminology from George Mason University in 2019.

Taryn Zastrow is a doctoral student in the Department of Criminology, Law and Society at George Mason University and a graduate research assistant for the Center for Evidence-Based Crime Policy.

David Weisburd is Distinguished Professor at George Mason University and Executive Director of the Center for Evidence-Based Crime Policy, and Walter E. Meyer Professor of Law and Criminal Justice at the Hebrew University Faculty of Law in Jerusalem. He has received many awards for his contributions to criminology and crime prevention including the Stockholm Prize in Criminology (2010), the Sutherland and Vollmer Awards from the American Society of Criminology, and the Israel Prize. Professor Weisburd is the faculty mentor for the Police Research Group.

Advances in Police Theory and Practice Series
Series Editor: Dilip K. Das

Cold Cases: Evaluation Models with Follow-Up Strategies for Investigators, Second Edition
James M. Adcock and Sarah L. Stein

Crime Linkage: Theory, Research, and Practice
Jessica Woodhams and Craig Bennell

Police Investigative Interviews and Interpreting: Context, Challenges, and Strategies
Sedat Mulayim, Miranda Lai, and Caroline Norma

Policing White-Collar Crime: Characteristics of White-Collar Criminals
Petter Gottschalk

Honor-Based Violence: Policing and Prevention
Karl Anton Roberts, Gerry Campbell, and Glen Lloyd

Policing and the Mentally Ill: International Perspectives
Duncan Chappell

Security Governance, Policing, and Local Capacity
Jan Froestad and Clifford Shearing

Police Performance Appraisals: A Comparative Perspective
Serdar Kenan Gul and Paul O'Connell

Policing in France
Jacques de Maillard and Wesley G. Skogan

Women in Policing around the World: Doing Gender and Policing in a Gendered Organization
Venessa Garcia

Police Behavior, Hiring, and Crime Fighting: An International View
Edited by John A. Eterno, Ben Stickle, Diana Peterson, and Dilip K. Das

Translational Criminology in Policing
Edited by The George Mason Police Research Group with David Weisburd

Translational Criminology in Policing

*Edited by The George Mason Police Research Group
with David Weisburd*

Routledge
Taylor & Francis Group

NEW YORK AND LONDON

Cover image: © Getty Images

First published 2022
by Routledge
605 Third Avenue, New York, NY 10158

and by Routledge
4 Park Square, Milton Park, Abingdon, Oxon, OX14 4RN

Routledge is an imprint of the Taylor & Francis Group, an informa business

Library of Congress Cataloging-in-Publication Data
Names: Weisburd, David, editor. | George Mason University. Police Research Group, editor.
Title: Translational criminology in policing/edited by The George Mason Police Research Group with David Weisburd.
Description: New York, NY: Routledge, 2022. | Includes bibliographical references and index.
Identifiers: LCCN 2021057256 (print) | LCCN 2021057257 (ebook) | ISBN 9780367716325 (hardback) | ISBN 9780367713126 (paperback) | ISBN 9781003153009 (ebook)
Subjects: LCSH: Criminology–Research. | Law enforcement–Research.
Classification: LCC HV6024.5 .T73 2022 (print) | LCC HV6024.5 (ebook) | DDC 364.072–dc23/eng/20211208
LC record available at https://lccn.loc.gov/2021057256
LC ebook record available at https://lccn.loc.gov/2021057257

ISBN: 978-0-367-71632-5 (hbk)
ISBN: 978-0-367-71312-6 (pbk)
ISBN: 978-1-003-15300-9 (ebk)

DOI: 10.4324/9781003153009

Typeset in Bembo
by KnowledgeWorks Global Ltd.

Contents

Contributors

Note: This reflects affiliation at time of original published date.

Geoffrey Alpert, University of South Carolina and Griffith University

Sarah Bennett, University of Queensland

Katharine Boyd, University of Exeter

Chris Burbank, John Jay College of Criminal Justice

Michal Dayan, The Israel Police

Hannah Farrimond, University of Exeter

Dreolin Fleischer, University of Exeter

Phillip Atiba Goff, John Jay College of Criminal Justice

William Graham, Abertay University

John Andrew Hansen, Western Carolina University

Jordan M. Hyatt, Drexel University

Tal Jonathan-Zamir, The Hebrew University of Jerusalem

Erin Kerrison, University of California, Berkeley

Anne Kringen, Austin (TX) Police Department and University of New Haven

Iain A. Lang, University of Exeter

Mia-Maria Magnusson, Swedish Police

Peter Martin, University of Queensland

Lorraine Mazerolle, University of Queensland

Michael Newman, Queensland Police Service and University of Queensland

Mark Pearson, University of Exeter

Debbie Platz, Queensland Police Service and University of Queensland

Alexis Poole, Devon and Cornwall Police

Neil Ralph, Devon and Cornwall Police

Brian Rappert, University of Exeter

Jeff Rojek, Michigan State University

Claudia Gross Shader, City of Seattle Office of City Auditor

Rachel B. Santos, Radford University

Roberto G. Santos, Radford University

John A. Shjarback, Rowan University

Eve Stephens, Austin (TX) Police Department

Cody W. Telep, Arizona State University

Heather Toronjo, George Mason University

David Weisburd, The Hebrew University of Jerusalem and George Mason University

James Willis, George Mason University

Kath Wilkinson, University of Exeter

Maia Zisso, The Israel Police

Preface

In the previous century, you would be hard pressed to find criminologists who are concerned with the idea of translational criminology. Translating research evidence to practitioners was not a key question raised in journals or by scholars. At the same time, criminologists were not alone in failing to recognize the importance of translation. Indeed the evidence-based medicine movement more generally can be traced only as far back as 1981 (Thoma & Eaves, 2015). And the term evidence-based policing was not coined until Sherman's Police Foundation Ideas in Policing Lecture titled "Evidence-based Policing" in 1998 (Sherman, 1998). In turn, while Sherman noted the methods through which evidence is diffused in policing, the idea of a specific academic interest in translating research into practice was not raised until a decade later by the then Director of the National Institute of Justice, John Laub.

Laub, who was on leave from his position as a University Professor in the Department of Criminology and Criminal Justice at the University of Maryland, formally proposed the idea of translational criminology in 2011 in a National Institute of Justice publication (Laub, 2011). He wrote:

> The idea of translational criminology is simple, yet powerful: If we want to prevent, reduce and manage crime, we must be able to translate scientific discoveries into policy and practice.

This idea seems so obvious that one might wonder whether Laub had to coin the term at all. But it is worthwhile to remember that many important scientific ideas seem obvious once they are identified. Sigmund Freud, for example, introduced the idea that dreams represent the deep-seated emotional lives of his patients (Freud, 1913). Today that is an obvious observation, but when Freud introduced the idea in the 19th century, it was a radical one.

Translational criminology has since 2011 gained much traction in academia and in practice and policy. A simple Google search yields almost a million hits, suggesting the penetration of translational criminology into the popular vernacular. The Magazine, *Translational Criminology*, produced by the Center for Evidence-based Crime Policy at George Mason University, has become a key outlet for ideas about translation, and is distributed widely to the academic and practice communities. There is a Springer briefs series on Translational Criminology, edited by two leading scholars in this field, both from George Mason University, Cynthia Lum and

Christopher Koper. It is fair to say that translational criminology, like translational medicine, has become an established part of the world of evidence-based policy in criminology.

In this context, it is surprising that there has not been more attention paid to translational criminology in policing. Policing was one of the first areas of criminology where evidence-based science was identified as a key idea. Sherman's 1998 Ideas in Policing Lecture led the way not only for evidence-based science in policing, but more generally in crime and justice. Policing has been at the center of advances in evidence-based science in criminology, and there has been a series of volumes that are devoted to introducing, explaining, and critiquing evidence-based policing (Fielding et al., 2019; Knutsson & Tompson, 2017; Lum & Koper, 2017). But to date, there has not been an edited volume focused on translational criminology in policing.

The George Mason Department of Criminology, Law and Society's "Police Research Group" (PRG) recognized this gap in its yearly discussions of projects that the group could work on. It has been the tradition of the PRG to develop publications on policing topics, and three years ago, the group worked to put together a special issue of Police Practice and Research on translational criminology in policing (Wire et al., 2019). The special issue was very well received, and this led to the idea of expanding the research identified for the special issue into a full-scale edited volume.

The students worked together to identify authors, and to edit contributions, and worked directly with Routledge in advancing the volume to publication. My role in the PRG and the development of the volume was to provide mentorship and to give the students guidance in moving this work forward. It is truly an accolade that the students were able to develop and bring this project to fruition. I am very proud of their efforts and have gotten much pleasure in working with them and guiding them along the way.

We think that this volume adds important new ideas and research findings to the field of translational criminology in policing. We hope as well that it spurs on other scholars to advance translational criminology in policing, and that the work is useful in spurring on a new generation of research in this area.

David Weisburd
George Mason University, USA
& Hebrew University of Jerusalem

References

Fielding, N., Bullock, K., & Holdaway, S. (2019). *Critical Reflections on Evidence-Based Policing* (1st Edition). Routledge. https://doi.org/10.4324/9780429488153
Freud, S. (1913). *The Interpretation of Dreams* (A. A. Brill, Trans.; 3rd Edition). The Macmillan Company. https://doi.org/10.1037/10561-000
Knutsson, J., & Tompson, L. (2017). *Advances in Evidence-Based Policing* (1st Edition). Taylor & Francis. https://doi.org/10.4324/9781315518299
Laub, J. H. (2011). Strengthening NIJ: Mission, Science and Process. *NIJ Journal, 268,* 6.
Lum, C., & Koper, C. (2017). *Evidence-Based Policing: Translating Research into Practice.* Oxford University Press.
Sherman, L. W. (1998). *Evidence-Based Policing.* Police Foundation. https://www.ojp.gov/ncjrs/virtual-library/abstracts/evidence-based-policing
Thoma, A., & Eaves, F. F., III. (2015). A Brief History of Evidence-Based Medicine (EBM) and the Contributions of Dr David Sackett. *Aesthetic Surgery Journal, 35*(8), NP261–NP263. https://doi.org/10.1093/asj/sjv130
Wire, S., Scherer, A., Wu, X., Sloan, M., & Nichols, J. (2019). Remarks by Guest Editors. *Police Practice and Research, 20*(6), 535–536. https://doi.org/10.1080/15614263.2019.1657624

PART I

An Introduction to Translational Criminology in Policing

1

Translational Criminology in Policing

Jordan Kenyon, Sean Wire, Kevin Petersen, Kiseong Kuen, and Muneeba Azam

DEPARTMENT OF CRIMINOLOGY, LAW AND SOCIETY, GEORGE MASON UNIVERSITY, FAIRFAX, VA, USA

Introduction

Bridging the gap between research and practice represents a fundamental challenge and an opportunity. Research is a powerful instrument for increasing the effectiveness and efficiency of society's most important institutions, but it cannot stand alone. Without translation into policy and practice, research tells us the benefits we might expect from an intervention without conferring those benefits. In medicine, enacting empirical findings through responsive policies has been responsible for many of the cutting-edge advancements we enjoy today (Fontanarosa & DeAngelis, 2002). Leveraging research findings regarding prevention and treatment of illness and injury, evidence-based policies and practices take action. Protocols to prevent or treat injuries and illnesses are based on research, but do not represent research on their own. Rather, they require an additional step whereby empirical knowledge is processed through organizational and occupational contexts to develop reliable, replicable methods of delivering interventions research has found effective in addressing outcomes of interest.

For a variety of reasons, researchers' efforts to integrate empirical knowledge into policing practices continue to encounter resistance in the field (Lum & Koper, 2017; Weisburd & Neyroud, 2011). The standard model of policing values direct experience, the application of rules and procedures, and the production of "justice" (Sherman, 1984; Sherman, 1998). On their face, these values can appear to run counter to those advanced by proponents of evidence-based policing. Yet, evidence-based policing does not present itself as an alternative to standard policing values such as discretion or professional experience. Instead, it argues that research should "have a seat at the table" (Lum & Koper, 2017, p. 3) to inform policy and practice decisions when it is well-positioned to do so. Evidence-based policing does not propose that science replace experience or dictate practice, if for no other reason than its inability to attain the level of exhaustive knowledge that would be necessary to do so.

As the evidence-based movement in policing has gained momentum, police leaders' and organizations' receptivity to scientific research appears to have increased in tandem (Alpert et al., 2013; Rojek et al., 2012a; Sherman, 2013). However, acknowledging the value of scientific evidence in policing is only part of the equation. Receptivity to and awareness of research cannot engender evidence-based policing without effective processes and procedures to convert scientific insights into action. The National Research Council's (2014) conclusion that scientific

DOI: 10.4324/9781003153009-2

research exerted little impact on public policy, despite the significant funding stakeholders have allocated to do so, illustrates this difficulty. These observations signify the need to look beyond the empirical identification of "what works" in policing to focus on the process of research utilization itself. In other words, what mechanisms may prevent the use of research in practice? What can be done to help facilitate this exchange? What roles and responsibilities do researchers and academics play in this process? How can researchers and practitioners work together to coproduce knowledge regarding policing policy?

Translational criminology is concerned with precisely these questions. Coined by John Laub (2012) during his time as director of the National Institute of Justice (NIJ), *translational criminology* seeks to address the gap between research and practice by evaluating the "processes by which scientific evidence is converted to politics and by forming interactive relationships between policymakers and criminologists" (Laub & Frisch, 2016, p. 52). This process involves linking scientific theory and evidence with practice, to inform systematic solutions embedded in policy and other regulatory mandates. In doing so, translational criminology extends program evaluation's traditional focus on program implementation to formulate effective approaches to convert research into policy and, thereby, practice. Thus, building on the foundation of data-driven decision-making models such as evidence-based policymaking, diffusion of innovations, and policy analysis (see Lum & Koper, 2017), translational criminology specifically focuses on obstacles to and facilitators of evidence development, dissemination, and utilization.

This edited volume assembles a broad range of scholarship on translational criminology in policing. It is imperative to understand the specific mechanisms required to create collaborative structures to produce and disseminate information. This progressive collection of articles addresses the growing interest in nurturing evidence-based policing by bringing the full weight of translational mechanisms to bear on the pressing challenges the field of policing faces today. It describes a varied, dynamic, and iterative decision-making process, in which researchers and practitioners work simultaneously to generate and implement evidence-based research. In addition to outlining a process for translating criminological information, this book offers varying perspectives on researcher-practitioner partnerships through both a domestic and international lens. We first begin by identifying and describing the major components of translational criminology in policing with examples of successful strategies for each component. The chapters that follow provide in-depth examples of the translational process and researcher-practitioner partnerships from a variety of different perspectives.

Researcher-Practitioner Partnerships

Researcher-practitioner partnerships are at the core of translational criminology's premise: dynamic processes through which researchers and practitioners coproduce knowledge regarding the effects of criminal justice interventions to improve research utilization. Successful partnerships aim to identify potential research or practitioner partners and make the case for a mutually beneficial collaboration. These partnerships allow independent institutions to combine their resources, skills, and knowledge in a way that empowers police agencies to achieve better results through data-driven decision-making. In step with these organization-specific benefits, these partnerships provide researchers with access to police personnel and data, generating opportunities for researchers to pursue unique ideas that contribute to research agendas that are responsive to the field's needs.

Despite their potential benefits, researcher-practitioner partnerships are not yet widespread in policing. Alpert and colleagues (2013) found that less than one-third of the 871 police agencies that responded to their survey partnered with a researcher during the five years preceding data collection. Challenges related to resources, staffing, and trust impose barriers to successful partnerships (see Alpert et al., 2013; Pesta et al., 2019; Rojek et al., 2012b). Successful partnerships require significant effort and planning from both researchers and practitioners. Collaboration strategies must start by recognizing that each partner has unique motivations that must be considered in formulating productive and sustainable partnerships.

Research Partners

There are a variety of motivations for police agencies to work with research partners. Researchers typically enhance practitioners' teams by providing specialized knowledge, skills, and abilities that increase an agency's operational capacity (see Bureau of Justice Assistance, 2017; Nichols et al., 2019). Research partners also typically enhance teams by introducing unique perspectives that can improve studies' objectivity and credibility with external stakeholders (Bureau of Justice Assistance, 2017). When effectively institutionalized, research partnerships can improve an agency's ability to address public safety issues and strengthen relationships with the communities they serve. It is important to note here that the term "research partners" encompasses a variety of disciplines that can add value to police agencies. Police agencies can find valuable partnerships in a variety of fields, including criminology, sociology, public policy, organizational psychology, economics, urban planning, and more.

Police agencies do not have to begin their search for a research partner alone and should consider whether they have any existing relationships that can assist them on their journey. This may include personal relationships that agency personnel may have with individual researchers or research institutions, like universities or think tanks. Agencies may also consider whether they have access to industry networking channels that could expand the aperture of their search for a research partner. These could include professional association memberships (e.g., International Association of Chiefs of Police, Police Executive Research Forum), conference networks (e.g., the American Society of Criminology lists its members by state on its website), or industry networking tools (e.g., George Mason University's eConsortium for University Centers and Researchers for Partnership with Justice Practitioners; Justice Research and Statistics Association's network of state Statistical Analysis Center directors). Lastly, agencies may increase their chances of successfully creating research partnerships by attempting to increase buy-in within the agency itself and prepare staff to view themselves as field researchers and partners in the research that will follow.

Police agencies may also benefit from making clear determinations regarding who will take the leadership role in communication with research partners. That is, who will review the agency's existing data resources and research capacity? Who will communicate that capacity to potential research partners and be responsible for managing resulting collaborations? It is also important to take stock of the resources that the agency has and is willing to devote to research efforts, the skills that the agency possesses, and the gaps that researchers might be able to fill. Researchers also vary widely along key dimensions, including subject matter expertise and capacity for complex research projects. To increase the likelihood of identifying the best research partner, agencies may wish to examine more than one potential partner and work with key decision-makers within their agency to develop a list of questions that can be used to determine which researcher might be the best partner based on the agency's needs and expectations.

Practitioner Partners

While researcher-practitioner partnerships can be effectively initiated by either side, Rojek and colleagues' (2012b) study suggests that practitioners may expect researchers to take the lead on initiating partnerships. For example, when asked why they were not participating in a research partnership, the second most prevalent response was that the agency had not been approached by a research partner (27%). However, Weisburd and Neyroud (2011) argue that police practitioners need to take ownership of science for evidence-based policing to be fully integrated into policing. These partnerships can yield impressive returns on investment for those who proactively and intentionally initiate and nurture them. Active partnerships provide researchers with access to both agency personnel and data, infuse unique ideas that inspire research agendas responsive to the field's needs, and may confer opportunities to shape what and how data is collected within the agency.

Much like research partners, practitioner partners can be identified by examining agencies that are close in proximity to the research institution, or agencies that others from the research institution have collaborated with in the past. Additionally, researchers should consider the needs of potential agencies and try to increase buy-in for research that fits those needs. Defining and assigning leadership roles is equally important for coordinating with practitioner partners. Someone from the research team must be responsible for communicating the team's capabilities and interests to potential practitioner partners. Additionally, after a partnership is initiated, someone from the research team must be responsible for managing communication with the police agency to facilitate the flow of information to and from the partner agency. Research teams that have successfully engaged in prior partnerships may also benefit from providing examples of practitioner-oriented research products as examples of how findings can be delivered.

Focusing on cultivating relationships with champions at potential partner agencies can help to grow the demand for collaboration and set the stage for long-term capacity for evidence-based policymaking, but it is important to take the second step to establish institutional commitments. Missing this step introduces risk, as partnerships based on a personal relationship with a champion can fall apart if that champion leaves the agency. Setting an expectation of co-ownership over research is also critical to realizing the promise of translational criminology. Given the importance of conducting research with—and not on—police, consideration of the research team's capacity for co-locating with practitioners is vital. Shared workspaces can open informal communication channels and reinforce co-ownership over the research and its results throughout the partnership.

Planning for Successful Partnerships

The most successful partnerships are designed to help researchers and practitioners focus on coproducing work in a way that makes the most of each party's unique contributions and increases the others' capacity to implement lessons learned from their partner. Strategically planning for long-term partnership is critical to realizing the benefits of translational criminology, where the true value is in the co-owned research relationship and collaborative model, rather than any one particular endeavor. Translational criminology is more concerned with *how* research generates knowledge than the specific knowledge an individual study generates. When researchers focus on delivering specific evidence to practitioners, they miss opportunities to conduct context-informed studies that account for a policy or practice's history and the emotions that surround it. When practitioners focus on identifying a research partner with the methodological expertise to answer a specific question of interest (and only that question of interest), they miss opportunities to critically examine what is motivating their initial question and whether there are other ways to pursue it. A commitment and plan for co-ownership increases research's potential impact and affects each stage of the research lifecycle from operationalizing core constructs in context-informed ways to framing findings to resonate with practitioners and policymakers to reduce barriers to evidence implementation (Neyroud & Weisburd, 2014).

Successful partnerships carry the expectation that there will be a mutual understanding of each partners' goals, roles, responsibilities, research agenda priorities, timelines, and account-ability mechanisms. Discussing team goals openly and honestly is a dynamic process that will evolve over time, requiring each partner to clearly communicate their limitations, needs, and interests. These conversations should also seek consensus regarding how results should be meas-ured, monitored, and shared. When in each research endeavor's lifecycle will the team begin disseminating preliminary results? Does the project involve sufficient capacity building to ensure sustainability?

While there are appreciable barriers to researcher-practitioner partnerships (Alpert et al., 2013; Rojek et al., 2012b; Rojek et al., 2015), successful partnerships can be achieved. In fact, some perceived impediments, such as lacking external funding, may not preclude partnerships. With sufficient planning and strategic scoping, researchers and practitioners can initiate part-nerships and projects without external investment. Telep, Michell, and Weisburd's (2014) study of hot spots policing in Sacramento, California provides a great example of an in-house exper-imental evaluation that did not require external funding. New researcher-practitioner part-nerships may focus on starting small with projects that do not require external funding and expanding over time.

It is also important to accept that not every project of interest to one party will be of max-imum utility for the other. Academics will not be able to publish the results of every project in outlets valued in academia. However, researchers should pursue formative evaluations and participatory action research projects that are of high value to their practitioner partners even if publication is less likely. The incentive structure of sustained relationships goes far beyond the count of publications. Similarly, agencies should explore options to compromise by extending timelines in some cases to enable the research partner to adopt more rigorous methodologies that are not only beneficial for enhancing confidence in study findings, but also more likely to lead to publication and other academic outcomes of interest.

Implementation and Dissemination

Even when research knowledge is successfully coproduced by researcher-practitioner partner-ships, challenges involving the use of that research both within and across policing agencies remain. These issues are pivotal to the concept of translational policing, as the focus of the translational process is on both the generation of empirical results and the conversion of those results into practice (Lum & Koper, 2017; Nichols et al., 2019). On one level, utilizing and implementing research findings within the police agency carries unique difficulties related to receptivity and deviation from the standard model of policing. On a second level, the traditional forms of publication and dissemination may be ineffective ways to put research results in the hand of police executives.

Improving Research Receptivity Within the Agency

One of the major challenges to the translation and successful distillation of lessons learned is police practitioners' awareness of and receptivity to research results. Lum and colleagues (2012) note that over three-fourths of officers report no exposure to academic journals or profes-sional publications. Furthermore, fewer than half of these officers read information provided by their agency and a small minority were exposed to other sources of information. The reliance on, and preference for, experience over research results is well documented, demonstrating the need for introducing evidence-based approaches during academy training and reinforcing those principles throughout officers' careers. Telep (2017) finds variability in receptivity across agencies, implicating organizational differences and responsibility beyond that of broader police culture. Recognizing gaps in police leaders' receptivity and understanding of the evidence base, Telep and Winegar (2015) find that leadership can play a role in integrating evidence-based policing as standard procedure. Further, the power of evidence-based practice lies in its implementation, not its recognition. Simplifying the presentation of evidence-based approaches as department standards can improve knowledge of effective policing practices even if their origin in academic literature remains unknown.

A second key component of utilizing research within the agency supporting its generation is effectively communicating research results to officers. Telep and colleagues (2014) note that even positive research results may not be understood in the agencies where those studies took place. This demands further efforts to communicate the research that is conducted within agencies to officers and stakeholders, as well as research being adopted into regular trainings and policies. At the same time, researchers need to recognize that the tendency to prefer experience over scientific findings is not simply the result of a failure to communicate scientific evidence, but also the result of a natural proclivity to rely on professional experience (Jonathan-Zamir, Weisburd, Dayan, & Zisso, 2019).

In addressing issues with research implementation and receptivity, partnerships should consider the communication of research results to frontline officers, as well as the changes to officer training or the academy that can reasonably be made to better integrate evidence-based policing as the standard operating procedure. Implementing evidence-based policies may also require cultural shifts within the organization to improve the receptivity of officers to evidence-based policing. However, as proposed by translational scholars (see Lum & Koper, 2017), the implementation of evidence-based policies should not completely replace professional experience. Indeed, the belief among frontline officers that their professional experience is being supplanted by research may lead to cultural resistance. Tomkins (2020) argues that a sole focus on "what works" can be perceived as a one-size-fits-all solution that ignores the experiences of particular agencies and officers, and science does not disagree. Researchers may start with the preliminary question of "what works," but their real question is "what works, for whom, under what circumstances?"

Receptivity may also be improved if the agency can identify a thought leader whose support may improve receptivity or awareness of evidence-based practices among their peers. This also signifies the importance of how research can be framed. For example, body-worn cameras framed as an officer accountability tool may generate less support than when framed as a tool to protect officers from frivolous complaints. The adoption of any research or knowledge can be contingent on how well it aligns with current interests. Understanding officers' needs and how an evidence-based policy aligns with those needs can improve receptivity.

Planning Successful Dissemination

Successful dissemination extends beyond "primary" methods of dissemination, such as academic journals, to "secondary" methods of dissemination (Rossi, 2004, p. 381; see also Lum & Koper, 2017), such as trade journals, briefings, professional conferences, or resources such as the Center for Evidence-Based Crime Policy's *Evidence-Based Policing Matrix* (Lum et al., 2011). Telep and Winegar's (2015) survey findings suggest that fewer than 10% of police executives review academic journals, while over 90% of police executives review practitioner-focused outlets such as *The Police Chief* and the *FBI Law Enforcement Bulletin*. Additionally, only about 22% of criminological research is available to people without journal subscriptions, about half as much as in other disciplines (Ashby, 2020). This makes outreach exceedingly important. Based on work done by Johns Hopkins University in communicating public health research (Fernández-Peña et al., 2008), a focus on creating a dissemination plan, communicating results to study participants or relevant populations, and disseminating findings directly to service providers is critically needed.

When creating a dissemination plan, it is important to consider budgets and timelines, as well as who the target audience should be and what avenues best cover that population. Successful dissemination can also be aided by professional connections with outside agencies, research institutions, and universities. The primary risk to successful research, especially as it relates to dissemination, is *not* taking these steps. A well-planned and executed research project is diminished if it does not make its way into the hands of service providers and practitioners to ensure its lessons learned are accessible. In determining target groups, it is important to consider how quantitative and qualitative results should be formatted for non-research audiences in a clear way that is inclusive of all research findings, including positive, negative, and null results. All findings may add value to the field and reduce grey literature, or non-positive findings which are often inaccessible.

The Chapters That Follow

Despite growing efforts to bridge the gap between research and practice in policing, dedicated attention toward the translation of research into practice continues to represent a critical need (Lum & Koper, 2017). There are still many questions to be answered around the translation of policing research into policy and practice: What factors prevent the use of scientific evidence in practice? What can be done to help facilitate the exchange of knowledge between researchers and practitioners? What roles and responsibilities do researchers and practitioners play in this process? In what specific ways can researchers and practitioners work together to coproduce scientific knowledge for policing policy?

In this chapter, we described two main components of effective translation of policing research into practice: building sound partnerships between practitioners and researchers and disseminating and implementing lessons learned from scientific study. A sound partnership benefits both researchers and police practitioners. Strong partnerships provide researchers with great opportunities to produce unique ideas that can contribute to research agendas and gather data that fit their research questions while fully understanding how the data are collected within the agency. At the same time, practitioner teams can be provided theoretically sound knowledge, unique perspectives, and advanced skills, which may help to enhance an agency's operational capacities (see Bureau of Justice Assistance, 2017; Nichols et al., 2019). Successful partnerships require effective dissemination of findings from research. As a large body of studies suggest (Lum et al., 2012; Lum & Koper, 2017), police officers are rarely exposed to research and rely on their own experience over scientific evidence. Thus, improving officers' receptivity to research is one of the important tasks for the successful translation of research into practice. As a way of improving their receptivity to research, efforts are needed in devising ways to nurture co-ownership of research and to effectively disseminate findings to practitioners.

Based on the importance of these two themes, this book focuses on how to build strong researcher-practitioner partnerships and how to disseminate lessons learned from research. This book also incorporates processes for translating policing research into practice. Moreover, it offers diverse perspectives on researcher-practitioner partnerships, both domestically and abroad. This book consists of three main parts. Part II covers procedures for translating evidence from research to practice. In Chapter 2, Santos and Santos introduce a four-phase research-to-practice translation process drawing on the knowledge to action (KTA) model prevalent in medicine and public health. In Chapter 3, Telep and Gross Shader introduce a new tool for translational criminology in policing, the 'What works in policing?' website that they developed. The case study indicates that a local government can play a major role in helping and supporting translational work. In Chapter 4, Willis and Toronjo summarize the results from the National Academies report on proactive policing (Weisburd & Majmundar, 2018) to provide substantive considerations that police practitioners (in particular, police leaders) should keep in mind when designing and implementing proactive policing for reducing crime and disorder. This chapter also outlines an agenda through which future research may examine more comprehensive evidence (e.g., collateral consequences of policing strategies) that would be helpful to police practitioners. In Chapter 5, Wilkinson and colleagues review the development and evaluation of their 'Making Sense of Evidence' training program, which encourages the use of research evidence in practice. They find encouraging evidence that the trainings led police practitioners to not only build knowledge and skills around evidence-based policing, but also advocate for cultural changes towards using scientific evidence from research to inform practice.

Part III addresses a diverse range of dynamics in researcher-practitioner partnerships in policing. In Chapter 6, Rojek and colleagues examine the correlates of researcher-practitioner partnership using a nationally representative sample of law enforcement agencies in the United States. The results of the study provide potential ways to promote the partnership between researchers and practitioners. In Chapter 7, Kerrison and colleagues present a case study of recruitment practices of the multimethod National Justice Database. It covers the quality of researcher-practitioner relationships, which has implications for resolving the often-contradictory aims of police practitioners and researchers. In Chapter 8, Julie Grieco provides valuable insight into the impacts of trainings on police officers' openness to evidence-based policing with unique data from two police academies across four cohorts. Grieco's findings highlight the importance of training organizations' role in promoting or undermining officers' openness to evidence-based policing. In Chapter 9, Kringen and Stephens' case study demonstrates implementation challenges by focusing on a mentoring program for female cadets in the Austin Police Department's training academy. This study provides valuable insight from both a research standpoint and a practitioner standpoint on challenges surrounding the implementation of the program. In Chapter 10, Mia-Maria Magnusson presents a process for mapping and analyzing illicit drug markets in Stockholm, Sweden developed by collaboration between researchers and practitioners. This chapter shows how a collaborative approach can produce a better understanding of the mechanisms or contexts of interest than could be developed with practice or scientific knowledge alone.

In Part IV, unique insights are provided from international perspectives on translational criminology in policing. In Chapter 11, Jonathan-Zamir and colleagues use survey data from high-ranking police officers in the Israeli police to examine high-ranked officers' proclivity to rely on professional experience rather than scientific evidence. This chapter has implications for understanding psychological drivers of resistance to evidence-based policing. In Chapter 12, William Graham describes a case study of policy transfer of a gang violence reduction program using a focused deterrence strategy in Cincinnati (USA) into Glasgow, Scotland. This study shows that policy transfer involves complex processes and can have both intended and unintended outcomes, which provides valuable lessons for future studies. In Chapter 13, Mazerolle and colleagues describe the experience of research translation in the Australian and New Zealand context drawing from the Queensland Community Engagement Trial (QCET). This study has implications in providing four key components (i.e., the importance of theory, the significance of partnerships, the need for supportive environments to evidence-based policing, and the role of collaborative dissemination) necessary for success in translational research in policing.

Taken together, these chapters provide important contributions to the primary areas of translational criminology in policing. This book is geared not only to researchers but also to police practitioners. We hope each chapter in this book provides practical principles to help researchers, practitioners, and policymakers facilitate evidence translation and researcher-practitioner partnerships.

References

Alpert, G., Rojek, J., & Hansen, J. A. (2013). *Building bridges between police researchers and practitioners: Agents of change in a complex world (Report for the National Institute of Justice)*. Washington, DC: U.S. Department of Justice.

Ashby, M. P. (2020). The open-access availability of criminological research to practitioners and policy makers. *Journal of Criminal Justice Education*, *32*(1), 1–21. https://doi.org/10.1080/10511253.2020.1838588

Bureau of Justice Assistance (2017). Identifying and Working with a Research Partner. Accessed at: https://psn.cj.msu.edu/tta/researchpartnerqa_version-2_june2017.pdf

Fernández-Peña, J. R., Moore, L., Goldstein, E., DeCarlo, P., Grinstead, O., Hunt, C., … & Wilson, H. (2008). Making sure research is used: Community-generated recommendations for disseminating research. *Progress in Community Health Partnerships: Research, Education, and Action*, *2*(2), 171–176. https://doi.org/10.1353/cpr.0.0013

Fontanarosa, P. B., & DeAngelis, C. D. (2002). Basic science and translational research in JAMA. *JAMA*, *287*(13), 1728. https://doi.org/10.1001/jama.287.13.1728

Jonathan-Zamir, T., Weisburd, D., Dayan, M., & Zisso, M. (2019). The proclivity to rely on professional experience and evidence-based policing: Findings from a survey of high-ranking officers in the Israel Police. *Criminal Justice and Behavior*, *46*(10), 1456–1474. https://doi.org/10.1177/0093854819842903

Laub, J. H. (2012). Translational Criminology. *Translational Criminology*, (3), 4–5.

Laub, J. H., & Frisch, N. E. (2016). Translational criminology: A new path forward. In T. G. Blomberg, J. M. Brancale, K. M. Beaver, & W. D. Bales (Eds.), *Advancing Criminology and Criminal Justice Policy* (pp. 78–88). London: Routledge.

Lum, C., & Koper, C. S. (2017). *Evidence-based policing: Translating research into practice*. Oxford, UK: Oxford University Press.

Lum, C., Koper, C. S., & Telep, C. W. (2011). The evidence-based policing matrix. *Journal of Experimental Criminology*, *7*(1), 3–26. https://doi.org/10.1007/s11292-010-9108-2

Lum, C., Telep, C. W., Koper, C. S., & Grieco, J. (2012). Receptivity to research in policing. *Justice Research and Policy*, *14*(1), 61–95.

National Research Council (2014). *The Growth of Incarceration in the United States: Exploring Causes and Consequences*. Washington, DC: The National Academies Press.

Neyroud, P., & Weisburd, D. (2014). Transforming the police through science: The challenge of ownership. *Policing: A Journal of Policy and Practice*, *8*(4), 287–293. https://doi.org/10.1093/police/pau048

Nichols, J., Wire, S., Scherer, A., Sloan, M., & Wu, X. (2019). Translational criminology and its importance in policing. *Police Practice and Research*, *20*(6), 537–551. https://doi.org/10.1080/15614263.2019.1657625

Pesta, G. B., Blomberg, T. G., Ramos, J., & Ranson, J. W. A. (2019). Translational criminology: Toward best practice. *American Journal of Criminal Justice*, *44*(3), 499–518. https://doi.org/10.1007/s12103-018-9467-1

Rojek, J., Alpert, G., & Smith, H. (2012a). The utilization of research by the police. *Police Practice and Research*, *13*, 329–341. https://doi.org/10.1080/15614263.2012.671599

Rojek, J., Smith, H. P., & Alpert, G. P. (2012b). The prevalence and characteristics of police practitioner-researcher partnerships. *Police Quarterly*, *15*(3), 241–261. https://doi.org/10.1177/1098611112440698

Rojek J., Martin P., & Alpert G. (2015). The literature and research on police–research partnerships in the USA. In J. Rojek, P. Martin, & G. Alpert, *Developing and Maintaining Police-Researcher Partnerships to Facilitate Research Use* (pp. 27–44). New York: Springer.

Sherman, L. W. (1984). Experiments in police discretion: Scientific boon or dangerous knowledge. *Law & Contemporary Problems*, *47*, 61.

Sherman, L. W. (1998). Evidence-based policing. *Ideas in American Policing Series*. Washington, DC: The Police Foundation.

Sherman, L. W. (2013). The rise of evidence-based policing: Targeting, testing, and tracking. *Crime and justice, 42*(1), 377–451.

Telep, C. W. (2017). Police officer receptivity to research and evidence-based policing: Examining variability within and across agencies. *Crime & Delinquency, 63*(8), 976–999. https://doi.org/10.1177/0011128716642253

Telep, C. W., & Winegar, S. (2015). Police executive receptivity to research: A survey of chiefs and sheriffs in Oregon. *Policing: A Journal of Policy and Practice, 10*(3), 241–249. https://doi.org/10.1093/police/pav043

Telep, C. W., Mitchell, R. J., & Weisburd, D. (2014). How much time should the police spend at crime hot spots? Answers from a police agency directed randomized field trial in Sacramento, California. *Justice Quarterly, 31*(5), 905–933. https://doi.org/10.1080/07418825.2012.710645

Tomkins, L. (2020). *Bridging the theory/practice gap in policing: 'What Matters' versus 'What Works' in evidence-based practice and organizational learning.* Accessed at: http://oro.open.ac.uk/73315/

Weisburd, D., & Majmundar, K. (Eds.) (2018). Proactive policing: Effects on crime and communities. Washington, DC: National Academies Press.

Weisburd, D., & Neyroud, P. (2011). Police science: Toward a new paradigm. In *New Perspectives in Policing* (pp. 1–24). National Institutes of Justice, U.S. Department of Justice. https://www.ncjrs.gov/pdffiles1/nij/228922.pdf

PART II

The Process for Translating Evidence

2

A Four-Phase Process for Translating Research into Police Practice

Roberto G. Santos and Rachel B. Santos

DEPARTMENT OF CRIMINAL JUSTICE, RADFORD UNIVERSITY, RADFORD, VA, USA

Introduction

The purpose of this chapter is to present a framework that extends the discussion of translational criminology and the dynamic process of translating research into practice. Our goal is to provide a dissection of the translation process into four phases to help outline a structured way of thinking about how to incorporate research into police practice. We focus on proactive crime reduction carried out by police; however, we believe this process will also be relevant to other aspects of policing and criminal justice.

Our ideas are founded in models of translation from medicine, the current translation activities occurring for proactive policing strategies, and our experience as practitioners, researchers, and 'translators' over the last 25 years. In the last 15 years, we have worked together, conducting experimental research as well as implementing and evaluating proactive crime reduction strategies in police agencies. Out of this work, we have created stratified policing, which is a structure of processes and procedures that standardizes crime analysis, problem solving, and accountability mechanisms for proactive crime reduction within a police organization. Stratified policing is not a crime reduction strategy itself, but its primary goal is to operationalize and sustain evidence-based crime reduction strategies within everyday operations of a police organization (Santos & Santos, 2015a).

We have done a lot of work in this area, so have thought a lot about how the translation process occurs both from the police practitioner and researcher perspectives. This chapter breaks down the translation process into four distinct phases and reflects our views of what is necessary to truly translate research into practice. What follows is a brief discussion of the challenge of translating research into practice and a description of a medical framework used as the basis of the process we outline. The remainder of the article details the four-phase translation process and ends with our conclusions.

The Challenge of Translating Research into Practice

As director of the National Institute of Justice (NIJ), Laub (2012) defined translational criminology as taking scientific knowledge and 'translating' it into policy and practice. He argued that translational criminology should be focused both on the creation of knowledge and its dissemination to influence policy and change operational practices. He tasked NIJ with several

DOI: 10.4324/9781003153009-4

directives, which included communicating research findings without academic jargon, making research accessible for practitioners and policy makers, and facilitating researcher-practitioner partnerships (Laub, 2012). Similarly, Lum and Koper (2017) define translational criminology as the 'theory and study of how the products of criminological and criminal justice research turn into outputs, tools, programs, interventions, and actions in criminal justice practice' (p. 266).

Criminologists and police practitioners have recognized that science has not often translated effectively into policy and practice, and more work must be done to that end (Bueermann, 2012; Laub, 2012; Lum & Koper, 2017; Rojek, Martin, & Alpert, 2015; Weisburd, 2011). The medical field recognizes the same challenge. Green and Seifert (2005) assert that even though there has been significant research identifying the factors of adoption, there is a gap in the research on how adoption actually occurs. They find that even when physicians understand the research related to their practice, there are often barriers to implementing the strategies into everyday diagnosis and treatment. These authors discuss how once the research shows that something works, physicians are left on their own to determine how and when to change their everyday practices based on the research evidence (i.e., 'just do it'). Interestingly, Green and Seifert (2005) go on to say that 'physicians are expected to accomplish these changes within an already overcrowded, demanding clinic schedule' (p. 542). This statement is eerily similar to what we have heard from police leaders about successfully implementing evidence-based crime reduction strategies.

Importantly, translational criminology involves understanding both how to translate one language (i.e., research results) into another (i.e., policies, procedures, processes, tools, etc.). However, it is also important to recognize that the goal of translation is not simply to ensure practitioners understand and consider research findings and evidence-based tools presented to them, but that the results of the research are institutionalized into everyday practice. In an attempt to overcome these challenges, we present a process that is the outgrowth of our own research and partnerships with police agencies as well as of our examination of translation activities in policing and models within the medical field.

Foundation in Implementation Science

As a foundation for the translation process we propose, we look to the medical field, in particular, the 'knowledge to action' (KTA) approach (Graham et al., 2006). In a recent review of the frameworks, models, and theories associated with research translation, Milat and Li (2017) identified 41 approaches within 98 articles within the medical and public health fields between 1990 and 2014. They conclude there is broad agreement that the translation process is dynamic and collaboration between researchers and practitioners is key. They also find the KTA model (Graham et al., 2006) to be one of the most frequently applied frameworks.

Under the auspices of 'implementation science,' which is the study of methods that promote the systematic adoption of clinical research findings into day-to-day practice (Manojlovich, Squires, Davies, & Graham, 2015), the KTA framework includes two interrelated but distinct cycles (Graham et al., 2006). The first, called the 'knowledge creation' cycle, is a process which includes knowledge inquiry, synthesis, and tool/product development. Results of knowledge inquiry funnels into the more specific synthesis of results and subsequently to products and tools provided to the field. Graham and his colleagues (2006) suggest an analogy for the knowledge creation cycle 'would be to think of the research being sifted through filters at each phase so that, in the end, only the most valid and useful knowledge is left' (p. 18).

Within the KTA framework, the knowledge creation cycle is linked to the 'action' cycle (i.e., application) through the identification of specific problems, assessment of barriers to application, and selection of knowledge relevant to the local context. The action cycle is the process in which selected knowledge and tools developed from the 'knowledge creation' cycle are tailored to the local environment, implemented, monitored, evaluated, and sustained (Graham et al., 2006). Importantly, according to Milat and Li (2017), the key implication of the KTA framework is it outlines both knowledge creation, its application and the importance of practitioners in each cycle.

For policing, there have been a large number of experimental and evaluation studies informed by police practice (Weisburd & Majimundar, 2017) that were accomplished by partnerships between researchers and police departments (Alpert, Rojek, & Hansen, 2013). In addition, there have been many meta-analyses conducted and a focus on communicating research findings in digestible and informative ways to police (Laub, 2012). Yet, it seems that most of the translation activities for police research fall within the knowledge creation cycle of KTA. Consequently, we believe there is a void in the development of application knowledge (i.e., action cycle of KTA) and how to implement and sustain evidence-based practices.

The Four-Phase Research-to-Practice Translation Process

Our goal here is to expand the current framework of translation in policing from inquiry, synthesis, and dissemination to include operationalization of evidence-based strategies into practice. To do so, we introduce the 'four-phase research-to-practice translation process' that breaks down the two cycles of the KTA model (Graham et al., 2006) into two phases each:

- Phase I: 'Does it Work?' Research and Evaluation
- Phase II: 'What Works?' Synthesis and Dissemination
- Phase III: 'How to Make it Work?' Implementation and Evaluation
- Phase IV: 'Make it Work!' Institutionalization and Sustainability

Phase I and II fall under the knowledge creation cycle of the KTA framework, and Phase III and IV fall under the action cycle or application of knowledge. All four phases are interconnected, build upon the previous phases, and overlap to some extent.

The rest of the chapter discusses each phase using police research and practice to provide context and illustrate the concepts. Each section includes the phase's purpose, the methods used to carry out the phase's activities, and its outcomes. Translation models in medicine put high importance on the participation of practitioners (Manojlovich et al., 2015), and in our framework, both researchers and practitioners play a role in each phase. Thus, we discuss the roles of each, the nature of the partnerships and collaboration necessary to accomplish the work, and major barriers to success for each phase.

Phase I: 'Does it Work?' Research and Evaluation

Phase I includes producing findings by conducting original and rigorous research studies. In the KTA framework, this phase is thought of as first-generation knowledge in which there are a large number of primary studies on similar topics (Graham et al., 2006). Similarly, in his discussion of evidence-based policing, Sherman (1998) stressed the importance of creating knowledge through both experimental research and evaluations of ongoing operations. He emphasized the research should be based in theory and examine different strategies and/or solutions that improve current practices. For example, opportunity theory hypothesizes and research has established that crime concentrates by place (Weisburd, 2015). Thus, the police research conducted in Phase I tests realistic strategies that police can implement to reduce crime at places – hot spots policing (Braga, Papachristos, & Hureau, 2014). Importantly, simply knowing crime concentrates by place does not show how police can actually prevent crime at place. The fundamental principle of Phase I is that innovative strategies are identified or created and then tested for effectiveness using the most rigorous methods.

Methods

The methods used in Phase I include academic research that serves two purposes. The first is to identify, describe, and understand ongoing police practices. These methods typically include national surveys of agencies, departmental surveys of personnel, and/or observational research. These studies identify common practices, challenges, and new trends in policing. For example, much of the research on Compstat and crime analysis has focused on their prevalence and nature of their implementation (Santos, 2014). Two such comprehensive studies include the Police Foundation's research on Compstat implementation (Weisburd, Mastrofski, McNally, Greenspan, & Willis, 2003) and the Police Executive Research Forum's (PERF) research on the implementation of crime analysis into patrol (Taylor & Boba, 2011). In both of these studies, a comprehensive research strategy was used in which a national survey was followed by qualitative assessment of a smaller number of agencies and several in-depth case studies with the goal of describing the state of police practice in these areas.

The second purpose of research in Phase I is to evaluate the impact and test the effectiveness of either current or newly developed strategies through rigorous evaluation methodology and experimental methods. Experiments test the effectiveness of isolated strategies in controlled conditions to achieve high internal validity (Weisburd, 2010). For example, many experiments have been conducted to test various types of police strategies implemented in crime hot spots, such as foot patrol (Ratcliffe, Taniguchi, Groff, & Wood, 2011), offender-based strategies (Groff et al., 2015; Santos, 2018a; Santos & Santos, 2016), and directed patrol (Santos & Santos, 2015b; Telep, Mitchell, & Weisburd, 2014).

Outcomes

Outcomes of Phase I are particularly salient for the academic side of the translation process. Results from national surveys help determine the state of policing to identify gaps in research and needs for new strategies. The research methods used, strategies tested, and limitations identified in each evaluation and experiment help to inform and improve future studies on similar concepts, since this is how science works. Each study's findings contribute to the body of knowledge, so the purpose of Phase I is to identify, evaluate, and test strategies in a variety of circumstances to establish empirical generalizations.

Because Phase I is focused on knowledge creation, police agencies generally do not directly benefit operationally from the research process or the results. Even in those police departments that actively seek research opportunities, the implementation often occurs in silos within an agency merely for the sake of the research (i.e., researchers work exclusively with a few hand-picked personnel). In addition, the strategy tested may not be sustainable beyond the study period, so once the study is over, police operations go back to normal.

Role of Researchers and the Police

Phase I involves direct collaboration between researchers and the police since the purpose is to understand ongoing practices or proactively test the effectiveness of practical and oftentimes new strategies. Police researchers require participation from police agencies and individual police practitioners to complete surveys, participate in focus groups and interviews, allow observation of practices, share data, and implement strategies as part of an experiment or evaluation.

Phase I research is not often initiated by police departments, which makes sense since they are not in the business of research but in the business of policing. That is not to say police departments do not solicit research studies and would pay for them with internal funds. Typically, however, when police agencies do seek out a research partner, it is often a requirement of grant funding (Griffith, 2014).

Consequently, researchers take the lead in Phase I, but their collaboration with police agencies and individual practitioners is absolutely necessary. Not only do researchers need a place to study, they also require police to provide them input about what is reasonable for research. It is important that the researcher articulates how a particular study is beneficial for research, the agency, and the overall field. There must also be activities that establish trust and understanding between police and researchers, so partnerships can develop and the translation process can begin. Examples include researchers presenting at practitioner conferences, developing informal relationships with agencies, and providing education and research opportunities to police agency employees.

Potential Barriers to Success

The first potential barrier, and perhaps the most challenging, is the process of researchers finding police leaders who see the importance of research and play an active part by allowing their agencies to participate in research studies. In the last two decades, more departments have opened their doors to researchers; however, researchers still argue that they tend to carry a significant load initiating and conducting these studies (Grieco, Vovak, & Lum, 2014).

Another potential barrier is that even when a police leader agrees that his/her agency will participate in a study, the agency's culture, capabilities, and participation by personnel may not be conducive to successful implementation. The need to combine rigorous research methodology with practical considerations can often cause conflict between researchers and the police. And while the research process is never perfect, there is potential for mismanagement by researchers who do not fully understand police culture and practice and for undermining by internal police personnel who may not agree with adjusting or changing police business for the sake of research.

Importantly, these barriers are most likely to arise when researchers seek to test strategies that are new to policing or new to the agency because they require a continued commitment of time and resources. They are less likely to arise when researchers seek to survey and interview personnel, observe routine practices of the agency, or test police strategies with minimal interruption, since there is a minimum commitment of time, allocation of resources, or need for systemic change.

Summary

At the beginning of the research-to-practice translation process, even though research tests new and innovative ideas, it is important that the strategies examined in Phase I are realistic in practice. Researchers should strongly consider what police resources and capabilities are required and whether a strategy is reasonable for the typical police department to sustain. As is emphasized in the KTA framework, a collaboration between 'knowledge producers-researchers' and 'knowledge implementers-users' is imperative (Graham et al., 2006, p. 18). Finally, the outcomes of Phase I are very important because they provide a wide range of knowledge, yet each study does not stand on its own and the information must be 'sifted.' Thus, Phase II must take place to synthesize findings and communicate those results to practitioners.

Phase II: 'What Works?' Synthesis and Dissemination

In the KTA framework, the knowledge creation cycle includes second-generation knowledge produced through systematic reviews and meta-analyses (Graham et al., 2006). Graham and his colleagues (2006) also include the production of third-generation knowledge in the knowledge creation cycle of KTA, which is the development of tools that present knowledge in 'clear, concise, and user-friendly formats and ideally provide explicit recommendations with the intent of influencing what stakeholders do ...' (p. 19).

Thus, Phase II includes a synthesis of findings from Phase I to establish 'what works' (Sherman et al., 1997) and the effective communication of the findings and tools to the police. Instead of relying on anecdotal evidence from one study, or on individuals' opinions, favorite programs, or political agendas, the evidence is collectively and critically examined to establish empirical generalizations. Phase II also includes removing research language and effectively disseminating the results to both police and researchers.

Methods

Phase II activities have been a significant focus of police researchers and government funding in the last two decades. The extensive report by Sherman and his colleagues (1997) was the first of many iterations of synthesis of police research on 'what works.' The most recent iteration was published in late 2017 by the National Academy of Sciences (Weisburd & Majimundar, 2017).

To start the synthesis process, police researchers have used the Campbell systematic review methodology (Campbell Collaboration, 2018) to evaluate research conducted about strategies in a particular topic area. The Campbell Collaboration's meta-analysis methodology sets criteria for selecting the highest quality studies and evaluating their results to make conclusions about effectiveness. The Campbell systematic reviews cover a range of disciplines, and in the area of crime and justice, there have been a number of systematic reviews of proactive policing strategies, including hot spots policing, focused deterrence, community policing, disorder policing, and problem-oriented policing (Campbell Collaboration, 2018).

With a broader purpose, researchers then collaborate with police leaders and experts to review the meta-analyses results and make recommendations for practice. The National Academy of Sciences report, entitled *Proactive Policing: Effects on Crime and Communities* (Weisburd & Majimundar, 2017), is the most recent result of this activity. The following describes its method (p. iv):

> Consensus Study Reports published by the National Academies of Sciences, Engineering, and Medicine document the evidence-based consensus on the study's statement of task by an authoring committee of experts. Reports typically include findings, conclusions, and recommendations based on information gathered by the committee and the committee's deliberations. Each report has been subjected to a rigorous and independent peer-review process and it represents the position of the National Academies on the statement of task.

The importance of this process lies in its foundation in theory, assessment of the research, and on establishing consensus among researchers and police experts.

Police practitioners also come together to identify and recommend 'best practices.' While informed by research, the recommendations made by practitioner groups about strategies are often based on experience and practice of police experts and their agencies. For example, organizations like PERF, the International Association of Chiefs of Police, the Major City Chiefs, and the Police Foundation often bring police leaders and experts together for focus groups and discussions to develop consensus and make recommendations to improve and/or implement particular strategies.

Outcomes

An important component of Phase II is the dissemination of the synthesis results. The findings from Phase I and of the meta-analyses from Phase II are primarily published in academic journals for which policy makers and practitioners typically do not have regular access. As Laub (2012) emphasized, to impact the field, research findings must be communicated effectively in non-research jargon as well as made accessible to practitioners and policy makers. There is a wide variety of dissemination media and central electronic repositories for this information that have been established over the last two decades. The following are three examples for evidence-based policing strategies:

- Campbell Plain Language Summaries: These are short one-to-two page briefs in a flyer format that are based on the larger report and are 'published as part of our [Campbell Collaboration's] commitment to helping people use and interpret research evidence' (Campbell Collaboration, 2018).
- Crimesolutions.gov: This is a website maintained by the Office of Justice Programs in the U.S. Department of Justice that includes easily understandable ratings about whether a strategy achieves its goals and profiles of programs and practices.
- Evidence-Based Policing Matrix Software: This is software that guides practitioners through the research evidence on proactive policing strategies so they can 'more easily access and understand the field of knowledge than by reading individual research articles or even systematic reviews' (Lum & Koper, 2017, p. 46).

Many federal agencies, academic, non-profit, and practitioner organizations have created publications and maintain websites that pare down the research results and remove jargon, including:

- *Research in Brief*, National Institute of Justice
- Problem and response guides, Center for Problem-Oriented Policing, Arizona State University
- *Ideas in American Policing* series, Police Foundation
- *The Police Chief* magazine, International Association of Chiefs of Police
- *Crime Analysts Research Digest*, International Association of Crime Analysts

Academics, police experts, and government officials also disseminate information about how to access these and other resources through a wealth of direct communication opportunities. Police membership organizations have direct contacts with their members through listservs and mailing lists. Presentations are made at membership conferences, in congressional briefings, and at state, city, and local government non-police conferences.

The Role of Researchers and Police

Researchers have an obvious and significant role in Phase II. They conduct the 'research on the research' that rigorously establishes what works. They collaborate with practitioners to make recommendations for the field. In addition, practitioners often lead their own efforts to establish best practices and serve an important role in helping to pare down the research and communicate it to other practitioners.

However, unlike Phase I, research in Phase II does not involve working directly with police departments to test interventions or engaging agencies and practitioners for national surveys. In Phase II, researchers and practitioners collaborate to synthesize knowledge, so there is more crosspollination than a direct partnership.

Potential Barriers to Success

To ensure synthesis and dissemination are successful, the information must be relevant to its customers (i.e., police and policy makers). It is important that findings from meta-analyses conducted by researchers are illustrated in the context of everyday police practice. Also, simply publishing in practitioner journals and posting on websites does not ensure the material is being read since people first have to know it is there. Thus, efforts must be made both to make the material accessible as well as engaging.

Summary

Together, Phases I and II represent the knowledge creation cycle of the KTA framework. They establish whether strategies work and communicate what works to researchers and the police. It is at this point where police are often told to take the information and 'just do it' as Green and Seifert (2005) assert happens in medicine. We argue even with effective communication, the 'what works' message is still fairly conceptual. For instance, based on theory and research, Lum and Koper's (2017) layout describes a number of 'plays' (i.e., strategies) for different crime reduction situations. One example, 'The Burglary Prevention Play,' includes the following (p. 186):

CONDITION: An increase in residential burglaries in an area; the occurrence of a burglary in a block or high rise.

1. Research indicates that once a home or apartment unit is burglarized, homes and units next door and/or very nearby have a heightened risk of burglary, particularly over the next 2 weeks.
2. After a burglary, warn neighbors immediately of their heightened risk and suggest methods to target harden their homes …
3. Work with place managers and residents of buildings to determine the underlying mechanism that may be contributing to burglaries …
4. Work with place managers and residents for longer-term solutions …
5. Have the agency's Crime Prevention through Environmental Design (CPTED) unit conduct an environmental analysis of the area to determine what opportunities are contributing to crime …
6. Research indicates burglaries often commit crimes within one mile of their own residence or activity space. Knowing, monitoring, and making contact with burglary probationers and parolees nearby may help prevent future crime.

This is an excellent example of translation that occurs in Phase II, as the recommended strategies are clearly informed by evidence created from Phase I that burglaries occur near one another in a short time and offenders commit crimes near where they live or frequent. However, the play does not provide guidance for operationalizing the strategies into the everyday police practice so it is systematic and sustained. Questions immediately come to mind for implementation:

• What constitutes an 'increase'?
• Who identifies the 'increase'?

- What is distributed to police for a response?
- How is implementation facilitated across different times of day, based on operational schedules, and/or among different units and divisions?
- Who makes sure this all happens and determines whether its working?

This is not a critique of the Burglary Play, but we use it to illustrate how more translation is necessary before evidence-based strategies and tools developed in Phase II are implemented into everyday practice. Consequently, Phases III and IV, which represent the 'action cycle' within the KTA framework, address this need.

Phase III: 'How to Make It Work?' Implementation and Evaluation

Police researchers can play a vital role in providing assistance to practitioners about 'how to make it work.' That is, recommending specific processes and practices for implementation without testing them is not enough to ensure successful translation. Graham et al. (2006) note the KTA action cycle is not only determining what knowledge is best applied in different environments and situations, but is also evaluating whether the implementation of knowledge makes a difference in practical processes and outcomes. Thus, Phase III includes the study of organizational implementation of evidence-based strategies as well as the synthesis and dissemination of those results to directly assist adoption. Now that we know which strategies are effective from Phases I and II, Phase III is the creation and testing of models, mechanisms, and structures to implement those strategies.

Methods

Police experts recognize that research results about crime reduction are not common knowledge among police practitioners, and they are not used as a regular part of police practice (Lum & Koper, 2017; Weisburd, 2011). Thus, to achieve translation for 'how to make it work,' researchers and the police must work together to implement evidence-based strategies, conduct research to test their effectiveness in routine practice, and understand how they are successfully implemented in the 'real world' and sustained.

We look to medicine again for guidance and what they call 'practice-based research,' which is the research of routine practice (Boba, 2010). Psychiatrists have recognized the need for research to be conducted in the therapeutic environment in addition to being gathered in an experimental setting where the real-world circumstances of therapy are not taken into account (Hellerstein, 2008; Marginson et al., 2000; McDonald & Viehbeck, 2007). More specifically, Marginson et al. (2000) argue that to complement random controlled trials, research based on good quality data collected from routine psychiatry practice may provide direction for the implementation of treatments as well. For policing, there are several methods that can accomplish a practice-based research approach.

First, police departments that have identified an effective strategy to implement can enlist researchers to conduct an evaluation of the process and impact of the strategy. This is important research because police agencies that are successfully implementing effective strategies do not always have the time, capabilities, or inclination to conduct sound evaluations and share the findings with the field.

Second, researchers can become involved with police departments that are seeking to implement innovative strategies. In this situation, the researcher actively assists in developing processes and mechanisms for implementation, provides technical assistance, and then conducts the evaluation. Since 2009, the Bureau of Justice Assistance has funded projects as part of their Strategies for Policing Innovation (SPI) program with the goal to provide:

> … financial and technical assistance to police departments to help them identify effective tactics for addressing specific crime problems in data-driven ways. Some key components of SPI include using various data sources when developing their strategies, seeking community input on crime issues and solutions, promoting organizational change in using data-driven strategies, and working with a research partner to implement and evaluate the outcomes of their strategies" (CNA, 2018).

Over the past 15 years, we have worked with a range of police departments without grant funding to provide assistance in implementing proactive crime reduction strategies, crime analysis, and accountability mechanisms. In each case, we have evaluated and critically analyzed the process of implementation (e.g., Boba, 2011; Santos, 2018b). Another method to accomplish practice-based research is through demonstration and field application projects where researchers and police work together to implement and study the operational processes necessary to implement evidence-based strategies. Some examples include the "Field Applications of POP Guides" in Savannah, GA, Chula Visa, CA, and Raleigh, NC as well as "Applying POP in Charlotte, N.C." (POP Center, 2018).

Finally, NIJ created a program in 2014 called LEADS Scholars program (Law Enforcement for Advancing Data and Science), which 'develops the research capacity of mid-career law enforcement personnel who are committed to advancing and integrating science into law enforcement policies and practice' (NIJ, 2018a). Merit-based scholarships are awarded to mid-rank officers and executives who have effectively infused research into policy development within their departments. The goal of the program is to encourage and develop future police leaders to value and conduct research in their agencies. NIJ has also created the LEADS Agency program, which is 'designed to help law enforcement agencies become more effective by improving their internal capacity for collecting data, analyzing data, conducting research, and using evidence' (NIJ, 2018b). While not offering support through grants, NIJ provides technical assistance to selected police departments to support internal research activities and help publish results.

Outcomes

Similar to Phase I, the findings of research studies conducted in Phase III should be published in academic journal articles to ensure rigor. However, the nature of the research and findings might be best published in specific journals that target a collective academic and practitioner audience. Examples include *Police Practice and Research: An International Journal*; *Policing: A Journal of Policy and Practice*; and *Policing: An International Journal of Police Strategies & Management*.

As in Phase II, the results from individual studies need to be synthesized and disseminated. The results of Phase III would be published in similar practitioner-focused outlets as in Phase II, such as monographs, short research briefs, summaries, and articles in practitioner magazines. In our own work, we have published academic journal articles related to implementation of proactive crime reduction strategies through stratified policing covering topics, such as process evaluation (Boba, 2011), impact on organizational culture (Santos, 2018b), the role of leadership (Santos & Santos, 2012), and the impact on crime (Santos & Santos, 2015c). We have also published articles about stratified policing in practitioner magazines, such as *Translational Criminology* (Santos & Santos, 2015a) and the *FBI Law Enforcement Bulletin* (Santos, 2011).

Yet, because the focus here is on guidance for implementation, it is important the findings are also translated into specific practical products that can be taken and used directly by police departments. For example, for stratified policing, we have produced a guidebook with funding from the COPS Office, which provides examples for developing crime reduction goals, creating required policies and action-oriented crime analysis products, assigning crime reduction responsibilities by rank, and establishing an accountability meeting structure (Boba & Santos, 2011).

Because the intention of Phase III is to provide instruction on how to make it work, it is important to have specific hands-on tools and products that can be taken and easily adapted for daily use. Accordingly, we have created and disseminated a 'Stratified Policing Toolkit' that contains over 25 different text documents, spreadsheets, and presentation files that police departments can download and use along with the guidebook to support implementation. The toolkit includes sample crime reduction policies, accountability meeting agendas, and presentation templates, crime analysis product templates, as well as sample organizational structures that have been implemented effectively in a host of police departments. Each file contains a short explanation for how to tailor it to the agency's purpose and use it for proactive crime reduction.

Face-to-face training is also a big part of delivering the results of Phase III. In Phase II, the results are presented at meetings, police conferences, and other seminars. However, because Phase III provides practical guidance for implementation, the results would be more appropriately delivered as training either for personnel from different agencies and/or for all personnel in one agency implementing new strategies. For example, our stratified policing training program includes an overview of foundation and framework of the model as well as separate sessions for different ranks and divisions based on their specific roles in the crime reduction process.

Finally, evaluation results of the implementation are important outcomes on two fronts as practice-based research. Assessing the strengths and weaknesses of an agency before implementation can help tailor strategies to resources, culture, and nature of the department and serves as a baseline for comparison. The results of an evaluation both inform the wider community about 'how to make it work' as well as help a particular department adjust and improve its implementation and sustainability.

The Role of Researchers and Police

Because evidence-based crime reduction practices are new to police generally and researchers do not always know the 'ins and outs' of the police organization, Phase III requires close collaboration between individual departments and researchers who have particular knowledge about the nature of police organizations and cultures. Not every researcher is well suited to both assist implementation and conduct the evaluation. Similarly, not every police leader and/or department is well suited to this type of collaboration. Even those agencies that work well with researchers to conduct research for Phase I may not be ideal partners here because Phase III requires them to make meaningful, permanent changes to the organizational structures and processes. The ideal partnership is between a police department that is truly looking to change and a researcher with both knowledge and experience in practice-based research and police operations.

The roles of the researcher and the police in Phase III are the most balanced of all the phases. Yet, it is important to recognize that even established partnerships will ebb and flow based on the circumstances. We suggest it is the researcher's responsibility to stay connected because the police department may continue implementation whether or not a researcher is involved. Since one desired outcome of Phase III is to produce findings for the field, the researcher must continually facilitate the connection and lead the publication of the results to the field.

Potential Barriers to Success

Having done much practice-based research ourselves, we have seen and experienced a number of challenges both to the implementation of evidence-based strategies and to carrying out the research. One example is the lack of or inconsistent leadership that can leave the implementation of innovative practices and/or facilitation of the research in the hands of uninformed, uncommitted, and/or unmotivated personnel. Other circumstances can overwhelm the agency's resources and morale making it more difficult to maintain the implementation of strategies not yet institutionalized. These can include budget crises, a critical incident gone bad, officer contract disputes, organizational push back, and mass retirement. Lastly, when practice-based research is funded by grants, a delay in the implementation can result in running out of time and/or funding, making it more difficult for the researcher to maintain involvement.

Summary

Like Phases I and II, Phase III requires individual research studies, synthesis, dissemination, and partnerships between police and researchers. But this is not the final step of the translation process because even when knowing what strategies are effective and how to implement them, the actual implementation in one department or throughout policing does not typically occur on its own. The results of Phases I, II, and III together are still not enough to complete the translation process.

Phase IV: 'Make it Work!' Institutionalization and Sustainability

Phase IV is concerned with the institutionalization and maintenance of evidence-based strategies by practitioners – 'Make it work!' It is consistent with the final part of the KTA action cycle, which is centrally focused on sustaining knowledge use (Graham et al., 2006). Conducting research is not the focus of Phase IV since the previous phases determined what strategies are effective and how to implement them. Phase IV is the culmination of the translation process but it is often overlooked, its importance and difficulty underestimated, or all together taken for granted. We maintain that the translation of research to practice does not occur until Phase IV is achieved.

To clarify the importance of Phase IV, we compare processes and procedures for crime reduction efforts to those for answering police calls for service. An entire system of technology, policies, procedures, training, and resources is clearly established in policing to answer calls for service. These processes and procedures are sustained through the police hierarchal structure, through formal accountability, and informally through the organizational culture. The system is more similar than different across police departments, and there are profession-wide standards and consistent expectations by police, governments, and the community about how police should answer citizen-generated calls for service. Thus, this function of police has been fully institutionalized and is sustained in practice.

On the other hand, proactive crime reduction efforts do not have such established mechanisms. While some police departments may have specific analysis and response processes, it is not the norm, but rather an exception, that an agency has institutionalized proactive crime reduction efforts with the same emphasis, standards, and expectations as calls for service. In the case of proactive crime reduction by police, the National Academy of Sciences report (Weisburd & Majimundar, 2017) asserts that to be effective, police leaders cannot simply prescribe to one approach. The committee recommends that not only should police combine place-based, problem-based, and offender-based approaches, but they should also incorporate a community-based approach to enhance legitimacy, trust, and cooperation with the community. Doing all this is not a simple task, and requires a concerted effort to infuse these practices into the field as well as into individual agencies.

Methods

We advocate that if the police are to fully operationalize proactive crime reduction, implementation and sustainability should focus both on individual police agencies and the entire profession itself. In our opinion, the essential requirement to 'make it work' and change the way an organization or a professional field operates is effective leadership. Leaders within individual agencies and leaders of the police professional community both have roles to play in Phase IV.

Individual police department leaders should seek to implement strategies in their own agencies based on evidence. However, this is often not as easy as it seems, and some police department executives say they are innovative but have not done what is necessary to institutionalize proactive crime reduction strategies. We found in a national study of police departments that even when patrol commanders prioritized evidence-based strategies, such as hot spots policing, problem-oriented policing, and crime analysis, they did not report changing their standard policing practices (Smith, Santos, & Santos, 2018). Our findings are similar to those of Weisburd and his colleagues (2003) who reported that Compstat adoption enabled police agencies to promote their progressive and innovative nature, when in reality Compstat adopters were largely functioning in an identical manner to non-adopters. In other words, agency executives claiming to be innovative were, in fact, not leading substantive change in their departments.

Then, what is the difference between departments that have made sustainable organizational change and those that only say they have? We strongly believe robust and consistent leadership is the difference. According to Carnall (2009) and Crank (2004), leadership, accountability, communication, and transparency are all important and necessary factors for true organizational change. Remember, at this point, leaders know which programs work, how to make them work, and have been provided the tools to support implementation.

Importantly, leaders can not only introduce a set of policies and procedures to their agencies, but must also 'articulate a vision, set standards for performance, and create focus and direction' (Bolman & Deal, 2008, p. 345). We have found that creating committees, providing funding, allowing feedback, conducting training, and increasing analysis capabilities were not enough for an agency to accomplish organizational change (Santos & Santos, 2012). We have found that it is the strong, consistent CEO who has a clear message and holds people accountable who tips the scale.

Even further, we have seen police departments where the status quo prevailed even when morale was good, personnel were open to the new ideas, leaders wanted change, and adequate training was provided. We believe the reason for this is the leaders often do not reinforce the organizational systems for the new strategies as systematically and vehemently as they do for handling calls for service. The police departments we have seen that are most successful are those in which the CEO takes ownership of the implementation, becomes directly and consistently involved, and creates processes and mechanisms that are unavoidable. The result is a system in which there are clear expectations, for everyone from the line-level officer to the chief, to carry out crime reduction strategies.

Leadership at the professional level is also crucial to 'make it work.' At the national level, Federal and state governments can strongly advocate and encourage change through words and action (i.e., funding) for practitioners to adopt evidence-based practices. Efforts here should emphasize the need and provide guidance for organizational change. For example, police leadership organizations, such as the International Association of Chiefs of Police and the National Sheriff's Association, as well as police commander training schools, such as the FBI National Academy and the Southern Policing Institute, should emphasize research findings in their classes, promote evidence-based practices, and support police executives, not simply to consider these practices but strongly encourage implementation. There are examples of this type of support from these entities, but we maintain even more needs to be done.

Outcomes

The outcomes, as noted earlier, are the result of the entire translation process. They are not easily accomplished but are straightforward to state. The outcome for individual police agencies is the institutionalization of new evidence-based strategies within the organizational structure with the same intensity, focus, and accountability as responding to calls for service and investigating crimes.

For the professional community, the outcome is establishing expectations that research 'should' and does inform practice at every level. This is a paradigm shift to being fully committed to incorporating evidence-based strategies into practice. In the context of proactive policing, an outcome is incorporating evidence-based strategies into the standard model of policing. Expectations of the community, local governments, and the police should be that specific evidence-based crime reduction strategies are not 'optional' but are part of every police department's mission and day-to-day operations just like the response to calls for service and investigating crimes are.

Importantly, at this point in the KTA action cycle, there is a feedback loop in which the attempts to sustain knowledge inform the first part of the action cycle and strategies are adapted and subsequently re-evaluated and implemented. Similarly, in this four-phase translation process, the successful and failed outcomes of Phase IV inform the future implementation and evaluation that continually takes place in Phase III.

The Role of Researchers and Police

The role of researchers is limited in Phase IV, as it is up to practitioners to implement and sustain evidence-based practices at the local, regional, and national levels. That is not to say researchers and police experts do not have a role at all. On the contrary, their role is to support the professional community and individual police departments in implementation, evaluation, and adjustments, just like they do when they assist in improving other areas of police practice.

To support a paradigm shift, we, and others, maintain that it will be beneficial for police departments to create an internal full-time, permanent capacity for supporting the translation process. This involves creating and maintaining a research and analytical capacity that can assist in the implementation and evaluation of evidence-based strategies. This capacity is fulfilled by a specific designated position(s) within the agency. While it may not be realistic for police departments with limited resources to create a new position, some small and most medium-to-large-sized agencies are well suited to create one or more of the following:

- Crime analyst: An employee of the agency who conducts crime analysis to support crime reduction efforts, investigations, patrol activities, and evaluation and has specific education and training related to research and analysis with a balance of knowledge about police culture, the organization, and technology (Santos, 2017). The crime analyst profession is fairly well established and most medium to large police agencies have individuals who do this work (Bureau of Justice Statistics, 2018).
- Pracademic: A sworn officer (at any level) who has a graduate degree and training in research. Ideally, individuals in these positions identify evidence-based practices, assist in their implementation, and conduct evaluations. They may also serve to clarify jargon and

research methods, so relevant research is effectively communicated to police management for decision making (Willis, 2016).

- Embedded criminologist: A person with a doctorate degree and/or a researcher who is not working *with* the police department but is working *within* the police department. The individual is an independent, unbiased full-time employee with expertise in criminology, criminal justice practices, analysis, statistics, research methodology, and evaluation (Braga, 2013). Embedded criminologists carry out independent research that supports an organization's mission and collaborate to develop programs by introducing and implementing evidence-based practices (Braga & Davis, 2014).

Potential Barriers to Success

As in Phase III, potential barriers to success in Phase IV are related to the leadership and commitment that is necessary to change an organization for any purpose. For example, the historical nature of police executive longevity is a major factor. Researchers have found the average tenure of a police chief is only around 3 years (Rainguet & Dodge, 2001), and experts say real organizational change often takes several years (Todnem & MacLeod, 2009). Thus, even a chief who begins the implementation process immediately upon starting the job might not be in the position long enough to follow through. We have seen initiatives fizzle out and abruptly stop when there is a change in top leadership and push back from middle managers. However, we have also seen organizational change sustained across leaders. In our work with the Port St. Lucie, FL Police Department, stratified policing has been carried out and made better by five consecutive police chiefs over 15 years.

Another potential barrier, also intrinsic to policing, is there is not often pressure on police leaders to innovate and/or incorporate research into their operations. Local government, political leaders, citizens of individual communities, and the public, in general, are satisfied when police answer calls for service quickly and conduct thorough investigations. In our experience, implementation of proactive policing strategies is most often sparked by police leaders and rarely is it insisted upon by an outside entity of any type. Thus, a difficult challenge is educating the government and the general public to understand the value of research so they expect the implementation of evidence-based strategies.

Summary

Of course, there are many practical factors that are required to accomplish this final phase of the translation process, such as funding, additional personnel, and resources. In many circumstances, however, strong leaders who place a priority on implementation of evidence-based strategies can overcome these practical barriers by prioritizing funding, reallocating resources to change the organization and the profession. We only briefly touch on the mechanisms that would make organizational change successful as there is a wide range of literature and research in many disciplines on this topic. However, the main point here is that Phase IV is important, yet very difficult, and should not be underemphasized or ignored in any discussion of the translation process.

Conclusions

Our purpose has been to provide a framework that extends the current discussion of translational criminology and, more specifically, the dynamic process of translating research to practice related to proactive policing. We provide a framework for the translation process based on the two cycles of the KTA process – knowledge creation and the action cycle (Graham et al., 2006). The four phases presented here overlap to some extent with one another and expand what has been discussed in previous translational criminology literature:

- *'Does it work?'* Phase I is led by researchers with the purpose of conducting high-quality rigorous research and evaluate innovative, realistic strategies. The outcomes are findings from individual studies and researcher/police partnerships are imperative to carry out the research.
- *'What works?'* Phase II is also led by researchers with the purpose of conducting meta-analyses of the individual study findings from Phase I. Researchers and practitioners collaborate to establish recommendations for the field and communicate the results to practitioners. The outcomes are evidence-based strategies (i.e., empirical generalizations).
- *'How to make it work?'* Phase III is the collaboration between researchers and organizations for both implementation of evidence-based strategies into organizations as well as the evaluation of that implementation. Practitioners and researchers must partner since this research requires implementation into the day-to-day operations of an organization as well as systematic evaluation. The outcomes include organizational models, policies, processes, mechanisms, and products that support implementation and are found to work in practice.
- *'Make it work!'* Phase IV is the institutionalization of evidence-based practices into individual organizations and within a profession. The outcomes are real organizational change in individual agencies as well as a paradigm shift in the field. Leaders are key to demanding and facilitating change at the local, regional, national, and international levels. While established practitioner/researcher partnerships are not required, researchers assist in this process and organizations build internal capacities for analysis and research.

Importantly, all four phases of the research-to-practice translation process are equally important. Graham and his colleagues (2006) recognize the transfer of KTA is 'complex and challenging' as well as an iterative process (p. 22). We assert if the goal of translational criminology is for practitioners to consistently use evidence-based strategies, translation is not accomplished until the strategies are operationalized across the field and in organizations' day-today operations as presented in Phase IV.

Consequently, the easiest way to determine whether something is fully translated is by comparing it to strategies and practices that are already institutionalized. We use the process for answering calls for service as our standard to assess proactive crime reduction efforts by police. Our conclusion is the translation of evidence-based crime reduction is not yet complete because police have not adopted consistent policies, systematic processes, and operational mechanisms as they have for carrying out a call for service.

While current translation of crime reduction research to police practice seems to have focused on Phases I and II, we hope that by parsing out Phases III and IV, more attention will be paid to the operationalization of the effective strategies, so police agencies and the field can be better equipped to 'make it work.' Finally, it is our hope that the four-phase translation process will assist researchers and police leaders to identify and fill gaps in current and future translation activities.

Disclosure Statement

No potential conflict of interest was reported by the authors.

Funding

No grant or other funding supported the writing of this article.

References

Alpert, G. P., Rojek, J., & Hansen, A. (2013). *Building bridges between police researchers and practitioners: Agents of change in a complex world.* Final Report to the National Institute of Justice. Columbia, SC: University of South Carolina.

Boba, R. (2010). A practice-based evidence approach in Florida. *Police Practice and Research, Special Issue: the Evolving Relationship between Police Research and Police Practice, 11*(2), 122–128.

Boba, R. (2011). *Institutionalization of problem solving, analysis, and accountability in the Port St. Lucie, FL police department.* Washington DC: Office of Community Oriented Policing Services.

Boba, R., & Santos, R. G. (2011). *A police organizational model for crime reduction: Institutionalizing problem solving, analysis, and accountability.* Washington DC: Office of Community Oriented Policing Services.

Bolman, L. G., & Deal, T. E. (2008). *Reframing organizations: Artistry, choice, and leadership.* San Francisco, CA: Jossey-Bass.

Braga, A. (2013). *Ideas in American policing: Embedded criminologists in police departments.* Washington DC: Police Foundation.

Braga, A. A., & Davis, E. F. (2014). Implementing science in police agencies: The embedded research model. *Policing: A Journal of Policy and Practice, 8*(4), 294–306.

Braga, A. A., Papachristos, A. V., & Hureau, D. M. (2014). The effects of hot spots policing on crime: An updated systematic review and meta-analysis. *Justice Quarterly, 31*(4), 633–663.

Bueermann, J. (2012, March). Being smart on crime with evidence-based policing. *National Institute of Justice Journal, 269,* 1–5.

Bureau of Justice Statistics. (2018). Law Enforcement Management and Administrative Statistics (LEMAS), 2013. Retrieved from http://www.icpsr.umich.edu/icpsrweb/NACJD/studies/36164

Campbell Collaboration. (2018). Retrieved from https://www.campbellcollaboration.org/

Carnall, C. (2009). A convergence analysis of strategic change: The national trust case. In R. Todnem & C. Macleod (Eds.), *Managing organizational change in public services* (pp. 97–110). New York: Routledge.

CNA. (2018). Strategies for policing innovation. Retrieved from http://www.strategiesforpolicinginnovation.com

Crank, J. P. (2004). *Understanding police culture.* Cincinnati: Anderson Publishing Co.

Graham, I. D., Logan, J., Harrison, M. B., Straus, S. E., Tetroe, J., Caswell, W., & Robinsons, N. (2006). Lost in knowledge translation: Time for a map? *Journal of Continuing Education in Health Profession, 26*(1), 13–24.

Green, L. A., & Seifert, C. M. (2005). Translation of research into practice: Why we can't "Just Do It." *Journal of American Board of Family Medicine, 18*(6), 541–545.

Grieco, J., Vovak, H., & Lum, C. (2014). Examining research–practice partnerships in policing evaluations. *Policing, 8*(4), 368–378.

Griffith, E. (2014). Translating research to practice and building capacity to use data, research, planning, and problem-solving. *Translational Criminology, 1*(6), 9–11.

Groff, E. R., Ratcliffe, J. H., Haberman, C. P., Sorg, E. T., Joyce, N. M., & Taylor, R. B. (2015). Does what police do at hot spots matter? The Philadelphia policing tactics experiment. *Criminology, 53*(1), 23–53.

Hellerstein, D. (2008). Practice-based evidence rather than evidence-based practice in psychiatry. *Medscape Journal of Medicine, 10,* 141.

Laub, J. H. (2012). Translational criminology. *Translational Criminology, 3,* 4–5.

Lum, C., & Koper, K. (2017). *Evidence-based policing: Translating research to practice.* Oxford, UK: Oxford University Press.

Manojlovich, M., Squires, J. E., Davies, B., & Graham, I. D. (2015). Hiding in plain sight: Communication theory in implementation science. *Implementation Science, 10*(58), 1–11.

Marginson, F. R., Barkham, M., Evans, C., McGrath, G., Clark, J. M., Audin, K., & Connell, J. (2000). Measurement and psychotherapy: Evidence-based practice and practice-based evidence. *British Journal of Psychiatry, 177,* 123–130.

McDonald, P. W., & Viehbeck, S. (2007). From evidence-based practice making to practice-based evidence making: Creating communities of (research) and practice. *Health Promotion Practice, 8,* 140–144.

Milat, A. J., & Li, B. (2017). Narrative review of frameworks for translating research evidence into policy and practice. *Public Health Research and Practice, 27*(1), e2711704.

National Institute of Justice (NIJ). (2018a). The Law Enforcement Advancing Data and Science Scholars Program. Retrieved from https://nij.gov/topics/law-enforcement/Pages/nij-iacp-leads-program.aspx

National Institute of Justice (NIJ). (2018b). The Law Enforcement Advancing Data and Science Agencies Program. Retrieved from https://nij.gov/topics/law-enforcement/Pages/leads-agencies.aspx

POP Center. (2018). Retrieved from www.popcenter.org

Rainguet, F. W., & Dodge, M. (2001). The problems of police chiefs: An examination of the issues in tenure and turnover. *Police Quarterly, 4*(3), 268–288.

Ratcliffe, J. H., Taniguchi, T., Groff, E. R., & Wood, J. D. (2011). The Philadelphia foot patrol experiment: A randomized controlled trial of police patrol effectiveness in violent crime hotspots. *Criminology, 49*, 795–831.

Rojek, J., Martin, P., & Alpert, G. P. (2015). The literature and research on police–research partnerships in the USA. In J. Rojek, P. Martin, & G. P. Alpert (Eds.), *Developing and maintaining police-researcher partnerships to facilitate research use* (pp. 27–44). New York, NY: Springer.

Santos, R. B. (2014). The effectiveness of crime analysis for crime reduction: Cure or diagnosis? *Journal of Contemporary Criminal Justice, 30*(2), 147–168.

Santos, R. B. (2017). *Crime analysis with crime mapping* (4th ed.). Thousand Oaks, CA: Sage Publications.

Santos, R. B., & Santos, R. G. (2012). The role of leadership in implementing a police organizational model for crime reduction and accountability. *Policing: A Journal of Policy and Practice, 6*(4), 344–353.

Santos, R. B., & Santos, R. G. (2016). Offender-focused police strategies in residential burglary and theft from vehicle hot spots: A partially blocked randomized controlled trial. *Journal of Experimental Criminology, 12*(3), 373–402.

Santos, R. G. (2011, February). Systematic pattern response strategy: Protecting the beehive. FBI Law Enforcement Bulletin. https://leb.fbi.gov/2011/february/systematic-pattern-response-strategy-protecting-the-beehive

Santos, R. G. (2018a). Offender and family member perceptions after an offender-focused hot spots policing strategy. *Policing: An International Journal, 41*(3), 386–400.

Santos, R. G. (2018b). Police organizational change after implementing crime analysis and evidence-based strategies through stratified policing. *Policing: A Journal of Policy and Practice, 12*(3), 288–302.

Santos, R. G., & Santos, R. B. (2015a). Evidence-based policing, "What works" and stratified policing, "How to make it work." *Translational Criminology, 8*, 20–22.

Santos, R. G., & Santos, R. B. (2015b). An ex post facto evaluation of tactical police response in residential theft from vehicle micro-time hot spots. *Journal of Quantitative Criminology, 31*(4), 679–698.

Santos, R. G., & Santos, R. B. (2015c). Practice-based research: Ex post facto evaluation of evidence-based police practices implemented in residential burglary micro-time hot spots. *Evaluation Review, 39*(5), 451–479.

Sherman, L. W. (1998). *Evidence-based policing: Ideas in American policing.* Washington, DC: Police Foundation.

Sherman, L. W., Gottfredson, D., MacKenzie, D. L., Eck, J., Reuter, P., & Bushway, S. (1997). *Preventing crime: What works, what doesn't, what's promising: A report to the attorney general of the United States.* Washington, DC: U.S. Department of Justice, Office of Justice Programs.

Smith, J., Santos, R. B., & Santos, R. G. (2018). Evidence-based policing and the stratified integration of crime analysis in police agencies: National survey results. *Policing: A Journal of Policy and Practice, 12*(3), 303–315.

Taylor, B., & Boba, R. (2011). *The integration of crime analysis into patrol work: A guidebook.* Washington DC: Office of Community Oriented Policing Services.

Telep, C. W., Mitchell, R. J., & Weisburd, D. (2014). How much time should the police spend at crime hot spots? Answers from a police agency directed randomized field trial in Sacramento, California. *Justice Quarterly, 31*(5), 905–933.

Todnem, R., & MacLeod, C. (2009). *Managing organizational change in public services.* New York, NY: Routledge.

Weisburd, D. (2010). Justifying the use of non-experimental methods and disqualifying the use of randomized controlled trials: Challenging folklore in evaluation research in crime and justice. *Journal of Experimental Criminology, 6*(2), 209–227.

Weisburd, D. (2011). From the director. *Translational Criminology, 1*, 1.

Weisburd, D. (2015). The 2014 Sutherland address: The law of crime concentration and the criminology of place. *Criminology, 53*(2), 133–157.

Weisburd, D., Mastrofski, S. D., McNally, A. M., Greenspan, R., & Willis, J. J. (2003). Reforming to preserve: Compstat and strategic problem solving in American policing. *Criminology and Public Policy, 2*, 421–456.

Weisburd, D. L., & Majimundar, M. K. (2017). *Proactive policing: Effects on crime and communities.* Washington DC: National Academy of Sciences.

Willis, J. J. (2016). The romance of police pracademics. *Policing: A Journal of Policy and Practice, 10*(3), 315–321.

3

Creating a 'What Works' Translational Tool for Police

A Researcher-City Government Partnership

Cody W. Telep

SCHOOL OF CRIMINOLOGY AND CRIMINAL JUSTICE, ARIZONA STATE UNIVERSITY, PHOENIX, AZ, USA

Claudia Gross Shader

CITY OF SEATTLE OFFICE OF CITY AUDITOR, SEATTLE, WA, USA

Introduction

The policing evaluation literature has grown rapidly in recent years. The Evidence-Based Policing Matrix (Lum, Koper, & Telep, 2011), a research-to-practice tool designed to summarize the rigorous crime control evaluation literature, now includes more than 160 quasi-experimental and experimental evaluation studies. Close to 70% of these have been published in the two decades since Lawrence Sherman (1998, p. 2) introduced evidence-based policing and argued that 'police practices should be based on scientific evidence about what works best.' Today, there is a much larger evidence base for police practitioners and policymakers to draw upon in making decisions about which strategies and tactics are most likely to be fair and effective.

This larger evidence base also creates challenges. It has become far more difficult for anyone to keep up with the policing evaluation literature and increasingly unrealistic to expect busy police practitioners and policymakers to read all of these studies. This is especially true when many evaluations are behind paywalls and only accessible at a high cost or through university library subscription services that are unavailable to most practitioners (Laycock, 2014). Prior research on receptivity to research in policing suggests that the average officer does not regularly read academic journals to learn about policing effectiveness (Lum, Telep, Koper, & Grieco, 2012; Telep & Lum, 2014).

Translational criminology has become an important focus in recent years as a response to this challenge in policing and across criminal justice research (see Lum & Koper, 2017; Mayhew, 2016). Former National Institute of Justice Director John Laub (2011) focused on the federal government's role in translation, noting that translational criminology is defined by both bringing research into practice and systematically studying how dissemination occurs and what techniques and strategies are effective. Thus, the idea of translational criminology is to make research more accessible and easier to digest for the policy and practice community. Examples of this recent emphasis include the creation of the magazine *Translational Criminology*, housed in the Center for Evidence-Based Crime Policy (CEBCP) at George Mason University. The publication began in 2011 and now has 16 issues focused on brief summaries of cutting-edge scientific work that has policy relevance.[1] The *SpringerBriefs in Translational Criminology* publication series, which began in 2014, now includes nine brief monographs that showcase examples of research being integrated into practice.

DOI: 10.4324/9781003153009-5

In the area of policing, translational tools have also developed to make research evidence more accessible and useful for practitioners and policymakers (Lum, 2009). National government organizations have played a key role in sponsoring tools in the United States and the United Kingdom. In the U.S., the National Institute of Justice's CrimeSolutions.gov is a 'what works' clearinghouse designed to provide practitioners and policymakers with a comprehensive resource on what works in criminal justice. All studies included on CrimeSolutions.gov are scored by multiple researchers and categorized as effective, promising, no effects, or inconclusive evidence. In the law enforcement topic area, as of June 2019, there are 102 programs and 12 practices with an evidence rating from the site.

In the United Kingdom, the What Works Centre for Crime Reduction in the College of Policing has created a crime reduction toolkit.[2] The toolkit reviews interventions using the EMMIE framework (Johnson, Tilley, & Bowers, 2015). EMMIE stands for impact on crime (Effect), how it works (Mechanism), where it works (Moderator), how to do it (Implementation), and what it costs (Economic cost). The ability to look at the impact of practices is similar to CrimeSolutions.gov, but the focus on implementation and cost makes the toolkit unique.

A third prominent translation tool is the Evidence-Based Policing Matrix (Lum et al., 2011)[3] mentioned earlier. The Matrix is a three-dimensional figure updated annually that displays the experimental and quasi-experimental evaluation literature in policing focused on crime control. Studies are placed in the figure as dots based on the scope of their target, the specificity of their prevention mechanism, and their level of proactivity. The dot color indicates the study results, with black dots representing studies with a statistically significant impact on crime. The figure makes it possible to view the dots and thus the evaluation literature collectively and see where effective studies cluster.

While the initial creation of the Matrix was unfunded, the federal government played a role in enhancing the Matrix and subsequent projects that developed out of the Matrix. A grant from the Bureau of Justice Assistance (BJA) made it possible to create a more sophisticated interactive website. Additionally, the grant funded a series of field projects, collectively called the Matrix Demonstration Project.[4] These projects all drew from the Matrix to institutionalize research into practice in multiple agencies (see Lum & Koper, 2017).

In this chapter, we focus on a fourth police translation tool, and in this case the role of local government in funding translational work. The 'What works in policing?' website (hereafter the 'What works' site) was created through a contract between the City of Seattle Office of City Auditor (OCA) and George Mason University and updated with a contract between OCA and a researcher at Arizona State University. This is the only case we are aware of in which a local government has funded the creation of a translational tool. This site is housed within CEBCP's website and, as we describe below, is well integrated with the Matrix. This is the first paper to describe the site in detail and its similarities to and differences from existing translation tools, as well as the rationale for a local government's involvement in translation. We begin with some background on the OCA and its reasons for funding a 'What works' site. We then describe the tool and its contents, focusing on efforts to link the site with work of the Seattle Police Department (SPD) through a case study approach. We then examine utilization of the site and close with thoughts on next steps for the site.

Background

The OCA was established by City Charter in 1991 to conduct performance audits of City of Seattle programs, departments, grantees, and contracts. In 2009, the City Council asked OCA to develop capacity to help the City conduct rigorous program evaluations and to ensure that the

City was incorporating findings from research into its programs. OCA has built its capacity for program evaluation in three ways.[5] The first is through City Council-funded evaluations. OCA manages contracts with research partners to conduct rigorous evaluations of City legislation and programs. This includes research partner selection and ongoing communication, input on evaluation design, and oversight of contract deliverables.

The second approach is through OCA's involvement in federal grants for crime prevention evaluations. In 2012, OCA collaborated with CEBCP researchers to examine the research base for 63 City-funded crime prevention programs (Gill et al., 2012). The study found that only five of these programs were based on rigorous research evidence indicating that they might be effective in reducing crime. Since 2012, OCA has co-written and/or actively participated in over $5.1 million of federally-funded research evaluations of several new City crime prevention efforts directed at crime hot spots. These include large-scale grants from the Department of Justice (see Gill, Vitter, & Weisburd, 2016).

Finally, OCA has developed in-house technical expertise to perform research activities that do not require additional funding for data collection or technical subject matter expertise. These reports provide insight to City Council on a host of topics relevant to policing. Recent reports include a process evaluation of street outreach for youth (Gross Shader & Jones, 2015), as well as research briefs on police technology and the evaluation of an acoustic gunshot locator system (OCA, 2016a), opportunities for a safe prescription drug disposal program (OCA, 2016b), evaluating Seattle's new police accountability system (OCA, 2017a), and evaluating the city's police-led Navigation Team approach to dealing with homelessness (OCA, 2017b).

OCA has thus played an important role in the creation and translation of rigorous research evidence. Because the Office often responds directly to requests from Councilmembers, their reports are actually read and designed to be actionable for policy and funding decisions. We recognize that cities vary, and the OCA may not be an appropriate home for translational work in other jurisdictions. But we suggest researchers think more about ways to partner with local agencies that play a key role in reviewing (and in the case of Seattle creating) research for policymakers. Depending on the structure of the local government, there may be a number of agencies or departments well-suited for translation work and researcher/practitioner partnerships, including budget, finance, planning, and public health.

Why a Website?

OCA began working with researchers at CEBCP on the 'What works' website in 2012. While under investigation by the Department of Justice in 2012, SPD rolled out an effort to implement 20 reforms in 20 months (the 20/20 plan).[6] These included an effort to be more data-driven to enhance the crime prevention effectiveness of the agency. A 'What works' website was viewed as a potential mechanism to provide guidance on effective strategies and a way for SPD to assess the extent to which its practices aligned with research.

Three key factors motivated OCA's investment in a 'What works in policing?' website. The first was a goal of reducing the potential for harm in Seattle's crime prevention work (see McCord, 2003). The website was designed to identify policing strategies that have been widely shown to be ineffective or even have 'backfire effects.' In these cases, it was deemed to be especially important that SPD practices were aligned with research evidence.

A second goal of the site was to increase the City's capacity for using proven practices. An important component of the site, described more below, was a self-assessment feature, which allowed SPD to assess how its strategies aligned with research evidence. The self-assessment feature makes it possible for the department and City to track how it incorporates the best-available research in its practices. The website's research summary was also viewed as a way to help the City discern whether there was a police strategy with sufficient supporting evidence that might address a specific City problem.

Finally, the site was viewed as a way to ensure sustainability in incorporating research into practice. The website and SPD case study were seen as a way to maintain consistency in institutional knowledge and practice in a City and police department that had undergone significant leadership transitions. From 2013 to 2018, Seattle went through five mayors (two interim), five police chiefs (three interim), and nine captains in SPD's South Precinct (one interim).

Although the focus of the website is on policing practices, another benefit of the website is in its potential to help develop a broad base for research-informed crime prevention. Certain crime prevention activities might best be conducted by regulatory agencies (Eck, 2015), social service providers, or community organizations. Understanding 'what works in policing' can also help local governments understand more about where it might be best for an entity other than the police to play a leadership role in crime prevention.

'What Works in Policing?' Site

The 'What works' site was officially launched by OCA on 10 November 2014.[7] The site includes four main components: a review of the research evidence that summarizes all of the strategies covered, a resource library with more information about what works in policing and evidence-based policing in general, individual pages for each research strategy that provide more information and resources, and the SPD case study. The site initially covered studies published through 2013. One of the authors updated the review in spring 2018 to cover studies published through the end of 2017.

The review of the research evidence draws from a number of prior studies and reviews to categorize strategies based on what works, what is promising, what does not work, and what we need to know more about. These categorizations draw largely from updating a review by Telep and Weisburd (2012) designed to provide more guidance to police on what they should (and should not) be doing to effectively reduce crime. Our focus was largely on crime control evaluations, but we also examine 'what works?' for increasing fairness and improving citizen perceptions of police legitimacy.

The goal was to create a translation tool that presented new information in a unique way. While CrimeSolutions.gov presents information on both programs and practices, its focus is more on the impacts of particular studies, and because the site covers the entire criminal justice system, it provides a broader overview of policing. Our goal was to more specifically focus on research knowledge on policing interventions. This is in line with the College of Policing toolkit (the 'What works' site was developed prior to the toolkit), with an emphasis on reviewing what works and providing guidance, when possible, on how to implement effective strategies.

While the site is well integrated with the Evidence-Based Policing Matrix, it is more driven by strategies. The Matrix differentiates studies not by the type of intervention, but by the target of the intervention and the level of focus and proactivity. This is a useful framework but does not easily allow a user to identify all problem-oriented policing studies, for example (which can focus on people or small or large places). The site thus complements the Matrix, while allowing visitors to assess the research evidence by strategy more easily.

In Table 3.1, we summarize the information available on our main 'Review of the research evidence' page, which displays our categorizations for 16 strategies included in our review. We chose strategies that cover common crime fighting strategies for which there was interest from police in knowing what worked and where there was at least some empirical evidence on effects.

TABLE 3.1 Summary of the 'Review of the Research Evidence' Page and the Categorization of All Studies Covered on the 'What works' Site

Category	Strategy	Outcome
What works?	Hot spots policing	For reducing crime and disorder
	Problem-oriented policing	For reducing crime and disorder
	Focused deterrence strategies (focus on high-rate offenders)	For reducing gang and drug market violence
	Directed patrol for gun violence	For reducing gun violence
	DNA for police investigations	For clearing more property crimes
What's promising	Information-gathering interrogation approach	For making investigations fairer/reducing false confessions
	Community policing and procedural justice	For improving police/community relations
	Closed circuit television (CCTV)	For reducing property crime
What doesn't work?	'Standard model' policing tactics (random preventive patrol, rapid response to 911 calls, general increases in arrests)	For reducing crime and improving efficiency
		For reducing subsequent family violence
	Second responder programs	For reducing youth drug/alcohol use
	Drug Abuse Resistance Education (D.A.R.E.)	
What do we need to know more about?	Broken windows policing	For reducing serious crime
	Increasing department size	For reducing crime
	Investigations by detectives	For clearing cases and reducing crime
	Counterterrorism strategies	For reducing crime and preventing attacks
	Police technology (ShotSpotter, drones, license plate readers)	For reducing crime and improving efficiency

In some cases, we also included strategies and tactics that were especially relevant to Seattle. This was the case, for example, for our discussion of drones on the police technology page, which had been a controversial issue in the city following the creation and then termination of an SPD drone program in 2013 (Clarridge, 2013).

We include many of the sources we used for categorizing strategies on the resource library page. These include prior narrative reviews of the policing evidence, such as the National Research Council's (2004) report on fairness and effectiveness in policing (see Weisburd & Eck, 2004), as well as more systematic reviews of the policing evidence, such as the updated Maryland Report chapter on policing (Sherman & Eck, 2002). We drew extensively from Campbell Collaboration systematic reviews on policing topics. These systematic reviews, which often include a meta-analysis combining effect sizes from multiple rigorous studies, are available for many of the policing strategies included on the site (Telep & Weisburd, 2016).

We describe examples of our reasoning for categorization below, but note that while this was ultimately a subjective process, we tried to be as consistent as possible in coding. We thus only categorized strategies under 'what works' if there was a published systematic review suggesting the strategy has an overall significant impact on reducing crime (see Braga, Papachristos, & Hureau, 2014; Braga & Weisburd, 2012; Braga, Weisburd, & Turchan, 2018; Koper & Mayo-Wilson, 2006; Weisburd, Telep, Hinkle, & Eck, 2010; Wilson, McClure, & Weisburd, 2010). Similarly, we required systematic evidence of a strategy's ineffectiveness for it to be placed under 'what does not work.' The 'promising' category was utilized for strategies where there is some systematic evidence of effectiveness and a largely positive systematic review, but where the research is too limited in some way (typically rigor or a lack of field trials) to draw strong conclusions about effectiveness. Finally, when the evidence base was more mixed or limited (or in some cases almost nonexistent), we categorized strategies as ones we need more research on to reach firm conclusions.

We coded five strategies under 'What works?' These included hot spots policing and problem-oriented policing for reducing crime and disorder in general, directed patrols specifically focused on gun violence, and focused deterrence strategies to reduce gang and drug market violence committed by groups. We also included the use of DNA evidence in police investigations as an effective strategy for solving more property crimes. We coded strategies under 'What works?' when the bulk of the research evidence suggested the approach is effective in reducing crime. For example, we coded hot spots policing under 'What works?' because there is a large rigorous evidence base summarized in the micro place slab of the Evidence-Based Policing Matrix (Lum et al., 2011) that suggests hot spots policing is an effective approach for reducing crime and disorder. This conclusion was echoed by the National Research Council (2004) and by an update of a Campbell Collaboration systematic review by Braga et al. (2014).

In the promising category, we included three strategies, information-gathering interrogation approaches to make investigations fairer, community policing and procedural justice to enhance police-community relationships, and closed-circuit television to reduce property crime. The promising category includes our two strategies that focus more on fairness than on simply crime control effectiveness as primary outcomes of interest. We coded strategies under 'What's promising?' when the available research evidence suggests the approach is effective in reducing crime and/or increasing legitimacy and fairness, but the evidence base remains limited in size or scope. For example, we coded the information-gathering interrogation approach under 'What's promising?' because a systematic review by Meissner et al. (2014) concluded that the strategy can help elicit confessions from suspects while also minimizing the number of false confessions when compared to the accusatorial interrogation approach. All of the studies comparing the two approaches in an experimental setting used laboratory studies, typically with college student volunteers. While the evidence to date shows the promise of information-gathering approaches, we did not code this as 'What works?' because of a lack of field trials on interrogation methods.

We included two strategies and one suite of strategies under 'What doesn't work?' These were second responder programs, which involve follow-up home visits with domestic violence victims by police and service providers, to reduce repeat family violence; Drug Abuse Resistance Education (D.A.R.E.) to reduce adolescent drug and alcohol use; and strategies that Weisburd and Eck (2004) defined as 'standard model' policing tactics. These 'standard model' tactics represent traditional policing approaches that dominated the professional era of policing and remain popular in many agencies today. These include random preventive patrol, rapid response to 911 calls for service, and general efforts to increase arrests (e.g., zero tolerance approaches). While many officers view these as effective strategies in addressing crime (Telep & Lum, 2014), there is little evidence that such approaches are effective in reducing crime or closing cases (see Kelling, Pate, Dieckman, & Brown, 1974; Spelman & Brown, 1984).

We coded strategies here when the bulk of the research evidence suggests the approach is ineffective in reducing crime. For example, we coded D.A.R.E. under 'What doesn't work?' because there is a large, rigorous evidence base of studies suggesting D.A.R.E. has little or no impact on adolescent, drug, alcohol, or tobacco use (Rosenbaum, 2007). This was also the conclusions of a systematic review examining the effectiveness of D.A.R.E. (West & O'Neal, 2004). It is important to point out that nonstatistically significant findings do not always mean that a program is ineffective; it could indicate issues with the implementation of the program or with the ability of the evaluation method to detect a program effect. With D.A.R.E., however, the overwhelming evidence that D.A.R.E. has little or no effect on adolescent drug use led us to place this program in the 'What doesn't work?' category.

Finally, we coded five strategies under 'What do we need to know more about?' For these strategies, the research was too limited to reach strong conclusions about whether the approach was effective in reducing crime or the current evidence was too mixed to reach an assessment of whether the strategy works or does not work. The line between 'promising' and 'what we need to know more about' is fuzzy, but we were generally conservative, and chose only strategies for which the systematic review had largely positive conclusions in categorizing the reviews described earlier as 'promising.' For the 'what we need to know more about' strategies, there was sometimes no systematic review yet, and at other times, the existing review was very mixed or drew upon almost no rigorous evidence. This included research on the effects of increasing department size or adding more officers, studies of counterterrorism tactics, research on investigations by detectives, and studies of most police technologies. Under the police technology umbrella, we discussed limited empirical research on acoustic gunshot locator systems (ShotSpotter) and drones, the mixed research on license plate readers, and the growing but also mixed body of research on body-worn cameras. For body-worn cameras in particular, the evidence base is expanding quickly, and we may revisit its placement as researchers complete more systematic reviews of this literature (see Lum, Stoltz, Koper, & Scherer, 2019).

We also coded broken windows policing (Wilson & Kelling, 1982) under 'What do we need to know more about?' because of conflicting results from the literature on the crime control effectiveness of this approach and the difficulties of evaluating most broken windows strategies. Some scholars conclude that broken windows policing was a major contributor to the New York City crime decline (e.g., Kelling & Sousa, 2001), while others argue the approach had a smaller impact (e.g., Rosenfeld, Fornango, & Rengifo, 2007), and still others conclude there was no impact of broken windows policing on crime (e.g., Harcourt & Ludwig, 2006). These divergent findings make it difficult to reach strong conclusions about the effectiveness of this strategy.

Each strategy described in the review of the research evidence site has its own page. These generally follow a similar format, starting with a definition of the strategy and a review of the research evidence for the strategy. For strategies that have evidence of effectiveness, the page also provides guidance on what police should be doing in implementing this strategy. The final section of the page includes a table with links to all relevant studies from the Evidence-Based Policing Matrix. We also include additional resources along the left-hand side of the page. These include government or organization reports, articles, and videos with more information about the strategy and its implementation.

As an example, the hot spots policing page first provides an overview of research suggesting the strong concentration of crime at a place (Weisburd, 2015) before defining hot spots policing as increased police attention in small geographic areas. The page also notes the variety of tactics that can fall under hot spots policing. As noted earlier, the evidence reviewed includes the National Research Council (2004) report and Braga et al. (2014) systematic review. The spring 2018 update included more current evidence, with a description of the new Center for Problem-Oriented Policing guide to identifying and responding to hot spots (Telep & Hibdon, 2019) and a summary of the findings of a new National Academies of Sciences, Engineering, and Medicine (2017) report on proactive policing, which also concluded that the evidence is persuasive for place-based policing strategies.

The section on 'what should police be doing at hot spots?' includes brief summaries of effective strategies from prior rigorous studies, ranging in complexity from simply increasing patrols for approximately 15 minutes at a time (e.g., Telep, Mitchell, & Weisburd, 2014) to problem-oriented approaches at hot spots (e.g., Braga & Bond, 2008). Finally, the page is integrated with the Evidence-Based Policing Matrix and includes information for the more than 25 micro place evaluations in the Matrix that qualify as hot spots studies. All of the Matrix study pages were updated in 2016 in collaboration with the Police Foundation to both better integrate the Matrix with the Police Foundation's new evidence-based policing app and link the 'What works' site into Matrix study pages. All hot spots policing study pages in the Matrix now include links to the hot spots 'What works' site page (and the problem-oriented policing page if applicable). Thus, visitors to either site can easily access information on the strategy or individual studies evaluating the strategy.

Seattle Police Department Case Study

For each strategy listed in Table 3.1, SPD provided a brief statement on the degree to which it was incorporating this research in its practices as of March 2014. This was intended to provide a frame of reference for SPD as it continues to build its capacity to apply scientific research on what is effective in policing. For each strategy, we used written information provided by SPD to assess whether the department was emerging in its use of research or could take steps to incorporate this research. The overall goal was to assess to what extent SPD was doing what works and what is promising (and ideally not doing what does not work) (see Veigas & Lum, 2013 for a similar example using the Evidence-Based Policing Matrix). In the case of department size, we did not give an assessment because department size is part of the settlement agreement for the consent decree. In the case of D.A.R.E., we noted that SPD has appropriately discontinued this practice.

In no case did we feel that SPD (or any agency) has fully used guidance from research to influence practice, but in many instances, the department has implemented evidence-based practices. These include multiple hot spots policing projects and drug market initiatives. In some cases, we recommended further efforts for the department to follow research, particularly in the area of problem-oriented policing, which has not been commonly used in the department in recent years. Thus, the case study provides an overall assessment of SPD's use of research evidence, while also providing a place for examples of innovative SPD strategies that are in line with research and areas where further work would be useful to better align practice with research evidence.

In terms of OCA's goals for the site, the case study demonstrates that SPD has suspended or is working towards limiting the use of less effective or ineffective strategies in an effort to do no harm. We recognize the challenge of fully eliminating standard model tactics such as random preventive patrol or rapid response to 911 calls. Our recommendation would be for SPD to prioritize more focused use of officer downtime between calls to target hot spots. For response time, we certainly see the value of quick police response for priority calls, but would encourage the department to continue to deemphasize response time as a primary performance metric for crime control.

The site also helped to spur some further efforts by SPD and OCA. The site, in conjunction with the Gill et al. (2012) crime prevention review, provided the momentum to examine SPD practices where research indicates that there may be some risk of potential harmful effects such as police officers in schools (see Gill, Gottfredson, & Hutzell, 2015). The site also provided timely information for policy makers who were considering implementing an acoustic gunshot locator system (AGLS). OCA's (2016a) report describing considerations for an evaluation of an AGLS included a number of factors that should be tracked to ensure that project did not result in unintended undesirable or harmful consequences.

In terms of building the City's capacity to use effective strategies, SPD and other City partners have continued to engage in a series of research projects in recent years. SPD collaborated with researchers from the Police Foundation on an innovative experiment designed to reduce use of force (Owens, Weisburd, Amendola, & Alpert, 2018). SPD and the research team worked together to develop a brief training intervention. During the intervention, supervising sergeants would ask the officers to recall a recent routine interaction with a citizen in a 'risky' place. The sergeant's script itself followed the principles of procedural justice and allowed the officers to reflect on the incident using 'slow thinking.' This report offered strong findings that officers who received this rather small supervisory intervention were less likely to be involved in subsequent arrests or use of force.

In another example, the 'Rainier Beach: A Beautiful Safe Place for Youth'[8] project was initiated in 2013 and funded until December 2015 through a BJA grant to the City. This innovative project addresses five hot spots of juvenile crime in an extremely diverse Seattle neighborhood utilizing research-informed, place-based, non-arrest strategies. The interventions, designed and implemented by non-police agencies and community partner organizations in collaboration with SPD, focus on increasing guardianship, improving collective efficacy, changing rules and policies, and altering the physical design at the hot spots. In 2016, the City began providing ongoing funding for the project coordination and interventions, as well as ongoing evaluation by CEBCP. Preliminary findings from the quasi-experimental evaluation conducted by Gill and Vitter (2017) show promising, but not statistically significant, results.

Our main challenge with the case study has been keeping it updated, particularly with high levels of turnover in SPD. Our goal is to work with SPD to update the case study to more accurately reflect recent work on a number of initiatives. If updated, the case study will allow the department and City to assess its growth over time in incorporating research into practice and allow the site to better achieve the goal of providing a repository for institutional knowledge about SPD research projects. In spring 2018, we updated articles and reports on the case study site, but further information provided by SPD would be helpful in ensuring the page is fully up to date. We revisit the need for further collaboration with SPD on the site in our conclusions below.

Utilization of the Site

It is difficult to track the extent to which the 'What works' site has been used by policymakers and practitioners in Seattle. Anecdotally, the site was well received by City Council members, who all were emailed a link to the site and, as we noted above, the site has influenced the subsequent work of OCA. We are less certain about the extent to which officers and leaders in the SPD are using the site on a regular basis. Moving forward, we hope to identify ways to better track the extent to which the site is a useful translational tool for practitioners at all levels, an issue we revisit below.

We can, however, track the influence of the site in two ways. The first is by examining the extent to which the site has been cited in media reports and academic sources. Unlike citations to academic articles, it is more challenging to track citations to a website. We used Moz, an inbound link tracker, in conjunction with Google and Google News searches of 'Center for Evidence-Based Crime Policy' (which is how the site is typically cited), to look for instances in which the 'What works' site was mentioned in an article as of March 2018. We identified a total of four citations in books and book chapters, nine mentions in law review articles, and three references in journal articles (in papers published in *Qualitative Inquiry, Criminal Justice Studies,* and *Urban Research & Practice*). The community policing strategy page was also included as a resource for applicants in the FY 2018 BJA solicitation for Project Safe Neighborhoods.[9]

Since websites are infrequently cited in academic work, we suspected the site might be more commonly linked to in news articles about policing effectiveness. We identified 15 newspaper, news company, or magazine articles from local and national publications that mentioned the site and included a link to the site in general or to a specific strategy page. These included national publications, such as a *Newsweek* article on how much the New York Police Department spends on misdemeanor arrests that referenced the broken windows page and the mixed effects of broken windows policing on crime (Bekiempis, 2014). Similarly, an NBC News report on Mayor Rahm Emanuel's plans to fight crime in Chicago cited the hot spots policing strategy page in describing how patrol deployments can be most effective in reducing crime (Ali, 2016). The site has also been included in local publications, including a *Richmond Times-Dispatch* article on neighborhood revitalization that cited the broken windows page and noted that aggressive enforcement strategies tend to be less effective than situational strategies to address disorder (Remmers, 2017).

The second way to assess site utilization is to examine the number of visitors to the site. Google Analytics tracks data on visitors and page views for each individual page within the CEBCP website. In Table 3.2, we include the total number of page views for each of the 21 pages that make up the 'What works' site for the four-year period of 1 March 2014 to 28 February 2018. We chose a start date prior to the official launch of the page because the site was up and live by spring 2014, although it was not heavily promoted until its official release in November. Overall, during this four-year period, there were about 1.82 million page views for the entire CEBCP website (all pages housed under cebcp.org). Approximately 46.3% of these were of pages within the 'What works' site. We should note that page view counts are not the same as visitors and one visitor may load a page multiple times on a single visit to a website. But these overall findings suggest a significant proportion of visitors to CEBCP's website were accessing the 'What works' site.

TABLE 3.2 Page Views for 'What works in policing?' Website Pages, 1 March 2014–28 February 2018

Rank	Page	Page Views
1	Broken Windows Policing	490,622
2	Hot Spots Policing	68,928
3	Problem-Oriented Policing	62,900
4	Community Policing and Procedural Justice	41,461
5	Review of the Research Evidence	28,900
6	Focused Deterrence Strategies	19,606
7	Police Technology	19,295
8	'Standard Model' Policing Tactics	17,930
9	DNA for Police Investigations	16,721
10	What Works in Policing? Main Page	14,543
11	Seattle Police Case Study	13,862
12	Closed Circuit Television (CCTV)	9,217
13	Information-Gathering Interrogation Approach	8,547
14	Resource Library	6,981
15	Drug Abuse Resistance Education (D.A.R.E.)	6,853
16	Directed Patrol for Gun Violence	5,595
17	Investigations by Detectives	4,409
18	Increasing Department Size	3,384
19	Counterterrorism Strategies	2,341
20	Second Responder Programs	1,863
	Methodology and Intervention Coding	972
	Total	844,930

The results in Table 3.2 suggest a great deal of variability within the 'What works' pages in terms of number of visitors. The broken windows policing website had far and away the most page views, with 490,622, representing 26.9% of all page views to CEBCP's website for the four-year period and more than 58% of all page views for the 'What works' site. The hot spots policing page was a distant second, with about 69,000 page views followed by the problem-oriented policing page. We are not certain as to why the broken windows page so dominates the total page views for the site, but Table 3.2 does give us some sense of the interests of site visitors. Broken windows policing has remained in the news, particularly in relation to policing tactics in New York City and thus likely remains a popular topic for both practitioners and the public. The page is one of the first hits on Google if you search for 'broken windows policing,' and thus we suspect the site has been an educational tool for those looking to learn more about the strategy and its effects.

The other popular 'What works' pages suggest an interest in better understanding evidence-based strategies, such as hot spots policing and problem-oriented policing, that have remained popular in recent years and which have strong evidence of effectiveness. We view this as promising for translation efforts. The community policing and procedural justice site was fourth most popular, which also seems logical in an era where police-community relationships are strained in many communities and where legitimacy was a major focus of the President's Task Force on 21st Century Policing (2015) and recent National Academies of Sciences, Engineering, and Medicine (2017) report on proactive policing.

Both of these indicators of utilization suggest the site is being used and visited a great deal. As we noted, we do not have clear data on the extent to which the site is being used by policing practitioners within and outside Seattle, but we do have evidence that the site is being utilized by journalists and a number of visitors interested in learning more about what works in policing. We further examined Google Analytics data in an attempt to understand the kinds of visitors coming to the site. We had hoped data on users' internet service provider might provide some insight. While a number of universities and some international police departments did show up in the service provider data, network data was most commonly either unavailable or pointed to a large national internet service provider. We also examined the city from which visitors accessed the site, based on user IP address. Here we see some evidence suggesting that the site is being accessed by users in Seattle, although again we cannot say for sure who these users are. The Seattle case study site, for example, was viewed most frequently by users in Seattle (457 views).

Overall, we recognize that there are not clear benchmarks as to what makes a translational tool successful. We note that in the same four-year period, the Evidence-Based Policing Matrix had 64,067 page views, suggesting that our site was well-visited in relation to another translation tool housed on the CEBCP site. Data from the Office of Justice Programs (OJP, 2017) suggests CrimeSolutions.gov receives an average of 2,600 views per day. The 'What works' site averages about 578 views a day, suggesting fewer visitors, but still a significant number, when considering the site is focused only on policing and is not an official government website. Overall, we think our citation, media, and web traffic data all suggest the 'What works' site is being used rather extensively, and is thus meeting our goal of making the policing effectiveness literature more accessible, but we note below the need for future work assessing the site's effectiveness.

Next Steps

In this chapter, we have described the creation of a 'What works in policing?' translational tool through a collaboration between local government and universities. The website provides accessible summaries of what we know is effective (and ineffective) based on prior findings. Importantly, the city government funding also led to a localized customization of the website, both in terms of the research and strategies covered and the SPD case study. We are not aware of any other partnerships of this kind, but we think this is a useful framework for researchers collaborating with local government agencies.

Before concluding, we offer some suggestions for next steps on the 'What works' site specifically and translational tools in policing in general. First, we recognize the main limitation of our work is our lack of knowledge about the extent to which SPD is utilizing the site. We plan to continue to work with SPD to both update the case study page and ensure the site is used. Moving forward, it would be helpful to talk directly to SPD leaders and officers about the site to get feedback on its perceived usefulness and ways it could be improved. We think some combination of surveys, interviews, and focus groups would allow for better data collection on site utilization. We received feedback from SPD personnel, including IT professionals, when the site first launched, but it would be valuable to take stock of the site collaboratively almost five years after its launch.

Second, we think more work is needed to promote the site and maximize its potential as a resource for police practitioners and policymakers in Seattle and beyond. Some of this work could be done in conjunction with efforts to better understand site utilization. This is also an opportunity to introduce SPD personnel not familiar with the tool to its features and usefulness as a free resource. Presentations and briefings would help further get the word out about the site, and examining site traffic before and after such outreach efforts would help with assessing their effectiveness. In the long term, the site could be integrated into academy, in-service, and supervisor training (Lum & Koper, 2017) in Seattle or other jurisdictions to provide new and current officers with recommendations for evidence-based strategies to reduce crime and increase fairness.

Third, we think additional research is needed on translation tools in general. We believe the federal government should play a key role both in funding this work and in translation efforts. CrimeSolutions.gov continues to be updated and expanded, although the federal infrastructure for translation in the Justice Department could be further expanded. In health and medicine, for example, the National Institutes of Health has a new National Center for Advancing Translational Sciences[10] established in 2011 to promote the use of innovative ways to more efficiently bring medical research into practice. While it is difficult to compare criminal justice funding to medical funding, the fiscal year 2017 budget for the agency was $684.1 million, suggesting a significant investment in translational work. As a contrast, CrimeSolutions.gov has not received dedicated funding since fiscal year 2014 (Office of Justice Programs, 2017).

Conclusion

Our case study suggests local governments can play a key role in funding and supporting translational work. While we are limited in our ability to fully assess the benefits of the 'What works' site for OCA, the costs were relatively minor to fund researcher time to create and update the site. Most American policing is funded at the local level, and we hope to see future examples of local government engaging with researchers to better ensure that police policies and practices are in line with research evidence. We think in particular that the case study approach is an important means for agencies to regularly assess their strategic portfolio, and, as noted above, we hope to continue to update the SPD case study as the policing evidence base continues to expand. Now more than ever, translational tools can play an important role in ensuring fairer and effective policing. For policing to truly be more evidence-based, such tools are necessary to ensure government employees, both inside and outside of the police department, can access and understand the latest research on what works.

Disclosure Statement

No potential conflict of interest was reported by the authors.

Funding

The creation of the website described in this work was supported by the City of Seattle Office of City Auditor under agreement number OCA-2016-01.

Notes

1. See http://cebcp.org/tcmagazine/.
2. See http://whatworks.college.police.uk/toolkit/About-the-Crime-Reduction-Toolkit/Pages/About. aspx.
3. See http://www.policingmatrix.org.
4. See http://cebcp.org/evidence-based-policing/the-matrix/matrix-demonstration-project/.
5. Reports from the Office of City Auditor are available at: http://www.seattle.gov/cityauditor.
6. See http://spdblotter.seattle.gov/2012/03/29/spd-2020-a-vision-for-the-future/.
7. See http://cebcp.org/evidence-based-policing/what-works-in-policing/.
8. See http://www.rb-safeplaceforyouth.com/.
9. See https://www.bja.gov/funding/PSNFormula18.pdf.
10. See http://www.ncats.nih.gov/.

References

Ali, S. S. (2016). Mayor Rahm Emanuel's tension with Chicago cops complicated crime fighting. *NBC News*, September 22. Retrieved from https://www.nbcnews.com/storyline/chicagos-cruel-summer/rahm-emanuel-s-tension-chicago-cops-complicates-crime-fighting-n651496

Bekiempis, V. (2014). How much does the NYPD spend on misdemeanor arrests? *Newsweek*, December 15. Retrieved from http://www.newsweek.com/embargoeddec-156-pm-policing-costs-291948

Braga, A. A., & Bond, B. J. (2008). Policing crime and disorder hot spots: A randomized controlled trial. *Criminology, 46*, 577–607.

Braga, A. A., Papachristos, A. V., & Hureau, D. M. (2014). The effects of hot spots policing on crime: An updated systematic review and meta-analysis. *Justice Quarterly, 31*, 633–663.

Braga, A. A., & Weisburd, D. (2012). The effects of focused deterrence strategies on crime: A systematic review and meta-analysis of the empirical evidence. *Journal of Research in Crime and Delinquency, 49*, 323–358.

Braga, A. A., Weisburd, D., & Turchan, B. (2018). Focused deterrence strategies and crime control: An updated systematic review and meta-analysis of the empirical evidence. *Criminology & Public Policy, 17*, 205–250.

Clarridge, C. (2013). Seattle grounds police drone program. *The Seattle Times*, February 7. Retrieved from https://www.seattletimes.com/seattle-news/seattle-grounds-police-drone-program

Eck, J. E. (2015). Who should prevent crime at places? The advantages of regulating place managers and challenges to police service. *Policing: A Journal of Policy and Practice, 9*, 223–233.

Gill, C., Gottfredson, D., & Hutzell, K. (2015). *Process evaluation of the Seattle youth violence prevention initiative's school emphasis officer program*. Seattle, WA: City of Seattle Office of City Auditor.

Gill, C., Lum, C., Cave, B., Dario, L., Telep, C., Vitter, Z., & Weisburd, D. (2012). *Evidence-based assessment of the City of Seattle's crime prevention programs*. Seattle, WA: City of Seattle Office of City Auditor.

Gill, C., & Vitter, Z. (2017). *Rainier Beach: A beautiful safe place for youth. 2017 evaluation update*. Fairfax, VA: Center for Evidence-Based Crime Policy, George Mason University.

Gill, C., Vitter, Z., & Weisburd, D. (2016). *Rainier Beach: A beautiful safe place for youth. Final evaluation report*. Fairfax, VA: Center for Evidence-Based Crime Policy, George Mason University.

Gross Shader, C., & Jones, D. G. (2015). *The City of Seattle could reduce violent crime and victimization by strengthening its approach to street outreach*. Seattle, WA: City of Seattle Office of City Auditor.

Harcourt, B. E., & Ludwig, J. (2006). Broken windows: New evidence from New York City and a five-city social experiment. *University of Chicago Law Review, 73,* 271–320.

Johnson, S. D., Tilley, N., & Bowers, K. J. (2015). Introducing EMMIE: An evidence rating scale to encourage mixed-method crime prevention synthesis reviews. *Journal of Experimental Criminology, 11,* 459–473.

Kelling, G. L., Pate, A. M., Dieckman, D., & Brown, C. (1974). *The Kansas City Preventive Patrol Experiment: Technical report.* Washington, DC: Police Foundation.

Kelling, G. L., & Sousa, W. H. (2001). *Do police matter? An analysis of the impact of New York City's police reforms* (Civic Report No. 22). New York: Manhattan Institute for Policy Research.

Koper, C. S., & Mayo-Wilson, E. (2006). Police crackdowns on illegal gun carrying: A systematic review of their impact on gun crime. *Journal of Experimental Criminology, 2,* 227–261.

Laub, J. H. (2011). Strengthening NIJ: Mission, science and process. *NIJ Journal, 268,* 16–21.

Laycock, G. (2014). Crime science and policing: Lessons of translation. *Policing: A Journal of Policy and Practice, 8,* 393–401.

Lum, C. (2009). *Translating police research into practice. Ideas in American policing.* Washington, DC: Police Foundation.

Lum, C., Koper, C., & Telep, C. W. (2011). The evidence-based policing matrix. *Journal of Experimental Criminology, 7,* 3–26.

Lum, C., & Koper, C. S. (2017). *Evidence-based policing: Translating research into practice.* New York: Oxford University Press.

Lum, C., Stoltz, M., Koper, C. S., & Scherer, J. A. (2019). Research on body-worn cameras: What we know, what we need to know. *Criminology & Public Policy, 18,* 93–118.

Lum, C., Telep, C. W., Koper, C., & Grieco, J. (2012). Receptivity to research in policing. *Justice Research and Policy, 14,* 61–95.

Mayhew, P. (2016). In defense of administrative criminology. *Crime Science: An Interdisciplinary Journal, 5,* 1–10.

McCord, J. (2003). Cures that harm: Unanticipated outcomes of crime prevention programs. *Annals of the American Academy of Political and Social Science, 587,* 16–30.

Meissner, C. A., Redlich, A. D., Michael, S. W., Evans, J. R., Camilletti, C. R., Bhatt, S., & Brandon, S. (2014). Accusatorial and information-gathering interrogation methods and their effects on true and false confessions: A meta-analytic review. *Journal of Experimental Criminology, 10,* 459–486.

National Academies of Sciences, Engineering, and Medicine. (2017). Committee on Proactive Policing: Effects on crime, communities and civil liberties. In D. Weisburd & M. K. Majmundar (Eds.), *Proactive policing: Effects on crime and communities.* Washington, DC: National Academies Press.

National Research Council. (2004). Committee to review research on police policy and practices. In W. Skogan & K. Frydl (Eds.), *Fairness and effectiveness in policing: The evidence.* Washington, DC: National Academies Press.

Office of City Auditor (OCA). (2016a). *Ten things the City of Seattle should consider when evaluating a pilot implementation of an acoustic gunshot locator system.* Seattle, WA: Author.

Office of City Auditor (OCA). (2016b). *Prescription drug disposal: Opportunities for the City of Seattle.* Seattle, WA: Author.

Office of City Auditor (OCA). (2017a). *Five new recommendations for evaluating Seattle's new police oversight system.* Seattle, WA: Author.

Office of City Auditor (OCA). (2017b). *Reporting plan for navigation team.* Seattle, WA: Author.

Office of Justice Programs (OJP). (2017). *FY 2018 program summaries.* Washington, DC: Author.

Owens, E., Weisburd, D., Amendola, K. L., & Alpert, G. P. (2018). Can you build a better cop?: Experimental evidence on supervision, training, and policing in the community. *Criminology and Public Policy, 17,* 41–87.

President's Task Force on 21st Century Policing. (2015). *Final report of the President's Task Force on 21st Century Policing.* Washington, DC: Office of Community Oriented Policing Services, U.S. Department of Justice.

Remmers, V. (2017). Chesterfield creates new hub for revitalization of neighborhoods, and residents' responses vary. *Richmond Times-Dispatch,* April 9. Retrieved from http://www.richmond.com/news/local/chesterfield/chesterfield-creates-new-hub-for-revitalization-of-neighborhoods-and-residents/article_58b59940-519d-558dabc8-cd6eff784cb2.html

Rosenbaum, D. P. (2007). Just say no to D.A.R.E. *Criminology and Public Policy, 6*, 815–824.

Rosenfeld, R., Fornango, R., & Rengifo, A. F. (2007). The impact of order-maintenance policing on New York City homicide and robbery rates: 1988–2001. *Criminology, 45*, 355–384.

Sherman, L. W. (1998). *Evidence-based policing: Ideas in American Policing.* Washington, DC: Police Foundation.

Sherman, L. W., & Eck, J. E. (2002). Policing for crime prevention. In L. W. Sherman, D. P. Farrington, B. C. Welsh, & D. L. MacKenzie (Eds.), *Evidence-based crime prevention* (pp. 295–329). New York: Routledge.

Spelman, W., & Brown, D. (1984). *Calling the police: A replication of the citizen reporting component of the Kansas City response time analysis.* Washington, DC: Police Executive Research Forum.

Telep, C. W., & Hibdon, J. (2019). *Understanding and responding to hot spots. Problem-Oriented Guides for Police.* Problem-Solving Tools No. 14. Phoenix, AZ: Center for Problem-Oriented Policing, Arizona State University.

Telep, C. W., & Lum, C. (2014). The receptivity of officers to empirical research and evidence-based policing: An examination of survey data from three agencies. *Police Quarterly, 17*, 359–385.

Telep, C. W., Mitchell, R. J., & Weisburd, D. (2014). How much time should the police spend at crime hot spots?: Answers from a police agency directed randomized field trial in Sacramento, California. *Justice Quarterly, 31*, 905–933.

Telep, C. W., & Weisburd, D. (2012). What is known about the effectiveness of police practices in reducing crime and disorder? *Police Quarterly, 15*, 331–357.

Telep, C. W., & Weisburd, D. (2016). Policing. In D. P. Farrington, D. Weisburd, & C. E. Gill (Eds.), *What works in crime prevention and rehabilitation: Lessons from systematic reviews* (pp. 137–168). New York: Springer.

Veigas, H., & Lum, C. (2013). Assessing the evidence base of a police service patrol portfolio. *Policing: A Journal of Policy and Practice, 7*, 248–262.

Weisburd, D. (2015). The law of crime concentration and the criminology of place. *Criminology, 54*, 133–157.

Weisburd, D., & Eck, J. E. (2004). What can police do to reduce crime, disorder, and fear? *The Annals of the American Academy of Political and Social Science, 593*, 42–65.

Weisburd, D., Telep, C. W., Hinkle, J. C., & Eck, J. E. (2010). Is problem-oriented policing effective in reducing crime and disorder? Findings from a Campbell systematic review. *Criminology & Public Policy, 9*, 139–172.

West, S. L., & O'Neal, K. K. (2004). Project D.A.R.E. outcome effectiveness revisited. *American Journal of Public Health, 94*, 1027–1029.

Wilson, D. B., McClure, D., & Weisburd, D. (2010). Does forensic DNA help to solve crime? The benefit of sophisticated answers to naïve questions. *Journal of Contemporary Criminal Justice, 26*, 458–469.

Wilson, J. Q., & Kelling, G. L. (1982). Broken windows: The police and neighborhood safety. *Atlantic Monthly, 211*, 29–38.

4

Translating Police Research into Policy

Some Implications of the National Academies Report on Proactive Policing for Policymakers and Researchers

James Willis and Heather Toronjo

DEPARTMENT OF CRIMINOLOGY, LAW AND SOCIETY, GEORGE MASON UNIVERSITY, FAIRFAX, USA

Introduction

Recently, a Committee on Proactive Policing, appointed by the U.S. government's prestigious National Academies of Sciences, Engineering, and Medicine, concluded a rigorous review of scientific research on the effects of various proactive policing strategies on key outcomes. Unlike traditional policing approaches with their emphasis on responding to crime in process, or that had already occurred, the Committee's focus was on evaluating proactive strategies that emphasize 'prevention, mobilizing resources based on police initiative, and targeting the broader underlying forces at work that may be driving crime and disorder' (Weisburd & Majmundar, 2018, p. 1).

Several proactive police innovations have emerged over the past few decades, including community-oriented policing and stop-question-and-frisk (SQF), raising crucial questions about their consequences for public safety and the proper uses of police authority. In light of the latest crisis in U.S. policing due to perceptions of abusive police practices against African-Americans and other minority groups, the Committee went beyond an evaluation of simply identifying 'what works' in reducing crime and disorder. Rather, it examined the evidence on whether proactive policing was applied in ways that were discriminatory, illegal, or harmful to the democratic principle that exercises of police power are derived from popular consent. Thus, the Committee acknowledged the implications of proactive policing for important values other than crime control, such as liberty, accountability, and parsimonious uses of police authority (Weisburd & Majmundar, 2018, p. 17).

The report has obvious relevance for policymakers, especially police chiefs who must make difficult choices about which policing strategies to pursue while balancing fundamental values. Knowing to what degree a policy delivers a given outcome is obviously vital to making informed decisions, but the successful translation of research into policy involves confronting challenges other than the availability of high-quality program evaluations (Lum & Koper, 2017; Nutley, Walter, & Davies, 2007).[1]

When it comes to the greater integration of science into policy, proponents of the evidence-based policing movement have focused on ways that science can be harnessed to existing bureaucratic structures. These include police agencies documenting the outcomes of different policing strategies and offering comprehensive training programs (Sherman, 2015). But while valuable,

DOI: 10.4324/9781003153009-6

this approach overlooks other key obstacles that can hinder the translation process. Some of these were raised by the Committee, but we take occasion to develop here. To support the implementation of more effective policies, we suggest policymakers will benefit from a broader research agenda that takes into account: (1) the mistrust of science and its experts; (2) the paucity of cost-efficiency analyses on proactive policing strategies; and (3) the challenge of managing competing values. For each of these, we describe the nature of the problem before identifying some possibilities for mitigating or overcoming it. Our goal is not to suggest 'one size fits all' prescriptions, or to imply that what we propose is effective (that would require scientific study). It is our hope that in exploring these complex issues in light of the Committee's work, we accomplish two goals: (1) we provide some considerations that police leaders might consider when deciding on how to 'take action' for ensuring more 'effective, efficient, and equitable agency operations' (Schafer, 2013, p. 129); and (2) we illuminate useful avenues for future studies.

Mistrust of Science

Science as a basis for decision making has long competed against other forms of knowledge, such as religion, intuition, and everyday experience (Greene, 2014). Recent events suggest this conflict is far from over. Even when there is widespread scientific consensus on an issue, such as climate change or childhood vaccinations, there continues to be significant resistance from broad segments of the public (Suhay & Druckman, 2015). The Committee's report appears at a time of skepticism toward scientific experts and their views, with popular concerns over misinformation or 'fake news' appearing to have spiked since the U.S. 2016 Presidential Election (Pew Research Center, 2016; Vraga & Bode, 2017). In a university commencement address, Atul Gawande (2016), the surgeon and writer, explored this prevailing 'mistrust of science,' noting that 'even where the knowledge provided by science is overwhelming, people often resist it – sometimes outright deny it.' Rejecting evidence not only undermines informed debate on which democracy depends, it can result in other harmful consequences, such as a rise in childhood illnesses due to a decline in vaccination rates (Center for Disease Control [CDC], 2017), or an increase in juvenile delinquency through an ineffective, but popular, program such as Scared Straight (Petrosino, Turpin-Petrosino, Hollis-Peel, & Lavenberg, 2013).

Why do people choose to reject science? Some of this doubting can be attributed to the nature of the scientific approach itself. Even though science strives to answer questions with facts and systematic methods, it also recognizes its own limitations. From a scientific perspective, all knowledge is conditional, so that 'a contradictory piece of evidence can always emerge' (Gawande, 2016). Thus, in its attempts to produce valid knowledge, science acknowledges variability, eschews overgeneralization, and is cautious in its judgments, often calling for additional research to provide a firmer basis for action. Unsurprisingly, the Committee was circumspect in stating its scientific conclusions and in presenting recommendations. Thus, it found strong evidence that individuals' perceptions of procedural justice treatment are strongly associated with subjective assessments of police legitimacy and cooperation with the police. But at the same time, the Committee noted that the research base is insufficient to conclude that procedural justice *causally influences* these outcomes and delivers crime prevention benefits (Weisburd & Majmundar, 2018, pp. 248–249).

One of the dangers of such scientific caution is that skeptics may use it to unduly undermine science's claims, such as using subtle differences between climate change models to assert that predictions on rising temperatures are invalid (Nuccitelli, 2017). In the case of procedural justice, it would be wrong-headed for people to infer from the Committee's report that the absence of strong evidence on its causal effects on certain outcomes justifies overlooking its significance to positive police-community relations (Nagin & Telep, 2017). Moreover, a strong argument can be made that the process of treating people fairly and with dignity and respect is intrinsically valuable whatever the outcome.

But the problem for scientific explanation runs much deeper than these challenges. Even a person's general level of education and scientific literacy seems to matter little to a willingness to embrace empirical evidence (Gawande, 2016). Indeed, education is only 'modestly predictive of the public's general attitudes toward and trust in science,' with some research suggesting that this association disappears altogether over contentious political issues (Lewandowsky & Oberauer, 2012, p. 218). In fact, a large body of research suggests that the 'perceived credibility' of scientific information and experts often depends on a person's existing worldviews or values (Suhay & Druckman, 2015, p. 8). When people confront information that confirms or strengthens their existing values, identities, and policy preferences, they are more likely to consider it relevant and accurate. Conversely, the more that scientific evidence conflicts with these values or beliefs, the more likely it will be rejected.

A study conducted by Dan Kahan and his colleagues (2010) is a powerful illustration of this tendency toward the 'motivated rejection' of science (Lewandowsky & Oberauer, 2012). They captured two dimensions of people's worldviews and tested how these influenced individuals' assessments of the level of scientific consensus on a number of controversial issues, and of the trustworthiness of a fictional scientific expert. Worldviews were distinguished by a preference for a hierarchical society stratified by fixed attributes such as race, gender, and class, or for a more egalitarian society (Hierarchy-egalitarianism), and by beliefs on how much government or society should be allowed to interfere in an individual's life choices (Individualism-communitarianism).

Their findings demonstrated that people significantly disagreed in their assessments of the level of scientific consensus on an issue based on their cultural predispositions. For example, people holding hierarchical and individualistic outlooks were much more likely to perceive that most scientists agreed that carrying concealed handguns reduced violent crime. In comparison, 'egalitarian communitarians' were more likely to believe that scientific experts *disagreed* on this point. Similarly, those with hierarchical and individualistic preferences were more likely to perceive the authors' description of a fictional scientist as a trustworthy and knowledgeable expert when he was assigned the position that concealed handguns reduced violent crime and much less so when they held different cultural values (Kahan, Jenkins-Smith, & Braman, 2010). Given the influence of prior values or beliefs, it seems likely that the Committee's conclusion on the mixed effects of controversial policies on crime, such as SQF, will be embraced as providing support for both its proponents and detractors.[2]

So where does this leave police leaders willing to use science to correct misinformation about the effects of different policing strategies, and to elevate science in the eyes of diverse constituents (including their own officers) as a basis for rational decision-making? Insights from organizational theory can provide some guidance.[3] According to one model, a rational response to a 'technical' concern, such as a rise in the crime rate, is to implement a policing strategy which has a high probability of being effective (Mastrofski, 1998). Thus, from the perspective of the technical-rational model, a police chief can garner support from stakeholders by using an evidence-based strategy that reduces crime. Over time, implementing approaches that 'work' could help win over doubters about the benefits of science for effective policing.

But there are considerable risks to this approach for a police chief hoping to acquire resources and support, such as the problem of external validity. Just because a proactive policing strategy worked in one police department does not guarantee it will be successful in a different time and place (Weisburd & Majmundar, 2018, p. 323). In fact, even in the case of hot spots policing, which evidence suggests is one of the most promising crime reduction strategies, there is much that is still unknown about 'the circumstances under which this approach will be most suc-cessful and least likely to generate undesirable side effects' (Mastrofski & Willis, 2010, p. 105). The translational process of evidence into policy requires careful attention to local context and to the specific mechanisms through which outcomes are accomplished (Sampson, Winship, & Knight, 2013). Should a police chief implement an evidence-based strategy that fails to produce the intended results in his or particular jurisdiction or worse, produce unintended and harmful results, this could undermine overall trust in an evidence-based policing approach. And some police chiefs themselves might be skeptical of science, and so rather than merely proselytizing about the virtues of science, researchers should take the time to understand the bases of these concerns, including being forthright about the strengths and limitations of their studies. For those chiefs who are convinced of science's merits, a different strategy to cultivate support for police science would be to inform stakeholders of its overall benefits, particularly in relation to untested strategies based on tradition or other questionable factors, whether or not they always result in desirable outcomes such as crime reduction. From the alternative perspective of 'institutional theory,' a chief is seen as legitimate simply because he or she is adopting a strat-egy that has become widely accepted as an example of what it means to be a progressive police department (Willis, Mastrofski, & Weisburd, 2007). A police chief could justify her approach by evoking the experiences of professional peers and the backing of occupational and professional organizations, such as the International Association of Chiefs of Police (IACP), but she could also seek to influence the outlooks of her own constituents more directly and within the rele-vant context of their own lives. As we have seen, overcoming deeply-entrenched worldviews is difficult, but research in communication science suggests there are some promising techniques for communicating contested findings in order to increase the likelihood of their acceptance (Lewandowsky, Ecker, Seifert, Schwarz, & Cook, 2012).

One of those techniques is framing, or 'the casting of information in a certain light to influ-ence what people think, believe, or do' (Committee on the Science of Science Communication, 2017, p. 36). Research suggests that framing a problem and responses to it in ways that resonate with a person's values and assumptions can 'enhance acceptance of information that would be rejected if it were differently framed' (Lewandowsky et al., 2012, p. 120). For example, a political rally for a hate crime group will evoke very different reactions should it be presented as an issue of free speech, or as a risk to public safety (Chong & Druckman, 2007). Similarly, a police chief wishing to implement hot spots policing to reduce violent crime in a disadvantaged neighborhood could frame it in ways that increase its appeal to a range of worldviews. Rather than focusing solely on this strategy's crime reduction benefits, the chief might anticipate that some might challenge this approach (despite strong evidence of its effectiveness), because it shifts resources away from their own communities, or because it could result in overly aggressive policing. Adopting an egalitarian frame that justifies the concentration of police resources as a fair means of protecting those at the highest risk of victimization might help allay some of these concerns. Moreover, focusing resources in a very small area could also be presented as minimizing the risk of widespread intrusions into the lives of broad segments of the community (Weisburd, 2016, p. 661). This could be supplemented with a 'constitutional frame' underscoring the chief's commitment to ensuring officers in the hot spots are in strict compliance with individual rights, such as Fourth Amendment protections against illegal search and seizure. The chief could rein-force this message by implementing measures to increase police accountability, such as collecting data on stops which are routinely audited by an independent bureau and making these data public (Mastrofski, 1999). To help convey this information to a broad audience, police departments could use their existing website and other social media tools, such as Twitter and Facebook. Importantly, police leaders would need to frame a problem aptly, and not frame it in a way that deceives people into accepting scientific conclusions that they are justifiably skeptical of.

A second communication technique that could help overcome skepticism toward science-based strategies supported by strong evidence is the use of narratives or storytelling. Narratives describe 'the cause-and-effect relationships between events that take place over a particular time period that impact particular characters' (Dahlstrom, 2014, p. 13, 614). Research suggests that people are more likely to understand narratives and more likely to find them interesting than the traditional mode of presenting science with its focus on logic, generalizability, and abstract truths (Dahlstrom, 2014; Green, 2006).

Unlike science's emphasis on rationality and general principles, stories use specific, context-rich cases to engage with people's emotions, and to build support for particular policies. Restorative justice is one example of storytelling's potential for changing the attitudes and behavior of those who participate in frank discussions of crimes or harms and their consequences (Gladwell, 2006). Lawrence Sherman has advocated for research that engages with people's emotions (2003), and others have recognized the limitations of an evidence-based approach that overlooks the 'affective' dimension to criminal justice policy (Freiberg & Carson, 2010). In the case of hot spots policing, a chief might tell the story of a person fearful of walking in the high crime area where she lives, and how her life has been deeply affected by the threat of being victimized. Such a story could be used as an opportunity to communicate scientific findings, while also appealing to deeply-rooted feelings about the high costs of living in fear.

In sum, the entrenched values possessed by different groups can provide a formidable obstacle to the acceptance of evidence-based policies. Consequently, police leaders could profit from considering different ways of communicating science's benefits that go beyond simply stating empirical facts to framing them in ways that try to affirm the cultural values of different groups, and to productively engage with people's emotions. Of course, those who use framing must recognize that it can be used by different groups to serve the broadest range of political values, including ways that could undermine a chief's message. At the very least, the research community whose work is being framed should speak out when framers step out of bounds in terms of the accurate interpretation of their work. Researchers might also assume a more active role in communicating their research findings to help ensure that their results are as widely available as possible. Future police research could draw from an extensive communications literature to test different approaches for communicating about proactive policing strategies, including any possible backfire effects.

Cost-Efficiency Analyses

Effectiveness is not a 'free good' (Horowitz & Zedlewski, 2006, p. 51), and research on proactive policing strategies raises the issue of whether their benefits justify their costs. Government officials operate in times of fiscal constraint and the 'bottom line' is an important factor when deciding how best to allocate resources among different programs (RAND, 2010). What return can a police chief expect for a $100,000 investment in community policing given the Committee's finding that it results in only a moderate improvement to community satisfaction (Mastrofski, Forth.)? What are the comparative effects of removing this resource from another program for which it could have been used? Answering these kinds of questions in the real -world of budget decision making requires an examination of the costs and benefits of proactive policing strategies, but, as the Committee observes, there are few studies that combine a program evaluation of what 'works' with an assessment of whether it is 'worthwhile' from a policy perspective (Weisburd & Majmundar, 2018, p. 322).

Fortunately, the literature on cost–efficiency assessments (cost effectiveness and cost-benefit analyses)[4] of crime prevention policies continues to grow and provides an analytical framework on which policing scholars can build (Cohen, 2000; Dominguez & Raphael, 2015; Journal of Benefit-Cost Analysis, 2017). But answering the question of whether a proactive strategy justifies its costs also raises complex theoretical, practical, and ethical issues: What should be counted as a cost or a benefit? Crime reduction benefits are obviously important, but so are public perceptions of legitimacy, and even potential costs to patrol officer satisfaction. What time-frame should be used given that some costs or benefits may take years to materialize? For example, street stops undermining legitimacy may contribute to future crime, resulting in a possible trade-off between crime today and crime tomorrow (Tyler, Fagin, & Geller, 2014). Moreover, attention must be paid to the distribution (as opposed to the net level) of costs and benefits, and to considering whether it is appropriate (or even possible) to put a value on the less tangible costs of crime, such as pain, suffering, and loss of quality of life (Horowitz & Zedlewski, 2006; Rossi, Lipsey, & Freeman, 2004). These complexities mean that cost-efficiency assessments rarely provide definitive answers and must be supplemented with other forms of moral evaluation. At the same time, their merit lies in encouraging a careful and disciplined examination of the relationship between program outlays and results. By exposing assumptions and quantifying outcomes with consistent measures, they can be a useful, but not definitive, tool for assessing the comparative advantages and disadvantages of different approaches (Nagin, 2015, p. 583).

In general, guidance on identifying and monetizing the costs or inputs of a particular intervention is better developed and less controversial than converting outcomes into monetary units. Even modest attempts to embed cost estimates in evaluations of crime control can provide decision makers with useful information (Rossi et al., 2004, p. 340). In policing, some of the most obvious inputs include the labor costs of police officers and community partners, and estimates of capital consumption, such as supplies and equipment. For example, in their study on the effects of hot spots patrol on gun violence in Kansas City, Sherman and Rogan (1995) included details on the treatment content and dosage of reallocating police patrols to specific areas where gun crime was concentrated. Even though the evaluators did not conduct a cost-benefit analysis, their accounting figures provide a means for calculating this strategy's overall efficiency. Assigning officers to the 8-by-10-block target beat involved 200 nights of patrol, 4,512 officer-hours, and 2,256 patrol car-hours of hot spot patrol (Sherman & Rogan, 1995, p. 680). Using salary information, these hours could be converted into labor expenses by multiplying them by an average wage rate. This could then be used to estimate the program's cost effectiveness by calculating dollars expended in relation to the specific percentage reduction in crime, and it could even serve as a means of comparison to other crime reduction approaches. However, a more ambitious cost-benefit analysis would involve evaluating the net benefit of policing gun hot spots by converting outcomes into monetary savings. So, for example, using measures that researchers have developed in the cost-of-crime literature, some of the value due to reductions in gun injuries could be estimated using hospitalization charges or workers compensation claims (Dominguez & Raphael, 2015).

One of the most well-known and systematic attempts to monetize the cost and benefits of crime prevention policies is provided by the Washington State Institute for Public Policy (WSIPP). WSIPP conducts systematic evidence reviews and then translates these research findings into dollars and cents (Lee, Aos, & Pennucci, 2015). In addition to providing an assessment of the economic consequences of a policy, WSIPP takes into account uncertainty in the research findings and in its cost-benefit tabulations to calculate a risk metric for each policy option. When results are presented to the state legislature, the evaluators provide an expected benefit-cost ratio and an estimation of 'the chance that a program will at least break even, that is, that the current value of benefits will outweigh the current value of costs' (Aos, 2015, p. 638).

WSIPP examines nearly 300 education, social welfare, public health, and criminal justice programs, including an assessment of the benefit of deploying one additional officer to hot spots policing compared with random preventive patrol. Currently, this is the only proactive policing strategy that is analyzed. Included in the calculation is the effect size for hot spots policing on violent and property crime, the tangible and intangible costs of victimization (including medical expenses, property loss, reductions in future earnings, and pain and suffering, in part computed from jury awards), and criminal justice costs (including the average cost of a police arrest) (see Washington State Institute for Public Policy [WSIPP], 2017). According to this estimation, hot spots policing generates about $5 of benefits for every $1 of cost, with a 100% chance that this approach will produce benefits greater than the costs (WSIPP, 2017b).

Of course, the challenge of building cost estimates tightly coupled to crime control outcomes is that it may fail to take into account other relevant social costs. For example, recent scholarship has illuminated the consequences of the police decision to make a misdemeanor arrest on other components of the criminal justice system, including unjust bail practices and weak prosecutorial screening (Natapoff, 2015). Other costs include those 'associated with abridging individual rights, or exacerbating a sense of unfairness in the way that police do their business' (Moore, 2006, p. 335). The latter possibility is particularly germane when it comes to more intrusive policing practices, such as SQF and broken windows policing. Because the laws and policies governing responses to minor offenses and stops and frisks 'permit officers generous discretion,' they increase opportunities for questionable police practices, and can also contribute to disparate racial impacts, both of which can undermine community confidence and trust in the police (Weisburd & Majmundar, 2018, p. 85). To what extent racial disparities associated with the targeting of high-risk people or places through proactive policing strategies are indicators 'of statistical prediction, racial animus, implicit bias, or other causes' requires further testing (Weisburd & Majmundar, 2018, p. 301). But this caveat aside, historical evidence, ethnographic studies, and correlational research suggests these strategies often have harmful 'distributional consequences, exposing individuals to additional scrutiny because of perceived or actual neighborhood characteristics, which often correlate with race and economic status' (Weisburd & Majmundar, 2018, p. 93).

In light of these larger social costs, Manski and Nagin have proposed a formal model for exploring the tradeoff between any public safety benefits of confrontational proactive policing strategies and the 'cost of their intrusion on the privacy of innocent persons, and their disparate impact on racial and other groups' (2017, p. 9308). In highlighting costs which are often overlooked in debates on police strategies, Manski and Nagin illuminate the advantages of considering policy judgments that assess alternatives to SQF (e.g., problem-oriented policing). These alternatives may be comparably effective in reducing crime but do not raise the same concerns about overly aggressive policing (2017, p. 9310). Moreover, using data for the period 2002–2013, during which 88% of the nearly 5 million stops in New York City did not result in a summons or arrest (i.e., 'innocent' stops), they demonstrate that attributable risk of an innocent stop (the differences in the innocent stop rates between black men and white men for specified ages) and not relative risk (the ratio of the innocent stop rate for black men compared to white men) is a more appropriate measure of the social cost of this confrontational strategy on innocent persons. Unlike relative risk, attributable risk varies directly with the scale of the phenomenon, or, in this case, the number of SQFs conducted, which declined precipitously after 2011. Thus, attributable risk captures what matters most when it comes to racial disparity, namely 'how much more frequently blacks are subjected to the tactic than innocent whites, not the ratio of group experiences' (Manski & Nagin, 2017, p. 9312).

In addition to the harmful effects of SQF on community perceptions of police legitimacy, evidence is starting to emerge of other costs that should be taken into account. These include the mental health costs of intrusive police strategies on different groups, particularly young men living in neighborhoods with high levels of involuntary police contact (Goff, 2018). Due to the large racial disparities associated with many proactive practices, they have the potential to exacerbate 'long-standing racial disparities in health' (Geller, Fagan, & Tyler, 2017, p. 6). Being stopped by the police can be a stressful event and contribute to anxiety about being stopped in the future. If people feel they are being targeted unfairly because of their race, it can also provoke feelings of shame, anger, and powerlessness, and a sense of being a second-class citizen unworthy of equal treatment under the law (Epp, Maynard-Moody, & Haider-Markel, 2014).

Cross-sectional studies demonstrate that young urban men living in neighborhoods with high frisk rates are more likely to report mental health issues than those with less exposure to the police (Sewell, Jefferson, & Lee, 2016), while a recent longitudinal study seeks to identify changes in an individual's mental health over time based on their encounters with the police. Controlling for past police contact and other relevant factors, the study found that stops, particularly those experienced as particularly intrusive because they involved invasive tactics such as a frisk or threat of force, were significantly associated with increased anxiety and post-traumatic stress disorder symptoms (Geller et al., 2017).

In developing the Committee's claim about the utility of complementing evaluations of effectiveness with assessments of cost efficiency, we have highlighted some points to consider about the rationale for this approach and its complexities. Future evaluation designs should include measures of a wide range of collateral consequences of proactive policing strategies to see how, and if, it might be possible to maximize crime control gains while minimizing harm to police legitimacy, lawfulness, mental health, and other possible effects (Weisburd, 2016). Research on proactive policing that is more valid and relevant to policymakers will also benefit from the development of standard principles and measures for conducting cost-benefit and cost effectiveness studies (Horowitz & Zedlewski, 2006). This would allow for more meaningful comparisons of the gains and losses across interventions and contribute to the development of a more coherent and generalizable body of research than currently available.

Competing Values

Our discussion has identified the influence of values on audience receptivity to scientific inquiry and their role in cost-efficiency assessments. Here we examine the challenge that police chiefs and policymakers invariably face in pursuing different values simultaneously, values which often compete with one another, like public safety, liberty, and equality. Moreover, external pressures on police chiefs, who generally have short tenures, to demonstrate quick results can lead to a focus on short-term crime issues and easily demonstrated outputs (e.g., pedestrian or traffic stops), rather than other values, such as improving legitimacy, that might take much longer to accomplish. The tension between the short-term goals of practitioners and longer-term goals of researchers can also be a source of value conflict, but due to space limitations, we focus on the role of values in the context of the larger police-community relationship.

Several decades ago, Philip Selznick defined a leader not in terms of his or her competency in accomplishing instrumental tasks like crime control or law enforcement, but as 'primarily an expert in the promotion or protection of values' (1957, p. 28). As the Committee acknowledged, tensions between these values lie at the heart of the current policing crisis, where concerns about crime are accompanied with criticisms over racial discrimination, arbitrary enforcement, and overreaches of police authority. Police researchers have long recognized the difficulties of value conflicts between crime control and due process (Skolnick, 1966), but similar to social scientists in general, they have often been reluctant to study and propose practical ways that these conflicts might be better managed given the conventional scientific divide between facts and values, or 'is' and 'ought' (Flyvbjerg, 2001, ch. 1, p. 5).

One exception is David Thacher, who has been a consistent proponent of police scholarship that contributes to the kind of practical reasoning on which normative judgments depend (2001, 2006). We draw on his work to describe some conventional strategies that policymakers have used to manage value conflicts around the use of their discretionary authority. We then consider the possibility of using police-community meetings as venues for the kind of public deliberation that can advance understanding about values, and that can contribute to principled and morally defensible decisions. Our premise is that effective police governance in a democracy does not depend on consensus, but on consent, and this 'is rendered when the process of government is known and accepted, even when there is discord over the substance of policy' (Mastrofski, 1988, p. 66, emphasis in original).

A common refrain to goals that conflict is to encourage policymakers to find a trade-off between them that is balanced or 'good enough' (Bowling, 2007; Neyroud, 2017). This conceptualization evokes Aristotle's golden mean, where the right decision lies somewhere between two extremes, with deficiency at one end of a scale and excess at the other (Willis & Mastrofski, 2017). As Thacher and Rein (2004) note, in practice, this balancing strategy can be overwhelming. It asks policymakers to identify ahead of time all the values relevant to a particular decision and the best means for achieving them. Then policymakers must weigh all of these against one another, as though different priorities can be 'assessed along a single metric' (Sunstein, 1994, p. 780). Thus, a police leader must seek to balance the gains to public safety through a proactive policing strategy, while also weighing potential harms to police legitimacy, or police-community relations. This approach to guiding decisions has been criticized extensively for being too abstract, for making unrealistic demands on policymakers when there are many factors to consider, and for assuming that values can somehow be assigned general weights and ranked according to importance (see Thacher & Rein, 2004, pp. 457–458).

Other strategies for managing the ambiguities surrounding value conflicts are not based on this instrumentalist logic, but are based on models of practical reasoning. These models rely on policymakers 'making situated judgments about what is appropriate in particular times, places, and contexts' (Thacher & Rein, 2004, p. 458). Their underlying assumption is that we are often more capable of making considered judgments about what should be done in a given situation than we are at identifying the abstract principles that justify those decisions (Thacher, 2006, p. 1656). One such strategy in policymaking is 'cycling,' whose justification lies in the idea that it is not yet known how trade-offs between conflicting values should be made, and so this needs to be discovered in practice. This is achieved by temporarily assigning primary responsibility to one set of values and then shifting attention to another set, as the need arises. Thacher and Rein (2004, p. 468) give the example of the New York City Police Department's Compstat program, a performance management system designed to focus laser-like on reducing crime (Willis et al., 2007). Aggressive policing tactics associated with Compstat, such as broken windows policing, gave rise to community concerns about abuses of police authority, which then shifted attention back to the department's obligation to protect civilians' rights and build positive police-community relationships (Auletta, 2015). One advantage of simplifying value choices is that it can act as a catalyst for the creation of new tactics or programs (like Compstat) whose design can be modified and improved in response to changing circumstances. However, a major limitation of a cycling approach is the harms that can arise by failing to consider adequately, or at least monitor, other values that are being sacrificed in pursuit of one overarching goal.

An alternative strategy to managing value conflicts is for a police leader to assign primary responsibility for pursuing different values to separate units within the organization, so they can be pursued simultaneously. For example, a police department might create a specialist problem-oriented policing unit focused on addressing specific community problems, such as illegal parking. This allows the rest of the agency to continue its traditional activities of answering calls for service and responding to serious crime. Dividing values in this way helps minimize disruption by buffering the organization's core structures and practices from change (Mastrofski & Willis, 2010, p. 58), but it is much less helpful when values, such as liberty and order, are not easily separated: 'It is incoherent to say that we might give the job of crime control entirely to one part of the patrol force and the job of minimizing intrusions on our liberty entirely to another part' (Thacher & Rein, 2004, p. 476).

An obvious limitation of both strategies is their inward focus on police operations and priorities, with less regard for giving community members opportunities to express their preferences for what constitutes an acceptable trade-off between competing values, or for creating opportunities to clarify and reflect on what values matter most and why, and whether they are being embodied in actual police practice. Building consent and eliciting public approval requires forums for regular and sustained feedback from those outside the organization. These forums can help surface concerns that department members might not have anticipated or misjudged, and they can also allow for the kind of give-and-take exchanges necessary for resolving any differences. Improving community participation in (and influence over) police decision making is a key element of community policing, an approach that a recent blue-ribbon commission reaffirmed as a central pillar to American policing (President's Task Force on 21st Century Policing, 2015). Learning how well this works can give insights into how it might help generate outcomes that are both fair and effective.

Much of what we know about attempts to give civilians input on what the priorities of police leadership should be and how these should be pursued comes from a lengthy, in-depth study of Chicago's community policing reform efforts known as the Chicago Alternative Policing Strategy (CAPS). Implemented in the 1990s, a key component of this model was the organization of police officers into 279 neighborhood beat teams, most of which held regularly monthly meetings with residents (Skogan, 2006). Deliberations at these beat meetings were structured around identifying, prioritizing, and finding solutions to community problems, but they also provided an opportunity for civilians to shape police policies and operations directly. What can police leaders learn from these meetings as forums for 'open deliberation and fair exchange about how best to advance public ends?' (Fung, 2001, p. 94).

Perhaps one of the major take-aways is that this approach is fraught with many challenges. One we have alluded to above: the pressure on agency executives to reduce crime, which can lead to a focus on short-term crime control goals rather than longer-term outcomes that can be difficult to achieve, such as building community partnerships or improving police legitimacy. Research suggests the participatory or partnership element of community policing is the one most weakly implemented (Maguire & Katz, 2002). A multi-wave national survey assessing community policing in the 1990s and early 2000s concluded that when it comes to police-community partnerships, the police are reluctant 'to give the community real authority and responsibilities' (Roth, Roehl, & Johnson, 2004, p. 10). Similarly, in Chicago, 'the police, not the community, selected residents to co-lead meeting with an officer, and more often than not, the officer ran the meeting' (Mastrofski, Forth., p. 15). Meetings dominated by the police would seem to limit opportunities for community members to voice their concerns, thereby making it difficult for police leaders to identify and clarify which values matter most to their constituents and how they are being brought to bear on a specific situation.

The potential of these meetings for promoting meaningful deliberation on conflicting values might also be undermined should only certain community interests be represented while others are excluded. In Chicago, beat meetings did a 'better job' of representing established stakehold-ers, particularly homeowners, than they did at 'integrating marginalized groups' such as young and poor African-American and Latino men (Skogan, 2004, p. 73). The danger here is that those groups who show up may have different views on police priorities and what constitutes an appropriate police response than those who are absent, and yet most likely to be the focus of police attention. In responding to the concerns of the better off and not those 'whose poverty, powerlessness, and unpopularity make it particularly difficult to be heard' (Mastrofski, 1988, p. 66), a police leader risks taking a course of action that is regarded by many as an unacceptable compromise between reducing crime or disorder and appropriate uses of police authority. Thus, some groups might embrace the use of broken windows policing as a means of reducing drug crime in their neighborhood, while others would consider this a strategy that too easily runs rough-shod over the rights of suspected offenders who live there. Added to these difficulties, residents might be fearful of reprisal for helping the police, or might simply be unenthusiastic at the prospect of closer police-community partnerships.

Even if these obstacles can be overcome, there is no guarantee of consensus. Where values conflict, reasonable people can be expected to disagree on what trade-off constitutes the right action. Oftentimes, the views of police differ from those of the public, sometimes markedly (Morin, Parker, Stepler, & Mercer, 2017). But there are examples of cases where, at their best, solutions are reached that many people can agree are justifiable and legitimate, solutions that depend heavily on police leaders attending to the 'methods and conditions of debate' (Thacher, 2001b, p. 4). In Lowell, Massachusetts, the police chief was able to mitigate the dilemma of sacri-ficing the value of responsiveness for equity in police-community partnerships by using objective information to identify the specific nature of the crime problem, and by inviting an under-represented group to a community meeting. In this case, the chief was under pressure to respond to the wishes of a powerful community group to locate a police substation in their neighborhood, but doing so would mean not placing it in an area of the city with a worse crime problem. By using crime data to explain the public safety benefits of having the sub-station in one location over the other, and by ensuring diverse perspectives were represented, he was able to reach a mutual agreement with the community that served the larger public good (equity) while also preserving his partnership with the powerful community group (responsiveness) (Thacher, 2001b, p. 9).

Focused deterrence programs, identified by the Committee as effective in reducing crime, embody similar features for helping channel police discretion along more 'principled routes' for managing conflicting values, particularly between public safety and liberty (Thacher, 2016, p. 105). For example, Boston's Operation Ceasefire used crime data and other relevant informa-tion to deliver a targeted police response to specific offenders minimizing the likelihood that non-offenders were subject to overuses of police authority, such as indiscriminate searches and unwarranted surveillance. Using crime data was also evidence that police decisions were based on facts and not assumptions shaped by a lack of objectivity. Moreover, the creation of collabo-rative working groups around the specific problem, including those community members most likely to be affected by a police decision, helped the police consider and implement strategies that demonstrated restraint. For example, warning drug offenders that there was evidence to arrest them unless they stopped dealing minimized the 'use of enforcement authority by making the threat so credible that it would never need to be carried out' (Thacher, 2016, pp. 126–127). According to Thacher, the use of police-community forums to help articulate 'explicit and defensible criteria' can be a promising means of reducing the risk that police authority will be 'used in arbitrary, inscrutable, and rights-violating ways' (2016, p. 105).

A willingness to listen to and reflect on community members' concerns (rather than to sim-ply direct them according to police interests) and to include relevant publics helps police leaders learn what is at stake so they can make better judgments about how to proceed. Gawande touches upon the benefits of these kinds of frank discussions in the context of difficult conversations over end-of-life decisions that involve trade-offs between improving the patient's health while reducing her quality of life. This is how he summarizes his conversation with Susan Block, a palliative care specialist:

> There is no single way to take people with terminal illness through the process, but there are some rules, according to Block. You sit down. You make time. You are not determining whether they want treatment X versus Y. You're trying to learn what's most important to them under the circumstances – so that you can provide information and advice on the approach that gives them their best chance of achieving it. This process requires as much listening as talking. If you are talking more than half of the time, Block says, you're talking too much (2014, p. 182).

Unlike doctors or surgeons, police leaders cannot entrust their final decisions to members of the public, but this analogy helps illustrate the importance of a process that allows for input and thoughtful reflection on a wider set of values than just crime control.

The implication is that police leaders stand to benefit from research that seeks to establish the causal relationship between proactive interventions and their various outcomes, but also scholarship that advances knowledge about how police leaders might best manage the problem of conflicting values. Adopting a case study approach, researchers could conduct in-depth examinations of how police leaders try to respond to this challenge in their collaborations with different segments of the community.

As these case studies accumulate, it might be possible to identify general principles for informing practices as well as providing leaders with examples they could draw upon to develop their practical reasoning skills (Thacher, 2001). Along with identifying the values at stake and the situational context which shapes them, attention could also be paid to the ethical obligations of police leaders and the approaches they use to justify decisions that many people consider legitimate. For William Ker Muir (1977), those patrol officers who were best equipped to handle the difficult ethical choices of street-level police work were morally reconciled to using their coercive authority and also capable of understanding the tragic nature of the human condition. Understanding how this 'professional political model' or other perspectives may apply to police leaders would be an important first step for learning how police organizations could better prepare their chief executives to make sophisticated normative judgments about the implementation of proactive police policies.

Finally, in trying to accomplish longer-term goals, such as improving police legitimacy and meaningful public deliberations, police chiefs need the support of mayors and city managers, so that they have the time and resources to invest in practices that help improve public trust and confidence. Recent research has exposed some of the complexities of defining and measuring legitimacy, but there are also examples of police agencies who have attempted to do so that are instructive (Worden & McLean, 2017), including practical approaches to measuring police legitimacy and other aspects of organizational performance at the local level (Rosenbaum, Lawrence, Hartnett, McDevitt, & Posick, 2015).

Conclusion

In evaluating the evidence base on specific proactive policing strategies, particularly in terms of their causal effects on crime, the Committee has provided policymakers with valuable information for making informed decisions. Scientific knowledge elevates the importance of facts and helps ensure that discretion becomes 'somewhat less a matter of public debate or police guess-work' (Klockars, 1988, p. 110). The Committee's report has also contributed to an important narrative that empowers police leaders to search for ways to enhance public safety, unlike the 'nothing works' narrative of the 1970s (Weisburd, 2016).

At the same time, the Committee's report pays less attention to some of the major obstacles to the successful translation of science into policy. No matter how persuasive the research evidence, policymakers must confront a skeptical public and tight budgets, and seek acceptable trade-offs between competing values. To help them make good decisions in such a challenging environment, researchers will need to go far beyond evaluating the crime prevention outcomes of different proactive policing strategies and their effects on other values, including the legality of police behavior and concerns about equity.

We have suggested that a mistrust of science can undermine attempts to advance policy recommendations based on evidence, even though this evidence is vital to any kind of meaningful and objective assessment. Thus, in their efforts to translate research into policy, police leaders will profit from studies that help demonstrate which communication strategies are most effective in minimizing the likelihood that rigorous empirical findings will be rejected simply because they are incongruent with someone's existing values and beliefs. Police leaders will also benefit from cost-efficiency analyses that take into account the wide variety of costs and benefits associated with different proactive strategies, so they are better positioned to make decisions on whether their benefits justify their costs and to make comparisons across different strategic alternatives. Finally, police leaders will gain from research that produces practical knowledge on how better trade-offs between competing values can be made, particularly in terms of a process that allows diverse perspectives to be heard and that contributes to consent. While any final decision might not necessarily fulfil everyone's expectations for justice, its primary advantage might lie in its potential for minimizing abusive or unfair policing practices. In short, we advocate for a narrative of policing that helps advance our understanding of what works and what ought to be.

Acknowledgments

We are grateful to Stephen Mastrofski, Robert Norris, Laurie Robinson, David Thacher, and Tom Tyler for their very helpful insights on an earlier version of this chapter.

Disclosure Statement

No potential conflict of interest was reported by the authors.

Notes

1. We recognize that the research needs of street-level practitioners differ from those of policymakers, but our focus in this chapter is mainly on the implications of scientific evidence for policy. This involves police leaders having to evaluate alternative strategies to address specific problems and to deal with concerns about how best to allocate their organization's scarce resources (Thacher, 2008, p. 48).
2. The Committee concluded that the crime reduction effects of SQF were mixed when it is implemented as a general policy, but that it had significant short-term effects on controlling crime when targeting specific places with violence or serious gun crimes and when focusing on high-risk repeat offenders (Weisburd & Majmundar, 2018, pp. 150–151).
3. We are grateful to Stephen Mastrofski for this observation.
4. In cost-effectiveness analyses, outcomes are expressed in substantive terms (e.g., X dollars expended on a problem-oriented policing approach helped reduce crime by 10%). In contrast, cost-benefit analyses express both the cost and benefits in monetary terms and thus allow for a calculation of the net

benefits (benefits minus costs) of a given policy (e.g., every dollar spent on a problem-oriented policing approach delivered a benefit of $4 in savings). Both cost-effectiveness and cost-benefit analyses are assessments of efficiency.

References

Aos, S. (2015). What is the bottom line? *Criminology and Public Policy, 14,* 633–638.

Auletta, K. (2015, September 7). Fixing broken windows. *The New Yorker.* Retrieved from https://www.newyorker.com/magazine/2015/09/07/fixing-broken-windows

Bowling, B. (2007). Fair and effective policing methods: Towards 'good enough' policing. *Journal of Scandinavian Studies in Criminology and Crime Prevention, 8,* 17–32.

Center for Disease Control [CDC] (2017). What would happen if we stopped vaccinations? Retrieved from https://www.cdc.gov/vaccines/vac-gen/whatifstop.htm

Chong, D., & Druckman, J. (2007). Framing theory. *Annual Review of Political Science, 10,* 103–126.

Cohen, M. A. (2000). Measuring the costs and benefits of crime and justice. In D. Duffee (Ed.), *Criminal Justice, Vol. 4: Measurement and analysis of crime and justice* (pp. 263–315). Washington, DC: National Institute of Justice.

Committee on the Science of Science Communication. (2017). *Communicating science effectively: A research agenda. Division of behavioral and social sciences and education.* Washington, D.C.: The National Academies Press.

Dahlstrom, M. F. (2014). Using narratives and storytelling to communicate science with nonexpert audiences. *Proceedings of the National Academies of Sciences, 111,* 13614–13620.

Dominguez, P., & Raphael, S. (2015). The role of the cost-of-crime literature in bridging the gap between social science research and policy making. *Criminology and Public Policy, 14,* 589–632.

Epp, C. R., Maynard-Moody, S., & Haider-Markel, D. (2014). *Pulled over: How police stops define race and citizenship.* Chicago: University of Chicago Press.

Flyvbjerg, B. (2001). *Making social science matter: Why social inquiry fails and how it can matter again.* Cambridge: Cambridge University Press.

Freiberg, A., & Carson, W. G. (2010). The limits to evidence-based policy: Evidence, emotion, and criminal justice. *The Australian Journal of Public Administration, 69,* 152–164.

Fung, A. (2001). Accountable autonomy: Toward empowered deliberation in Chicago schools and policing. *Politics and Society, 29,* 73–103.

Gawande, A. (2014). *Being mortal.* New York, NY: Picador.

Gawande, A. (2016, June 10). The mistrust of science. *The New Yorker.* Retrieved from https://www.newyorker.com/news/news-desk/the-mistrust-of-science

Geller, A., Fagan, J., & Tyler, T. R. (2017). Police contact and mental health. Columbia public law research paper No. 14-571. Retrieved from https://ssrn.com/abstract=3096076

Gladwell, M. (2006, April 10). Here's why. *The New Yorker.* Retrieved from https://www.newyorker.com/magazine/2006/04/10/heres-why

Goff, P. A. (2018, January 7). On stop-and-frisk, we can't celebrate just yet. *New York Times.* Retrieved from https://nyti.ms/2FbWgFj

Green, M. C. (2006). Narratives and cancer communication. *Journal of Communication, 56,* s163– s183.

Greene, J. R. (2014). New directions in policing: Balancing prediction and meaning in police research. *Justice Quarterly, 31,* 5–40.

Horowitz, J., & Zedlewski, E. (2006). Applying cost-benefit analysis to policing evaluations. *Justice Research and Policy, 8,* 52–65.

Journal of Benefit-Cost Analysis. (2017). *Special Issue on Policing, 8,* 305–398.

Kahan, D. M., Jenkins-Smith, H., & Braman, D. (2010). Cultural cognition of scientific consensus. *Journal of Risk Research, 14,* 147–174.

Klockars, C. B. (1988). *The idea of police.* Newbury Park, CA: Sage.

Lee, S., Aos, S., & Pennucci, A. (2015). *What works and what does not? Benefit-cost findings from WSIPP (Doc. No. 15- 02–4101).* Olympia: Washington State Institute for Public Policy.

Lewandowsky, S., Ecker, U. K. H., Seifert, C., Schwarz, N., & Cook, J. (2012). Misinformation and its correction: Continued influence and successful debiasing. *Psychological Science in the Public Interest, 13,* 106–131.

Lewandowsky, S., & Oberauer, K. (2012). Motivated rejection of science. *Current Directions in Psychological Science, 25,* 217–222.

Lum, C., & Koper, C. (2017). *Evidence-based policing: Translating research into practice.* Oxford: Oxford University Press.

Maguire, E. R., & Katz, C. M. (2002). Community policing, loose coupling, and sensemaking in American police agencies. *Justice Quarterly, 19,* 501–534.

Manski, C. F., & Nagin, D. S. (2017). Assessing benefits, costs, and disparate racial impacts of confrontational proactive policing. *Proceedings of the National Academy of Sciences, 114,* 9308–9313.

Mastrofski, S. D. (1988). Community policing as reform: A cautionary tale. In J. R. Greene & S. D. Mastrofski (Eds.), *Community policing: Rhetoric or reality?* (pp. 47–67). New York, NY: Prager.

Mastrofski, S. D. (1998). Community policing and police organization structure. In J. P. Brodeur (Ed.), *Community policing and the evaluation of police service delivery* (pp. 161–189). Thousand Oaks, CA: Sage.

Mastrofski, S. D. (1999). Policing for people. In *Ideas in American policing.* Washington, DC: Police Foundation.

Mastrofski, S. D., & Willis, J. J. (2010). Police organization: Continuity and change. In M. Tonry (Ed.), *Crime and justice: A review of research, Vol. 39* (pp. 55–144). Chicago: University of Chicago Press.

Mastrofski, S. D. (Forth). Community policing: Critic. In D. Weisburd & A. A. Braga (Eds.), *Police innovation: Contrasting perspectives* (2nd ed.) (pp. 45–70). Oxford: Oxford University Press.

Moore, M. H. (2006). Improving police through expertise, experience, and experiments. In D. Weisburd & A. A. Braga (Eds.), *Police innovation: Contrasting perspectives* (pp. 322–338). Oxford: Oxford University Press.

Morin, R., Parker, K., Stepler, R., & Mercer, A. (2017). *Behind the badge.* Washington, DC: Pew Research Center.

Muir, W. K., Jr. (1977). *Police: Streetcorner politicians.* Chicago: University of Chicago Press.

Nagin, D. S. (2015). Cost-benefit analysis of crime prevention policies. *Criminology and Public Policy, 14,* 583–587.

Nagin, D. S., & Telep, C. W. (2017). Procedural justice and legal compliance. *Annual Review of Law and Social Science, 13,* 5–28.

Natapoff, A. (2015). Misdemeanors. *Annual Review of Law and Social Sciences, 11,* 255–267.

Neyroud, P. W. (2017). Balancing public safety and individual rights in street policing. *Proceedings of the National Academy of Sciences, 114,* 9231–9233.

Nuccitelli, D. (2017). Climate scientists just debunked deniers' favorite argument. *The Guardian.* Retrieved from https://www.theguardian.com/environment/climate-consensus-97-per-cent/2017/jun/28/climate-scientists-justdebunked-deniers-favorite-argument

Nutley, S., Walter, I., & Davies, H. T. O. (2007). *Using evidence: How research can inform public services.* Bristol, United Kingdom: The Policy Press.

Petrosino, A., Turpin-Petrosino, C., Hollis-Peel, M., & Lavenberg, J. G. (2013). Scared straight and other juvenile awareness programs for preventing juvenile delinquency: A systematic review. *Campbell Systematic Reviews, 9,* 1–55.

Pew Research Center (2016). Many Americans believe fake news is sowing confusion. Retrieved from http://www.journalism.org/2016/12/15/many-americansbelieve-fake-news-is-sowing-confusion/

President's Task Force on 21st Century Policing. (2015). *Final report of the President's Task Force on 21st Century policing.* Washington, DC: Office of Community Oriented Policing Services.

RAND (2010). Hidden in plain sight: What cost-of-crime research can tell us about investing in policing. Santa Monica, CA: Author. Retrieved from https://www.rand.org/content/dam/rand/pubs/occasional_papers/2010/RAND_OP279.pdf

Rosenbaum, D. P., Lawrence, D. S., Hartnett, S. M., McDevitt, J., & Posick, C. (2015). Measuring procedural justice and legitimacy at the local level: The police–community interaction survey. *Journal of Experimental Criminology, 11,* 335–366.

Rossi, P. H., Lipsey, M. W., & Freeman, H. E. (2004). *Evaluation: A systematic approach* (7th ed.). Thousand Oaks, CA: Sage Publications.

Roth, J. A., Roehl, J., & Johnson, C. C. (2004). Trends in the adoption of community policing. In W. G. Skogan (Ed.), *Community policing: Can it work?* (pp. 3–29). Belmont, CA: Wadsworth.

Sampson, R. J., Winship, C., & Knight, C. (2013). Overview of: "Translating causal claims: Principles and strategies of policy-relevant research.". *Criminology and Public Policy, 12,* 1–29.

Schafer, J. A. (2013). *Effective leadership in policing: Successful traits and habits.* Durham, NC: Carolina Academic Press.

Selznick, P. (1957). *Leadership in administration: A sociological interpretation.* New York, NY: Harper and Row.

Sewell, A. A., Jefferson, K. A., & Lee, H. (2016). Living under surveillance: Gender, psychological distress, and stop-question-and-frisk policing in New York City. *Social Science and Medicine, 159*, 1–13.

Sherman, L. (2003). Reason for emotion: Reinventing justice with theories, innovations and research—The American Society of Criminology 2002 Presidential Address. *Criminology, 41*, 1–41.

Sherman, L. (2015). A tipping point for "totally evidenced policing": Ten ideas for building an evidence-based police agency. *International Criminal Justice Review, 25*, 1–29.

Sherman, L. W., & Rogan, D. P. (1995). Effects of gun seizures on gun violence: "Hot spots" patrol in Kansas City. *Justice Quarterly, 12*, 673–693.

Skogan, W. G. (2004). Representing the community in community policing. In W. G. Skogan (Ed.), *Community policing: Can it work?* (pp. 57–75). Belmont, CA: Wadsworth.

Skogan, W. G. (2006). *Police and community in Chicago*. Oxford: Oxford University Press.

Skolnick, J. (1966). *Justice without trial*. New York, NY: John Wiley and Sons.

Suhay, E., & Druckman, J. N. (2015). The politics of science: Political values and the production, communication, and reception of scientific knowledge. *The Annals of the American Association of Political and Social Science, 658*, 6–15.

Sunstein, C. R. (1994). Incommensurability and valuation in law. *Michigan Law Review, 92*, 779–846.

Thacher, D. (2001). Policing is not a treatment. *Journal of Research in Crime and Delinquency, 38*, 387–415.

Thacher, D. (2001b). Equity and community policing: A new view of community partnerships. *Criminal Justice Ethics, 20*, 3–16.

Thacher, D. (2006). The normative case study. *American Journal of Sociology, 111*, 1631–1676.

Thacher, D. (2008). Research for the front lines. *Policing and Society, 18*, 46–59.

Thacher, D. (2016). Channeling police discretion: The hidden potential of focused deterrence. *The University of Chicago Legal Forum, Article 13*, 101–150.

Thacher, D., & Rein, M. (2004). Managing value conflict in public policy. *Governance: An International Journal of Policy, Administration, and Institutions, 17*, 457–486.

Tyler, T. R., Fagin, J., & Geller, A. (2014). Street stops and police legitimacy: Teachable moments in young urban men's legal socialization. *Journal of Empirical Legal Studies, 11*, 751–785.

Vraga, E. K., & Bode, L. (2017). Using expert sources to correct health and misinformation in social media. *Science Communication*, 1–25. doi:10.1177/1075547017731776

Washington State Institute for Public Policy [WSIPP]. (2017). *Benefit-cost technical documentation (December)*. Olympia, WA.

Washington State Institute for Public Policy [WSIPP]. (2017b). *Deploy one additional police officer with statewide average practices*. Olympia, WA.

Weisburd, D. (2016). Does hot spots policing inevitably lead to unfair and abusive police practices, or can we maximize both fairness and effectiveness in the new proactive policing? *University of Chicago Legal Forum, Article 16*, 661–689.

Weisburd, D., & Majmundar, M. K. (Eds.). (2018). *Proactive policing: Effects on crime and communities. Committee on proactive policing: Effects on crime, communities, and civil liberties. Committee on law and justice, division of behavioral and social sciences and education*. Washington, DC: The National Academies Press.

Willis, J. J., & Mastrofski, S. D. (2017). Contrôler l'autonomie policière par un équilibre des forces: Le cas des caméras portées. *Cahiers de la Sécurité et de la Justice, 40*, 90–102.

Willis, J. J., Mastrofski, S. D., & Weisburd, D. (2007). Making sense of Compstat: A theory-based analysis of organizational change in three police departments. *Law and Society Review, 41*, 147–188.

Worden, R. E., & McLean, S. (2017). *Mirage of police reform: Procedural justice and police legitimacy*. Oakland, CA: University of California Press.

5

Making Sense of Evidence

Using Research Training to Promote Organisational Change

K. Wilkinson

NIHR COLLABORATION FOR LEADERSHIP IN APPLIED HEALTH RESEARCH & CARE SOUTH-WEST PENINSULA (CLAHRC), INSTITUTE OF HEALTH RESEARCH, UNIVERSITY OF EXETER MEDICAL SCHOOL, EXETER, UK

K. Boyd

DEPARTMENT OF SOCIOLOGY, PHILOSOPHY AND ANTHROPOLOGY, UNIVERSITY OF EXETER, EXETER, UK

M. Pearson

NIHR COLLABORATION FOR LEADERSHIP IN APPLIED HEALTH RESEARCH & CARE SOUTH-WEST PENINSULA (CLAHRC), INSTITUTE OF HEALTH RESEARCH, UNIVERSITY OF EXETER MEDICAL SCHOOL, EXETER, UK

H. Farrimond

DEPARTMENT OF SOCIOLOGY, PHILOSOPHY AND ANTHROPOLOGY, UNIVERSITY OF EXETER, EXETER, UK

I. A. Lang

NIHR COLLABORATION FOR LEADERSHIP IN APPLIED HEALTH RESEARCH & CARE SOUTH-WEST PENINSULA (CLAHRC), INSTITUTE OF HEALTH RESEARCH, UNIVERSITY OF EXETER MEDICAL SCHOOL, EXETER, UK

D. Fleischer

DEPARTMENT OF SOCIOLOGY, PHILOSOPHY AND ANTHROPOLOGY, UNIVERSITY OF EXETER, EXETER, UK

A. Poole and N. Ralph

DEVON AND CORNWALL POLICE, EXETER, UK

B. Rappert

DEPARTMENT OF SOCIOLOGY, PHILOSOPHY AND ANTHROPOLOGY, UNIVERSITY OF EXETER, EXETER, UK

Introduction

Internationally, the evidence-based practice movement has grown in momentum across many countries over the past 30 years in the areas of medicine, education, management, social care, and more recently in policing. This movement is driven by the aspiration to have informed

DOI: 10.4324/9781003153009-7

and effective practice by reducing the gap between the research knowledge often generated by academics and organisations' policy or practice. Recent work by Avby, Nilsen, and Dahlgren (2014) has drawn attention to the demands of achieving evidence-based practice, such as how practitioners can be helped to use evidence-based knowledge in their roles. All institutions seeking to become more evidence-based need to train personnel and staff about what evidence-based practice means, how to incorporate it into their work, and how to encourage practitioner-led research. This training often requires collaboration between organisations and relevant academics.

The current study focuses on the collaborative development of workshops to train police in evidence-based practice. The chapter elucidates the methods used to develop evidence-based policing (EBP) training, the delivery of these workshops, and efforts made to assess how such training impacted police practice.

Background

EBP has been defined by Sherman (2013) as 'a method of making decisions about "what works" in policing: which practices and strategies accomplish police missions most cost-effectively' (p. 377). It is often promoted as a means of enabling more informed decisions and thereby producing greater 'value for money'. Other aims include providing a better service for the public, reducing risk to the community, and enhancing policing legitimacy. In the United Kingdom, while these reasons serve as the dominant rationales associated with EBP, there are those who think that this agenda privileges certain kinds of methodologies and forms of knowledge over others in harmful ways (Lumsden & Goode, 2016). The College of Policing for England & Wales (2017) has sought to frame EBP as resting on the 'best available' evidence, rather than a uniform methodological standard.

Against the ongoing discussion about the place and meaning of EBP, this chapter describes and assesses a police-university collaboration intended to promote the place of research evidence within policing. Training workshops for officers and staff in south-west England were designed to develop participants' understanding, critical appraisal, and application of research evidence. As many have argued, promoting effective EBP depends, at least in part, on those in law-enforcement agencies understanding the potential of EBP and having appropriate training in methods of research and analysis (e.g., Beal & Kerlikowske, 2010; Knutsson, 2010; Rosenbaum, 2010; Telep & Lum, 2014; Tillyer et al., 2014). Despite this, there are few detailed accounts of such training, how it might reconfigure academic-police interactions, or whether training by academics can align with priorities within policing organisations (Fleming & Wingrove, 2017).

This chapter addresses these issues and in doing so also considers the appropriateness of a research training model originally designed for use in the healthcare sector. Our workshops sought to provide officers and staff with the knowledge, skills, and confidence to engage with research evidence and EBP. But more than this, in seeking to further attendees' willingness and capacity to alter their day-to-day practice, the workshops were necessarily bound up with wide-ranging issues about how to bring about organisational change. As a result, far more was at stake with them than relatively narrow choices about classroom pedagogy. The design and undertaking of workshops relied on, put to the test, and helped generate theories about the barriers and facilitators of employing research evidence to inform practice in policing. It also helped to unpack the challenges of collaborative working between academics and police practitioners through making the workshops a two-way dialogue.

The analysis that follows is divided into three sections. By way of context, the first provides a brief overview of the intertwined topics of police-university collaborations and EBP, with specific reference to the UK. Section two details the workshops undertaken, including how they evolved as collaborative efforts that purposefully sought to transform existing organisational practices through iterative cycles of reflection and action. The final section offers a discussion of lessons learnt.

Promoting Evidence and Collaboration

The primary origin of the research training workshops examined in this chapter is the current drive for EBP. In part, the intensification of interest in EBP today derives from an acknowledgement that despite the long-standing interest in ensuring that practice is informed by research, bringing about the kind of integration sought has often proven elusive (e.g., Engel & Whalen, 2010; Fyfe & Wilson, 2012). The recognised challenges of realising the aspirations of EBP include the existing skill sets of many officers, a lack of time, and the ever-shifting demands of operational practice (e.g., Beal & Kerlikowske, 2010; Hunter, May, & Hough, 2017).

Previous studies have identified various barriers to police use of research knowledge in practice: a lack of familiarity with what research exists, uncertainty about where to find it, individual and organisational cultural resistance, and an inability to change practice (e.g., Carson & Rooy, 2015; Hunter et al., 2017; Rojek, Alpert, & Smith, 2012). For some, the problem is not only having appropriate information (e.g., Bullock & Tilley, 2009), or even the ability to act on it (e.g., Innes, 2010), but to the manner in which policing agencies routinely perform in ways known to be ineffective (Kennedy, 2010). One crucial issue is how practitioners' experiences, routines, and values get reconciled with the conclusions of research (e.g., Boba, 2010; Bradley & Nixon, 2009). For instance, the extent to which the attention to research evidence either builds on or attempts to usurp professional experience has been identified as a critical factor in the realisation of EBP (e.g., Ekblom, 2002; Fleming & Wingrove, 2017; Hunter et al., 2017; Telep & Lum, 2014).

This regard for EBP has been accompanied by the promotion of collaborations between police practitioners and those with expertise in gathering and assessing research evidence, notably academic researchers (Fyfe & Wilson, 2012; Murji, 2010).[1] The advancement of EBP and police-university relations is often regarded as demanding because both are understood as requiring far more than the ability to gather and disseminate relevant information. Instead, issues about organisational priorities and entrenched working routines are widely seen as conditioning the place of research evidence in police practices (e.g., Bradley & Nixon, 2009). There is also research indicating that differing priorities and ways of working between academics and practitioners makes collaboration even more challenging (e.g., Steinheider, Wuestewald, Boyatzis, & Kroutter, 2012).

In many respects, the debates about the how, why (and why not) of police-university collaborations present a microcosm of broader debates about the place of research in policing. Much of the discussion has been animated by the belief in mutual benefit. For the police, working with academics is said to increase their ability to do more with less resources, improve outcomes for the public, enhance organisational transparency, and improve the credibility of policies. For academics, the ability to study otherwise unapproachable topics, to undertake well-informed research, and to affect change are some of the cited benefits (see Engel & Whalen, 2010 for an overview). And yet, despite this potential, it is acknowledged there is still some way to go in fostering collaborations that provide enhanced research capacity, especially with regard to informing policing practice (e.g., Hunter et al., 2017; Weisburd & Neyroud, 2011).

Various barriers have been identified to fostering impactful collaborative research: the lack of police interest in social sciences, the failure of academics to communicate in accessible ways, the mismatch in topic priorities, the contrasting orientations toward intellectual rigour and pragmatic operational demands, and incompatibilities in organisational decision-making (e.g., for surveys of these issues, see Steinheider et al., 2012; Stephens, 2010). Academic researchers have been portrayed as too critical and disengaged from the day-to-day experiences of policing or as too set on working with traditional 'objective' and 'scientific' forms of research validation that are poorly suited to informing organisational practice (e.g., Bradley & Nixon, 2009). It is not surprising, then, that much of the literature reflecting on police-university collaborations has been framed in terms of the need to build bridges between separate worlds (e.g., Murji, 2010).

What Works?

Within the UK, interest in promoting EBP and police-university collaborations has led to various funding initiatives. For instance, the establishment of the College of Policing in 2012 as well as its hosting of the 'What Works Centre for Crime Reduction' were in part justified as a way of drawing on expertise and knowledge within the police force and elsewhere to improve the identification, utilisation, and undertaking of research that could support EBP. Of specific relevance to the workshop examined in this chapter, in 2015, the College of Policing, the Higher Education Funding Council for England, and the Home Office launched the £10m Police Knowledge Fund to foster research collaborations between universities and police forces in the UK. The Fund aimed to: build sustained capability amongst officers and staff to understand, critique, use and undertake research; to embed or accelerate understanding of crime and policing issues, and evidence-based problem-solving approaches; and demonstrate innovation in building the research evidence base and applying it through knowledge exchange and translation across all levels of policing (College of Policing and HEFEC, 2015, p. 1).

The Exeter Policing, Evidence, and Research Translation (ExPERT) project was one of the awards made under this Fund. It entailed a strategic partnership between Devon and Cornwall Police (DCP); the Office of the Police and Crime Commissioner for Devon, Cornwall, and Isles of Scilly; and a cross-disciplinary group of staff members from fields including medical sociology, criminology, and public health at the University of Exeter. The project aimed to develop and sustain capacity amongst police officers and staff to engage in EBP, to undertake research relevant to strategic priorities, and to improve knowledge transfer between the police and academia.

This chapter describes and assesses one element of this project: the use of 'Making Sense of Evidence' training workshops as a vehicle to promote the use of research evidence.[2] Four two-day workshops were delivered in 2016 – each stand-alone, with a new set of attendees (up to 25 per event). The workshops were modelled on related efforts to promote EBP by the National Institute for Health Research Collaboration for Leadership in Applied Health Research and Care for the South-West Peninsula (PenCLAHRC). For nearly ten years, PenCLAHRC has delivered evidence-based medicine workshops to participants drawn from across the public sector including health, local authority, and third-sector organisations.[3] This well-established and tested method of training was considered a useful starting point for the delivery of similar training in a policing context.

Workshop Development

The exploratory and yet goal-driven orientation for the collaborations envisioned as part of the workshops gave a primacy to the need for reflection and revision. In aid of making such adjustments, we adopted a research design inspired by Action Research (AR). According to Reason and Bradbury (2001), AR entails cycles of dialogue, intervention, and reflection that lead to the generation of practical knowledge. AR is often contrasted with traditional research in the social sciences because it eschews the aim of undertaking value-free, objective forms of research with its stark contrast between researchers and the researched in favour of forms of inquiry undertaken 'in order to acquire actionable knowledge that enables improvement' (James, 1999, p. 85). The emphasis on improvement as an outcome goes hand in hand with working in partnership. AR is both a tool for investigating positive change and a means for achieving it. As a result, the goal of this chapter is not only to specify how the undertaking of research training can inform an understanding of the organisational limits of EBP implementation (e.g., Fleming & Wingrove, 2017), but to describe how collaborative academic-police research training provided the basis for organisational change, which in turn helped inform an understanding of the limits and promise of EBP.

With the emphasis placed on undertaking rigorous cycles of planning, action, observation, and reflection that bring together theory and practice to realise improvement, AR in general has been invested with much promise to address problems within criminal justice as well as a means of enhancing the skills of those involved (Bradley & Nixon, 2009; Tillyer et al., 2014). Although the novelty of AR in contrast to previous forms of police-university partnerships is debatable (Rosenbaum, 2010), in recent years, projects under an AR label have been credited with improving the effectiveness of policing, building relations of trust, overcoming sources of opposition to research on the police, and surfacing differences in how evidence and professional identities are conceived (e.g., Beal & Kerlikowske, 2010; Stott, West, & Radburn, 2016; Wuestewald & Steinheider, 2010).[4] In relation to the specific topic of this chapter, a participatory AR methodology has previously been used to introduce a problem-based general police training pedagogy in India where it was found to provide space for voicing concerns otherwise side-lined within hierarchical and regimented police settings (Rai, 2012).

In line with the overall AR methodology, the development and delivery of our research evidence training workshops entailed undertaking cyclical activities of planning, action, evaluation, and reflection of a range of activities. Evaluation sought to be both formative (to inform ongoing workshop development) as well as summative (to assess workshop impact). These workshops are situated within the wider efforts in the ExPERT project as well as within DCP more generally to foster organizational change in the direction of EBP (see Discussion section). Figure 5.1 depicts how the development of workshop nested within these wider efforts.

In the rest of this section, we briefly recount our experience of developing the workshops, assessing their impact, and considering how well they supported wider organisational change in DCP.

Workshop Planning

As part of the initial planning stage, a number of decisions were made on the content and structure of the workshops; choices that reflected the overall aim of further embedding research evidence within the practices in the DCP. Planning was a collaborative process, shaped by both the university and police staff authoring this chapter.

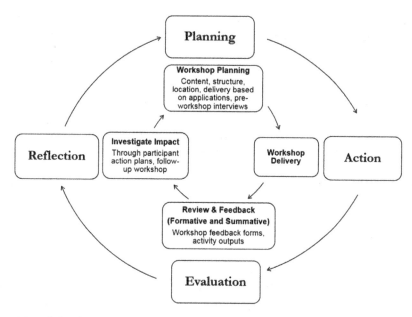

FIGURE 5.1 Nested development cycles

Engagement

DCP colleagues foresaw a number of potential barriers workshop attendees might encounter when attempting to embed evidence in their practice: limited organisational support for EBP, balancing 'what works' with 'what matters' within the often publicly fraught space policing occupies, and senior managers with little research expertise viewing EBP as a direct challenge to innovation. This supports findings in the existing literature detailing practitioner preferences for making decisions based on their personal experience over research evidence (e.g., Telep & Lum, 2014). To ensure the perceived relevance of the material examined and to enable practitioners' operational knowledge to come to the fore, the workshops invited attendees to consider questions arising from their operational experience and how to transfer the learning into the practice setting.

Messaging

The Deputy Chief Constable (second-highest-ranked officer in the organisation) opened the workshops to demonstrate his support and commitment towards EBP. Other senior professionals were also integral to the delivery of the workshop, to provide grounding and credibility to the content. The workshops were located at the Police Headquarters on day one and at the University on day two to emphasise their collaborative spirit.

Attendees

In light of the ultimate goal of achieving organisational change across the police force, the workshops were open to officers and staff at all levels. Participation was initially advertised at the Society of Evidence Based Policing's regional annual conference and via the organisation's intranet system, with applicants completing a written application form. Places were also subsequently offered through word-of-mouth and directly through the police contacts who recommended individuals. This was to ensure that those who were both keen and integral to the organisational movement attended. To demonstrate continued support for regional links, a small number of spaces were made available to police staff from neighbouring forces.

Through informal feedback gathered from individuals attending similar workshops within PenCLAHRC, our experience tells us that best results are reported to be obtained when teams attend the same workshop together. However, in the context of policing, removing too many people from any particular department at one time was thought to present a service risk. Therefore, there was no intended grouping of individuals based on their current roles or teams.

Pre-delivery data gathering

Attendee applications and pre-workshop interviews were undertaken for the first two workshops to confirm that the draft plan was fit for purpose. Interviews were conducted with approximately half the participants of the first two workshops (workshop 1: 13/20; workshop 2: 9/23), and took place either face-to-face or on the telephone. All participants were emailed an invitation to interview and those who positively replied made up the final sample. Responses to the questions did not differ significantly across the two interview time-points.

During the interviews, participants were asked about their understanding, knowledge, and use of EBP and any personal examples of EBP they may have. Almost all interviewees said they had a basic understanding of the notion of EBP but their experience and knowledge were varied, with some staff working in analyst roles and commissioning research while others had no research experience at all. Three-quarters of interviewees rated themselves and their teams as being somewhat evidence-based (a 3/5 rating on average). Ratings for the organisation as a whole were slightly lower, with around three-quarters rating EBP as 2 or 3 out of 5.

Interviewees were also asked what helped and hindered them to be evidence-based in the way that they work to identify the key facilitators and barriers to EBP. Responses were collated and themed, resulting in three broad categories: Organisational Characteristics (support from colleagues, reactive vs proactive management, target-driven culture, research vs professional-judgement mentality, sharing information across teams); Individual Characteristics (time to look for and review research, knowledge about how and where to find research, staff training, competing demands); and Networks and Processes (access to local and national data, links with other professionals, clear organisational processes). Interviewees were generally positive about the upcoming training and the organisation's investment in EBP.

Through gathering such information, the pre-workshop interviews were intended as a way of ensuring the needs of police attendees were embedded from the start.

Action: Workshop Delivery

Workshops were delivered to 83 police staff (Workshop 1, $n = 20$; Workshop 2, $n = 23$; Workshop 3, $n = 18$; Workshop 4, $n = 22$). Each workshop was delivered over two days and began in a plenary format with the consideration of evidence-based medicine and EBP so as to inspire attendees and bring attention to the importance of framing research questions. A series of largely small-group breakouts dedicated to assessing varied forms of research methods (e.g., qualitative, quantitative, Randomised Control Trials), ethics, and resources followed. After these breakout sessions, the afternoon of the second day returned to plenary format in order to promote collective discussion of how to encourage ethical EBP within DCP and elsewhere.[5] With some modifications (see below), their basic structure remained consistent.

Facilitators and barriers activity

The themes around barriers and facilitators to EBP identified in the pre-workshop interviews formed the basis of a workshop activity looking at this in more detail. Attendees were asked to highlight and categorise barriers and facilitators under one of the three themes (Individual Characteristics, Organisational Characteristics, Networks and Processes) and to share these with the group. The intention of this activity was to encourage discussion and problem-solving amongst attendees and to gather information to support the organisation's ongoing strategy for embedding EBP.

Organisational survey for EBP

Attendees completed a survey rating of how well they felt their organisation supported EBP. The rationale behind the organisational survey was two-fold: first, to identify what staff perceive to be the organisation's strengths and weaknesses with regards to EBP; and second, to use this data as a baseline measure for how far EBP is embedded within the organisation. The survey was developed by one of the authors, adapted from one used by Research in Practice (2012) within the social care sector. Respondents were asked to rate their agreement on a five-point scale (from '1-strongly agree' to '5-strongly disagree') about a number of factors relating to the organisation's practices with regards to EBP including Leadership, Culture, Building Capacity, and Sharing Learning. In addition to containing questions about the organisation, the survey asked about individuals' feelings towards research and their use of research to inform decision-making over the past 12 months (see Appendix 1 for complete survey). Surveys were collected and responses collated together. Ten members of the DCP Business Board (senior managers from across the force) also completed the survey.

Action planning

At the end of the workshops, attendees were asked to complete action plans detailing up to three actions they intended to take forward into practice and what they would need to complete each one (e.g. resource, time, support, etc.). Copies of the action plans were taken in order to follow up on future progress.

Workshop evaluations

End-of-session evaluation forms including questions about the impact of the workshop, as well as how well it met its aims, were completed and collected for analysis after each workshop. The responses were also used to inform amendments to subsequent workshops.

Evaluation: Workshop Review & Feedback

Facilitators and barriers activity

Attendees from all four workshops identified similar barriers and facilitators to EBP, including staff working in different roles across the organisation (see Table 5.1). The barriers and facilitators fit into the three main themes identified following the pre-workshop interviews (Organisational

TABLE 5.1 Overview of barriers and facilitators to EBP

Barriers	Facilitators
Organisational Characteristics	
• Lack of resources – time, money, technology	• Resources – knowledge, time, money, access to data and technology
• Limited management support – lack of understanding/buy-in, competing demands, hierarchy, training gaps, manager expectations for quick results	• Need/desire for evidence – appetite, recognition of value/ importance, increased efficiency
• Unwillingness to change – entrenched views/ established practice, risk aversion, 'one-size-fits-all' mentality	• Management support – buy-in, encouragement, role modelling
• (small-p) politics	• Willingness/recognition of need to change
Individual Characteristics	
• Limited time	• Knowledge/understanding/ skills
• Lack of skills	• Willingness to change – open-minded, confidence and passion
	• Flexible/protected time
• Resistance to change – reactive vs proactive, valuing experience over research knowledge	• Management support – encouragement, increased confidence, inspiring others
Networks and Processes	
• Lack of access to data/information – legal barriers, inefficient police data systems	• Resources – access to software and data, tools and information
• Not sharing information	• Communication and support – between forces, multi-agency working, College of Policing
• Lack of knowledge/training – knowing where to access support/info	• Knowledge/training

Characteristics, Individual Characteristics, and Networks and Processes) and built on the information already gathered from this activity. This information served as essential intelligence for DCP in considering how best to drive forward organisational change in the direction of EBP.

Organisational survey for EBP

Table 5.2 summarises how DCP workshop attendees (from all four workshops; $n = 57$) and Business Board members ($n = 10$) rated the organisation in terms of EBP with regards to leadership, culture, building capacity, and sharing learning (the factors considered important for

TABLE 5.2 Average ratings for organisational EBP by DCP workshop attendees and Business Board members [Ratings 1(low) – 5(high)]

	Workshop attendees (n = 57)	Business Board members (n = 10)
	Mean rating (SD)	Mean rating (SD)
Leadership (vision, strategy, clear evidence-base to policies and procedures)	2.44 (0.51)	3.28 (0.38)
Culture (values, expectations, evidence champions, sharing learning)	3.06 (0.48)	3.43 (0.41)
Building Capacity (learning opportunities, investment, access and support)	2.94 (0.69)	2.82 (0.70)
Sharing Learning (networks, conducting evaluations, involving stakeholders, and communication)	3.19 (0.48)	3.33 (0.61)

organisational EBP). The results show fairly average ratings across the board, with means ranging between 2.44 and 3.43 out of 5 (where 1 is low and 5 is high). Overall, ratings for Building Capacity were slightly lower than the other categories for both groups with greater standard deviations, suggesting greater disagreement amongst those who responded. Given the small sample size, we did not perform any statistical analyses to look for differences in ratings between the groups. Despite this, although the ratings did not differ enormously, the results suggest that the Business Board may have viewed the organisation's overall progress more favourably than the staff group, which could present a potential barrier to EBP implementation.

The survey also asked about individuals' feelings towards research and their use of research to inform decision-making over the past 12 months. Fifty-three per cent of all DCP staff who attended the workshops and completed the survey agreed or strongly agreed with the statement: 'Research evidence plays an important role in my day-to-day decision-making' (mean rating = 3.32; SD = 1.14); 30 per cent of the Business Board agreed (mean rating = 3.00; SD = 0.82). Seventy-five per cent of DCP attendees and 80% of Business Board members also agreed that they lacked the time to seek research evidence out, once again highlighting a lack of time as a barrier to EBP.

Action planning

Actions set out in attendees' individual plans were loosely themed into categories around searching for evidence, building EBP into daily practice or using it to approach a new project, sharing learning, networking with others, challenging current practice, and undertaking further research training (a full list is outlined in Table 5.3). A follow-up survey (described later) sought to investigate attendees' progress on their action plans as a means of measuring longer-term workshop impact.

Workshop evaluations

In the end-of-session workshop evaluations, attendees were asked about how well the workshop achieved its core aims. Table 5.4 summarises the findings from all four workshops (with mean ratings and standard deviations presented in bold). It suggests that the majority of attendees thought the workshop achieved all of its aims 'very well' or 'quite well'. Fifteen per cent thought that the workshop only somewhat achieved its aim to support attendees to share and learn from colleagues about applying EBP.

TABLE 5.3 Action plan themes (*n* = 75; 204 actions in total)

Theme identified based on action	Frequency of actions fitting this theme (percentage)
To search for research evidence or investigate sources of data/information	27
To use EBP to approach a new research project or area of work (e.g., using PICO [population/participant, intervention/indicator, comparator/control, outcome])	19
To share learning and champion EBP	18
To build EBP into my daily practice/the practice of my team	16
To network or collaborate with others	9
To challenge or review current ways of working	7
To undertake training or a professional research qualification	3

TABLE 5.4 Collated feedback about workshop aims*

How well do you think the workshop achieved its aims? To support attendees to:	Very well (%)	Quite well (%)	Somewhat (%)	Not very well (%)	Not at all well (%)	Mean rating (1–5)	SD
...formulate a focused and answerable research question.	47	45	8	0	0	4.4	.63
...find and organise the best evidence.	45	46	8	1	0	4.4	.68
...critically appraise the evidence.	54	35	10	1	0	4.4	.72
...understand the benefits and limitations of various research methodologies.	42	49	6	3	0	4.3	.70
...understand research ethics.	60	35	5	0	0	4.6	.59
...reflect on what helps and hinders evidence-based practice.	53	39	6	1	0	4.4	.68
...share and learn from colleagues about applying evidence-based practice.	49	35	15	0	0	4.3	.73

* $N = 79$ or 80, depending on the question.

After reviewing the feedback and reflecting on each workshop, a number of changes were made to the plans for subsequent workshops. For example, more pre-course information was provided about the sessions and the research papers that would be used, and some of the sessions' content was revised, such as the breakout session about tracking down research evidence.[6] Further, small groups were mixed in terms of role and experience rather than splitting according to the extent of their EBP knowledge or experience, and more networking time was built into the workshops, including grouping attendees with similar professional interests to work together to develop ideas for taking work forward (e.g. domestic violence, vulnerable groups, processual change such as evaluating changes to working practices such as gender balance, shift patterns, etc.).

Reflection: Investigate Workshop Impact

Workshop evaluations

At the conclusion of each workshop, attendees were asked to report their knowledge, skills, and confidence in applying EBP in practice at the start of the workshop compared to the end (i.e., retrospective pre-test). Ratings were on a 5-point scale (1 being 'very poor' and 5 being 'very

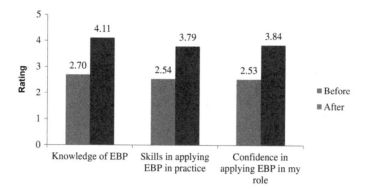

FIGURE 5.2 Knowledge, skills and confidence before/after workshop ratings [1 (very poor) – 5 (very good)] ($n = 80$)

good'). Before the workshop, most attendees rated themselves 'adequate' or 'poor' for all three factors, whereas after the workshop, the majority of attendees rated their knowledge, skills, and confidence as 'good' or 'very good'. Figure 5.2 shows the collated mean ratings for before and after from all four workshops ($n = 80$), demonstrating increases across all three variables. T-tests confirmed that the difference between before and after ratings was statistically significant separately for all three variables and for all four workshops ($p < 0.001$).

Follow-up survey

In addition to gathering feedback at the end of the workshops to gauge the immediate impact on attendees' knowledge, skills, and confidence around EBP, attendees were contacted five to six months after the workshop took place and asked to complete an online survey about the progress they had made against their action plans, allowing us to estimate the medium-term impact of the workshops on practice (see Appendix 2).

Forty-six out of the 83 attendees responded to the survey (18 from Workshop 1, 14 from Workshop 2, 5 from Workshop 3, 5 from Workshop 4, and 4 that did not state which workshop they had attended). We received reports that some invitations sent to attendees from Workshops 3 and 4 were redirected as email spam, which explains the lower response rate from attendees from these later sessions. Almost three-quarters of respondents stated that the progress on their action plans was underway; some respondents highlighted that their actions were ongoing and therefore could never be 'completed'.

Participants were asked to rate the impact of the workshop on their practice. Out of the 41 who responded to the question, the majority of participants rated the impact as medium ($n = 20$) or high ($n = 14$), which highlighted a great start considering the workshop itself only sought to provide the knowledge, skills, and confidence to change practice, and did not aim to change it directly. Six participants rated the impact as low, and one as very low. This was useful insight before the follow-up meeting and helped to shape the conversation.

Follow-up meeting

During the first and second workshops, many attendees expressed a desire to continue working together and to meet in person again with university colleagues. The follow-up survey stated the aims of the follow-up meeting and invited input for any additional items. These scheduled meetings lasted half a day and were held at the DCP Headquarters. A number of university and police project staff attended, a representative from the College of Policing, and the Deputy Chief Constable returned to close the session, continuing visible senior support. Fifteen police staff attended the first follow-up meeting, with all but one being from DCP; eight staff attended the second meeting.

The meetings were intended to give attendees the opportunity to share learning with colleagues about how they had used the workshop within their day-to-day work and to encourage conversations about how to move forward with EBP across their organisation. DCP colleagues involved in the project also outlined opportunities for staff secondments and shared actions the organisation was taking following the information provided by staff about the barriers and facilitators to EBP. A number of suggestions for organisational change were also proposed by attendees that were intended to further promote EBP within DCP. These included presenting the ExPERT project to others (e.g., through video), sharing workshop presentations and other EBP-related materials on the internal network and through putting on 'Lunch and learn' sessions. There were also suggestions about creating a practitioner forum where people can talk about things they are working on, develop ideas, and think through issues they are encountering with their ideas. Attendees were also keen to act as champions for EBP, and some suggested wearing a special badge or using an identifying email signature.

Feedback about the meeting provided through an end-of-session evaluation form was positive. Some attendees mentioned feeling 're-energised' and that the session had reinforced learning and provided further ideas to take forward. Attendees particularly valued the sharing of practice examples and highlighted their desire to maintain working relationships with colleagues they had met at the workshops.

Discussion

Our 'Making Sense of Evidence' workshops aimed to promote EBP within DCP and neighbouring forces in the south-west of England through addressing the need to promote the knowledge and skills required for police officers and staff to find, critique, utilise, and plan research. The workshops complemented national imperatives placed on police forces to make their operations more evidence-based by bringing officers and staff together for the purpose of individual and organisational transformation. The workshops appear to have been successful in raising awareness of EBP and in building capacity across the force in terms of research skills and appetite for EBP.

There are a number of lessons we can take from the development and delivery of the 'Making Sense of Evidence' workshops described in this chapter: how they helped contribute towards wider organisational change in relation to embedding EBP in practice, and the academic-police collaborations that underpinned it.

The first centres on the importance of approaching training workshops of this sort as a dialogue. The workshops were approached as a two-way information sharing activity – on the one hand, to support the embedding of EBP through raising awareness, understanding, and providing staff with the necessary skills, and on the other hand, to gather data about what staff perceived as the barriers and facilitators to EBP and to enable a conversation about how to respond to those. The ideas collected during pre-workshop interviews were confirmed and scrutinised during the workshops; this also fits with previous research findings about the identified barriers and facilitators to the implementation of research knowledge within a policing context (Hunter et al., 2017; Wilkinson et al., 2017).

Four workshops, targeting less than 100 individuals, are not sufficient to bring about large-scale change across an organisation of over 5,000 people. However, it was never the plan for these workshops to work alone – rather, they were intended to provide one means of overcoming some of the identified barriers to EBP (for instance, lack of skills) in supporting a wider cultural shift. Our experience has shown that these workshops can be valuable not only in tackling barriers but also in gathering information that can be used to inform other organisational activities taking place. More workshops, involving staff from a variety of roles across the organisation (including those with less of an initial interest in EBP), would further support this process.

We were very aware that almost all of the workshop attendees had chosen to apply for the course of their own initiative and therefore represented an enthusiastic and pro-EBP sample of DCP. Whether the workshops delivered here would work as well for staff who are less keen on EBP is unclear, but through the two-way conversation that forms an integral part of their delivery, vital learning is likely to be brought to the table in any case.

It is important to note, however, that just knowing how to utilise research does not mean that research will be utilised. For this reason, it is important that organisational policies support the embedding of EBP; for example, if the presentation of research evidence is required for policy and practice decision-making at all levels. Elsewhere, training transfer has also been shown to be most effective when the organisational transfer climate supports the use of learned skills (Burke & Hutchins, 2007). Publicly demonstrating that EBP is a priority for the organisation will provide a necessary backing for keen individuals, and a nudge for those who are yet to be convinced.

In the case of the ExPERT project involving DCP, the importance attached to embedding EBP and the demands recognised with doing so have led to the creation of an innovative job role: the DCP and the University of Exeter created a trial one-year 'embedded researcher' position for the ExPERT Research Fellow. Formally employed by the University of Exeter but located primarily at DCP Police Headquarters within the Performance & Analysis department, she will be working towards a number of organisational goals geared towards building resilient infrastructure to support continued development of EBP within DCP.

Whilst there is an obvious need for a strategic core to promote EBP (e.g., Fell, Lacey, & Voas, 2004), those taking a leadership role for EBP need to be situated across both departments and geographical locations. During both the workshops and follow-up meetings, attendees were asked how they thought the organisation, as well as individuals, could support the EBP agenda. Suggestions for lunchtime groups, sharing of training materials, and other ways to promote EBP to colleagues have subsequently been put in place by some of the attendees, and following networking at the workshops, working relationships have been formed as well as groups supporting the use of evidence in practice. It was noted by a number of staff during the workshops that DCP, like other police organisations in England and Wales, is highly fractured, with lots of people working in silos and with similar research being conducted simultaneously. Attendees reported great value in sharing practice examples and experience of EBP and the support from colleagues around this way of working. Increased and improved networking to share knowledge, skills, and learning is also therefore important if the workshops and other activities associated with EBP are to have wider impact.

As part of such efforts, the positioning of EBP will be important. There were a number of barriers consistently raised by police staff during the pre-workshop interviews, the workshop activities, and also in the follow-up surveys and meetings (also aligned with Fleming & Wingrove, 2017). One factor relating to both the culture of the organisation and the individual characteristics of police staff was staff attitude towards change. Some believed there were colleagues in their organisations who felt that EBP directly challenged innovation and professional judgement. This is also something that has been found in other studies investigating EBP (e.g., Telep & Lum, 2014). These points would suggest that if EBP is understood as a means of restricting decision-making or criticising the importance of professional experience, it is likely to be highly contested. On the other hand, if it is understood as providing a solid backing for decisions and support of the application of knowledge gained through experience, it is more likely to win acceptance.[7] As research has suggested (Lum, Telep, Koper, & Grieco, 2012), while police officers might initially regard professional experience as sufficient and as preferable to research findings, greater exposure to research can lead to a greater willingness to experiment and to incorporate research within conceptions of professional experience.[8]

For those in the police, examples of how others had managed to embed elements of EBP within their day-job was of particular relevance, and based on the feedback received, we propose that any future workshops of this type should include a session whereby practical examples are shared by colleagues as a means of inspiring others. Indeed, providing relevant and practical examples within a teaching environment increases the content relevance and has been found to greatly improve the extent of 'training transfer' – that is, the amount of learning from training that is subsequently transferred and implemented within the practice environment (see Burke & Hutchins, 2007).

Conclusion

Organisational change is not something that can happen instantly – it requires determined commitment over long periods of time. This chapter demonstrates the positive contribution of training workshops for police staff in building knowledge and skills around EBP and in supporting cultural change towards using research evidence to inform practice. Our collaborative approach to design and delivery along with a continuous cycle of reflection and review enabled the development of a successful workshop in addition to gathering invaluable information about staff needs and perceptions of organisational barriers to EBP more broadly.

Developing and delivering the workshops using an AR methodology allowed the research team to review as they went along and amend the plans to ensure they were as useful as possible. Some of the factors important in workshop design mentioned at the beginning of this chapter, including location, presenters, content, and structure, proved successful within this context with only minimal adjustments required. The collaborative planning of the workshops that drew on the framework PenCLAHRC developed for health no doubt led to this success, as discussions about requirements were had at the outset. However, despite the positive results observed in this study, we must recognise that the findings are based on a small sample of police staff situated within a single law enforcement agency. We therefore cannot assume that the workshops would be as successful or feasible in other law enforcement contexts.

In addition to testing this model in other law enforcement agencies and contexts, future research in this area would benefit from investigating the impact of such workshops when delivered to more staff across the organisation, and to consider the other activities employed to promote and bring about organisational change and how these interact and work together over a longer period of time. Longitudinal research to systematically investigate the sustainability of targeted activities and whether these workshops are successful in supporting organisations work towards real cultural change with regards to EBP (e.g., change that is evident in policy or practice) would also be interesting to explore.

Disclosure Statement

No potential conflict of interest was reported by the authors. The views and opinions expressed therein are those of the authors and do not necessarily reflect those of the National Institute for Health Research, National Health Service, or the Department of Health.

Funding

This report was undertaken as part of a project titled "The Exeter Policing, Evidence and Research Translation (ExPERT) project" funded by the Home Office and the Higher Education Funding Council for England and the College of Policing under award J10. The University of Exeter was supported in their contribution to the development of the original research proposal by the NIHR Collaboration for Leadership in Applied Health Research & Care South-West Peninsula (CLAHRC). With many thanks to the rest of the ExPERT project team as well as Nicky Miller at the College of Policing.

Notes

1. Just as EBP has been a long standing matter of consideration, so too has the promotion of police-university research collaborations. In the case of the US, for instance, Rojek et al. (2012) traced recent substantial efforts to link police practitioners and university researchers to a 1967 President's Commission on Law Enforcement and the Administration of Justice recommendation that criminal justice agencies make more use of social science research as well as the subsequent federal funding that accompanied the establishment of National Institute of Justice. Since that time, the need for greater collaborations has resurfaced as a major theme from time to time within the agendas of criminal justice organisations.
2. In practice, the elements of the project were inter-related and in particular in relation to promoting organizational change. The workshops elaborated in this paper, for instance, supported other forms of collaboration (e.g., the police-academic secondments).
3. http://clahrc-peninsula.nihr.ac.uk/making-sense-of-evidence.
4. Still, some concerns of AR in the police have been identified. These have included the limitations of case studies that typically characterise AR, the potential for closing working partnering researchers to refrain from criticism, and the danger that action-orientated research slides into law enforcement practice (Rosenbaum, 2010).
5. The full workshop programme can be found here: http://socialsciences.exeter.ac.uk/sociology/research/projects/policingandevidencegroup/makingsenseofevidenceandresearchworkshops/.
6. In relation to this session, while participants were eager to devise their own research projects, it initially proved difficult to get them to think about how to utilise existing secondary literature so the structure of the session was amended to support this further.
7. Referring to EBP as evidence-*informed* practice will help to support this, by recognising the equal importance and contributions of professional expertise and service-user experience in addition to evidence gathered through research.
8. Our thanks to Nicky Miller, College of Policing, for this suggestion.

References

Avby, G., Nilsen, P., & Dahlgren, M. A. (2014). Ways of understanding evidence-based practice in social work: A qualitative study. *British Journal of Social Work, 44*(6), 1366–1383.

Beal, P., & Kerlikowske, R. G. (2010). Action research in Buffalo and Seattle. *Police Practice and Research, 11*(2), 117–121.

Boba, R. (2010). A practice-based evidence approach in Florida. *Police Practice and Research, 11*(2), 122–128.

Bradley, D., & Nixon, C. (2009). Ending the 'dialogue of the deaf': Evidence and policing policies and practices. An Australian case study. *Police Practice and Research, 10*(5–6), 423–435.

Bullock, K., & Tilley, N. (2009). Evidence-based policing and crime reduction. *Policing, 3*(4), 381–387.

Burke, L. A., & Hutchins, H. M. (2007). Training transfer: An integrative literature review. *Human Resource Development Review, 6*(3), 263–296.

Carson, L., & Rooy, D. (2015). 'Commonsense psychology' is a barrier to the implementation of best practice child interviewing guidelines: A qualitative analysis of police officers' beliefs in Scotland. *Journal of Police and Criminal Psychology, 30*, 50–62.

CoP. (2017). What is evidence-based policing? Retrieved from http://whatworks.college.police.uk/About/Pages/Whatis-EBP.aspx

CoP and HEFCE. (2015). Police knowledge fund. Retrieved from http://whatworks.college.police.uk/Partnerships/Knowledge-Fund/Pages/Police-Knowledge-Fund.aspx

Ekblom, P. (2002). From the source to the mainstream is uphill. In N. Tilley (Ed.), *Analysis for crime prevention* (pp. 131–203). London: Sage.

Engel, R. S., & Whalen, J. L. (2010). Police–academic partnerships: Ending the dialogue of the deaf, the Cincinnati experience. *Police Practice and Research*, *11*(2), 105–116.

Fell, J. C., Lacey, J. H., & Voas, R. B. (2004). Sobriety checkpoints: Evidence of effectiveness is strong, but use is limited. *Traffic Injury Prevention*, *5*(3), 220–227.

Fleming, J., & Wingrove, J. (2017). 'We would if we could … but not sure if we can': Implementing evidence-based practice. *Policing*, *11*(2), 202–213. doi:10.1093/police/pax006

Fyfe, N. R., & Wilson, P. (2012). Knowledge exchange and police practice: Broadening and deepening the debate around researcher-practitioner collaborations. *Police Practice and Research: An International Journal*, *14*(4), 306–314.

Hunter, G., May, T., & Hough, M. (2017). *An Evaluation of the 'What works Centre for Crime Reduction' Final Report*. London: ICPR.

Innes, M. (2010). A 'mirror' and a 'motor'. *Policing*, *4*(2), 127–134.

James, P. (1999). Rewriting narratives of self. *Educational Action Research*, *7*(1), 85–103.

Kennedy, D. (2010). Hope and despair. *Police Practice and Research*, *11*(2), 166–170.

Knutsson, J. (2010). Nordic reflections on the dialogue of the deaf. *Police Practice and Research*, *11*(2), 132–134.

Lum, C., Telep, C. W., Koper, C. S., & Grieco, J. (2012). Receptivity to research in policing. *Justice Research and Policy*, *14*(1), 61–95.

Lumsden, K., & Goode, J. (2016). Policing research and the rise of the 'evidence-base': Police officer and staff understandings of research, its implementation and 'what works. *Sociology*, 1–17.

Murji, K. (2010). Introduction: Academic–police collaborations - beyond "two worlds". *Policing*, *4*(2), 92–94.

Rai, R. K. (2012). A participatory action research training initiative to improve police effectiveness. *Action Research*, *10*(3), 225–243.

Reason, P., & Bradbury, H. (2001). *Handbook of action research*. London: Sage.

Research in Practice (2012). *Organisational survey for evidence-informed practice*. Dartington: Research in Practice.

Rojek, J., Alpert, G., & Smith, H. (2012). The utilization of research by the police. *Police Practice and Research*, *13*(4), 329–341.

Rosenbaum, D. P. (2010). Police research: Merging the policy and action research traditions. *Police Practice and Research*, *11*(2), 144–149.

Sherman, L. W. (2013). The rise of evidence-based policing: Targeting, testing, and tracking. *Crime and Justice*, *42*(1), 377–451.

Steinheider, B., Wuestewald, T., Boyatzis, R. E., & Kroutter, P. (2012). In search of a methodology of collaboration. *Police Practice and Research*, *13*(4), 357–374.

Stephens, D. W. (2010). Enhancing the impact of research on police practice. *Police Practice and Research*, *11*(2), 150–154.

Stott, C., West, O., & Radburn, M. (2016). Policing football 'risk'? A participant action research case study of a liaison-based approach to 'public order'. *Policing and Society*, 1–16. doi:10.1080/10439463.2015.1126267

Telep, C. W., & Lum, C. (2014). The receptivity of officers to empirical research and evidence-based policing: An examination of survey data from three agencies. *Police Quarterly*, *17*, 359–385.

Tillyer, R., Tillyer, M. S., McCluskey, J., Cancino, J., Todaro, J., & McKinnon, L. (2014). Researcher–practitioner partnerships and crime analysis: A case study in action research. *Police Practice and Research*, *15*(5), 404–418.

Weisburd, D., & Neyroud. P. (2011). *Police science: Toward a new paradigm*. Cambridge, MA: Harvard University. Retrieved from https://www.ncjrs.gov/pdffiles1/nij/228922.pdf

Wilkinson, K., Lang, I., Rappert, B., Boyd, K., Farrimond, H., Reardon, E., … Pearson, M. (2017). *What do we know about the use of research knowledge in policing? A systematic scoping review*. Manuscript submitted for publication.

Wuestewald, T., & Steinheider, B. (2010). Practitioner-researcher collaboration in policing: A case of close encounters? *Policing*, *4*(2), 104–111.

Appendix 1. Organisational Survey for EBP

Audit Tool: How evidence-based is your organisation?

Research shows that using evidence to inform practice supports individuals and organisations to learn and improve, and to be more confident in what they do.

This audit aims to help you to think about your organisation and your practice and how evidence-based you are in the way that you work at the moment. Please work through the following sections and rate each point on the scale according to your experience, knowledge, and perceptions.

Section 1: Leadership	*Strongly agree*	*Agree*	*Neutral*	*Disagree*	*Strongly disagree*
The organisation has a clear vision and strategy for embedding evidence-based practice.					
Evidence based approaches are promoted by influential figures or leaders in the organisation.					
When new policies and procedures are introduced, we are made aware of the research evidence which supports them					
Staff know who to contact to ask questions about evidence-based practice.					

Section 2: Culture	*Strongly agree*	*Agree*	*Neutral*	*Disagree*	*Strongly disagree*
The organisation welcomes constructive challenge from all staff and their input into evidence-informed decisions.					
The organisation values and encourages reflection to learn from both positive and negative experiences.					
The organisation has individuals who act as 'champions' in promoting evidence-based practice.					
The organisation expects staff to draw on evidence to make decisions about how they do their jobs.					
The organisation reports on how it has used evidence in service planning and commissioning.					
The organisation rewards good practice in the use of evidence.					

Section 3: Building capacity	*Strongly agree*	*Agree*	*Neutral*	*Disagree*	*Strongly disagree*
The organisation encourages and supports its workforce to gain knowledge and understanding from research evidence.					
The organisation provides learning opportunities for staff to develop their skills and knowledge around gathering and implementing evidence in practice.					
The organisation provides sufficient support and resources to implement evidence-based practice.					
The organisation provides access to research for all staff.					
The organisation provides dedicated ongoing support to staff to appraise and applies evidence to its work.					

Section 4: Sharing learning	Strongly agree	Agree	Neutral	Disagree	Strongly disagree
Individuals, teams and multi-agency groups share and use learning from research and practice.					
The organisation supports staff to carry out their own research.					
The organisation systematically gathers and uses service-user views about experience and impact.					
The organisation carries out impact evaluations about how well it has done and the difference it has made.					
The organisation uses information gathered from research and evaluations to improve its services.					
The organisation shares learning with other forces and relevant organisations about best practice.					

Section 5: Individual factors	Strongly agree	Agree	Neutral	Disagree	Strongly disagree
Research evidence plays an important role in my day-to-day decision-making.					
I lack the time to be able to seek research evidence out.					

Snapshot
During the last 12 months....

	Strongly agree	Agree	Neutral	Disagree	Strongly disagree
I can think of at least one occasion where research evidence has affected how I allocate resources.					
I have used research evidence to help me understand a crime problem.					
I have used research evidence to justify existing practice.					
I have used research evidence to develop new practice.					
I have used research evidence to help think about ways that I might assess the impact of practice.					

Your responses are anonymous. However, it would be useful for us to know your role or area of work. If you are happy to provide this, please state it here:

Appendix 2. Post-workshop Follow-up Survey

Note that this survey was sent electronically using survey software
Making Sense of Evidence Workshop Follow-up Survey
This survey is for anyone who attended one of the 'Making sense of evidence' workshops, delivered by Devon and Cornwall Police and the University of Exeter in 2016.

The aims of this survey are:

- To capture the impact of the workshops on individuals' practice
- To understand how we can amend the workshops to be more useful in the longer term
- To explore alternative workshop follow-up options

- To understand what the organisation needs to do to support collaborative working and drive forward EBP
- To help plan the follow-up workshop

Responses are anonymous, unless you choose to leave your email at the end so that we contact you about your answers.

The survey should only take you 10 min to complete.

Thank you in advance for your time!

The ExPERT Team

1. **Are you planning to attend the follow-up meeting on [DATE OF FOLLOW-UP WORKSHOP]?**

   - Yes
   - No
   - Don't know

2. **Why are you not attending the meeting?**

   - I am unable to make the date/time
   - I do not have time/I am too busy
   - I do not feel the need to attend another meeting/workshop on the topic of EBP
   - Other (please specify)

3. **If you would have preferred a different kind of follow-up to the workshop, please let us know:**

   _____

4. **What two things are you hoping to get out of the follow-up workshop?**
   1.
   2.
   Comments:

   _____

5. **Which 'Making sense of evidence' workshop did you attend?**

   - 21–22 March 2016
   - 18–19 April 2016
   - 19–20 September 2016
   - 10–11 October 2016

6. **To which organisation do you belong?**

   - Devon and Cornwall Police
   - Other

7. **How evidence-based would you say you are currently in the way that you work?**

Not at all evidence-based		Somewhat evidence-based		Entirely evidence-based
1	2	3	4	5

8. **How would you rate the impact of attending the workshop on your practice to date?**

Very low	Low	Average	High	Very high
1	2	3	4	5

9. **Did you complete an Action Plan at the workshop?**

   - Yes
   - No

10. **Please select the categories below which best describe the actions you outlined in the workshop (please tick all that apply)**

    - To build EBP into my daily practice/the practice of my team
    - To challenge or review current ways of working
    - To network or collaborate with others
    - To search for research evidence or investigate sources of data/information
    - To share learning and champion EBP
    - To undertake training or a professional research qualification
    - To use EBP to approach a new research project or area of work (e.g., using PICO)
    - I don't remember
    - Other (please specify)

11. **Overall, how would you best describe your progress on your action plan?**

    - Not started
    - Underway
    - Complete

    Comments:

    _____

12. **Since the workshop, please outline anything that has helped you to achieve your actions/become more evidence-based in your practice (i.e., the facilitators):**

    _____

13. **Since the workshop, please outline anything that has prevented you from achieving your actions/becoming more evidence-based in your practice (i.e., the barriers):**

    _____

14. **Have you been in contact with colleagues you met in the workshop that you didn't work with previously?**
    If yes, please tell us how and why:

    _____

15. **Do you have an example of how you have changed your practice or how the workshop has helped you to progress in an area of work?**

    - Yes
    - No

• **If yes, please provide brief details below:**

_____

16. **If you are happy for us to contact you for more details about your responses, please leave your email here**

_____

Many thanks for taking the time to complete this survey.

PART III

Researcher Practitioner Partnership

6

Present but Not Prevalent

Identifying the Organizational Correlates of Researcher-Practitioner Partnerships in U.S. Law Enforcement

Jeff Rojek

SCHOOL OF CRIMINAL JUSTICE, MICHIGAN STATE UNIVERSITY, EAST LANSING, MI, USA

John A. Shjarback

DEPARTMENT OF LAW AND JUSTICE STUDIES, ROWAN UNIVERSITY, GLASSBORO, NJ, USA

John Andrew Hansen

cDEPARTMENT OF CRIMINAL JUSTICE, WESTERN CAROLINA UNIVERSITY, CULLOWHEE, NC, USA

Geoffrey P. Alpert

DEPARTMENT OF CRIMINOLOGY AND CRIMINAL JUSTICE, UNIVERSITY OF SOUTH CAROLINA/GRIFFITH UNIVERSITY

There has been a concerted effort over the last few decades to foster more researcher-practitioner partnerships in American law enforcement. For example, a number of federally funded programs have provided grant money to agencies with the requirement/stipulation that they partner with members of the research community. These programs include CeaseFire, Drug Market Analysis Program (DMAP), Locally Initiated Researcher Partnerships (LIRP), Strategic Approach to Community Safety Initiative (SACSI), Project Safe Neighborhoods (PSN), and, most recently, the Bureau of Justice Assistance's Smart Policing Initiative (SPI). The International Association of Chiefs of Police (IACP) is perhaps the most prominent advocate for such partnerships. In a 2004 report, IACP asserted that partnerships were 'critical to discovering and implementing best policing practices' (p. 3) – arguing that developing researcher-practitioner partnerships should be a primary goal for every law enforcement agency in the country. Additionally, the National Institute of Justice (NIJ) (2017), in its Strategic Research Plan through 2022, has pledged continued funding to promote research to examine police-researcher partnerships and their impact on public safety.

Yet, few studies have explored the growth and prevalence of research partnerships in policing. International Association of Chiefs of Police (2011) conducted a survey of its members in late 2009: finding that 45% of the 731 responding departments had collaborated in the past or were currently collaborating with college/university researchers. More recently, Alpert, Rojek, and Hansen (2013) conducted a nationally representative survey with 32% of responding agencies reporting involvement in partnerships. And while much more has been learned

DOI: 10.4324/9781003153009-9

about the prevalence of research partnerships in policing, little empirical work has examined the predictors of those partnerships. As such, the field lacks an understanding of which factors contribute to their successes or failures and the type of agencies that are willing to engage in them.

In an effort toward this goal and expanding on prior research, we examined the organizational correlates of researcher-practitioner partnerships in U.S. law enforcement.[1] Using a nationally representative sample of 871 agencies of all sizes (see Alpert et al., 2013; Rojek, Smith, & Alpert, 2012a), the current study employed multivariate analysis to investigate participation in what we term 'rigorous partnerships'. A particular focus is placed on agencies' orientation/openness to research as well as the specific sources of those research outlets.

Literature Review

Shared Governance, Research Utilization, and Knowledge Translation

Problems confronting public institutions have become more complex in recent years. A number of fields and disciplines (e.g., public administration, medicine) have recognized that one potential solution to address these concerns lies in the adoption of a 'governance framework' based on a process of shared responsibility among government institutions and stakeholders (i.e., 'shared governance'). The primary mechanism government institutions have used to foster such shared governance has been the formation of *partnerships* with other government agencies/ entities, community members and organizations, private organizations, and academic institutions (Vigoda, 2002). The rationale behind, as well as the underlying goal, of these partnerships is to combine the resources, skills, and knowledge of the actors in a way that allows them to achieve better results in managing problems more effectively and efficiently than could be accomplished either individually or by government agencies alone (Lasker, Weiss, & Miller, 2001). A wide variety of partnerships in law enforcement exist, including community policing and multi-jurisdictional task forces. However, it is the formation of police practitioner-researcher partnerships, because of their potential benefits, that are deserving of more scholarly attention.

Collaborations between law enforcement and the research community hinge on the interrelated concepts of 'research utilization' and 'knowledge translation' (see Green, Ottoson, Garcia, & Haitt, 2009; Henry & MacKenzie, 2012; Lang, Wyer, & Eskin, 2007). 'Translational criminology', in fact, fits neatly within this broader framework. While both sides of the practitioner-researcher partnership arguably benefit from said participation, the public policy consideration has largely focused on how the researcher can improve the law enforcement agency and/or its practices. The research partner, ideally, adds a degree of empirical knowledge, various methodologies, and analytical skills that can improve an agency's ability to identify problems and formulate effective responses. It is assumed that such relationships will lead practitioners/agencies to integrate findings from established and accepted scientific methodology into efforts to evaluate police responses and understand social problems (i.e., bringing research to practice). In turn, these results will, theoretically, make police agencies more effective in serving their respective communities (Braga & Hinkle, 2010; International Association of Chiefs of Police, 2004). As such, police practitioner-researcher partnerships represent an interpersonal form of research utilization by law enforcement agencies.

It is important to note that not all partnerships are created equally, and they vary in the degree to which they create opportunities for research utilization and knowledge translation. The most effective collaborations aim to foster more interactive, two-way exchanges of information between police practitioners and researchers. From a research utilization/knowledge translation standpoint, these types of interactive exchanges are, without a doubt, more desirable than passive forms, such as researchers publishing results from studies with the expectation that practitioners will locate and incorporate this knowledge on their own. We frame involvement in partnerships as a form of research utilization/ knowledge translation.

History, Advocacy, and the Prevalence of Researcher-Practitioner Partnerships[2]

Federal funding has provided perhaps the biggest impetus for the creation and growth of such partnerships. According to Sherman (2004), the NIJ-funded DMAP, with the goal of evaluating police efforts addressing illegal drug markets, was one of the first streams of grant initiatives requiring the partnership of practitioners with researchers. DMAP, however, ended in the mid-1990s. The next NIJ funding stream – the Locally Initiated Research Partnerships (LIRP) in policing program – occurred between 1995–1996; 41 police practitioner-researcher partnerships were granted money to engage in problem-oriented policing/ SARA-type (i.e., scanning, analysis, response/intervention, assessment) projects (McEwen, 2003). Aside from LIRP, NIJ also funded Operation CeaseFire – a collaboration between the Boston Police Department and researchers from Harvard University's John F. Kennedy School of Government (see Braga, Kennedy, Waring, & Piehl, 2001). Because of its success in reducing youth violence, NIJ funded replication efforts (with collaborative partnerships between law enforcement and researchers) in 10 U.S. cities under SACSI (Roehl et al., 2006). Similar efforts were followed by the PSN program (McGarrell et al., 2009) and, most recently, the Bureau of Justice Assistance's SPI. In fact, Rojek and colleagues (2012a: 252) found that the number one reason why agencies reported not participating in partnerships was 'not having the funding or resources'.

IACP has been at the forefront of advocacy for partnerships for some time now. In 2004, they took assertive effort in creating a link between law enforcement practitioners and the research community through the formation of a Research Advisory Committee. The committee is comprised of both researchers and law enforcement leaders, and its mission is to 'help guide the IACP and its partners in identifying and conducting law enforcement policy research on the most important issues facing police executives' (Wellford, Serpas, & Firman, 2007, p. 1). The committee has made promoting the development of police-researcher partnerships a priority. The NIJ (2017) also recently reported that it would continue to prioritize research on and the development of practitioner-researcher partnerships in its Strategic Research Plan for 2017–2022. In addition to organizations, a number of influential police leaders have called for the increase in partnerships. William Bratton (2006), then chief of the Los Angeles Police Department, delivering the keynote speech at the 2006 NIJ conference, stated, 'I embrace and encourage the need for research, because I am a change agent, who constantly needs timely accurate information to help shape my initiatives and understand my challenges' (p. 1). Similar insight and messages can be found by Darrel Stephens (2010) and Jim Bueermann (2012).

Despite the federal funding over the past few decades, particularly from the NIJ, and the encouragement from prominent law enforcement organizations (e.g., IACP) and executives (e.g., William Bratton), little is known about the development and prevalence of researcher-practitioner partnerships among U.S. law enforcement. Most of the research that has been done is limited to case studies. One of the few exceptions was a review conducted by McEwen (2003); however, it only focused on the 41 practitioner-researcher partnerships funded through the LIRP policing program. Additionally, there have been two special issues dedicated to the topic in *Police Practice and Research* (Rojek, Alpert, & Smith, 2012b; Stephens, 2010) and another in *Policing: A Journal of Policy and Practice* in 2010. This body of literature has discussed the benefits of partnerships, particularly for the police, and it has identified a number of interrelated factors that influence their development: trust, the involvement of the right individuals, communication, and the permanence of personnel.

International Association of Chiefs of Police (2011) conducted a survey of its 731 members in 2009, which explored their perceptions of research utilization and participation in partnerships. It represented an important first effort in measuring the prevalence of researcher-practitioner partnership; however, it was only conducted on a convenience sample of association agencies. While the majority of police organizations reported that they either 'often' or 'always' have an interest in learning about new research relevant to law enforcement and the justice system, their answers did not define the degree to which they use research to inform agency decisions/operations, or even what constitutes the term 'research'. For example, 30% of responding agencies reported that research 'often' or 'always' influence their decisions, and another 61% of agencies reported that research 'occasionally' influences their decisions (International Association of Chiefs of Police, 2011). When asked about the specific sources of research that they rely on, more than 90% of agencies reported 'professional law enforcement associations' and more than 70% reported 'conferences and training courses'. On the other hand, approximately 40% mentioned 'academic or technical journals' and 34% referenced 'universities and colleges' (International Association of Chiefs of Police, 2011). Some of the respondents, in fact, raised concerns in their survey responses about the 'relevance of academic or university-driven law enforcement research to the practical issues they face' (International Association of Chiefs of Police, 2011, p. 6).

In regard to the prevalence of police partnerships, 45% of the IACP member agencies reported that they had either collaborated with college/university researchers in the past or were currently collaborating with those researchers. Interestingly, proximity to a college/university did not seem to be a factor in contributing to research partnerships: as 60% of agencies who reported there was a college or university within 30 miles also reported having no experience in these collaborations. Knowledge of a local college or university's research capacity, however, did appear to influence participation, as 64% of those respondents who knew about the local research capacity had participated in collaborations. Conversely, 70% of agencies that were not aware of this local research capacity had never collaborated with a college or university researcher. The education level of the organization's chief executive also appeared to be a factor (International Association of Chiefs of Police, 2011). Police leaders with graduate degrees were more likely to have an interest in using research and their agencies were likely to have collaborated with a college/university researcher, followed by leaders with bachelor's or associate's degrees; chiefs with only high school diplomas reported the lowest rates on both measures – interest in research and history of collaboration.

Alpert and colleagues performed, arguably, the most rigorous evaluation of the prevalence of police practitioner-researcher partnerships to date. Using a nationally representative, stratified random sample, they uncovered a number of noteworthy findings regarding prevalence and distribution across agency size. Nearly one-third (32%) of departments in the sample indicated that they had engaged in a partnership with researchers within the past five years (Alpert et al., 2013; Rojek, Smith et al., 2012a) – a figure lower than the International Association of Chiefs of Police (2011) count but more generalizable and broader than the sample of IACP members. In addition, the likelihood of involvement in a research partnership was largely associated with agency size. Nearly half (48%) of departments in the sample with 100 or more sworn officers had engaged in a partnership compared to 25% of agencies with 50–99 officers, 22% of agencies with 25–49 officers, 10% of agencies with 10–24 officers, and just 7% of departments with less than 10 officers (Rojek, Smith et al., 2012a).

Current Study

Prior research on the topic has provided initial insight into the history, growth, and prevalence of practitioner-researcher collaboration in U.S. policing. Although these partnerships are certainly present and have likely increased in recent years, they are by no means prevalent – especially for smaller sized agencies. In addition to size, the education level of chief executives may also be related to the likelihood of participation while proximity to a college/university researcher might be inconsequential. Aside from these factors, which have largely been examined at the descriptive level, little empirical work has investigated other correlates, particularly organizational features, of willingness to engage in research partnerships. Given the framing of partnerships within the broader interest in research utilization/knowledge translation, we explored the potential link between orientation/openness to research and engagement in high-quality partnerships (i.e., where more opportunity for interactive knowledge exchange can take place). Moreover, due to the fact that there is reported variation in the sources of research findings (e.g., academic vs. professional journals; see International Association of Chiefs of Police, 2011), we examined the specific outlets where agencies are receiving knowledge (if at all) and whether it impacts participation in research collaborations. Because past studies have found that size matters, we paid particular attention to large agencies.

Methods

Data and Sample

This study used data from a NIJ-funded project on police partnerships as well as supplemental measures from the 2007 Law Enforcement Management and Administrative Statistics (LEMAS) survey. More specifically, it employed a national survey of a stratified random sample of 2,015 municipal, county, and state law enforcement agencies, which was drawn from the 2009 National Directory of Law Enforcement Agencies (NDLEA) database. The 2009 NDLEA database provides information on 15,759 state and local law enforcement organizations, including the name of the current chief executive and the agency address. In addition, it provides information on the type of agency (city/county police department; county sheriff; state police/highway patrol), population of the jurisdiction (under 10,000; 10,000–49,999; 50,000–99,999; 100,000–499,999; 500,000–999,999; 1,000,000+), and region of the country where the agency is located (northeast; Midwest; south; west) – all characteristics that were used for the stratified sampling criteria. All state law enforcement agencies ($n = 50$) and large municipal and county agencies serving populations of 100,000 or more ($n = 827$) were oversampled; the remaining sampling frame was randomly selected from agencies with jurisdictional populations of less than 100,000 and divided across the above population, region, and agency type categories.

Surveys were addressed to the chief executive of each agency and mailed between March and July 2010. Data collection included an initial survey mailing with two follow-up mailing reminders. A total of 871 agencies returned completed surveys, representing a 43% response rate. Four hundred and thirty-three (50%) of those were city/county police departments, 404 (46%) were county sheriffs, and 34 (4%) were state police/highway patrols. In terms of size, 91 agencies served jurisdictions with fewer than 10,000 residents (10%), 137 served jurisdictions with between 10,000 and 49,999 residents (16%), 165 served jurisdictions with between 50,000 and 99,999 (19%), and 439 agencies served jurisdictions with 100,000 or more residents (50%); population estimates were missing for 39 agencies in the sample (5%). One hundred and thirty-five agencies were located in the Northeast (16%), with 222 in the Midwest (26%), 297 in the South (34%), and 217 were located in the West (25%) (see Alpert et al., 2013; Rojek, Alpert et al., 2012b for a more detailed explanation of the data and sample). Agencies serve as the unit of analysis.

Measures

Dependent variable. The primary outcome of interest is whether an agency participated in a rigorous research partnership within the past five years, and it was constructed in two steps. First, the survey defined research partnership, broadly, as 'A relationship with a researcher with the goal to define or implement a research project. Examples include situations where police agencies and researchers work together to learn about training, leadership, policies, procedures, or other related matters. These efforts can also include police agencies and researchers working together to develop, implement, and/or monitor policies, new programs, and initiatives'. Two hundred and eighty departments (32%) reported involvement and 68% ($n = 591$) reported no involvement in a research partnership within the last five years.

Agencies that had indicated participation in a research partnership (i.e., the abovementioned $n = 280$) were then asked to define the nature of their partnership commitment in order to differentiate between both the formality and length of such partnerships. After all, not all partnerships are equipped to provide equal opportunity for research utilization/knowledge translation; the vast majority of prior research has not distinguished the nature of the police practitioner-researcher partnership (see Rojek, Smith et al., 2012a for an exception). Based on the three-category classification system outlined by the IACP (n.d. a, n.d. b; see also Rojek, Smith et al.,2012a), agency representatives were asked to choose among the following:

1. cooperation – defined as short term and informal partnerships that may involve such efforts as the agency seeking advice from a researcher or simply providing the research partner data for analysis;
2. coordination – defined as more formal partnerships that center on a specific project or goal, such as contracting a researcher to conduct a specific analysis or jointly securing grant funding with a researcher to evaluate a specific initiative; the partnership ends with the conclusion of the project; and
3. collaboration – defined as formalized long-term partnerships where police agencies and researchers work together on multiple projects over time (e.g., could involve a MOU or contract between an agency and university or researcher for engaging in ongoing and multiple research efforts).

In recognition that some agencies may have participated in more than one research partnership over the past five years, the respondents could identify more than one type if they have been involved in different types of partnerships. Thus, agencies that had been involved in a cooperation type partnership and a coordination type were asked to check both the cooperation and coordination categories. One hundred and eighty-five (21%) departments indicated they had engaged in a cooperation partnership, with fewer agencies reporting involvement in coordination ($n = 160$; 18%) and collaboration ($n = 83$; 10%) partnerships, respectively.

However, the three-category classification system was designed to be ranked according to the level of sophistication and opportunity for knowledge translation/exchange between researchers and practitioners, with 'cooperation' being the lowest followed by 'coordination' and then 'collaboration'. As such, we were not particularly interested in examining 'cooperation' partnerships (e.g., short-term/informal, with an agency sometimes simply providing data to researchers). Instead, the focus of the current study was placed on the 'coordination' and 'collaboration' partnerships. *Rigorous research partnership* was measured using a dummy variable (1 = *yes*) if an agency indicated that they had participated in either a coordination or collaboration partnership in the past five years.[3] One hundred and eighty-two departments (21%) – or approximately one-fifth of the sample – reported in the affirmative, and 667 agencies (79%) reported no such involvement in rigorous research partnerships.

Covariates (full sample). Given that the goal was to explore the influence of an agency's orientation to research on involvement in research partnerships, the survey asked respondents about two factors. For one, agencies were asked how often they use research to inform their decisions on policy development and operations. *Uses research to inform decisions* was measured at the ordinal level, with a response mode consisting of 0 ('never'), 1 ('seldom'), 2 ('sometimes'), and 3 ('very often'). The mean response was 1.95 (SD = .82). Next, and building on the International Association of Chiefs of Police (2011) study discussed earlier, the survey asked about the source of research outlets. Using a series of dummy variables (1 = *yes*), agencies were asked to indicate whether or not they used *academic journals*, *NIJ publications*, and/or *professional publications* (e.g., Police Chief Magazine, FBI Law Enforcement Bulletin). Thirty-three percent of the sample reported using academic journals ($n = 278$), 55% used NIJ publications ($n = 469$), and 82% reported using professional publications ($n = 692$).

Dummy variables (1 = *yes*) were used to measure the region of the country where the agency was located. They were broken down into the *northeast* ($n = 130$; 15%), *Midwest* ($n = 217$; 26%), *south* ($n = 291$; 34%), and *west* ($n = 211$; 25%) regions; northeast was used as the reference category. Type of agency was also captured using a series of dummies: police department ($n = 424$; 50%), county sheriff ($n = 392$; 46%), and state police/highway patrol ($n = 33$; 4%), with county sheriff as the reference group. Lastly, a dummy variable was created to account for the size of the agency; 1 = agencies with *100+ sworn officers* ($n = 427$; 50%).

Additional covariates (larger models). Prior descriptive analyses (see Alpert et al., 2013; Rojek, Smith et al., 2012a) of the current sample have indicated that larger agencies are most likely to engage in partnerships in general and in 'coordination' and/or 'collaboration'-style partnerships more specifically – although involvement is still far from universal. For this reason, an effort was made to take a deeper look into larger agencies with more than 100 sworn officers. Supplemental measures from the 2007 LEMAS survey were used to examine another set of organizational characteristics and their potential influence on the likelihood of forming a rigorous research partnership. LEMAS is administered by the Bureau of Justice Statistics every few years, and the 2007 iteration (like all previous versions) employs both a 'long form' format for all agencies with over 100 sworn officers and 'short form' format for smaller agencies that asks fewer questions (see Reaves, 2010). Therefore, the LEMAS sample of agencies with 100 or more sworn personnel was combined with the current sample of departments with 100+ sworn officers. Excluding state police/highway patrol, a total of 335 out of 397 local/municipal police departments and county sheriff's from the national survey were matched with organizational characteristics from the 2007 LEMAS survey.

In order to assess the impact of agency size, a series of six dummy variables (1 = *yes*) were created: *100–199 sworn* (n = 114; 34%), which was used as the reference category; *200–299 sworn* (n = 61; 18%); *300–399 sworn* (n = 45; 13%); *400–499 sworn* (n = 31; 9%); *500–999 sworn* (n = 35; 10%); *1,000+ sworn* (n = 49; 15%). LEMAS also provided a number of questions, which were used to create three scales. A *problem-solving scale* was measured as an additive index that consists of four questions regarding whether or not an agency (1 = *yes*; 0 = *no*): (1) actively encourages patrol officers to engage in SARA-type problem-solving projects, (2) includes collaborative problem-solving projects in the evaluation criteria of patrol officers, (3) upgraded technology to support the analysis of community problems, and (4) conducted or sponsored a survey of citizens on crime, fear or crime, or satisfaction with police services. Ranging from 0 to 4, the sample of agencies with 100+ officers had a mean of 1.95 (*SD* = 1.34).

A *partnership scale* was created using another additive index to capture the degree to which agencies partner with organizations and entities other than researchers. LEMAS inquired about nine such organizations/entities, including advocacy groups, business groups, faith-based organizations, local government agencies (non-law enforcement), other law enforcement agencies, neighborhood associations, senior citizen groups, school groups, and youth service organizations. The scale ranged from 0 to 9 with a mean of 5.99 (*SD* = 3.11). A similar approach was taken with the *computer analysis scale* – measured as an additive index of whether agencies used computers to accomplish: (1) analysis of community problems, (2) crime analysis, (3) crime mapping, (4) hotspot identification, and (5) intelligence gathering (*mean* = 3.95; *SD* = 1.42; range 0–5). Collectively, these three measures developed through the LEMAS data were intended to examine if the use of analytic approaches or openness to other partnerships predicts participating in partnerships with researchers. Summary statistics for each of the variables in both the full sample and sub-sample of larger agencies are presented in Table 6.1.

Analytic Strategy

The analysis was carried out in two phases – one for the full sample and another for the sub-sample of larger agencies, specifically local/municipal police departments and county sheriff's, with more than 100 sworn officers. Given that the dependent variable was measured dichotomously (0, 1), the data were estimated using a series of logistic regressions. There was a minor issue with missing data (22 agencies), which was addressed using the listwise deletion of cases. This reduced the sample size for the full models from 871 to 849. The sub-sample included 335 agencies.

Results

Full Model

Table 6.2 provides the results from the logistic regression equations. Model 1 on the left-side column presents the findings from the full sample, predicting whether an agency reported engaging in either a coordination or collaboration partnership – representing the more formal relationships of interest as opposed to a cooperation partnership – in the past five years. The coefficients listed are odds ratios (OR), with values greater than one denoting a positive relationship between the covariate and the outcome, whereas those values less than one indicate a negative relationship. The model fits the data well (Log-likelihood = 692.44; $p < .01$), and it

TABLE 6.1 Descriptive statistics

Variable	Mean (SD)	Range
Dependent Variable		
Rigorous Research Partnership	.21 (–)	0–1
Covariates (full models)		
Uses Research to Inform Decisions	1.95 (.82)	0–3
Uses Academic Journals	.33 (–)	0–1
Uses NIJ Publications	.55 (–)	0–1
Uses Professional Publications	.82 (–)	0–1
Northeast	.15 (–)	0–1
Midwest	.26 (–)	0–1
South	.34 (–)	0–1
West	.25 (–)	0–1
Police Department	.50 (–)	0–1
County Sheriff's	.46 (–)	0–1
State Police/Highway Patrol	.04 (–)	0–1
100+ Sworn Officers	.50 (–)	0–1
Covariates (larger models)		
Uses Research to Inform Decisions	2.16 (.68)	0–3
Uses Academic Journals	.45 (–)	0–1
Uses NIJ Publications	.67 (–)	0–1
Uses Professional Publications	.86 (–)	0–1
Northeast	.10 (–)	0–1
Midwest	.17 (–)	0–1
South	.47 (–)	0–1
West	.26 (–)	0–1
Police Department	.63 (–)	0–1
100–199 Sworn	.34 (–)	0–1
200–299 Sworn	.18 (–)	0–1
300–399 Sworn	.13 (–)	0–1
400–499 Sworn	.09 (–)	0–1
500–999 Sworn	.10 (–)	0–1
1,000+ Sworn	.15 (–)	0–1
Problem-Solving Scale	1.95 (1.34)	0–4
Partnership Scale	5.99 (3.11)	0–9
Computer Analysis Scale	3.95 (1.42)	0–5

explains 31% of the variance in the dependent variable. Agencies' use of research in general to inform decisions on policies and operations as well as the use of academic journals or NIJ publications increases the odds of partnership participation, respectively. In fact, the odds of partnership participation were more than three times greater for those departments who used NIJ publications compared to those who reported they do not (OR = 3.67; $p < .01$), which suggests that agencies who look to NIJ publications to inform their decisions are much more likely to engage in partnerships. Interestingly, the reported use of professional publications (e.g., Police Chief Magazine, FBI Law Enforcement Bulletin) decreased the odds of engaging in a partnership by 56% (OR = .44; $p < .01$).

Using the northeast as the reference category, there were no significant differences in partnership participation across regions of the country (Midwest, South, and West). Compared to county sheriff's, both local police departments (OR = 2.43; $p < .01$) and state police/highway patrols (OR = 3.54; $p < .01$) were more likely to be involved in partnerships. As expected, agencies with over 100 sworn officers were more than four times as likely to have reported involvement in a partnership within the past five than smaller departments – further justifying a deeper examination of those larger agencies.

TABLE 6.2 Full sample and larger agencies (100+ sworn)

Variables	Model 1 (Full) Odds Ratio (SE)	Model 2 (Sub-Sample) Odds Ratio (SE)
Uses Research to Inform Decisions	1.47* (.15)	1.21 (.23)
Uses Academic Journals	1.74** (.21)	1.58 (.31)
Uses NIJ Publications	3.67** (.25)	5.47** (.41)
Uses Professional Publications	.44** (.31)	.35* (.47)
Midwest	1.16 (.33)	1.07 (.59)
South	.97 (.31)	.88 (.53)
West	1.25 (.33)	1.21 (.55)
Police Department	2.43** (.21)	3.57** (.33)
State Police/Highway Patrol	3.54** (.42)	–
100+ Sworn Officers	4.23** (.23)	–
200–299 Sworn	–	1.48 (.42)
300–399 Sworn	–	1.83 (.47)
400–499 Sworn	–	5.65** (.53)
500–999 Sworn	–	4.82** (.48)
1,000+ Sworn	–	11.39** (.49)
Problem-Solving Scale	–	1.23 (.12)
Partnership Scale	–	1.04 (.06)
Computer Analysis Scale	–	.97 (.13)
Log-likelihood	692.44**	317.63**
Pseduo-R^2	.31	.42
N	849	335

Note: Entries are odds ratios with standard errors in parentheses.

* $p < .05$;

** $p < .01$ (two-tailed test).

The specific research outlets where agencies seek out and receive information to make decisions on policies and operations warrant further discussion and examination. Agencies, for example, might rely on a combination of research outlets for information (i.e., interaction effects might be taking place). In other words, affirmative responses to the use of academic journals, NIJ publications, or professional publications are not mutually exclusive. Due to these scenarios, an additional set of dichotomous variables (1 = *yes*) was created to more effectively tease out the aforementioned findings: no use of any publications, academic journals only, NIJ publications only, professional publications only, as well as a number of combinations (e.g., professional and NIJ publications; academic journals and NIJ publications).

These supplemental analyses were conducted to examine the interactions of the various research/publication outlets – comparing the use of professional publications to both NIJ publications and academic journals. The newly created dummy variables were then entered into the multivariate analysis from Table 6.2, with the use of professional publications only serving as the reference category. Table 6.3 presents the results from the new analysis. The other covariates hold their prior levels regarding statistical significance and direction of association, and, therefore, were not reported. Comparing professional publications to NIJ publications (as well as combination between the two): agencies reporting only the use of professional publications had the lowest participation rate at 8.1%, followed by not using either outlet (11.3%), then the use of NIJ and professional publications (30.8%), and finally the use of only NIJ publications (41.7%) – the highest participation rate, although only 24 agencies fell within this category. Although agencies reporting no use of NIJ or professional publications have greater odds of partnership participation relative to agencies reporting only the use of professional publications, the relationship is not statistically significant.

TABLE 6.3 Odds ratios for interactions with professional publications and specific research-based outlets for all agencies

Interactions	# of Agencies in Category	% Reporting Partnership	Odds Ratio
NIJ Publication-Professional Publication			
Professional Only	(*n* = 247)	8.1%	Reference
No Professional or NIJ	(*n* = 118)	11.3%	2.12
NIJ Only	(*n* = 24)	41.7%	8.82★★
Professional and NIJ	(*n* = 445)	30.8%	4.19★★
Academic Journals-Professional Publications			
Professional Only	(*n* = 431)	14.2%	Reference
No Professional or Academic	(*n* = 141)	14.2%	1.52
Academic Only	(*n* = 16)	31.3%	1.81
Professional and Academic	(*n* = 262)	36.6%	2.36★★

★ $p < .05$;
★★ $p < .01$ (two-tailed test).

However, there is a significant relationship with agencies reporting only the use of NIJ publications, as well as NIJ and professional publications, relative to agencies reporting only the use of professional publications. Agencies reporting that they rely on NIJ publications are almost nine times as likely to participate in a partnership (OR = 8.82; $p < .01$) relative to agencies reporting professional publication use only, and agencies reporting the use of NIJ and professional publications have more than four times the likelihood of participation (OR = 4.19; $p < .01$). The results suggest that agencies that look to NIJ publications to inform their decisions are more likely to engage in partnerships, whether they use NIJ publications alone or in conjunction with professional publications.

A similar approach was taken to compare professional publications to academic journals (as well as a combination between the two). The only statistically significant difference that emerged was between the reference category (professional publications only) and a combination of using professional publications with academic journals (OR = 2.36; $p < .01$).

Sub-Sample (Agencies with 100+ Sworn Officers)

Model 2 on the right-side column of Table 6.2 shows the results from the sample of larger agencies with more than 100 sworn officers. One hundred and twenty-four agencies (37%) in the sub-sample reported involvement in such a partnership, and 211 departments (63%) indicated that they had not. Explaining more than 40% of the variance in the outcome of interest, it performed better than Model 1; however, it also included more variables. While the general use of research to inform decisions and the use of academic journals were no longer statistically significant, the pattern of significant relationships found for using NIJ publications and professional publications persisted. The odds of partnership participation were more than five times greater for those who used NIJ publications as opposed to those who reported they do not (OR = 5.47; $p < .01$). Similar to the full sample model, the reported use of professional publications decreased the odds of partnership participation by 65% (OR = .35; $p < .05$).

Again, there were no significant differences in partnership participation across the regions. Police departments were significantly more likely to participate in partnerships than sheriff's departments (OR = 3.57; $p < .01$). Setting agencies with 100–199 sworn officers as the reference category, the other agency size ranges illustrate a positive relationship. While the increased

TABLE 6.4 Odds ratios for interactions with professional publications and specific research-based outlets for large agencies (100+ sworn)

Interactions	# of Agencies in Category	% Reporting Partnership	Odds Ratio
NIJ Publication-Professional Publication			
Professional Only	(n = 76)	10.5%	Reference
No Professional or NIJ	(n = 36)	30.6%	3.32★
NIJ Only	(n = 11)	45.5%	13.29★★
Professional and NIJ	(n = 212)	47.2%	7.03★★
Academic Journals-Professional Publications			
Professional Only	(n = 146)	23.3%	Reference
No Professional or Academic	(n = 40)	32.5%	1.74
Academic Only	(n = 7)	42.9%	1.60
Professional and Academic	(n = 142)	52.1%	2.40★★

★ $p < .05$;
★★ $p < .01$ (two-tailed test).

odds for partnership participation were not significant for the first two categories (200–299 and 300–399 officers), agencies with 400–499 sworn personnel were just shy of being five times as likely and agencies with 1,000 plus sworn officers were more than eleven times as likely to report engagement in a rigorous partnership. All three scales derived from the 2007 LEMAS survey were not predictive of involvement in either a coordination or collaboration partnership over the last five years.

Similar to the approach taken with the full sample, we further explored the issue of specific research outlets. Results regarding only agencies with 100+ sworn officers are presented in Table 6.4. The supplemental analyses and presentation of findings are again similar to those for all responding agencies in Table 6.3. With agencies reporting only the use of professional publications set as the reference category, agencies who reported only using NIJ publications were thirteen times more likely to engage in partnerships (OR = 13.29; $p < .01$). The odds were seven times greater (OR = 7.03; $p < .01$) that an agency reporting the use of NIJ and professional publications engaged in a partnership relative to agencies who reported using only professional publications. The difference between the rates of partnership participation between agencies reporting the use of professional publications and neither outlet is also significant, where the odds are more than three times greater for agencies reporting neither (OR = 3.32; $p < .05$), holding all other covariates constant.

A similar approach was taken to compare professional publications to academic journals (as well as a combination between the two) among the sample of agencies with 100+ sworn members. The only statistically significant difference that emerged was between the reference category (professional publications only) and a combination of using professional publications with academic journals (OR = 2.40; $p < .01$).

Discussion

The current study focused on identifying factors that predict engagement in practitioner-researcher partnerships in U.S. law enforcement. To date, there have been no longitudinal examinations of the prevalence of such partnerships. The field lacks studies/surveys using comparable samples over time for comparison. Still, it is reasonable to assume – with the increase in federal funding as well as advocacy from key organizations and police leaders – that law enforcement engages in more research partnerships and looks to the empirical and theoretical works of the research community to inform their decisions and agency operations today than was the case 30 or 40 years ago. While the current level of participation in partnerships falls well short of the International Association of Chiefs of Police (2004) goal of every agency in the United States being involved in one, it is within reason to conclude that partnerships have grown in number and accomplishment over the years. Forming partnerships in every agency may be unrealistic and unattainable for a variety of reasons, particularly because there are not enough researchers to support them.

Prior work has highlighted the limitations and shortcomings on the part of the research community to support the growth in partnerships with law enforcement, specifically as it relates to the relative lack of reaching out to agencies and engaging in applied work. According to Rojek, Smith et al. (2012a), one of the primary reasons agencies have not participated in a partnership was due to the fact that they have not been approached by a researcher (27% of non-involvement). This suggests there has been a reluctance or lack of opportunity in both communities to interact and form personal relationships. As many police agencies and researchers who have collaborated with practitioners have noted, forming trust through personal links is a critical element for forming partnerships. In this way, the success of collaborations is similar to dating and every other type of relationship building and its subsequent maintenance.

The future expansion of police practitioner-researcher partnerships will also depend, at least in part, on the supply of researchers willing to engage in these efforts. From the researcher perspective, participation requires them to be pulled away from other research opportunities. For example, time spent trying to build relationships with police agencies or providing 'pro-bono' (i.e., non-funded) analyses/evaluation – with the hope that it translates into future opportunities and/or valuable department/officer data – means time not spent working on and attempting to produce research products (e.g., peer-reviewed academic articles). This is particularly relevant and challenging for untenured junior faculty members. It is unknown how many researchers desire to participate in partnerships with police practitioners, although it is reasonable to assume there are not enough willing researchers for every agency.

Relatedly, this research speaks to the broader issue of the effectiveness (or lack thereof) of researchers' ability to disseminate knowledge to police practitioners. It points to the specific outlets and mechanisms that connect with practitioners. Findings here do not reflect a strong connection of practitioners with the work of the research community (see also Rojek, Alpert et al., 2012b). The most common response (82%) provided by agency representatives when asked which research outlets they rely on to inform decisions were professional publications (e.g., Police Chief Magazine or FBI Law Enforcement Bulletin) – showcasing the importance of such outlets among practitioners. These are neither the outlets where members of the research community commonly publish their work, nor where academics are incentivized to publish. The overwhelming majority of academic researchers, who represent most of the police research community, publish their work almost exclusively in academic journals, which only 33% of agency respondents reported using as a research outlet. The findings of this research suggest that those practitioners who draw knowledge from research-based outlets – academic journals and NIJ publications – are more likely to engage in partnerships with researchers, presumably given their orientation toward research indicates a perceived value of working with researchers. Thus, if the goal is to increase these partnerships as advocated by NIJ, IACP, and others, then a strategy to increase the number of police practitioners that look to these outlets for knowledge and ideas would be valuable.

Alternatively, researchers also need to improve the dissemination of their work to the practitioner community by publishing in professional publications. The two-communities perspective on research utilization (i.e., research translation) argues practitioners and researchers reflect separate cultures that 'often have conflicting values, different reward systems, and different languages' (Caplan, 1979, p. 459). Academic journals represent one of the clear manifestations of this gap. These articles are written for academic peers with jargon and concepts that may be unfamiliar to practitioners, and they focus on theoretical and empirical conclusions that may not be readily apparent to a practitioner as to how it applies to their work. Furthermore, access to peer-reviewed academic journals is restricted by pay walls/firewalls, and a single article is costly (e.g., $36 for 24-hour access to download one article from *Police Quarterly*). Even among those willing to seek out such journals, particularly mid-level managers (e.g., lieutenants) in research/planning units, these studies remain isolated in outlets reserved, almost exclusively, for people with a university affiliation and subscription. One potential recommendation to alleviate this problem is placing more onus and responsibility on the part of the editors of peer-reviewed journals (particularly policing-related journals). Editors can accept program evaluations and policy-relevant papers with a stipulation that the author(s) at a minimum attempt to also disseminate the findings in professional publications.

Writing to professional publications forces the researcher to write to the practitioner audience more directly. However, it is important to note there are additional barriers that academics must first consider while attempting to do so. Similar to peer-reviewed journals, there are a limited number of professional outlets that have national prominence and broad reach among practitioners. Next, professional outlets possess their own editors/editorial boards, whose publishing philosophies must cater to their specific audience(s). An academic's desire to write for practitioners – not to mention his/her ability to effectively condense the findings and message of the work into a piece that is brief and easily consumable – is likely insufficient. There may be limited space to publish content from researchers, and work deemed 'too negative or critical' of law enforcement runs the risk of being rejected.

Despite these concerns, funding agencies, such as NIJ or the Community Oriented Policing Services (COPS) Office, can motivate researchers to engage in such efforts by stipulating publications in professional outlets as deliverable requirements. University faculty performance reviews that think more inclusively about research dissemination to include valuing publications in professional outlets would also provide support to these efforts. In connecting back to the present study, instead of waiting for more practitioners to start reading traditional research publications in the hope of expanding the pool of practitioners willing to partner with researchers, the latter should make more concerted efforts to expand this pool by directly disseminating their work in outlets that practitioners already value. If practitioners see researchers trying to communicate their work in more familiar formats – professional publications – they may find more value in the knowledge and skills that researchers can provide.

Although the degree of researcher-practitioner partnerships in American law enforcement has undoubtedly increased over the last few decades, the majority of police organizations have yet to foster meaningful relationships with members of the research community – as defined and measured by participation in a 'rigorous partnership'. We have characterized the level of collaboration between the two as 'present, but not prevalent' with much room for improvement. The current study uncovered more information about the organizational characteristics of police departments most open and willing to work with the research community. Because time and resources are limited, identification of such agencies should help motivated policing researchers to more efficiently attempt to partner with those departments – reducing the level of risk involved in doing so. This study, in addition to prior work on the topic, also illustrates the shortcomings on the part of the research community to engage with policing practitioners and focus on applied work. Researchers, especially those in academia, must acknowledge and shoulder part of the blame for the lack of collaboration. It shows that the research/academic community must change and adapt as well – on both the institutional and individual levels.

Acknowledgments

This research is supported by grant 2009-IJ-CX-0204 from the National Institute of Justice, the Office of Justice Programs, and the US Department of Justice. Points of view are those of the authors and do not necessarily represent the official position of the US Department of Justice.

Disclosure Statement

No potential conflict of interest was reported by the authors.

Notes

1. A review of the literature on organizational theories, particularly those related to law enforcement agencies (e.g., contingency theory, resources dependency theory, and institutional theory) was beyond the scope of this article. However, readers interested in more detail on the aforementioned organizational theories should consult King (2009) and Maguire (2014).
2. The review provided here only focuses on the history of police practitioner-researcher partnerships. For a more in-depth overview of the evolution of policing research – including the innovative efforts of August Vollmer, the 1967 President's Commission on Law Enforcement and Administration of Justice, the establishment of the National Institute of Justice, the growth in research on related topics that was spurred by funding from the Community Oriented Policing Services (COPS) Office – see Rojek et al. (2012b).
3. Therefore, the dummy variable 'rigorous research partnership' (1 = *yes*) compares these agencies to all other departments that reported no partnerships and partnerships characterized as 'cooperation' or 'coordination'.

References

Alpert, G. P., Rojek, J., & Hansen, J. A. (2013). Building bridges between police researchers and practitioners: Agents of change in a complex world. *Final Report to the National Institute of Justice*. Washington, DC: Department of Justice.
Braga, A. D., & Hinkle, M. (2010). The participation of academics in the criminal justice working group process. In J. M. Klofas, N. K. Hipple, & E. F. McGarrell (Eds.), *The new criminal justice: American communities and the changing world of crime control* (pp. 114–120). New York, NY: Routledge.
Braga, A. D., Kennedy, D. M., Waring, E. J., & Piehl, A. M. (2001). Problem-oriented policing, deterrence and youth violence: An evaluation of Boston's operation ceasefire. *Journal of Research in Crime and Delinquency, 38*(3), 195–226.
Bratton, W. J. (2006). Research: a practitioner's perspective, from the streets. *Western Criminology Review, 7*, 1–6.
Bueermann, J. (2012). Being smart on crime with evidence-based policing. *NIJ Journal, 269*, 12–15.
Caplan, N. (1979). The two-communities theory and knowledge utilization. *American Behavioral Scientist, 22*(3), 459–470.
Green, L. W., Ottoson, J. M., Garcia, C., & Haitt, R. A. (2009). Diffusion theory and knowledge dissemination, utilization, and integration in public health. *Annual Review of Public Health, 30*, 151–174.
Henry, A., & MacKenzie, S. (2012). Brokering communities of practice: A model of knowledge exchange and academic-practitioner collaboration developed in the context of community policing. *Police Practice and Research, 13*(4), 315–328.
International Association of Chiefs of Police. (2004). *Unresolved problems and powerful potentials: Improving partnerships between law enforcement leaders and university based researchers*. Washington, DC: Author.
International Association of Chiefs of Police. (2011). *Law enforcement research priorities for 2011 and beyond*. Washington, DC: Author.

International Association of Chiefs of Police. (n.d. a). *Establishing and sustaining law enforcement-researcher partnerships: Guide for researchers*. Washington, DC: Author.

International Association of Chiefs of Police. (n.d. b). *Establishing and sustaining law enforcement-researcher partnerships: Guide for law enforcement leaders*. Washington, DC: Author.

King, W. R. (2009). Toward a life-course perspective of police organizations. *Journal of Research in Crime and Delinquency, 46*(2), 213–244.

Lang, E. S., Wyer, P. C., & Eskin, B. (2007). Knowledge translation in emergency medicine: Establishing a research agenda and guide map for evidence uptake. *Academic Emergency Medicine, 14*(11), 915–918.

Lasker, R. D., Weiss, E. S., & Miller, R. (2001). Partnership synergy: A practical framework for studying and strengthening the collaborative advantage. *The Milbank Quarterly, 79*(2), 179–205.

Maguire, E. R. (2014). Police organizations and the iron cage of rationality. In M. D. Reisig & R. J. Kane (Eds.), *The Oxford handbook of police and policing* (pp. 68–98). New York: Oxford University Press.

McEwen, T. (2003). *Evaluation of the locally initiated research partnership program*. Washington, DC: National Institute of Justice.

McGarrell, E. F., Hipple, N. K., Corsaro, N., Bynum, T. S., Perez, H., Zimmerman, C., & Garmo, M. (2009). *Project Safe Neighborhood - A national program to reduce gun crime: Final project report*. Washington, DC: National Institute of Justice.

National Institute of Justice. (2017). *Policing: Strategic research plan, 2017-2022*. Washington, DC: U.S. Department of Justice.

Reaves, B. A. (2010). *Local police departments, 2007*. Washington, DC: Bureau of Justice Statistics.

Roehl, J., Rosenbaum, D. P., Costello, S. K., Coldren, J. R., Schuck, A. M., Kunard, L., & Forde, D. (2006). *Strategic Approaches to Community Safety Initiative (SACSI) in 10 US cities: The building blocks for Project Safe Neighborhoods*. Washington, DC: National Institute of Justice.

Rojek, J., Alpert, G., & Smith, H. (2012b). The utilization of research by the police. *Police Practice and Research, 13*(4), 329–341.

Rojek, J., Smith, H. P., & Alpert, G. P. (2012a). The prevalence and characteristics of police practitioner–researcher partnerships. *Police Quarterly, 15*(3), 241–261.

Sherman, L. W. (2004). Research and policing: The infrastructure and political economy of federal funding. *The ANNALS of the American Academy of Political and Social Science, 593*(1), 156–178.

Stephens, D. W. (2010). Enhancing the impact of research on police practice. *Police Practice and Research, 11*, 150–154.

Vigoda, E. (2002). From responsiveness to collaboration: Governance, citizens, and the next generation of public administration. *Public Administration Review, 62*(5), 527–540.

Wellford, C., Serpas, R., & Firman, J. (2007). IACP launches new committee to guide law enforcement policy research. *Police Chief Magazine*. Retrieved from http://www.policechiefmagazine.org/magazine/index.cfm?fuseaction=display_archandarticle_id=1294andissue_id=102007

7

On Creating Ethical, Productive, and Durable Research Partnerships with Police Officers and Their Departments

A Case Study of the National Justice Database

Erin M. Kerrison

School of Social Welfare, University of California, Berkeley, USA

Phillip Atiba Goff and Chris Burbank

Center for Policing Equity, John Jay College of Criminal Justice, New York, USA

Jordan M. Hyatt

Department of Criminology and Justice Studies, Drexel University, Philadelphia, USA

Introduction

How do you measure justice? Despite the philosophical, methodological, and logistical difficulty of this question, law enforcement executives are increasingly asked to turn over data with the aim of evaluating how fairly they are doing their jobs. At the same time, many community members perceive law enforcement activities to be targeted toward – and biased against – non-White people. Communities suffering from mass incarceration and highly publicized police shootings have called for greater transparency and accountability on the part of their local police. Research shows that positive police-community relationships are crucial for safer communities, as citizens are more likely to engage as witnesses and as partners in crime reduction if they believe in the legitimacy of police as equitable and impartial agents of the law (Kerrison, Cobbina, & Bender, 2018).

Increasingly, then, forward-looking law enforcement executives seek hard metrics on current practices as a way to identify effective policy reforms aimed at reducing racial discrimination and improving police-community relations. To that end, they are seeking out partnerships with prominent researchers to solve this riddle, and to lead with a model of policing that honors a commitment to civil rights and public accountability.

The goals of the police-researcher partnership are necessarily ambitious. The aim is for researchers and police departments to share skills and experiences, trade information, and produce answers that can inform sustainable policies that make safety and legitimacy that much more possible (Greene, 2014a). Interview data analyzed from a nationwide multi-method study of the prevalence of police-researcher partnerships conducted by Alpert, Rojek, and Hansen (2013)

DOI: 10.4324/9781003153009-10

suggest that there are four general benefits to both researchers and police practitioners who enter into police-researcher partnerships: (1) researchers from a wide range of disciplines, including criminology, sociology, and psychology, bring a useful theoretical, scientific, and methodological knowledge base and lens to the endeavor of solving problems; (2) confidence in presenting steps forward to an array of stakeholders is bolstered by the credibility departments can claim after having solicited the insights and expertise of an independent researcher; (3) partnering with researchers allows departments to expand their analytic, grant-seeking, and self-evaluation capacities; and (4) researchers can broker healthier exchanges between departments and community members (collecting civilian input by conducting surveys, etc.) and help to build trust and faith in the police departments' earnest commitment to public safety and wellbeing.

These are tremendous values that benefit researchers interested in actively engaging in applied police science (or 'active research'), police departments seeking to design tactics and initiatives grounded in a systematically measured truth, and community member constituencies who would prefer that policing practices be anchored in science rather than hunches. Reining in these competing agendas, however, can prove challenging. To that end, this chapter addresses the following research questions:

1. How can an action research model support ethical research conduct between social scientists and police departments seeking reductions in racially disparate policing outcomes?
2. If the action-research model is adopted, what are the tactical goals of a researcher-practitioner relationship aimed at reducing racial bias and discrimination in policing practice?
3. How might the research community seek research partnership buy-in from police executives as well as patrol personnel?
4. How can these partnerships foster a robust exchange of information and guidance between social scientists and police agencies?
5. What are the potential policing reform implications of police department-social science partnerships aimed at reducing racial disparities?

The following begins with a discussion of the aims and promises of translational criminological research focused on policing and the action research theoretical model that allows for a productive research praxis to unfold. Next, we offer a description of the Center for Policing Equity (CPE) and the international National Justice Database (NJD) partnership that the organization has built alongside agencies representing over one third of police jurisdictions in the United States and Canada. Then, we offer a case study analysis of how the relationships that comprise the data-driven NJD are cultivated and supported through ethical action research design and execution. Finally, we highlight some of the remaining unresolved challenges to these sorts of partnerships as well as a path forward for the expansion of police-researcher partnerships that allow for translational science focused on eradicating racial bias and discrimination in contemporary policing practice.

Theoretical and Methodological Model

Translational Policing Science

Some argue that the expansion of rigorous scientific processes is the primary vehicle for improving policing practice and outcomes (Weisburd & Neyroud, 2011), and that standards for rigorous research design in this domain must be clearly established (Sherman, 2013). Efforts to enhance policing science research methodologies may prove moot, however, if either findings are inaccessible to the very subjects who need most to understand them or research scientists are poorly equipped to grapple with the realities of policing practice and policing datasets. The growing, but potentially narrowing research community that emphasizes the significance of randomized controlled trial findings, must be mindful of the tendency to self-insulate and speak only to one another (Braga, Welsh, Papachristos, Schnell, & Grossman, 2014; Greene, 2014b). Furthermore, while a rich body of scholarship has explored which elements of a robust systematic evaluation of policing practices will yield the most reliable evidence of causal treatment effects with the minimum burdens imposed on police departments (Bedford & Mazerolle, 2014; Lum, Koper, & Telep, 2011; Weisburd, 2003), we argue that those schema neither fully address the needs of police agencies and the residents in their care, nor remedy all of the ethical challenges that experimental designs tend to surface.

As such, there is no shortage of opportunities for accessible, ethical, and translational policing research to address the needs and interests of departments oriented toward engaging in data-driven, equitable policing policy. What has been less clearly established is how to get rigorous evaluation research 'right' without relying exclusively on the standards of experimental design, or how to ensure those criteria always include stakeholder understanding and continuous input beyond securing permission from departments at the final stages of research dissemination (Kelty & Julian, 2013).

The Action Research Model

In order to address our first guiding research question (*how can an action research model support ethical research conduct between social scientists and police departments seeking reductions in racially disparate policing outcomes?*), we turn to the assumptions of the action research framework. Ideally, police personnel and researchers will work together in all phases of the research process to:

- select a focus or problem topic that is relevant for the needs of police and their communities, and can be tackled with as high a degree of scientific rigor as the available data will allow;
- develop a rigorous research design whose various elements were made clear to all stakeholders and were agreed on by all stakeholders;
- and jointly engage in the execution of the research, including data collection, analysis, final product preparation, and final product dissemination.

Because this ideal work plan inherently holds a number of contingencies and need-driven accommodations, it is best characterized as *action* research. Action research is an iterative problem-oriented and solution-driven methodological approach that involves joint input from researchers and those who are experiencing the problem, on diagnosing and solving the problem (Eikeland, 2012). Greenwood and Levin (1998a) assert that the simultaneous union of action and participation in research is what sets this approach apart from other applied research methodologies less focused on urgent social change. Below, we offer their thoughts as an explanation for how the research focused on reducing racial disparity and discrimination in policing might be well-served by a solution-oriented research design for confronting the problem:

> Action research refers to the conjunction of three elements: research, action, and participation. Unless all three elements are present, the process cannot be called action research. Put another way, action research is a form of research that generates knowledge claims for the express purpose of taking action to promote social change and social analysis. But the social change we refer to is not just any kind of change. Action research aims to increase the ability of the involved community or organization members to control their own destinies more effectively and to keep improving their capacity to do so (Greenwood & Levin, 1998b, p. 6).

Those who raise doubts about the feasibility of action research in police science have cited concerns that atheoretical and anti-intellectual practitioners might not (1) devote the requisite resources or commitment to launch a rigorous research endeavor (Lefkowitz, 1977), (2) might avoid ownership of the treatment or intervention implementation (Famega, Hinkle, & Weisburd, 2017), or (3) might exhibit a general reluctance to embrace scientific methods (Harris, 2012; Rousseau & Gunia, 2016). We propose instead that because police departments are closest to the nuanced problems of inequitable policing, they are also closest to its consequences and are uniquely motivated to devote as much commitment as this persistent policing problem requires. Others have suggested that researchers who embed themselves in police contexts risk 'going native' and introducing new politicized bias (Spano, 2005). These concerns run counter to the successes that have emerged from partnerships where researchers have worked alongside and within criminal justice agencies as 'embedded' research scientists and conducted research with the utmost integrity (Braga & Davis, 2014; Kerrison, 2018; Petersilia, 2008). First, we remind readers not only that building research partnerships with police departments neither requires researchers to become sworn peace officers, nor are researchers invited to actually do the work of their practitioner partners. Second, all researchers bring personal, disciplinary, and institutional biases to their work. Increasing their exposure to the ways in which their study populations of interest confirm or diverge from their unconscious understandings might actually help to shape the research community in truly productive ways.

Finally, we acknowledge suggestions that action research is unscientific as its lack of systematization does not allow for precise replication in other settings (van Wijngaarden, van der Meide, & Dahlberg, 2017). We argue that this is neither a weakness of the approach, nor is it an impediment to creating useful scientific advancement. A method whose assumptions are not burdened by systematic procedure (other than to iteratively modify research design and execution as needed) allows for nimble adaptation, which might be required in an organizational problem-solving effort. Further, inherent to action research is a more ethical, just, and flexible interactional approach for stakeholders who are less familiar with scientific methodology. Slowing down to accommodate the needs and constraints of police agencies that lack the infrastructure for systematic research that neatly fits the canonical mold creates space to educate their members about the possibilities to design, participate in, and rely on science. An action research model can empower practitioner stakeholders by inviting them to see how their day-to-day problems might be explained and resolved by measuring a broad array of observable inputs and outputs, relying on scientific theory, and building analytic methods (Telep, 2016). In other words, a more flexible and wider approach to research and learning might actually allow for a more productive bridging of theory and 'book smarts' with real-world contexts, concerns, and experiences. The results are more inclusive, informed, and accessible. Moreover, research scientists learn how to engage in scientific endeavors with, rather than in spite of, non-scientist partners.

We are also troubled by scientific practices focused disproportionately on the integrity of the final research products, and less so on the integrity of the ongoing research process. Translational research processes that evidence the meaning and value of research for a wider set of stakeholders address many of the shortcomings of other research models that leave stakeholders siloed, rather than supported and foregrounded (Lumsden & Goode, 2018; Telep & Somers, 2019). Thus, we argue that the validity of action research findings is only as robust as the study design and execution are ethically built and transparently communicated. Furthermore, because results that lack validity serve no purpose, engaging in ethical research practice (via experimental methods or not) is a scientific imperative (Bachman & Schutt, 2017). Achieving valid research results is contingent on the extent to which all study stakeholders adhere to ethical principles of research practice – from study design to dissemination – and we have explored the application of this philosophy in the discussion below.

In this chapter, we discuss the merits and challenges of adopting an action research model approach to measuring and eradicating nationwide racial disparity in American policing practices. We do this by providing evidence of the ethical and analytical merits of adopting the action research approach, and by sharing what we have found to be some best practices for addressing ethical and logistical hurdles that are inherent to empirical criminological research efforts focused on policing reform.

Center for Policing Equity

The CPE is a not-for-profit research consortium committed to helping law enforcement professionals cultivate stronger relationships with the communities they are sworn to protect and serve. At its core, it is a consortium of social scientists and law enforcement professionals dedicated to facilitating innovative research collaborations between law enforcement agencies (LEAs) and empirical social scientists. Ultimately, CPE aims to create collaborations that will improve issues of equity and effect better cultural relations between police and civilians. This undertaking comes with a series of benefits and challenges. The vitality of CPE's partnerships depends on a number of factors including its ability to expand knowledge in social science and criminal justice practitioner spaces, respond to political challenges within and around police departments, and enhance police-civilian relations. The answer to our second guiding research question, then (*if the action-research model is adopted, what are the tactical goals of a researcher-practitioner relationship aimed at reducing racial bias and discrimination in policing practice?*) is addressed below in our discussion of CPE's NJD.

National Justice Database

The NJD is a first-of-its-kind project that aims to collect, standardize, aggregate, analyze, and report on how justice is enforced by police departments across the United States and in Canada. The NJD was created by CPE and is led by an interdisciplinary team of researchers at CUNY John Jay College of Criminal Justice, New York University, and the University of California, Berkeley. With support from the National Science Foundation and a number of private organizations, the NJD works to fill the many gaps in our knowledge about police-public contact, including the causes of racially disparate policing. Each police department that joins the NJD receives a confidential report analyzing its own trends through a lens of race, gender, and age.[1] Reports include an analysis of use of force data, vehicle stops, pedestrian stops, the department's policy manual(s), officer climate survey results, as well as the city's local population demographics and crime statistics. CPE provides each participating department with this 'City Report,' which reviews all of the data provided by the department, and then shares recommendations based on the study findings.

CPE aims to address the needs of law enforcement and civilian communities. The NJD collects policing data to measure fairness and improve policing equity and to make its findings accessible to law enforcement and to community audiences. The NJD offers a rigorous analytic framework to make sense of policing data, seeking to identify and understand the consequences of policing activities and the sources of racial disparity.[2] Member departments of the NJD receive confidential empirical documentation of the degree of racial disparity in their policing practices, as well as analyses and interpretation of the factors that might contribute to such disparity. CPE analyses reveal encouraging trends, but also flag questions and disparities that warrant further investigation and reform.

A principal purpose of this framework is to demonstrate what can be learned by thoroughly analyzing open data. All City Reports aim to offer law enforcement officials a roadmap toward greater transparency and accountability in police practices, so they can transform agencies and adopt more just and equitable means of promoting public safety. As such, the NJD analytic framework aims to distinguish among three broad types of explanations for racial disparities in policing, all of which are likely to play some role in producing racial disparities in a given police department or jurisdiction:

1. Disparities that arise from *community characteristics*. For instance, high crime rates or poverty within a community may draw increased police attention. Individuals within a community may place a disproportionately larger volume calls for service to police.
2. Disparities that arise from *police characteristics*. For instance, police may patrol some neighborhoods with less commitment to the dignity of those who live there. Or deploying more officers to high-crime neighborhoods may produce a disproportionately greater number of interactions between police and non-White communities.
3. Disparities that arise from the *relationships between communities and police*. For instance, mistrust of law enforcement may incite members of some communities to flee approaching officers or resist arrest more than members of other communities do. Similarly, a sense that communities do not trust or respect police may cause officers to feel unsafe or defensive in some neighborhoods.

While the charge of identifying sources of racial disparity in policing likely incorporates elements of each of these explanations, the comprehensive NJD framework allows departments to learn about how all three contribute to racially disparate outcomes. Each City Report carefully analyzes the role that community- and police-level characteristics may contribute to racial disparities. The resulting analyses can be used to steer community engagement, relationship building, and continued departmental reform. It is important to emphasize that the persuasive power of analytics grows substantially the longer a department measures and analyzes important indicators. As a result, CPE encourages all LEAs involved in the NJD to see these analyses as an initial benchmark against which future progress can be measured.

To be clear, no police department in the country currently collects all of the data recommended by the NJD analytic framework. Voluntary partners, however, are very forthcoming in response to CPE requests for data-sharing and information. By combining police administrative data (e.g., citations issued, complaints received, pedestrian and vehicle stops) with local census-derived population data (e.g., income, education, racial demographics), officer climate survey data, and jurisdictional community surveys, CPE researchers and their LEA partners can begin to fulfill the goal of measuring the role that each explanation plays in the disparities that both police departments and communities want to reduce. The first step to taking on this charge effectively, efficiently, and ethically is to design a research partnership that considers and accommodates both partners' needs and concerns.

Data and Methods

To demonstrate how the aforementioned tactical goals of a racial justice-driven researcher-practitioner relationship are accomplished in a policing reform context, we deploy a mixed-method within-case study design of the NJD. Specifically, the first author conducted interviews with key CPE team members; conducted content analyses of NJD data acquisition, officer survey templates, and analytic materials shared with, and prepared by LEAs; and reviewed secondary quantitative analyses and police and community member testimonials on the impacts of reforms that emerged as a product of the research-practitioner partnership. A case study design is the appropriate investigative framework for us to explore how an NJD framework models an ethical and effective action research partnership. Our epistemological justification for the case study research approach relies on the belief that causal analyses should actually look more closely at causal mechanisms, or the underlying realities that might link inputs and outcomes (Bennett & Elman, 2006; Sayer, 2010). We can – and will – empirically demonstrate that positive outcomes follow NJD partnerships, but a more compelling objective is to illustrate what makes those results possible.

The following discussion topics explore themes that emerged during a series of semi-structured interviews that the first author conducted with the NJD's Project Director and Lead Project Manager, between March and September of 2018. Both respondents were interviewed for this study for 60–90 minutes, either two and five times, respectively. Field notes taken during the interviews were transcribed and coded for analysis of patterned explanations. These individuals were purposively sampled for this case study because they are primary stakeholders of the NJD project that are uniquely positioned to provide insights on the needs of law enforcement partners entering into a data-driven collaboration. For example, beyond police executives' understandable concerns about handing over their administrative data, these stakeholders work alongside NJD police department partners who are unable to share the full breadth of data that CPE requests. The nationwide incapacity to engage in rigorous secondary police data analysis is largely attributed to the poor quality of police data, as police departments' data collection and data management efforts are notoriously underfunded (Miller et al., 2017). Still, these team members work closely with departments to understand and improve their data collection protocols, both for the purposes of NJD participation and so that departments and communities can cultivate a clearer understanding of local policing practices.

Second, the team members who were interviewed bring a hybrid perspective of sorts in that they are CPE employees, but hail from professional backgrounds outside of the social science research canon (the NJD Project Director is a former law enforcement officer and the Lead Project Manager brings extensive expertise in building software engineering projects). Proponents of action research suggest that some of the strongest research partnerships include team members who not only share social justice as well as professional goals and backgrounds, but also leverage the commonalities of those overlapping positions (Ripamonti, Galuppo, Gorli, Scaratti, & Cunliffe, 2016; Wittmayer & Schäpke, 2014). Thus, both of these CPE team members who work closest with NJD partner departments have backgrounds and expertise in criminal justice administration and software engineering – rather than social science – and are well suited to engage in translational science efforts and facilitate the recruitment of non-scientist police executives into research partnerships. The following summary of those series of interviews highlights what they described as the 'pains of policing science,' or challenges that these CPE team members must navigate in order to build an ethical and generative action research partnership. They also described the practices that they employ to recognize how the biases and intentions derived from their identities as research community members can be identified and reduced.

The first author also conducted content analyses of the 41 existing Memorandums of Understanding (MOUs) for the police department partners, the data acquisition template, and management protocols created by CPE personnel. MOU content varies as each agreement is shaped by CPE's academic institutional data agreement protocol and the analysis and privacy needs of each department. All MOUs include details of which secondary data will be requested for analysis (e.g., pedestrian stops, officer complaints), the nature of primary data to be collected (e.g., officer climate surveys), and how data will be managed and protected (e.g., assurances of confidentiality, data ownership). Before entering into the NJD partnership, departments receive a preliminary data assessment identifying the scope of secondary data that CPE requests in order to produce the most robust City Report. Currently, none of the NJD partner departments have fulfilled all of the data requests, as the ask includes requests for at least five years of data on departments' record management systems, use of force, training curricula, among other policing practice domains. Still, the NJD Project Director and Lead Project Manager work very closely with departments to collect the administrative data that are available and to build an infrastructure for departments to pursue more encompassing data collection practices in the future.

Finally, while participation in the NJD is strictly confidential, some department leadership officers have spoken publicly about their partnership with CPE and how participating in the NJD has yielded results that inform their reform and racial equity enhancement agendas. Excerpts from those narratives were analyzed for this case study and are discussed below. That discussion will feature findings (publicized with the participating departments' express written permission) that include multi-year aggregated count and regression analyses of police practices captured within their administrative records, benchmarked against ethnoracial population proportions detailed in geo-coded census datasets. These analyses measure changes in racially disparate policing practices over time and were translated for police leadership and civilian use.

As the focus of this chapter is not to evaluate the impact of evidence-based interventions crafted by NJD partners, we will instead demonstrate how the nature of the partnership, taken together and as described by the police department executives or community members themselves, allows for large-scale, data-driven reductions in racially disparate policing and a move toward better police-community relations. This study features an exploration not only of *how* the convergence of NJD partner expertise and perspective (CPE and LEA personnel) allows for impactful and lasting positive policing reform, but also *why* this approach is desirable to law enforcement executives, the residents that they serve, and the research community committed to developing evidence-based suggestions for reform.

The Pains of Policing Science … And How to Address Them through Action Research

Building a true and lasting productive research partnership with police departments requires more than compromise on the part of parties with potentially divergent aims. Rather, a more ethical and effective approach to action research involves creating a research strategy that acknowledges the costs and inputs required of each partner, and continuously endeavors to create solutions to minimize associated harms and risks. The following discussion addresses our third and fourth guiding research questions:

- *How might the research community seek research partnership buy-in from police executives as well as patrol personnel?*
- *How can these partnerships foster a robust exchange of information and guidance between social scientists and police agencies?*

Below, we provide examples of the challenges and risks that interviewed NJD personnel suggested are responsible for some LEAs' initial hesitations about participating in the NJD data collection effort. Those descriptions are then followed by the strategies that the NJD team iteratively devised *alongside* its partner departments, as evidenced in the data collection and analysis protocols, in order to efficiently and adequately address those hurdles.

How Do Police Departments Learn About the NJD?

The NJD is the nation's first database tracking national statistics on police behavior and standardizes data collection across many of the country's police departments. Currently, more than 40 national police departments and LEAs have signed on to participate, and those jurisdictions represent half of all major cities, and service more than one third of the nation's population. Though CPE does not advertise the

NJD or actively recruit partner departments, the word has gotten out. While CPE representatives do participate in a host of discussions and convenings that bring police researchers and police executives together (e.g., CPE staff regularly attend meetings of the Major Cities Chiefs of Police Association and the International Association of Police Chiefs), the NJD Project Director shared that the overwhelming majority of the existing NJD partners have approached CPE on their own.

Chiefs from major cities as well as smaller jurisdictions have approached CPE with an interest in identifying the scope of racial disparity in their practices and the sources of that bias. Upon learning more about the depth of scrutiny required to measure those truths, however, concerns about the potential consequences of a data reveal emerge. Still, the NJD Project Director shared that all police executives are advised, 'we [CPE] will find disparity and we want you to know that so that you all aren't surprised by what the data show.' She also commented on the deep humility she has felt toward the chiefs who have replied, 'but I can't fix what I don't know.' Chief Andrew Greenwood of the Berkeley Police Department, for example, has publicly shared that he aimed to be 'all in to find out where we [Berkeley PD] stand and what we need to work on,' and has since published a draft of Berkeley PD's City Report.[3] NJD personnel work with partner department leadership like Chief Greenwood to identify a shared goal of cultivating a climate and process that will enable racial justice and equity, and then devise a research plan that will get them closest to an accurate measure of the gulf to be filled.

No department has ever been excluded from joining the NJD, and a wide cross-section of jurisdictions are represented in the database. With that variance, however, comes a need to identify different strategies for collecting data and honoring the needs and positions of different departments and their constituencies. Thus, NJD personnel communicated that there is no one way to work with a department. Each department does enter into the partnership supplied with the same information and continuous contact, however: as many conference call and in-person meetings as officer union representation, the chief, their designee(s), and their Information and Technology (IT) Lead desires; a mutually agreed upon and executed Memorandum of Understanding (MOU); a standard data request checklist; and the establishment of a secure data transfer protocol. All NJD data collection, storage and analysis practices adhere to the confidentiality standards of Institutional Review Board protocol approved by the University of California, Los Angeles. Just as data on any other vulnerable human subject population are secured by research institutions, NJD data are safeguarded with the same protections.

The abovementioned steps and materials are created in partnership with police leadership and all parties have consented to the scientific undertaking to come. Missing from these con-versations, regrettably, are the voices of the officers whose administrative behavioral data (while confidential) are included in the data extraction. In order to ethically address their individual concerns, CPE appoints an Outreach Coordinator to work on-site with officers who have ques-tions and concerns about what partnering with the NJD might mean for their careers and their reputations. The discussion below details the most frequently cited apprehensions.

Officers' 'us vs. them' Concerns

While police officer indoctrination into their multi-dimensional local cultures may take varied forms, studies suggest that one element of their culture is characterized by a shared sense of isola-tion from the public (Ingram, Paoline, & Terrill, 2013). As police work constitutes a charge and responsibility that most adults in the labor force will never confront, many officers raise concerns about the public's capacity to imagine the justifications that police offer for making unpopular choices – the deployment of lethal force, among them. Therefore, the collection and release of data that capture those behaviors, often without a consideration of the context or individual-level calculus that led to police behaviors (legitimate fear, for example), can leave officers feeling leery of participating in research that will invite judgment from an uninformed public or research community. Furthermore, as researcher-police partnerships are initiated at the discretion of LEA leadership, officers have told NJD team members that researchers are viewed with suspicion and as an arm of an administration looking to audit and discipline lower-ranked officers. Officer fears that research will be used against them is real in its implications, and so CPE has worked hard to ensure that officers feel more comfortable participating in the growth of the NJD.

As the NJD adopts a holistic approach to examining policing practice, the primary aim of the research project is not to identify 'bad apples' or individual actors whose behaviors may prove actionable to their supervisors or the public at large. Instead, CPE and its practitioner partners are committed to identifying how the environment in which officers are asked to police might contribute to racial bias and racially disparate policing outcomes.

This approach unfolds in three different ways. First CPE's primary police department outreach partners are former police officers themselves. By sending these ambassadors, CPE provides space for actors who are well-versed in research science, method, and utility to address officers' questions and concerns about the value of their input and how data will be used to support their efforts to keep everyone safe. By deploying these 'embedded researchers' (Braga, 2016; Braga & Davis, 2014), or thought partners who serve as an internal resource to the departments by regularly participating in meetings, troubleshooting hurdles, and collaboratively developing strategies for more efficient execution of research, officers come to see CPE as partners, and more like 'us' instead of 'them.' CPE recruits officers to anonymously describe their experiences by electronically completing a climate survey that examines officers' thoughts about departmental dynamics, interactions with their communities, and officer wellbeing. Finally, CPE works with NJD partners to provide a systematic review of the department's written orders and policies. This review also notes areas where department practices may not be formally represented in official policy language, but as ambiguities that create administrative blind spots for well-meaning officers. All of this work is done in part, to empower officers to participate in ethically crafted research design and to ensure them the research effort is executed with their best interests in mind.

Labor Unions

In order to meaningfully and ethically engage police officers in a given department, proceeding with a research study requires the earned trust and buy-in of that department's labor union. Guided by the presumption that police unions are overly defensive (Morabito, 2014; Rushin, 2017), some researchers are reluctant to work with police unions. CPE, instead, understands and appreciates that union leadership takes their responsibility to protect the best interests of patrol officers very seriously (Walker, 2008). Officers' concerns about maintaining personnel confidentiality sometimes emerge from union policies, labor contracts, or other legal restrictions that needlessly hide disciplinary processes and outcomes from the research community (DeCarlo & Jenkins, 2015). Additionally, union representatives do not necessarily know about the ethical principles to which social scientists engaged in human subjects research must adhere – and so their reluctance to accommodate scientists is more than reasonable. As such, the support of the police union is critical not only for the purposes of shoring up participation and officer response rates, but also for creating research designs that are meaningful to the larger patrol officer collective.

The NJD framework addresses the concerns of labor unions in several important ways. First, by surveying officers on departmental procedures and fairness and being an outside, legitimate expert, CPE amplifies the voices of officers and, therein, the union's concerns. Officer respondents are recruited with the permission of the departmental leadership. Second, CPE researchers make a point of meeting with union representation early in the research partnership proposal, in order to present evidence that the NJD framework and action research approach works and will be beneficial for their officers. Unions have repeatedly cited an appreciation for this reassurance, as absent that conversation, the MOU agreements drafted between CPE and the police department can appear to cast CPE as partnering with the department's administration arm, rather than the department as a whole. Finally, because the NJD aims to systematically measure departmental policy, practice, and procedure, any unfavorable data-related fallout that might worry union leadership and the officers that they represent is presented in the aggregate, alongside recommendations for improving structural weaknesses that leave officers at risk for policing less effectively.

Chiefs' Assumption of Risk

CPE has observed that the overwhelming majority of police chiefs that the NJD team has encountered wants very much to lead good departments focused on ensuring safety and welfare for all of their community members. For those chiefs charged with addressing a legacy of tense (or even violent) police officer-Black community relationships, many have expressed a keen interest in strengthening systems that will preclude high-profile incidents of racially-animated misconduct as well as everyday racism and racial discrimination. Despite this sincere interest, police chiefs have expressed fears about the fallout that data science might spark. 'What will the numbers say or reveal? What will it mean for my department? My city? My career?' These are all reasonable concerns for police chiefs to raise with NJD team members, particularly when confronted with local political pressure to perform in ways that appease multiple, but divergent constituency agendas (International Association of Chiefs of Police, 2004; Walker, 2004).

Consistent with research presented by Engel and Whalen (2010), prior to joining the NJD database, police chiefs cited some combination of four primary reasons for their reluctance to partner with research scientists, let alone adopt any instructions from the research community. First, chiefs were preoccupied by the idea that accountability for all successes, and more importantly, any assessed failures that emerge from scientific analysis, rests solely on the shoulders of the department chief. In other words, however flawed the advice offered by the research community, should that advice lead to poor outcomes for the police or the community, it is the chief who will be held responsible rather than the researchers from whom the counsel may have been derived. Second, many chiefs who have expressed hesitation around the partnership believed that innovation and departures from their local political and historical status quo might cost them their jobs. Third, while most scientists rely on quantitative data analyses to establish truths about policing science, there are a number of policing procedures, behaviors, and intentions that simply cannot be captured numerically. Hence, a number of police chiefs fear that an incomplete narrative will gain traction, especially if negative for the department. Finally, as research scientists have historically failed to partner with police departments through the implementation stage of their recommendations, many police chiefs hesitate to take on a research-based reform initiatives that will not be accompanied by the supports of the scientists who authored it.

The NJD framework includes several mechanisms to address police chiefs' concerns about engaging in research partnership. First, CPE's embedded researchers who intimately understand the perception of risk felt by police chiefs, assure leadership that departmental members of the NJD will be supported through the research execution effort, the public relations rollout of any unfavorable findings – should chiefs decide to publicize them – and the thoughtful implementation of any trainings, remedies, or recommendations derived from any report authored by CPE. Data are also collected from multiple sources – administrative officer behavioral data, residential survey data, and census crime data – to help departments construct a more holistic portrayal of what precisely is driving their practices and outcomes. This no-cost support helps to cultivate a positive and longstanding relationship between police officers, CPE research scientists, police chiefs, and their communities. Further, this public partnership models for other departments chiefs, the merits of transparency and the benefits of bravery. CPE also assists NJD partners actively working to involve their mayoral and city government colleagues in their department-wide reform efforts. Police executives have reported positive outcomes associated with cultivating buy-in for data-driven reform, across local stakeholder groups. The NJD Director expressed sincere admiration for the chiefs who seek out the details of what a research partnership can look like, and then consent to participate in the NJD. 'We have some pretty courageous chiefs,' she shared. 'They put their neck out there in order to improve their relationship with the community, and we will always stand by them through whatever comes.'

Data Access and Quality

Recall that every department receives a data request checklist upon joining the NJD and that CPE requests longitudinal data on a number of policing domains that departments cannot always fulfill. The most common missing data points include pedestrian stops; important vehicle stop variables (e.g., officer and suspect demographics, contraband hit metrics), use of force variables; and consistent dispatch records. That said, no department, however incomplete their data transfer to CPE, is ever excluded from joining the NJD. In fact, the majority of NJD partners represent smaller jurisdictions with relatively smaller budgets, and do not maintain some of the more robust data collection and storage protocols that departments in major cities have adopted in recent years.[4] These departments often need assistance even for determining *if* they have the data that the NJD team requests. In response, the NJD Project Director and Principal Data Acquisition Specialist work closely with police executive, IT, and/or records management personnel to shed light on data collection practices, extract whatever data are usable for rigorous statistical analyses, and build systems that will improve data collection efforts moving forward.

For example, because the NJD team consists of members who have a professional background in Criminal Justice Administration and software engineering, they help partner departments troubleshoot IAPro, Computer-Aided Dispatch (CAD), and an array of Records Management System (RMS) queries. The NJD Lead Project Manager even described instances where the team avoided burdening an often already taxed IT and records-keeping unit, and instead secured additional support from RMS vendors directly. She shared, 'they're out there, busy doing the work. If we can take this off their hands and keep things moving for them, then of course we will, and we should.'

Public Reception

While materials prepared for NJD member departments are not publicized by anyone other than the figures of leadership in that jurisdiction, CPE scientists encourage departments to make their efforts to leverage data science to hold themselves accountable and police more effectively, known to as many people as will listen. Departments whose practices and procedures lead to inequitable outcomes across ethnoracial groups are justifiably concerned that data science documenting their unsatisfactory practices will bring them into the purview of federal oversight (Powell, Meitl, & Worrall, 2017; Simonson, 2016). There are three reasons for which this hesitation should not preclude partnering in an ethical action research endeavor, however.

First, it is inappropriate to believe that there is only one audience poised to learn of the results of these action research partnerships. Stakeholders include police officers, police chiefs, command staff, and unions; mayoral staff; community members; and even funders (Carr &

Littler, 2015; Telep & Weisburd, 2014). As there are sometimes conflicting, but always overlapping needs, NJD output is designed to address the concerns, questions, and agendas of various stakeholders and partners within departments in the public-facing media rollout of any research product. By centering the biggest concern – safety and that everyone deserves to be seen and to get home – the NJD products provide a platform for forward thinking dialogue by naming and identifying everyone's needs and then devising methods, in partnership with departments, to meet them. Second, NJD report recommendations often leverage existing Department of Justice consent decree rationales. Therefore, departments are more likely to avoid consent decrees and official federal oversight if they proactively implement best practices for reform that are endorsed by federal governing bodies. Finally, NJD members are invited to co-author public-facing products with CPE scientists, signaling to audiences that they are involved in and committed to developing sustainable strategies to address problems that endanger safety (Birzer, 2002; Jenkins, 2015). Notably, CPE scientists also stand to learn a great deal from producing scholarship with thinkers who are not trained in science. Fostering a more balanced exchange of expertise and perspective between partners helps to center the phenomenon and the method, rather than some of the more abstract constructs that are interpretable by an almost exclusively academic readership.

Implications for Policing Research and Reform

Unless a department expressly publicized their involvement with the NJD, CPE does not reveal the identities of its police department partners. Several partners, however, have seen positive moves toward reform that they have publicly attributed to data analytic-driven suggestions derived from the NJD partnership. In order to address our final guiding research question (*what are the potential policing reform implications of police department-social science partnerships aimed at reducing racial disparities?*), we turn to examples of data-driven reforms cited by partners whose efforts stemmed directly from working with the NJD.

Toronto, Ontario

The Toronto Police Services (TPS) came to the Center for Policing Equity with concerns about their Field Interview Stops. Their leadership worried that their officers were stopping too many citizens, and that the stops were burdensome and racially disparate. As part of CPE's review, researchers tailored an officer climate survey that asked why officers were motivated to conduct field interviews. It turned out that TPS personnel promotional practices included a review of the number of officer field interviews conducted in a given year. So, while officers did not have a target number of interviews to conduct, they reported a need to maintain interview counts that appeared 'within the normal range' to make sure they were eligible for promotion. While not its original intent, the promotion policy encouraged a culture where more stops were seen as better for officers looking to move up the professional ladder.

Following a review of the officer survey and administrative field interview data, CPE worked with TPS to create and rollout an evidence-informed policy change. Two major changes were instituted; promotion criteria were no longer to include officer field interview counts or rates; and should a resident be stopped by TPS, each was to receive an interview card that included the name of the police officer(s) conducting the stop, the most common civil rights infractions committed during a field interview, and a municipal number to call to complain should the need arise. Since implanting this reform, field stops decreased from 7,000 per week to 96, jurisdiction-wide. TPS attribute these public welfare improvements to data-driven policy reform developed in partnership with action research scientists at CPE.

Additionally, when asked to explain why they had identified CPE as a research partner, Deputy Chief Peter Sloly offered that CPE would not only create and conduct a rigorous research plan, but would also do so without any expectation of payment from the department. As an indication of the department's sincere interest in objectively and effectively tackling their racial disparities in stops by leveraging data science, he shared, '[t]his is as independent and third-party as we can get.'[5] For this department, it was important to work with a thought partner who shared a stake in their moves toward ensuring equitable safety and nothing more.

Minneapolis, Minnesota

Minneapolis is one of six cities participating in the National Initiative for Building Community Trust and Justice. The initiative aims to combine leading social science interventions of procedural justice and psychological approaches to bias, with work on racial reconciliation to drive down burdensome and disparate policing (National Initiative for Building Community Trust and Justice, 2016). Minneapolis was selected as a pilot site for its demonstrated willingness and capacity to engage in the National Initiative's research, intervention, and evaluation process. 'We'll take a look at how we do business to make sure it is equitable,' said former Minneapolis Mayor, Betsy Hodges, who, along with former Police Chief Janeé Harteau, wrote letters to the federal government explicitly requesting that Minneapolis join the National Initiative effort.[6] As a principal on the National Initiative project, CPE developed a procedural justice training curriculum that officers then delivered to their colleagues, which focused on identifying risk factors for officer bias (both implicit and explicit), then used pre- and post-officer climate survey and administrative data to diagnose where bias in police behavior was largest and modifiable via the training curriculum.

Instead of looking at single measurements of public safety, CPE encouraged the Minneapolis Police Department (MPD) to examine environmental factors like social services utilization, substance abuse, and housing insecurity. The purpose was to see where Minneapolitans who needed help were and to empower other social service entities to show up with help before law enforcement was required. As a result of measuring the environmental context that gave rise to over-policing and identifying the organization that needed support to support local residents, MPD's total use of force rates was reduced by 48 percent. Additionally, CPE worked with the MPD to launch a public-facing data website that more transparently informs and educates community members about their local policing practices. 'Too often in policing – our culture, our history – we've shielded our communities from this data. . . they have a right to this data' said Minneapolis Police Chief Medaria Arradondo.[7] CPE worked with MPD to create a data dashboard that is illustrative, accessible, and offers a reliable start to productive police-community conversations about reform.

Austin, Texas

In 2015, the City of Austin partnered with the White House under the Obama administration on the Task Force on 21st Century Policing.[8] Austin Police Department (APD) was one of twelve departments committed to sharing administrative data to help strengthen the ability of police to identify factors that led to poor police-community interactions. Sharing data, APD quickly realized, was the easy part. Using the data to distinguish between racial disparities in outcomes and racial discrimination on the part of the institution, however, is a heavier lift. In order to help APD tackle this feat, CPE analyzed APD's data to provide the city – and the White House – with the first analyses of racial bias in open police data. Findings revealed that neither local crime, poverty, nor education attainment rates were sufficient to explain racial disparities in APD use of force data. In other words, there were racial disparities that APD could 'own' and, in turn, do something about.

Armed with those data, CPE worked with the city to develop recommendations and change the department's use of force policies. As a result, the police department partnered with local activists to revise their field training protocols in ways that reflected a focus on de-escalation and reducing racial disparities in officer reliance on force. Following the release of the data and the officer-involved shooting of Austin resident, David Joseph, then Chief Art Acevedo met with local activists about crafting evidence-driven police reform. 'The policy talk started [then],' said Chas Moore of the Austin Justice Coalition. 'We looked at that incident as something that's problematic with [APD] training. It was a bad shooting, and that's on [the cop]. But we stepped back and looked at how it happened – started looking at APD training, their response to resistance training. There were some things they could change internally. There was David Joseph and then Breaion King. After that, they realized "You know what, there are some things that we can change, so let's start working on that."'[9]

The community of Austin – including elected officials and local press – lauded the Chief of Police, Art Acevedo, for his work and he was later hired as Chief of the Police for Houston, Texas. President Barack Obama even cited the report on APD as the lone example of analyses that are possible with open police data and research partnerships aimed at understanding how police activities impact different communities (Obama, 2017).

Elevating Policing Science

The collaborations described above are not one-sided. Neither the NJD team members interviewed nor the larger CPE research group characterizes the work of entering these action partnerships as saviors for floundering police departments. Rather, researchers that engage in these partnerships – no matter the phase – are exposed to opportunities to learn a great deal about how everyday policing unfolds, how those practices are memorialized (or not) and why, and how public safety institutions position themselves as accountable to the public and to their own. Action research partners also learn that the analysis of secondary data may still require some 'primary' data infrastructural building efforts, too. The willingness to be nimble and unrushed in these efforts allows for the production of science that does not speed past the study subjects' needs or capacities (police departments, in this case of the NJD) and mandates space for scientists to learn more about the study subject's environment, beyond the more objective and anonymous data points that these departments provide. That nuanced and reflexive exchange and accommodation, we believe, will push the quality of the policing science findings forward and foster healthier relationships between police departments, research scientists, and all stakeholders waiting to access that knowledge base.

Conclusions: Possibilities for Translational Policing in the 21st Century

The Center for Policing Equity aims to address the needs of both law enforcement and communities, who can avail themselves of the aggregated findings produced by the NJD. The NJD collects policing data from multiple sources to measure fairness and improve policing equity, create a national picture of policing practice and impact, and to make its findings transparent to law enforcement and to community residents. The NJD offers a rigorous analytic framework to make sense of policing data, seeking to identify and understand the consequences of policing activities and the sources of racial disparity. Research reports provide empirical documentation of the degree of racial disparity stemming from policing practices, as well as an analysis and interpretation of the factors that might contribute to such disparity. As such, there are a number of departments moving toward transparency and are increasingly amenable to partnering with policing research scientists who are committed to ensuring health and safety.

This case study analysis reveals that one of the principal purposes of creating ethical action research partnerships with departments is to demonstrate the value of analyzing data, to empower all stakeholders to use them, and to build research practices that better accommodate the needs of institutions with overlapping aims. Outputs from these partnerships include real data that can provide both a holistic birds-eye scope and laser-focused view of operations; can be used to improve staffing, training, and professionalization initiatives (Cordner & Shain, 2011); and provide evidence for multiple sources of racial bias and discrimination. These findings allow scientist and practitioner partners to systematically work toward justice and safety outcomes that are specific to the local context, but also lend wisdoms to the larger policing science action research community.

The NJD partnership accomplishes those goals by building standardized longitudinal datasets; crafting rigorous descriptive and inferential statistical analyses; creating benchmarks across jurisdictions, cities, and states; and diagnosing emergent problems *earlier*. All of these efforts help to reduce the risk of departments engendering bias-related future events and/or causing harm to their members. In sum, these partnerships offer law enforcement officials and research scientists a roadmap toward greater transparency and accountability in police practices. The result yields a robust opportunity to transform agencies, adopt more just and equitable means of promoting public safety, and emerge as an exemplar of action research that enables public safety.

Disclosure Statement

No potential conflict of interest was reported by the authors.

Notes

1. With the exception of police departments adhering to mandates of the Sunshine Act, no department that contributes data to the NJD is required to publicize identifiable CPE findings. The *Government in the Sunshine Act* (P. L. 94–409, 90 Stat. 1241) amended the Freedom of Information Act and increased publicly available transparency of operations in the federal government, Congress, federal commissions, and other legally constituted federal bodies.
2. In this article, 'racial' is used as a shorthand for the ethnoracial demographic groups described in a given police department's administrative records. When NJD analyses compare a department's policing statistics to census data, these identities are mapped onto the following census categories: non-Hispanic Asian, non-Hispanic Black, non-Hispanic Native American, Hispanic (any race), and non-Hispanic White [and any other census categories mapping onto PD's descriptors, e.g., Native American/Alaska Native, Native Hawaiian/Pacific Islander]. This simplified terminology does not represent a claim that such persons belong to monolithic 'races,' or indeed that the category of 'race' has objective meaning independent of its social context. Furthermore, it should be noted that for most departments, racial categories only describe an officer's perception of a civilian's race or ethnicity. This perception may or may not match the individual's own racial or ethnic identity.
3. https://www.cityofberkeley.info/CPEDraftInterimReport.aspx.
4. CPE does not charge departments to enter the National Justice Database or receive the City Report.
5. http://tpsnews.ca/stories/2015/02/academic-aims-social-justice/.
6. https://www.minnpost.com/politics-policy/2015/08/professors-and-police-how-minneapolis-project-maychange-way-cops-everywhere/.
7. https://www.mprnews.org/story/2017/11/14/mpd-use-of-force-data-now-online.
8. https://obamawhitehouse.archives.gov/blog/2015/05/18/launching-police-data-initiative.
9. https://www.austinchronicle.com/news/2016-11-04/austin-police-consider-community-reforms/.

References

Alpert, G. P., Rojek, J., & Hansen, J. A. (2013). *Building bridges between police researchers and practitioners: Agents of change in a complex world.* Washington, DC: National Institute of Justice, US Department of Justice.

Bachman, R. D., & Schutt, R. K. (2017). *Fundamentals of research in criminology and criminal justice* (Fourth ed.). Thousand Oaks, CA: SAGE Publications, Inc.

Bedford, L., & Mazerolle, L. (2014). Beyond the evidence: Organizational learning from RCTs in policing. *Policing: A Journal of Policy and Practice, 8*(4), 402–416.

Bennett, A., & Elman, C. (2006). Qualitative research: Recent developments in case study methods. *Annual Review of Political Science, 9*(1), 455–476.

Birzer, M. (2002). Writing partnership between police practitioners and researchers. *Police Practice and Research: An International Journal, 3*(2), 149–156.

Braga, A. A. (2016). The value of "pracademics" in enhancing crime analysis in police departments. *Policing: A Journal of Policy and Practice, 10*(3), 308–314.

Braga, A. A., & Davis, E. F. (2014). Implementing science in police agencies: The embedded research model. *Policing: A Journal of Policy and Practice, 8*(4), 294–306.

Braga, A. A., Welsh, B. C., Papachristos, A. V., Schnell, C., & Grossman, L. (2014). The growth of randomized experiments in policing: The vital few and the salience of mentoring. *Journal of Experimental Criminology, 10*(1), 1–28.

Carr, D., & Littler, K. (2015). Sharing research data to improve public health: A funder perspective. *Journal of Empirical Research on Human Research Ethics, 10*(3), 314–316.

Cordner, G., & Shain, C. (2011). The changing landscape of police education and training. *Police Practice and Research: An International Journal, 12*(4), 281–285.

DeCarlo, J., & Jenkins, M. J. (2015). *Labor unions, management innovation and organizational change in police departments.* New York: Springer.

Eikeland, O. (2012). Action research: Applied research, intervention research, collaborative research, practitioner research, or praxis research? *International Journal of Action Research, 7*(2), 9–44.

Engel, R. S., & Whalen, J. L. (2010). Police-academic partnerships: Ending the dialogue of the deaf, the Cincinnati experience. *Police Practice and Research: An International Journal, 11*(2), 105–116.

Famega, C., Hinkle, J. C., & Weisburd, D. (2017). Why getting inside the "black box" is important: Examining treatment implementation and outputs in policing experiments. *Police Quarterly, 20*(1), 106–132.

Greene, J. R. (2014a). New directions in policing: Balancing prediction and meaning in police research. *Justice Quarterly, 31*(2), 193–228.

Greene, J. R. (2014b). The upside and downside of the "police science" epistemic community. *Policing: A Journal of Policy and Practice, 8*(4), 379–392.

Greenwood, D. J., & Levin, M. (1998a). Action research, science, and the co-optation of social research. *Studies in Cultures, Organizations and Societies, 4*(2), 237–261.

Greenwood, D. J., & Levin, M. (1998b). *Introduction to action research: Social research for social change.* Thousand Oaks, CA: SAGE Publications Inc.

Harris, D. A. (2012). *Failed evidence: Why law enforcement resists science.* New York: New York University Press.

Ingram, J. R., Paoline, E. A., III, & Terrill, W. (2013). A multilevel framework for understanding police culture: The role of the workgroup. *Criminology, 51*(2), 365–397.

International Association of Chiefs of Police. (2004). *Unresolved problems and powerful potentials: Improving partnerships between law enforcement leaders and university-based researchers.* Washington, DC: Author.

Jenkins, M. J. (2015). The use of qualitative methods and practitioners-as-authors in journal publications of police research. *Police Practice and Research: An International Journal, 16*(6), 499–511.

Kelty, S. F., & Julian, R. (2013). Looking through the crystal ball: Do others know what you expect from research projects? *Policing: A Journal of Policy and Practice, 6*(4), 408–417.

Kerrison, E. M. (2018). Risky business, risk assessment, and other heteronormative misnomers in women's community corrections and reentry planning. *Punishment & Society, 20*(1), 134–151.

Kerrison, E. M., Cobbina, J., & Bender, K. (2018). Stop-gaps, lip service, and the perceived futility of body-worn police officer cameras in Baltimore City. *Journal of Ethnic & Cultural Diversity in Social Work, 27*(3), 271–288.

Lefkowitz, J. (1977). *Problems of conducting research in organizations: The case of police departments.* New York: Baruch College, City University of New York.

Lum, C., Koper, C. S., & Telep, C. W. (2011). The evidence-based policing matrix. *Journal of Experimental Criminology, 7*(1), 3–26.

Lumsden, K., & Goode, J. (2018). Policing research and the rise of the "evidence-base": Police officer and staff understandings of research, its implementation and 'what works'. *Sociology, 52*(4), 813–829.

Miller, T. R., Lawrence, B. A., Carlson, N. N., Hendrie, D., Randall, S., Rockett, I. R. H., & Spicer, R. S. (2017). Perils of police action: A cautionary tale from US data sets. *Injury Prevention, 23*(1), 27–32.

Morabito, M. (2014). American police unions: A hindrance or help to innovation? *International Journal of Public Administration, 37*(11), 773–780.

National Initiative for Building Community Trust and Justice. (2016). *Reconciliation: Process overview.* New York: CUNY John Jay College of Criminal Justice.

Obama, B. (2017). The president's role in advancing criminal justice reform. *Harvard Law Review, 130*(3), 811–866.

Petersilia, J. (2008). Influencing public policy: An embedded criminologist reflects on California prison reform. *Journal of Experimental Criminology, 4*(4), 335–356.

Powell, Z. A., Meitl, M. B., & Worrall, J. L. (2017). Police consent decrees and Section 1983 civil rights litigation. *Criminology & Public Policy, 16*(2), 575–605.

Ripamonti, S., Galuppo, L., Gorli, M., Scaratti, G., & Cunliffe, A. L. (2016). Pushing action research toward reflexive practice. *Journal of Management Inquiry, 25*(1), 55–68.

Rousseau, D. M., & Gunia, B. (2016). Evidence-based practice: The psychology of EBP implementation. *Annual Review of Psychology, 67*, 667–692.

Rushin, S. (2017). Police union contracts. *Duke Law Journal, 66*(6), 1191–1266.

Sayer, A. (2010). *Method in social science: A realist approach* (Second ed.). New York: Routledge.

Sherman, L. W. (2013). The rise of evidence-based policing: Targeting, testing and tracking. In M. Tonry (Ed.), *Crime and justice in America, 1975–2025* (Vol. 42, pp. 1–75). Chicago: University of Chicago Press.

Simonson, J. (2016). Copwatching. *California Law Review, 104*(39), 391–445.

Spano, R. (2005). Potential sources of observer bias in police observational data. *Social Science Research, 34*(3), 591–617.

Telep, C. W. (2016). Expanding the scope of evidence-based policing. *Criminology and Public Policy, 15*(1), 243–252.

Telep, C. W., & Somers, L. J. (2019). Examining police officer definitions of evidence-based policing: Are we speaking the same language? *Policing and Society: An International Journal of Research and Policy, 29*(2), 171–187.

Telep, C. W., & Weisburd, D. (2014). Generating knowledge: A case study of the national policing improvement agency program on systematic reviews in policing. *Journal of Experimental Criminology, 10*(4), 371–398.

van Wijngaarden, E., van der Meide, H., & Dahlberg, K. (2017). Researching health care as a meaningful practice: Toward a nondualistic view on evidence for qualitative research. *Qualitative Health Research, 27*(11), 1738–1747.

Walker, S. (2004). Science and politics in police research: Reflections on their tangled relationship. *Annals of the American Academy of Political and Social Science, 593*, 137–155.

Walker, S. (2008). The neglect of police unions: Exploring one of the most important areas of American policing. *Police Practice and Research: An International Journal, 9*(2), 95–112.

Weisburd, D., & Neyroud, P. (2011). Police science: Toward a new paradigm. *New perspectives in policing.* Washington, DC: US Department of Justice, Office of Justice Programs, National Institute of Justice.

Weisburd, D. L. (2003). Ethical practice and evaluation of interventions in crime and justice: The moral imperative for randomized trials. *Evaluation Review, 27*(3), 336–354.

Wittmayer, J. M., & Schäpke, N. (2014). Action, research and participation: Roles of researchers in sustainability transitions. *Sustainability Science, 9*(4), 483–496.

8

Openness to Research and Partnerships in Policing

Julie Grieco

U.S. COMMISSION ON CIVIL RIGHTS[1]

Introduction

While the notion of evidence-based policing can hardly be described as a new movement anymore, it remains a key item of interest for policing scholars and many practitioners alike. Evidence-based policing involves many different types of activities (Lum & Koper, 2017, p. 4), and can also be thought of as a philosophical approach to police operations that suggests research should be a "part of the conversation" of police practices (Lum & Koper, 2013, p.1430), requiring that officers are receptive to this philosophy, as well as to ideas supported by research evidence (which may differ substantially from their existing practices) (see also Telep, 2016 for a discussion of thinking more broadly about evidence-based policing). Efforts to expand the movement have included increasing the use of research in policing by making it more accessible,[2] which has predictably also led to a greater interest in translational criminology – the practice of translating scientific findings into policy and practice (see Laub, 2012; Laub & Frisch, 2016). This translation is a core component of the evidence-based movement (Lum, 2009; Lum et al., 2012; Nutley et al., 2007).

The expansion of translational criminology has also been paired with the growing interest in partnerships between police practitioners and researchers, and the various ways these partnerships can form, thrive, and sustain. Research has examined existing partnerships, classifying their types as 'cooperation,' 'coordination' or 'collaboration' (see Rojek et al., 2012; Alpert et al., 2013), finding that most of these partnerships had ended or existed for less than two years. Another study found that unsurprisingly, researchers do the majority of initiating partnership-creating evaluations and that the majority of the products of such partnerships are scholarly (Grieco et al., 2014). Research identifying the organizational correlates of more formal, long-term research-practitioner partnerships found that larger agencies (more than 100 sworn officers) were more than four times likely to have been involved in a partnership within the past five years than smaller departments, and that an agency's reported use of academic journals or publications from the National Institute of Justice increased the odds of engaging in a partnership, whereas the reported use of professional publications decreased such odds (Rojek et al., 2019).

While the evidence-based policing movement is expanding in areas such as scholarly research (Lum & Koper, 2017; Sherman, 2013; Braga et al., 2013; see Lumsden & Goode, 2018 for a discussion of the rise of the evidence-base in the UK), translation (Laub & Frisch, 2016), and

DOI: 10.4324/9781003153009-11

the growth of research-practitioner partnerships, in practice it is still not the norm. Barriers to getting the police to pay attention to and use research evidence can include administrative constraints, a lack of resources, translation failures, and individual resistance to change. Some argue that the values of researchers and practitioners differ so widely that translation and implementation of research must overcome a cultural gap (see Buerger, 2010; Hirschkorn & Geelan, 2008). Some of the more rigorous forms of research, namely randomized controlled experiments, bring with them practical, ethical, and funding challenges of their own (Pawson & Tilley, 1997). There are also barriers filtering scientific knowledge from policy, such as prevailing paradigms, prevailing ideology, short-term political considerations, and short-term bureaucratic inertia (Tonry & Green, 2003). An obstacle toward the evidence-based policing movement can also stem from the research itself, as conventional research approaches in policing may address the concerns of management or policy-makers more so than police practitioners on the front line (Thacher, 2008). A review of the importance of translational criminology to the field of policing highlighted two pertinent challenges in translating evidence into practice: the quality of existing research and the disconnect between what researchers produce and what consumers and practitioners value (Nichols et al., 2019). The authors describe ambiguity in intervention characteristics and implementation environments, in which the information provided from evaluative work may not include enough information to allow others to replicate the program properly. Importantly, they also describe divergent values, time constraints, and rewards. The confluence of researchers preferring rigorous designs that often take years to complete and the need for decision-makers to act under time constraints impacts the ability for evidence-based policing to take hold in many circumstances. Additionally, research findings are most often housed in locations unavailable to many practitioners, such as academic journals (Nichols et al., 2019; see also Grieco et al., 2014 describing research-practitioner partnerships and the tendency to solely produce scholarly articles).

At the individual level of receptivity and use of research in policing, Lum and Telep developed a survey which has been administered and modified in several different departments (Lum et al., 2012; Telep & Lum, 2014a). The survey assesses officer knowledge about evidence-based policing, officer views on a variety of tactics and strategies supported by research evidence, officer perceptions and views of scientific knowledge versus experiential knowledge, as well as questions regarding opinions of innovation, new ideas, and also the importance of education to policing. When asked about the usefulness of information from research regarding police tactics, responses varied by department. In one department, 21.5% of officers said information from research is very useful, whereas in the other two departments, only 7.7% and 6.1% of respondents agreed that research could be very useful (Telep & Lum, 2014a). Officers in all three agencies examined overwhelmingly indicated that experience should play a greater role than research in day-to-day decision-making (over 70% of responding officers in all three agencies).

Police receptivity to research has continued to remain a topic of interest (Blaskovits et al., 2018; Lumsden, 2017; Telep, 2017). The extent to which attitudes may relate to this receptivity, whether these attitudes are malleable to change, remains a larger challenge in the field of translational criminology. One study interviewing 38 police executives in Canada found several individual characteristics impacting openness to evidence-based policing (Kalyal, 2020), finding that openness depended on levels of existing skills and knowledge base, as well as organizational culture, climate, and leadership (see also Koziarski & Kalyal, 2021). Wolfe et al. (2019) put forth a theoretical model of how certain predictors can impact training motivation, which in turn relates to receptivity to training. Internal locus of control – the belief that the specific training will improve their skills – significantly predicted training motivation. The study also examined training receptivity, assessed through measures of training satisfaction and perceived skill acquisition. Overall, the authors found that "officers with an internal locus of control had more training motivation and, as a result, tended to be more satisfied with the training and believed they acquired valuable skills from the training" (Wolfe et al., 2019, p.17).

While it has yet to be directly studied, a line may be drawn from individual receptivity among practitioners to engaging in evidence-based policing concepts, to participation in a research partnership. The police academy presents an opportunity to begin understanding the extent to which recruits are being taught about research findings, or how to incorporate scientific knowledge into their practices. Are officers trained to view and approach policing with a mindset that ensures their receptivity to innovations and reforms within evidence-based policing? Research shows that police academies are where recruits first acquire attitudes and assumptions about the field of policing (Chan et al., 2003) and that individuals may be more likely to be open to change and new ideas during their educational or transitional period (Aarons, 2004; Bercovitz & Feldman, 2008; Clarke, 1996; Garland et al., 2003; Ogborne et al., 1998). Perhaps over time, what we learn from the police academy might also apply to understanding how evidence-based policing is implemented in law enforcement agencies overall.

Current Study

A 2016 study sought to explore the concepts of attitudinal openness to evidence-based policing concepts among academy recruits. Some of the attitudinal dimensions are not specific to evidence-based policing literature and were captured using the philosophies of evidence-based policing (i.e., Sherman, 1998; Lum & Koper, 2017), the evidence stemming from the policing research itself (i.e., tactics and strategies that have been deemed 'evidence-based'), and knowledge about the use of scientific research in other fields.

Examining characteristics that may lead to a police officer being more receptive to the philosophy and practice of evidence-based policing and whether these attitudes change over the course of academy training created a unique challenge. Some literature provided what evidence-based policing is (as a philosophy), as well as information on receptivity to evidence-based policing and the use of research more generally. These sources provided indications as to the characteristics and attitudes an individual open to such ideas may have.

Individual attitudes and traits aligned with evidence-based policing, as well as whether these attitudes changed throughout the course of academy training, were examined across eight cohorts of recruits in two academies, referred to as Academy 1 and Academy 2. Both police academies primarily serve suburban jurisdictions in the mid-Atlantic region. Training for Academy 1 lasted 21 weeks, and the class sizes surveyed ranged from 69 to 80 recruits. In Academy 2, training lasted 26 weeks, and the class sizes examined ranged from 37 to 69.

There were some slight differences in the demographics of the recruits surveyed. Academy 1 had significantly more recruits with prior military experience and more recruits with prior police officer experience. Additionally, this academy served many more agencies than Academy 2, and the cohorts were larger. These departments vary from airport authority to community college police agencies. The academies also varied in size: one department in Academy 1 has 14 sworn officers in total, while others have over 300 sworn officers. It is reasonable to state that, with regard to the type of departments the recruits in Academy 1 were hired for, that academy was more heterogeneous than Academy 2.

Recruits from eight cohorts of academy training (four cohorts in Academy 1 and four cohorts in Academy 2) participated in this study. Recruits were surveyed at the beginning of each academy class, and then again within a week prior to that cohort's graduation. As Table 8.1 indicates, response rates ranged from 90% to 100% across cohorts. Data collection occurred

TABLE 8.1 Survey administration

	Academy 1		Academy 2	
	Beginning of academy	*End of academy*	*Beginning of academy*	*End of academy*
Cohort 1				
Administration	July 2013	November 2013	November 2013	April 2014
N (Response rate)	69 (90.8%)	66 (95.6%)	40★	30 (96.8%)
Cohort 2				
Administration	February 2014	June 2014	April 2014	September 2014
N (Response rate)	80 (97.6%)	78 (95.1%)	37 (100%)	33 (97.0%)
Cohort 3				
Administration	August 2014	December 2014	August 2014	February 2015
N (Response rate)	79 (96.3%)	75 (100%)	70 (100%)	58 (95.0%)
Cohort 4				
Administration	February 2015	June 2015	February 2015	July 2015
N (Response rate)	81 (96.4%)	80 (100%)	55 (100%)	45 (100%)
Total	309	299	202	166

★ Initial number of students in this session unknown; response rate cannot be calculated.

between July 2013 and July 2015. The survey provided a unique code for each recruit to enable linking pre- and post-training surveys, and only linked surveys were used in the final analysis. Academy 1 provided a total of 259 linked surveys, and Academy 2 provided 156, for a total of 415 recruits studied.

A smaller percentage of respondents in Academy 2 served as an officer in another jurisdiction or in the military before entering the academy than recruits in Academy 1 (see Table 8.2). Compared to national statistics found in the 2013 Law Enforcement Management and Administrative Statistics (LEMAS) (Reaves, 2015), both academies were male-dominated. Academy 1 had a larger proportion of non-white recruits compared to the national average. Although LEMAS data does not provide information on officer education, one study sampling a broad population of over 900 officers found that 27.6% had a four-year college degree (Weisburd et al., 2001). Another study found 63.7% of respondents from three agencies had a Bachelor's degree or higher (Telep & Lum, 2014b). Both academies studied appear to be on the higher end of the education spectrum, which may have implications for findings, as recruits may gain exposure to concepts of policing research and crime control evidence in their educational experiences.

The survey instrument utilized selected items from the National Police Research Platform's Longitudinal Study of New Officers (Rosenbaum et al., 2011) and the Receptivity Survey by Lum and Telep (Lum et al., 2012; Telep & Lum, 2014a). Relevant questions were selected using attitudinal dimensions described in the study's literature analysis (Grieco, 2016): openness to research,

TABLE 8.2 Recruit demographics

	Academy 1 Final Sample (N = 259)	Academy 2 Final Sample (N = 156)	LEMAS data (Nationwide)
% Male	78.2	81.3	87.8
% Under 30	71.1	74.8	★
% White	67.2	71.8	72.8
% College degree or higher	63.3	69.9	★
% Prior served (police)	18.5	10.9	★
% Prior served (military)	26.3	17.3	★

★ Data not provided by LEMAS.

proactivity, communication skills, community/civilian relations, and low levels of cynicism. Demographics collected included sex, age, race/ethnicity, current marital status, the highest level of formal education achieved, military service, prior police service, and employment history.

Principal components analyses were conducted (one for each attitudinal dimension) using recruit responses at the beginning of the training. Following a review of the factor loading scores, variation in responses, and theoretical justifications, several initial items were dropped from the analysis, leaving 12 attitudinal components. Table 8.3 provides the components and variables yielding from the principal components analyses for each of the attitudinal dimensions. The table also offers a brief explanation for what the component scores indicate.

Scale scores were created by averaging each recruit's responses that fell within the attitudinal components for both Wave 1 and Wave 2, and scale change scores were created by subtracting the Wave 1 scale scores from the Wave 2 scale scores. To determine whether individual or group (academy) characteristics influenced attitudinal dimensions, or changes in them, component scores and score changes were entered into regression models, specifically a heteroskedasticity-consistent covariance matrix (HCCM) approach.[3] Regression tables are available in the Appendix.

Findings

Recruits Began Training with Relatively Positive Attitudes; Ended with Lower Scores

Recall, a high score shows a strong agreeance of the component within the attitudinal dimensions. For example, a high score for communication skills indicates that recruits have high confidence in a variety of communication skills. The mean score for communication skills was approximately 4 at the beginning of the academy, and 4.14 at the end of the academy, indicating that recruits had high confidence in their communications skills at both survey times, but had more confidence at the end of their training. The communication items were measured on a 5-point Likert scale, with the higher number indicating higher confidence in communication abilities. Optimistically at the beginning of training, all scores were relatively high. The scores at the end of training were also quite high, closer to the maximum range than the minimum. However, all but four components had a lower average score at the end of the academy. Other than communication skills, empathy, obtaining compliance, and the congenial component, all other scores decreased on average. The proactivity component and one component under Community/Citizen Relations (customer service) were measured on a 4-point Likert scale. The remaining components were measured on a 5-point Likert scale.

Table 8.4 provides the findings from the paired-samples t-test analysis, comparing mean score changes from the beginning of the academy to the end of the academy.

All components, other than balancing research and experience, had a mean higher than the halfway mark of possible scores at both the beginning and at the end of training.[4] Most of these scores decreased in a negative manner by the end of training, and five of these decreases were statistically significant. However, two of the positive changes were also significant: recruits were statistically more positive in their confidence in their communication skills as well as their attitudes toward obtaining compliance by the end of their training.

Individual Predictors of Attitudes/Attitudinal Change

The independent variables entered into the regression models were age, being male, being a minority, being a sworn officer in a different organization before entering the academy, having prior military experience, and the highest level of education attained.

TABLE 8.3 Attitudinal components

Attitudinal Dimension	Variables (*indicates reverse coding)	Component	Brief explanation
Research Receptivity	How important is pursuing higher education for police officers?	Education Support	Education-related questions; ↑ score, ↑ agreement
	Minimum educational standard for new recruits? Balance between use of scientific knowledge and experience	Balance	Balancing research with experience; ↑ score, ↑ agreement
Proactivity	Encourage the use of negotiation and conflict resolution Improve methods and strategies for catching criminals Improve the investigations of crime Reduce the incidence of crime and violence	Proactivity	Questions related to proactively addressing crime problems; ↑ score, ↑ agreement
Communication	I know how to talk to people I know how to resolve conflict between people I can talk anyone into doing just about anything I have good communication skills I feel confident when using my communication skills I can talk my way out of trouble	Skills	Confidence in skills relating to communication; ↑ score, ↑ agreement
	I know how to make someone comfortable I am good at reading other people's emotions I know how to show empathy or compassion I know how to use nonverbal cues to communicate feelings to others	Empathy	Confidence in skills relating to making others comfortable; ↑ score, ↑ agreement
	People don't often take my advice* I don't like to make eye contact when telling people bad news*	Withholding	Confidence in reaching out with advice or delivering bad news; ↑ score, ↑ disagreement

(Continued)

TABLE 8.3 Attitudinal components (*Continued*)

Attitudinal Dimension	Variables (*indicates reverse coding*)	Component	Brief explanation
Community/Civilian Relations	If you let people vent their feelings first, you are more likely to get them to comply with your request	Obtaining Compliance	Obtaining compliance through procedural justice means; ↑ score, ↑ agreement
	Being professional with the public should be one of the highest priorities in law enforcement All people should be treated with respect regardless of their attitude	Professionalism	Rates importance of being professional with civilians; ↑ score, ↑ agreement
	Increase citizens' feelings of safety Involve the community in crime prevention Improve services to victims Increase public satisfaction with police service	Customer Service	Agreeance with issues relating to improving community relations through improving services to civilians; ↑ score, ↑ agreement
	Police officers are expected to gather information from victims of crime, not comfort them★ The time that officers spend chatting with average citizens could be better spent investigating crime and suspicious situations★	Congenial	Agreeance with issues relating to friendliness; ↑ score, ↑ disagreement
	In an emergency, most community members would come to aid of an officer who needs assistance The community shows a lot of respect for the police Most citizens have confidence in the police Many residents try to make the community look bad★ The community doesn't appreciate what the police do for them★	Community Relations	Measures the extent to which recruits believe there are poor relations between police and the community; ↑ score, ↓ cynicism
Low Cynicism	Residents don't understand problems officers face★ You can't help the community if they are unwilling to help themselves★ You can get tired of listening to citizens complain about everything ★	Us Vs. Them	Measures extent to which recruits believe there is a strong divide between police and the community; ↑ score, ↓ cynicism

★ Reverse coded.

TABLE 8.4 Comparing attitudes at the beginning and end of academy

	Beginning of academy mean score	End of academy mean score	Mean Change
Research Receptivity			
Education Support	3.643	3.598	−0.046
Balance Research & Experience	2.412	2.279	−0.132★★
Proactivity			
Proactivity	3.792	3.730	−0.062★★
Communication			
Communication Skills	4.009	4.137	0.128★★★
Empathy	4.174	4.221	0.046
Withholding	4.109	4.028	−0.081
Community/Civilian Relations			
Obtaining Compliance	3.958	4.139	0.180★★★
Professionalism	4.404	4.283	−0.121★★★
Customer Service	3.703	3.702	−0.001
Congenial	3.640	3.657	0.017
Low Cynicism			
Community Relations	3.352	3.118	−0.234★★★
Us Vs. Them	2.591	2.489	−0.102★★

★ $p < .05$;
★★ $p < .01$;
★★★ $p < .001$

Several individual variables were significant predictors of various attitudes at the beginning of training. Being a minority was found to be a positive predictor for the 'us vs. them' attitudinal component at the beginning of the academy. At the end of the training, being a minority was a positive predictor for education support, empathy, professionalism, and customer service. Some of these findings were similar to research discovering that Black officers tend to have a broader police role orientation, be less selective in their enforcement of the law, and have more positive attitudes toward legal restrictions (Sun, 2003). It has also been found that Black officers may be more likely to feel criticized and to believe they are perceived as militant (Dowler, 2005). These attitudes may contribute to minority officers tending to support ideals such as professionalism and customer service, as found in this study.

Having previously been a former sworn officer was a predictor for the low cynicism attitudinal dimensions: leading to more negative attitudes toward community relations at the beginning of training, and more negative attitudes toward the 'us vs. them' attitudes at the end of the academy. While little is known about veteran officer attitudes when embarking on a career in a new agency, it has been found that officers who reach a career plateau (15 or more years of service) had more cynicism than officers who had not (Burke & Mikkelsen, 2006).

Additionally, education predicted several items. At the beginning of the academy, higher education predicted more positive attitudes toward education support but negative attitudes toward customer service and the 'us vs. them' component. At the end of the academy, education predicted (again) positive attitudes toward educational support and for balancing research with experience, as well as empathy and the withholding component (from the Communications attitudinal dimension). Education at the end of training also predicted negative attitudes toward customer service.

Police officer education has long been researched, from assessing the state of police officer education (Carter et al., 1989) to examining the effects of education on a variety of outcomes. College-educated police officers have previously been found to be more likely to believe that a bachelor's degree should be required to join a police force (Telep & Lum, 2014b). Education has also been looked at concerning its effect on different attitudes. One study found that college education was not strongly related to professionalism attitudes (consistent with the findings here), but that education was not related to the measure of commitment to service (Shernock, 1992) – which is inconsistent with the finding that higher education predicted less support for customer service attitudes. More recently, an examination of education on the outlooks of officers found that officers with higher education were significantly less satisfied with their job and had less favorable attitudes toward top management, yet that educational attainment had no impact on officer views toward their role (law enforcement, order maintenance, community policing) (Paoline et al., 2015). Higher education predicting higher scores for empathy and withholding was unsurprising, as these components measure confidence within the communication dimension, and previous research has shown the effects of education in improving communication skills (Pascarella & Terenzini, 2005).

Organizational Differences and Predictors of Attitudes/Attitudinal Change

Surveying recruits at two different academies provided the ability to compare attitude scores, and changes in those scores, across the academies. The academies were located within the same state, reporting to the same state training guidelines. However, they had different instructors and served different police agencies.

Table 8.5 provides the paired samples t-test comparing mean score changes from the beginning of training to the end of training, separated by academy, assessing whether one academy experienced more significant change in attitudes than the other. While the academies had several similar significant changes in the same direction (communication skills, obtaining compliance, professionalism, and community relations), there were also some differences in how attitudes changed over time. In Academy 2, recruit attitudes significantly decreased for the balance research and experience question. Also in Academy 2, empathy, customer service, and

TABLE 8.5 Comparing change across academies

	Academy 1 Mean Change	Academy 2 Mean Change
Research Receptivity		
Education Support	−0.058	−0.026
Balance Research & Experience	−0.073	−0.231★★★
Proactivity		
Proactivity	−0.097★★★	−0.005
Communication		
Communication Skills	0.100★★	0.174★★★
Empathy	0.006	0.114★★
Withholding	−0.133★	0.0032
Community/Civilian Relations		
Obtaining Compliance	0.122★★	0.277★★★
Professionalism	−0.109★	−0.139★★
Customer Service	−0.036	0.059★
Congenial	−0.078	0.174★★
Low Cynicism		
Community Relations	−0.297★★★	−0.129★★
Us Vs. Them	−0.125★★	−0.064

★ $p < .05$;
★★ $p < .01$;
★★★ $p < .001$

the congenial component significantly increased. In Academy 1, attitudes about proactivity significantly decreased, as did the withholding component and the 'us vs. them' component.

Independent samples t-tests were conducted to examine scale scores at the beginning and end of training for each academy. At the beginning of their training, recruits in Academy 1 had lower mean scores in all components but three (communication skills, withholding, and the "us vs. them"), but none of the differences were statistically significant. By the end of the training, the differences in mean scale scores were more pronounced, with five differing significantly across academy. Academy 2 recruits had significantly higher mean scale scores for proactivity, obtaining compliance, customer service, congeniality, and community relations.[5]

Due to these interesting findings, being in Academy 1 was also entered into the regression models as a predictor variable,[6] and academy turned out to be the greatest predictor of attitudinal dimensions, as well as the most significant predictor of changes in those attitudes. Being in Academy 1 was a significant predictor of more negative attitudes toward proactivity, empathy, the obtaining compliance variable, customer service, congeniality, and community relations at the end. Academy 1 was also a significant predictor for negative coefficients in the change score regressions for proactivity, empathy, obtaining compliance, customer service, congeniality, and customer relations.

Discussion

Changes in attitudes may occur during the early socialization of officers, as well as throughout their careers. Academies may foster or reduce openness to the philosophy of evidence-based policing or to particular types of approaches known to be evidence-based. Much of our knowledge regarding the socialization process of becoming a police officer stems from rich, ethnographic work of policing scholars providing a qualitative analysis of their own observations and conversations with officers (i.e., Manning, 1977; Muir, 1977; Van Maanen, 1975). Van Maanen found that the training academy creates a powerful setting for individuals to start to cultivate an ideal of oneness with policing culture, as well as solidarity with other officers (see also Rosenbaum et al., 1994).

Socialization does occur in policing and occurs early, especially during training. Chan et al. (2003), following approximately 150 new police recruits in New South Wales, found that officers began to create cultural barriers between themselves and their friends and family members, quickly viewing members of the public as lacking an understanding of police work. Another study followed more than 500 new officers from the first day at the academy until they left the force, documenting variations in new officer attitudes and beliefs, finding that officers reported more aggressiveness after completing the academy than before they entered (Rosenbaum et al., 2011).

One important area of interest in the early socialization of officers is what officers are taught about policing in the academy. Very little is known about the content of academy training. In an observation study of recruit training, Chappell and Lanza-Kaduce (2010) concluded that the most salient lessons being provided to recruits reinforced paramilitary structure and culture and that instructors advised the recruits only to discuss problems among one another rather than with 'outsiders,' reinforcing the strong bond encouraged among recruits occurring within academy walls. Another study tried to examine curriculum data from each state agency responsible for certifying training, in order to assess how much of the curriculum was task-oriented versus cognitive in nature (Bradford & Pynes, 1999). It defined task-oriented training as instruction in basic repetitive skills (such as conducting a proper traffic stop), and cognitive-oriented training as moving beyond a task and including an integrated skill response that requires reasoning (such as simulated scenarios that require effective communication). The study of 22 curricula found that less than 3% of their sample's academy training time was spent in cognitive and decision-making domains, while most were spent in task-oriented activities, although only 22 (44%) of their responses provided enough information for curriculum analysis (Bradford & Pynes, 1999). This while intensified calls for police reform have only been increasing, little is known about what is being taught in academies.

The short-term and long-term effects of a police training program based on the principles of procedural justice have also been studied (Skogan et al., 2015). An examination of 2,681 officers found that the training increased recruit levels of trust in the public shortly after training, but that these effects wore off over the long term. In the long term, Black and older officers were significantly more likely to be supportive of the principle of respect they learned about in training, but in the long run, training did not appear to impact the willingness of the officers to trust the public (Skogan et al., 2015).

Studies have also shown that recruit attitudes can change over time. One followed a sample of 446 police recruits through their police academy basic training program, and then to their respective agencies where they proceeded through field training and the completion of a one-year probationary period (Haarr, 2001). It was found that after completing basic training, recruits expressed more positive attitudes toward community policing and problem-solving policing and felt more qualified to engage in problem-solving tasks related to the SARA (Scanning, Analysis, Response, and Assessment) model. These gains, however, were undone by field training. By the end of their field training, recruits believed that fewer resources should be devoted to community policing, expressed less favorable views toward community policing and its effectiveness, and felt less qualified to engage in problem-solving tasks related to the SARA model (Haarr, 2001). Overall, academy classes emerged as statistically significant variables, suggesting that police recruits that train together may develop a unique group culture that influences their attitudes. Understanding openness to evidence-based policing notions – to include willingness to engage in research partnerships – and how training may impact these attitudes, lends to an important and fruitful area of translational research (see Lum & Koper, 2017, p. 269).

Study Limitations

This study was not able to determine whether the attitudinal dimensions identified were linked to amenability to evidence-based policing after leaving the academy, or what the impact of training may have had on future efforts to implement evidence-based policing. Following officers long past academy completion to observe the outcomes of attitudes regarding actual behaviors would have provided greater insight into the implications of these attitudes. Additionally, the measures of openness to evidence-based policing used were only proposed measures and had not been validated as such.

Additionally, the content of training in the two academies was not carefully examined. While given the overall curriculum and class schedule for academy cohorts, systematically observing all formal lessons provided to recruits throughout the training was not feasible. Without knowing what recruits are specifically learning, it is difficult to pinpoint whether specific classes or lesson plans contributed to attitudes or attitudinal change.

In addition to the study being geographically unrepresentative, as the two academies studied were in the same geographic region, there was also an issue with timing. American policing had been experiencing a sea change of concurrent experiences over the past 15 years, from departmental budget cuts to the implementation of new technology, and importantly, to facing much of society's discontent with how departments handle police brutality and other high-profile incidents. Thus, the findings may be limited to the period in which these academy sessions took place (summer 2013 – summer 2015).

While the surveys captured changes in responses intended to measure personal ideas about evidence-based policing concepts, it is possible that these changes may have reflected temporary outlooks or positions based on current mood or a recent event, attempts to recall how one responded to the initial survey, or a random and quick selection of responses to complete the survey and move on with other tasks. Moreover, these changes merely suggested an alteration in how a recruit may have felt about some concepts that are evidence-based at a given time; these are attitudes that are likely not only amenable throughout the initial academy experience but may also change throughout the first several years in the field.

Future Research

More accurate scales are needed to measure these variables of interest. This study was unable to directly assess many of the attitudes proposed to reflect individual openness to the philosophy and tactics of evidence-based policing due to constraints in the survey instrument used. Future measures that can directly address the measurement of critical thinking skills in individuals are necessary for evaluating what might be an 'evidence-based police officer.' Some items measured receptivity to the philosophies of evidence-based policing, while others represented attitudes reflected in evidence-based policing; future measures would benefit by focusing more on the former attitudes, as the tactics based on the evidence may change over time.

New scales intended to measure attitudinal openness to evidence-based policing would allow for greater understanding of overall openness to introducing research evidence into day-to-day decision making. The creation of such scales, however, should rely on what we know about evidence-based policing and what we know about different types of attitudinal openness, perhaps including adapted items from Aarons' (2004) Evidence-Based Practice Attitudes Scale. Future research should create better measures of understanding evidence-based policing by understanding the individuals most amenable to using it and the traits they may possess. Further, using these scales would add to the knowledge of police attitudes toward things such as proactivity, critical thinking, and communication, of which the literature is currently lacking.

Scales that are more capable of identifying attitudes toward the use of evidence in practice, toward tactics backed by that research, and toward methods known to improve community relations would enable policing scholars to understand more accurately how officers view evidence-based ideas and assess how these attitudes change over time. A better-constructed survey would also be of use in evaluating training programs designed to increase receptivity to evidence-based policing.

More information is needed regarding the content of academy training. This study found that recruits from one academy had less open attitudes toward evidence-based policing at the end of the training, and the regression analysis found academy to be the greatest predictor of these attitudes, as well as attitudinal change. However, existing academy research mostly provides ethnographic information on the socialization of officers or studies examining individual predictors of academy performance. A large-scale content analysis of police academy curricula would provide the field with key differences across training organizations, as well as a base of understanding as the policing field moves toward developments in training aimed to defeat crime problems while building public trust.

Conclusion

As Lum and Koper argue, an important aspect of building the evidence for evidence-based policing involves increasing the field's knowledge of what leads to successful evidence-based practice, to include the "types of institutional infrastructure and systems...needed for agencies and their officers to be receptive to research" (2017, p. 267). Resources did not provide the opportunity for the above study to observe an entire academy session from beginning to end, yet this study provides potential insight into the impacts of training on openness to evidence-based policing. As evident in the regression findings, unknown variables led to certain attitudes, as well as attitude change over the course of training: something created an opening for change in attitudes during the academy experience. Another possibility was that there was not necessarily something specific that occurred during training that would reflect these changes, rather they are the result of the overall socialization process that introduces recruits to the culture of policing (Chan et al., 2003). If changes in openness to evidence-based policing are an outcome of a social process, rather than official teachings, trying to instill certain attitudes would require a sea change in the social culture of the academy rather than an overhaul of the curriculum.

For agencies hoping to hire recruits engaged in more research-based approaches, openness among a training academy is of critical importance. Academy instructors, for example, might provide important insight into some of the unexplained changes occurring in recruit attitudes. A recruit class provides many opportunities for instructors to influence cadets, either with personal attitudes or with more nuanced policing culture attitudes [such as the hegemonic masculinity of policing (see Prokos & Padavic, 2002)]. Ensuring that a training program provides instructors that are open to evidence-based policing ideas could, at the very least, ensure recruits receive a more open atmosphere for these philosophies and practices.

These findings contribute to the field's understanding of attitudes at an organizational level. Haarr (2001) found that recruits expressed less favorable views toward both community policing and engaging in problem-solving tasks by the end of their field training, but also that academy classes emerged as significant variables predicting these attitudes, suggesting class cultures could be shaped by instructor differences (which she was unable to examine). However, Haarr only looked at multiple classes within the same academy; the findings here add to the importance of training organization in shaping attitudes toward evidence-based policing concepts.

The regression analysis of the academies separated out indicates that, in fact, inter-academy differences are important to consider. At the beginning of training, in both academies, higher education predicted more positive attitudes toward education support. In addition, being a prior sworn officer significantly predicted more cynicism in the community relations attitudinal component. This is the extent of the similarities between the two academies. The Academy 1 regressions produced twice as many significant predictors of attitudes at the beginning of training than Academy 2. In Academy 1, being male significantly predicted lower cynicism in the community relations component; being minority significantly predicted more positive attitudes for the empathy and the 'us vs. them' component; and higher education predicted more positive attitudes toward empathy and congeniality but more negative attitudes toward customer service and the 'us vs. them' component. In Academy 2, being an older recruit predicted lower cynicism in the community relations component; being minority predicted more positive attitudes toward customer service; and prior military experience predicted more positive attitudes in communication skills.

In examining the regressions on change scores for each academy, there were no predictors of attitudinal change that stood across both training organizations. In Academy 1, being a minority predicted positive change for obtaining compliance and professionalism, but a negative change for the 'us vs. them' attitudinal component; having experience as a prior sworn officer predicted positive change in the professionalism component; and higher education predicted negative change (higher cynicism) for the community relations component. In Academy 2, only being a prior sworn officer predicted any negative attitudinal changes: in the withholding and congenial components. Also in Academy 2, having prior military experience predicted positive change in the professionalism component; and having higher education predicted positive change in the empathy and professionalism component.

In addition to the existence of attitudinal differences between academies at the starting point of training, there is the possibility that then the training differentially influenced the shaping of those attitudes over time. It may be possible that a 'one size fits all' approach to changing attitudes will not work across all academies. However, more research is needed to determine if that is the case.

Recruits tended to start their training with views compatible to the philosophy of evidence-based policing, but some of these attitudes changed in a negative direction. Either the training itself or the socialization that occurs during the academy may be undermining receptivity to evidence-based policing notions. Many overall attitudes did change significantly over the course of training and certain demographic variables significantly predicted these attitudes. The most poignant predictor, however, was academy. Being in one academy (versus the other studied here) predicted two negative attitudes at the beginning of training, but six at the end of training, indicating that something occurred during training to create antagonism toward ideas of proactivity, empathy, customer service, and community relations. Additionally, the two academies varied in predictors of attitudinal change. Thus, similar to earlier findings of organizational correlates and engagement in research-practitioner partnerships (Rojek et al., 2019), the importance of training organization and its relation to promoting (or undermining) such partnerships, and evidence-based policing overall, should not be overlooked.

Notes

1. The views expressed herein are my own and do not reflect the views of the U.S. Commission on Civil Rights or the federal government.
2. Online resources such as the Evidence-Based Policing Matrix (Lum et al., 2011) or the U.S. Department of Justice website CrimeSolutions.OJP.gov are strong examples of efforts undertaken to expand the accessibility of crime and justice research. The Strategies for Policing Innovation (SPI) site is a collaborative effort among DOJ's Bureau of Justice Assistance, national training and technical assistance partners, state and local law enforcement agencies, and researchers, intended to assist agencies in identifying innovative and evidence-based solutions to address jurisdictional crime problems. Additionally, the Campbell Collaboration's Crime and Justice Coordinating Group provides systematic reviews that cover a broad range of policing research, including strategies, technology, stress management, and legitimacy.
3. The dependent variables were highly skewed and remained skewed after various transformation attempts (log, natural log, square, square root). Due to the non-normality of the dependent variables, first a non-parametric regression was looked into (quantile regression), yet several models were unable to converge due to the small amount of variance among the variables. Thus, the regression analysis turned to a heteroskedasticity-consistent covariance matrix (HCCM) approach. This approach estimates corrected ordinary-least-squares standard errors without having to specify the particular form of heteroskedasticity and is argued to be the most appropriate choice for those preferring to avoid the risk of misspecification of the form of the error variance (Kaufman, 2013).
4. Academy recruits in this study, however, were still much more positive about balancing research with experience than current officers answering the same question (see Telep & Lum, 2014a).
5. Kruskal-Wallis tests compared the eight individual cohorts at the beginning and end of the academy. Each cohort had both negative and positive changes in the different components; all but one cohort had statistically significant changes in opposite directions (in which one component changed significantly in the positive direction, and another component changed significantly in the negative

direction). The differences were random and difficult to interpret, indicating that there was not one cohort driving the significant changes in the attitudinal components, or the significant differences between the academies at the end of training.

6. Two temporal predictor variables were initially entered into the regression models as well (if the recruit was in training prior to the shooting of Michael Brown in Ferguson, MO [August 2014] prior to death of Freddie Gray in Baltimore, MD [April 2015]), with no significant findings.

References

Aarons, G. A. (2004). Mental health provider attitudes toward adoption of evidence-based practice: The Evidence-Based Practice Attitude Scale (EBPAS). *Mental Health Services Research*, 6(2), 61–74. https://doi.org/10.1023/B:MHSR.0000024351.12294.65

Alpert, G. P., Rojek, J., & Hansen, J. A. (2013). *Building Bridges Between Police Researchers and Practitioners: Agents of Change in a Complex World*. Washington, DC: National Institute of Justice, U.S. Department of Justice.

Bercovitz, J., & Feldman, M. (2008). Academic entrepreneurs: Organizational change at the individual level. *Organization Science*, 19(1), 69–89. https://doi.org/10.1287/orsc.1070.0295

Blaskovits, B., Bennell, C., Huey, L., Kalyal, H., Walker, T., & Javala, S. (2018). A Canadian replication of Telep and Lum's (2014) examination of police officers' receptivity to empirical research. *Policing & Society*, 30(3), 276–294. https://doi.org/10.1080/10439463.2018.1522315

Bradford, D., & Pynes, J. E. (1999). Police academy training: Why hasn't it kept up with practice? *Police Quarterly*, 2(3), 283. https://doi.org/10.1177/109861119900200302

Braga, A. A., Welsh, B. C., Papachristos, A. V., Schnell, C., & Grossman, L. (2013). The growth of randomized experiments in policing: The vital few and the salience of mentoring. *Journal of Experimental Criminology*, 10, 1–28. https://doi.org/10.1007/s11292-013-9183-2

Buerger, M. E. (2010). Policing and research: Two cultures separated by an almost-common language. *Police Practice and Research: An International Journal*, 11(2), 135–143. https://doi.org/10.1080/15614261003593187

Burke, R. J., & Mikkelsen, A. (2006). Examining the career plateau among police officers. *Policing: An International Journal of Police Strategies & Management*, 29(4), 691–703. https://doi.org/10.1108/13639510610711600

Carter, D. L., Sapp, A. D., & Stephens, D. W. (1989). *The State of Police Education: Policy Direction for the 21st Century*. Washington, DC: Police Executive Research Forum.

Chan, J. B., Devery, C., & Doran, S. (2003). *Fair Cop: Learning the Art of Policing*. Toronto, Ontario, Canada: University of Toronto Press.

Chappell, A. T., & Lanza-Kaduce, L. (2010). Police academy socialization: Understanding the lessons learned in a paramilitary-bureaucratic organization. *Journal of Contemporary Ethnography*, 39(2), 187–214. https://doi.org/10.1177/0891241609342230

Clarke, J. S. (1996). *Faculty Receptivity/Resistance to Change, Personal and Organizational Efficacy, Decision Deprivation and Effectiveness in Research I Universities*. ASHE Annual Meeting Paper.

Dowler, K. (2005). Job satisfaction, burnout, and perception of unfair treatment: The relationship between race and police work. *Police Quarterly*, 8(4), 476–489. https://doi.org/10.1177/1098611104269787

Garland, A. F., Kruse, M., & Aarons, G. A. (2003). Clinicians and outcome measurement: What's the use? *The Journal of Behavioral Health Services & Research*, 30(4), 393–405. https://doi.org/10.1007/BF02287427

Grieco, J. (2016). *Attitudinal dimensions and openness to evidence-based policing: Perspectives of academy recruits*. [Doctoral dissertation]. George Mason University.

Grieco, J., Vovak, H., & Lum, C. (2014). Examining research–practice partnerships in policing evaluations. *Policing: A Journal of Policy and Practice*, 8(4), 368–378. https://doi.org/10.1093/police/pau031

Haarr, R. N. (2001). The making of a community policing officer: The impact of basic training and occupational socialization on police recruits. *Police Quarterly*, 4(4), 402–433. https://doi.org/10.1177/109861101129197923

Hirschkorn, M., & Geelan, D. (2008). Bridging the research-practice gap: Research translation and/or research transformation. *Alberta Journal of Educational Research*, 54(1).

Kalyal, H. (2020). "Well, there's a more scientific way to do it!": Factors influencing receptivity to evidence-based practices in police organizations. *Police Practice and Research*, 21(6), 609–623. https://doi.org/10.1080/15614263.2019.1608548

Kaufman, R. L. (2013). *Heteroskedasticity in Regression: Detection and Correction: Detection and Correction* (Vol. 172). Thousand Oaks, CA: Sage Publications.

Koziarski, J., & Kalyal, H. (2021). Resistance to evidence-based policing: Canadian police executives' perceptions as to which level of Canadian policing is most resistant. *Police Practice and Research*, 22(1), 763–776. https://doi.org/10.1080/15614263.2020.1786690

Laub, J. (2012). Translational Criminology. In *Translational Criminology* (Fall, pp. 4–5).

Laub, J. H., & Frisch, N. E. (2016). Translational criminology: A new path forward. In *Advancing Criminology and Criminal Justice Policy* (pp. 78–88). New York, NY: Routledge.

Lum, C. (2009). *Translating police research into practice*. Ideas in American Policing. Washington, DC: Police Foundation.

Lum, C., Koper, C. S., & Telep, C. W. (2011). The evidence-based policing matrix. *Journal of Experimental Criminology*, 7(1), 3–26. https://doi.org/10.1007/s11292-010-9108-2

Lum, C. M., & Koper, C. S. (2017). *Evidence-based Policing: Translating Research into Practice*. Oxford, UK: Oxford University Press.

Lum, C., Telep, C. W., Koper, C. S., & Grieco, J. (2012). Receptivity to research in policing. *Justice Research and Policy*, 14(1), 61–96. https://doi.org/10.3818/JRP.14.1.2012.61

Lum, C., & Koper, C. S. (2013). Evidence-based policing. In G. Bruinsma & D. Weisburd (Eds.), *Encyclopedia of Criminology and Criminal Justice* (pp. 1426–1437). New York, NY: Springer.

Lumsden, K. (2017). Police officer and civilian staff receptivity to research and evidence-based policing in the UK: Providing a contextual understanding through qualitative interviews. *Policing: A Journal of Policy and Practice*, 11(2), 157–167. https://doi.org/10.1093/police/paw036

Lumsden, K., & Goode, J. (2018). Policing research and the rise of the 'evidence-base': Police officer and staff understandings of research, its implementation and 'what works.' *Sociology*, 52(4), 813–829. https://doi.org/10.1177/0038038516664684

Manning, P. K. (1977). *Police Work: The Social Organization of Policing*. Cambridge, MA: MIT Press.

Muir, W. K. (1977). *Police: Streetcorner Politicians*. Chicago, IL: University of Chicago Press.

Nichols, J., Wire, S., Wu, X., Sloan, M., & Scherer, A. (2019). Translational criminology and its importance in policing: A review. *Police Practice and Research: An International Journal*, 20(6), 537–551. https://doi.org/10.1080/15614263.2019.1657625

Nutley, S. M., Walter, I., & Davies, H. T. (2007). *Using Evidence: How Research can Inform Public Services*. Bristol: Policy Press.

Ogborne, A. C., Wild, T. C., Braun, K., & Newton-Taylor, B. (1998). Measuring treatment process beliefs among staff of specialized addiction treatment services. *Journal of Substance Abuse Treatment*, 15(4), 301–312. https://doi.org/10.1016/S0740-5472(97)00196-7

Paoline, E. A., Terrill, W., & Rossler, M. T. (2015). Higher education, college degree major, and police occupational attitudes. *Journal of Criminal Justice Education*, 26(1), 49–73. https://doi.org/10.1080/1051 1253.2014.923010

Pascarella, E. T., & Terenzini, P. T. (2005). *How College Affects Students: A Third Decade of Research. Volume 2*. San Francisco, CA: Jossey-Bass.

Pawson, R., & Tilley, N. (1997). *Realistic evaluation*. Thousand Oaks, CA: Sage.

Prokos, A., & Padavic, I. (2002). 'There oughtta be a law against bitches': Masculinity lessons in police academy training. *Gender, Work & Organization*, 9(4), 439–459. https://doi.org/10.1111/1468-0432.00168

Reaves, B. A. (2015). *Local Police Departments, 2013: Personnel, Policies, and Practices*. U.S. Department of Justice, Office of Justice Programs, Bureau of Justice Statistics.

Rojek, J., Shjarback, J. A., Hansen, J. A., & Alpert, G. P. (2019). Present but not prevalent: Identifying the organizational correlates of researcher-practitioner partnerships in US Law Enforcement. *Police Practice and Research*, 20(6), 552–566. https://doi.org/10.1080/15614263.2019.1657626

Rojek, J., Smith, H. P., & Alpert, G. P. (2012). The prevalence and characteristics of police practitioner–researcher partnerships. *Police Quarterly*, 15(3), 241–261. https://doi.org/10.1177/1098611112440698

Rosenbaum, D. P., Schuck, A. M., & Cordner, G. (2011). *The National Police Research Platform: The Life Course of New Officers*. U.S. Department of Justice, National Institute of Justice.

Rosenbaum, D. P., Yeh, S., & Wilkinson, D. L. (1994). Impact of community policing on police personnel: A quasi-experimental test. *Crime & Delinquency*, 40(3), 331–353. https://doi.org/10.1177/0011128794040003003

Sherman, L. (1998). *Evidence-based policing*. Ideas in American Policing. Washington, DC: Police Foundation.

Sherman, L. W. (2013). The rise of evidence-based policing: Targeting, testing, and tracking. *Crime and Justice*, *42*(1), 377–451. https://doi.org/10.1086/670819

Shernock, S. K. (1992). The effects of college education on professional attitudes among police. *Journal of Criminal Justice Education*, *3*(1), 71–92. https://doi.org/10.1080/10511259200082531

Skogan, W. G., Van Craen, M., & Hennessy, C. (2015). Training police for procedural justice. *Journal of Experimental Criminology*, *11*(3), 319–334. https://doi.org/10.1007/s11292-014-9223-6

Sun, I. Y. (2003). Police officers' attitudes toward their role and work: A comparison of black and white officers. *American Journal of Criminal Justice*, *28*(1), 89–108. https://doi.org/10.1007/BF02885754

Telep, C. W., & Lum, C. (2014a). The receptivity of officers to empirical research and evidence-based policing: An examination of survey data from three agencies. *Police Quarterly*, *17*(4), 359–385. https://doi.org/10.1177/1098611114548099

Telep, C. W., & Lum, C. (2014b, February). *The Impact of Departmental and Officer Characteristics on Receptivity to Research and Evidence-based Policing*. Philadelphia, PA: Academy of Criminal Justice Sciences.

Telep, C. W. (2016). Expanding the scope of evidence-based policing. *Criminology & Public Policy*, *15*, 243. https://doi.org/10.1111/1745-9133.12188

Telep, C. W. (2017). Police officer receptivity to research and evidence-based policing: Examining variability within and across agencies. *Crime & Delinquency*, *63*(8), 976–999. https://doi.org/10.1177/0011128716642253

Thacher, D. (2008). Research for the front lines. *Policing & Society*, *18*(1), 46–59. https://doi.org/10.1080/10439460701718567

Tonry, M., & Green, D. (2003). Criminology and public policy in the USA and UK. In L. Zedner & A. Ashworth (Eds.), *The Criminological Foundations of Penal Policy – Essays in Honour of Roger Hood* (pp. 485–525). Oxford, Clarendon: Oxford University Press.

Van Maanen, J. (1975). Police socialization: A longitudinal examination of job attitudes in an urban police department. *Administrative Science Quarterly*, *20*(2), 207–228. https://doi.org/10.2307/2391695

Weisburd, D., Greenspan, R., Hamilton, E. E., Bryant, K. A., & Williams, H. (2001). *The Abuse of Police Authority: A National Study of Police Officers' Attitudes*. Washington, DC: Police Foundation.

Wolfe, S. E., McLean, K., Rojek, J., Alpert, G. P., & Smith, M. R. (2019). Advancing a theory of police officer training motivation and receptivity. *Justice Quarterly*, 1–23. https://doi.org/10.1080/07418825.2019.1703027

Appendix

Regression tables provide regression coefficients and t scores for the attitudinal components.

TABLE 8.A Predictors of research receptivity attitudes

	Beginning of Training		End of Training	
	Education Support $R^2 = .277$	Balance Research and Experience $R^2 = .014$	Education Support $R^2 = .23$	Balance Research and Experience $R^2 = .05$
Age	−.009 (−1.16)	−.0003 (−.05)	−.009 (−1.00)	.0007 (.1)
Male	.067 (.68)	−.051 (−.61)	.095 (.83)	−.149 (−1.71)
Minority	.122 (1.42)	.105 (1.44)	.214 (2.18)★	.034 (.41)
Prior Sworn	−.139 (−1.15)	−.056 (−.51)	−.156 (−1.20)	−.166 (−1.58)
Military	.045 (.47)	−.079 (−.98)	.161 (1.62)	−.048 (−.56)
Education	.378 (12.11)★★	.023 (.81)	.371 (10.78)★★	.076 (2.59)★
Academy	.005 (.07)	−.027 (−.39)	−.046 (−.51)	.135 (1.83)

★ $p < .05$;
★★ $p < .01$;
★★★ $p < .001$

TABLE 8.B Predictors of proactivity attitudes: Beginning of training

	Beginning of Training	End of Training
	Proactivity $R^2 = .012$	Proactivity $R^2 = .04$
Age	−.000 (−.06)	−.002 (−.53)
Male	−.03 (−.88)	−.018 (−.4)
Minority	.031 (.68)	.095 (2.05)★
Prior Sworn	−.014 (−.32)	−.028 (−.45)
Military	.002 (.05)	.043 (.87)
Education	−.002 (−.14)	−.021 (−1.28)
Academy	−.060 (−1.69)	−.143 (−3.68)★★

★ $p < .05$;
★★ $p < .01$;
★★★ $p < .001$

TABLE 8.C Predictors of communication attitudes

	Beginning of Training			End of Training		
	Communication Skills $R^2 = .024$	Empathy $R^2 = .018$	Withholding $R^2 = .011$	Communication Skills $R^2 = .03$	Empathy $R^2 = .06$	Withholding $R^2 = .03$
Age	.005 (.80)	.006 (1.15)	.012 (1.73)	.006 (1.04)	.004 (.70)	.005 (.60)
Male	.005 (.08)	−.091 (−1.38)	.026 (.31)	.073 (1.07)	−.101 (−1.61)	.038 (.44)
Minority	.014 (.23)	.087 (1.54)	−.0611 (−.79)	.049 (.74)	.179 (2.89)★★	−.053 (−.59)
Prior Sworn	.122 (1.63)	−.009 (−.13)	−.018 (−.17)	.145 (1.8)	−.077 (−.88)	−.191 (−1.62)
Military	.129 (1.92)	−.040 (−.62)	−.051 (−.65)	.125 (1.83)	.074 (1.07)	−.026 (−.26)
Education	.009 (.39)	.015 (.80)	.027 (1.05)	.006 (.28)	.052 (2.13)★	.067 (2.19)★
Academy	.037 (.68)	−.009 (−.19)	.023 (.34)	−.045 (−.78)	−.124 (−2.32)★	−.103 (−1.40)

★ $p < .05$;
★★ $p < .01$;
★★★ $p < .001$

TABLE 8.D Predictors of low cynicism attitudes

	Beginning of Training		End of Training	
	Community Relations $R^2 = .08$	Us Vs. Them $R^2 = .07$	Community Relations $R^2 = .13$	Us Vs. Them $R^2 = .02$
Age	.027 (4.14)★★	.015 (1.91)	.036 (7.21)★★	.011 (1.49)
Male	.141 (2.18)★	−.044 (−.55)	.031 (.43)	.009 (.11)
Minority	.012 (.17)	.240 (2.92)★★	−.079 (−1.14)	.129 (1.57)
Prior Sworn	−.300 (−3.42)★★	−.185 (−1.82)	−.179 (−1.96)	−.266 (−2.51)★
Military	−.046 (−.66)	.032 (.37)	−.028 (−.41)	.054 (.59)
Education	.011 (.46)	−.0638 (−2.33)★	−.020 (−.79)	−.048 (−1.70)
Academy	−.069 (−1.2)	.048 (.68)	−.258 (−4.15)★★	.003 (.04)

★ $p < .05$;
★★ $p < .01$;
★★★ $p < .001$

TABLE 8.E Predictors of community/civilian relations attitudes

	Beginning of Training				End of Training			
	Obtaining Compliance $R^2 = .004$	Professionalism $R^2 = .02$	Customer Service $R^2 = .03$	Congenial $R^2 = .02$	Obtaining Compliance $R^2 = .04$	Professionalism $R^2 = .03$	Customer Service $R^2 = .05$	Congenial $R^2 = .05$
Age	.001 (.14)	.009 (1.61)	-.002 (-.55)	.002 (.36)	-.008 (-1.33)	.004 (.64)	-.002 (-.44)	-.004 (-.66)
Male	-.041 (-.43)	-.021 (-.29)	-.025 (-.52)	.141 (1.68)	.047 (.55)	.056 (.69)	-.082 (-1.82)	.063 (.76)
Minority	-.030 (-.38)	.003 (.05)	.075 (1.79)	-.101 (-1.27)	.124 (1.70)	.190 (2.64)**	.111 (2.65)**	-.112 (-1.44)
Prior Sworn	-.044 (-.43)	-.138 (-1.46)	-.081 (-1.43)	.028 (.28)	.043 (.45)	.051 (.51)	-.028 (-.46)	-.142 (-1.25)
Military	-.024 (-.27)	-.146 (-1.99)*	.044 (1.01)	.031 (.38)	-.027 (-.33)	-.024 (-.30)	.035 (.75)	-.142 (-1.25)
Education	.021 (.73)	-.009 (-.41)	-.034 (-2.19)*	.0002 (.01)	.044 (1.63)	.028 (1.05)	-.035 (-2.11)*	.011 (.39)
Academy	-.014 (-.18)	-.019 (-.32)	-.008 (-.23)	-.006 (-.09)	-.184 (-2.66)**	-.018 (-.27)	-.108 (-2.76)**	-.244 (-3.46)**

* $p < .05$;
** $p < .01$;
*** $p < .001$

9

Partnerships and Pitfalls

Insights from an Incomplete Evaluation of Police Training

Anne Li Kringen

Henry C. Lee College of Criminal Justice and Forensic Sciences, University of New Haven, West Haven, CT, USA

Eve Stephens

Austin Police Department, Austin, TX, USA

A common theme of discussion among criminal justice academics is the need for more evaluation work conducted in partnership with police organizations. Several processes and practices demand evaluation to render evidence to guide what departments should do to address problems facing modern policing. Among evidence-based policing advocates, agreement largely exists that substantially more evaluation is needed. This view reflects the understanding that many issues in policing remain unstudied, and, of the issues that have been studied, there are few that have been studied in depth. Moreover, even when research about a topic is available, given the jurisdictional nature of U.S. policing, local validation is still necessary when the strategies are employed in new departments. What works well in one jurisdiction simply may not work well in another.

Lack of agency interest in partnering with researchers is often discussed as a reason why more evaluation work is not conducted. It is unclear whether this assertion is correct; many well-known policing scholars manage multiple ongoing evaluations simultaneously across several departments. Another key issue, perhaps more impactful, is the substantial transactional cost associated with managing projects within police departments. A considerable amount of time working on research within a department is spent navigating the complexity of the organization and engaging in the interpersonal elements required to build and maintain the trust necessary to make working together successful.

Even with a substantial investment of time, many well-intentioned evaluations – including projects involving an excited researcher, a committed department, and, perhaps, even funding – fail to render meaningful evidence related to the initial line of inquiry. Common obstacles include projects getting sidelined or halted due to personnel changes within the department or projects experiencing implementation challenges that simply cannot be overcome. Personnel changes can be particularly tough; contacts within a department can change roles through promotion and reassignment. After a staffing change, replacement personnel may have very different views about research. As well, executive changes may alter the department's willingness to continue altogether. Many projects have been halted when a chief resigns and a replacement chief takes over the organization.

DOI: 10.4324/9781003153009-12

Implementation challenges do not always result in a project being terminated altogether. Yet, roadblocks may result in the research completing a substantially different project than was originally planned. Changes made within the department during the evaluation or alteration of the evaluation schedule can raise validity issues such as lack of fidelity, treatment diffusion, and potential history effects. While reports are typically written summarizing these evaluations providing some insight, the results of these efforts are generally less informative than the original plan would have been.

Given the challenges, researchers must ask themselves whether conducting evaluation works within police departments is worth the effort. Academic considerations, such as the substantial time commitment required to develop a single article from an evaluation project and potential that a project renders non-publishable findings, definitely play into the decision whether to work within departments or to choose another approach such as working with secondary data collected from police agencies. Still, many researchers believe in the value of in-agency evaluations. The results from these in-agency evaluations can be substantially more informative, often including important process details that studies conducted on secondary data alone cannot.

When an evaluation project fails, the outcome evaluation is typically substantially impacted. Given that many fundamental questions about what should be done in policing relate to outcomes, it can be easy to see this loss as complete. However, at times even failed evaluation projects effort can render valuable, albeit different, findings. Insights gleaned from other components of the overall evaluation, in particular, those uncovered through process evaluation, can render discoveries about policing that are informative to criminal justice academics and law enforcement practitioners alike. This chapter describes one such "failed" evaluation, the evaluation of a mentoring program for female cadets implemented in the APD's training academy. For reasons beyond the control of the research team and the department itself, the overall project was not completed. As a result, no conclusions can be drawn about the impact of the mentoring program; however, key insights into elements of both the mentoring program and female cadets' experiences in the academy were still unearthed.

An Ideal Start

In 2016, a lieutenant working at APD's training academy began tracking the attrition rate for female cadets. As part of the process, the lieutenant reviewed information from previous academy classes. Noting that the female academy attrition rate was approximately double the attrition rate for male cadets, the lieutenant began investigating programs that might be implemented at the academy to reduce attrition among female cadets. Unfortunately, there was only limited information available to the department on strategies that might help. What the lieutenant did find were recommendations from other departments suggesting that a mentoring plan might be helpful. Based on this information and information about mentoring women in other fields, the lieutenant designed a mentoring program for female cadets.

The mentoring program was adopted as part of APD's 140th cadet class in 2019, and the first cohort of female cadets to participate in the mentoring program entered the academy. The plan attempted to provide support to female cadets by providing female cadets with mentorship from more senior female officers within the department. The goal was to provide guidance, encouragement, and assistance to female cadets as they navigated the various complexities they might face in the academy. Despite high hopes, the mentoring program was not successful at reducing female attrition. Of the 17 women who began the 140th academy class, only four graduated. To understand why the program failed, the lieutenant partnered with an academic researcher, and the process of designing an evaluation strategy began. Working together, an evaluation plan and schedule were developed.

The research plan was ambitious. A research team was assembled that would collect data from the second, third, and fourth cohorts in the mentoring program as well as collect data from two academy classes where the mentorship program would not be offered. The data collection would involve pre and post surveys measuring a variety of personality, attitudinal, and situation factors for all cadets. The research team would also conduct extensive interviews with cadets throughout their time in the academy. The research plan involved interviewing female cadets prior to starting the academy and all cadets who left the academy before completing training. In addition, the research team would interview the female officers working as mentors as well as training staff at the academy. Finally, direct observation of training would be conducted to provide the context of cadets' initial experiences in the academy.

The initial evaluation started in June of 2019 with Austin's 141st academy class. The class included the second cohort of female cadets participating in the mentoring program. By January of 2020, the data from the initial class had been collected. Initial evaluation of the data began in preparation for the next academy class scheduled for evaluation, and both the research team and the department were optimistic. Over multiple academy classes, adequate data would be collected to help guide in developing the mentoring program into a program that might possibly help the department graduate more female cadets.

An Academy on Hold

The research team prepared to resume data collection from the 144th academy class, which was originally scheduled to start in June 2020.[1] As plans to continue work were finalized, the timeline changed. Expressing concerns over inadequate anti-bias and cultural sensitivity training in the academy curriculum, the City of Austin delayed the 144th academy class by 30 days. The research team adjusted their schedule and continued preparations. However, before the 30 days had past, Austin City Council passed Resolution 20191205-066. The resolution ordered the city to engage in several processes to address concerns about systemic racism and the disproportionate impact of policing, including use of force, on Austin's African American and Latino communities.

Among other things, the proposition mandated an external audit of the department and the training academy. As well, all training for new cadets was suspended until the audit had been performed and the training curriculum had been revised to address the concerns. Evaluation of the second cohort of female cadets in the 144th academy class was placed on hold, and, at the time of writing this analysis, the class had yet to commence.[2] While technically the evaluation plan is on hold, awaiting results from the audit and an evaluation of redeveloped curriculum, the training academy will be substantially changed when it admits the next group of cadets. As such, the history effect resulting from the curriculum overhaul and substantial changes to the academy's training processes renders the original evaluation plan and the data collected from the 141st academy class moot.[3]

"Evaluation" and "Results"

The data collected from the 141st academy class were insufficient to conduct a meaningful analysis of the impact of the mentoring program on female cadet attrition. In total, 71 cadets entered the academy. Of those, 68 agreed to take part in at least some part of the evaluation. Twenty-three members of the class were women (32.3% of cadets in the class; 33.8% of participants).

Initial analysis began by analyzing the pre-test survey, which was collected two weeks into the academy. Sixty-eight cadets responded to the survey (95.8%). Female cadets reported significantly lower levels of a sense of belonging within the organization (Smith, Lewis, Hawthorne, & Hodges, 2013). Regarding academy staff, female cadets reported significantly lower levels of comfort with instructors, belief that the instructors were good communicators, belief that the relationships between instructors and cadets were genuine, and belief that instructors facilitate individual development. As well, female cadets reported significantly lower levels of self-efficacy (Schwarzer & Jerusalem, 2010; Chen, Gully, & Eden, 2004) and significantly lower levels of belief in their ability to deal with pressure (Smith Schultz, Smoll & Ptacek, 1995).

Part of the overall design of the evaluation involved collecting these and other survey measures near the beginning of all academy classes being evaluated starting with the 141st. After collecting data from multiple classes, the research team would have adequate statistical power to estimate the impact of the mentoring program on female cadets controlling for personality, attitudes and beliefs, perceptions of the academy, and experiences during the academy. A variety of analyses were planned for the data, including models that predicted the impact of mentoring on completion as well as the impact of mentoring on changes in attitudes or perceptions that occurred between the time the academy began and ended. Without collecting data from the subsequent classes, none of these plans are possible.

The inability to move forward as planned rendered the outcome evaluation void. However, the process evaluation components, including interviews with cadets, mentors, and training staff, provide substantial detail into how the mentoring program functioned and challenges to implementation that arose. This information is likely useful to practitioners and researchers. For practitioners, it outlines a series of relevant issues related to how to design and implement mentoring programs. As such, it provides a starting place to begin consideration. While the information cannot answer questions related to which choices are correct, it can render a roadmap to help project designers make choices in advance to address similar pitfalls. As well, the insights may be of value to academics studying police training, since the details provide a glimpse into the internal dynamics in academy training from the perspective of the cadets, outside observers (i.e., the mentors), and academy instructors. As well, the issues that were discovered might serve as a useful guide for the implementation of training programs other than mentoring. The concerns that were raised and the challenges that impacted the program are likely important considerations for implementing and evaluating any type of training academy program. This value may be important for both practitioners and academics alike.

Interviews and Insights

Three different groups were interviewed for the evaluation of the 141st training academy: cadets, mentors, and instructors. While the initial questions differed between groups, all three groups were interviewed using a semi-structured interview protocol. This increased the likelihood that information obtained from the interviews would be comparable while allowing the interviews to move in unforeseen directions to explore attitudes, beliefs, and experiences more generally from individuals with all groups.

The interviews were confidential and took place in different locations. Cadet interviews were conducted offsite at various coffee shops. Instructor interviews were conducted at the academy, and mentor interviews were conducted both in mentors' offices within the department and offsite. The interviews were digitally recorded and transcribed for analysis.

Cadets

In total, 17 of the 23 female cadets that completed the initial survey agreed to be contacted about an interview. Of those, 14 participated in the interviews (82.4% response rate, 60.9% of female cadets). On average, the cadet interviews lasted 26 minutes with the longest interview being 61 minutes and the shortest being 9. Cadets were asked about their decisions to join the department, their expectations for the academy, concerns about starting the academy or a career in policing, and questions about mentoring. The mentoring questions included questions about experiences with previous mentoring, expectations for mentoring in the academy, and experiences with their academy mentor. Additionally, they were asked about prior law enforcement or military experience, whether they had friends or family in law enforcement or APD, and their educational backgrounds. Finally, they were asked to verify their demographic information including race/ethnicity and age.

Mentors

Out of 14 mentors, 7 agreed to be interviewed (50%). The mentor interviews were longer than the cadet interviews with an average of 35 minutes. Mentors discussed experiences with their mentees and expectations for themselves as mentors. As well, they discussed whether they ever received any mentoring in their careers, barriers to success they believed that women in the department face, and perceived changes in attitudes over their careers. In addition, mentors detailed their service within the department including length and assignments. Finally, they discussed their backgrounds including military experience, law enforcement experience prior to APD, educational background, and their demographics including race/ethnicity and age.

Instructors

Twelve instructors were asked to participate in interviews, and 8 instructors agreed to participate (67%). On average the instructor interviews were the longest with an average of 47 minutes. Instructors were asked about their perceptions of working at the academy including challenges faced by instructors and recent changes. As well, they were asked about training methods and challenges faced by cadets. Finally, like the mentors, they discussed their backgrounds including time as an instructor, military experience, law enforcement experience prior to APD, educational background, and their demographics including race/ethnicity and age.

Procedure

As previously noted, no outcome evaluation was possible; however, for context, in total 6 female recruits did not complete the 141st academy representing a passing rate of 73.9%. This compares to a male passing rate of 83.3% for the same class. Female cadets who did not complete the academy left for a variety of reasons including injuries, unsuccessful academic or training performance, and depression brought on by the physical demands of the training.

While the outcome evaluation is largely uninformative, the interview responses provided a unique capacity to triangulate the training process and cadets' experiences and perceptions of training and the academy instructors. The qualitative analysis of the interview data was completed using an indictive analytic coding strategy followed by an interpretative phenomenological analysis (IPA) framework to explore experiences and isolate themes that represent the core commonalties within experiences (Charmaz, 2014; Smith, 2004; Starks & Brown-Trinidad, 2007).

Findings

The interview data demonstrate that female cadets expressed concerns about aspects of the academy that worried them prior to starting. These related to all areas of the academy, but physical test (PT) was a common concern.

CADET: I expect it to be absolutely horrible for an extended amount of time and then for it to get better. I expect to excel academically, I'm going to have to study a lot, but that I can handle [that]. I am nervous about PT, and I'm nervous about driving.

Mentors were aware of these types of concerns and tried to provide various forms of support.

MENTOR: I really stress the fact that they're going to get tested physically. And it is because you're a female. And that's just the way it is. And they want to see how you hold up in a fight. And the key is just to never stop.

Cadets and mentors communicated through a variety of methods. Although some cadets preferred certain modes of communication, they generally expressed that the contact made them feel comfortable initiating contact with or responding to their mentor.

CADET: Right, yeah, a text or an email. But I mean, if she ever called me, I would never not answer her call.
CADET: She texted me and just kind of like, "Hey, my name is [NAME], I'm your mentor." It was kind of a quick, simple, which I was expecting a call, or a meeting in person. But we just texted back and forth.
CADET: I think texting or calling. I'm a phone call, I like talking on the phone. I think it's more personal, so I'd probably call her if I had anything.
CADET: So, she reached out to me, she left me a voicemail. I listened to that and she let me know that I could call her back and things like that. I did. We spoke initially on the phone where she kind of explained who she was. But since then, we've communicated via text.

Some cadets met their mentors personally either at a group event or one-on-one.

CADET: Well, we had a mentor luncheon about two weeks ago. It was myself and another cadet who's in the program. So we all went to lunch, and we were just talking about... She said, basically, "I'm here for you." So if you have any questions, ask her, she'll let us know what she can let us know. So it was really just authentic casual conversation.
CADET: So, it's been mostly text and she'll just randomly like pop in, be like, "Hey, are you feeling?"

While these encounters were valuable, they were challenging given the academy schedule. As well, meetings occurring when other academy activities were scheduled resulted in an irregular schedule for some cadets, and instructors worried other cadets would perceive this as special treatment.

INSTRUCTOR: The times that I did see a mentor here, it was like between breaks, which [are] 10 to 15 minutes, and then they have to be back in class. I'd rather see it on lunch or right after the academy being done. The breaks are their breaks. They need to, especially being a female, you need take off all your gear, go to the bathroom, and that takes 15 minutes in itself sometimes.
INSTRUCTOR: [A problem was mentors] dictating when there are interactions... We have had lieutenants popping in, and so we'd leave to lunch and suddenly there's a lieutenant at the door saying, "Hey, I want to talk and pop in," and they would pop in and pull out this one cadet on their off time. To me, once again, the perception of bias or anything like that, that's hard for me to explain away.

Need for relationships while in the academy: Female cadets expressed that they made friends while in the academy. As well, they expressed the need for these new relationships within the academy.

CADET: Whether it was through a type of workout program or just getting to know somebody as I went through the hiring process, and then also two of the female former cadets that are now officers, two of the four that graduated last semester, became close friends of mine.

CADET: This class has the most amount of females I think that they've ever had really starting out. Which is great. And we have a Facebook group, like a chat. I'm not very Facebook savvy. I basically have it just for this. We have a group with our entire class and we've got like a chat room with just the females which is awesome. Because we're here to support each other.

CADET: …which sucks, It'd be nice to not be completely alone.

Mentors noted that relationships within the department were important since relationships outside the department could be difficult during the academy.

MENTOR: But yeah, you've got to keep them strong, because it can be depressing. No one wants to date me. Nobody wants to be with me. All these other women are getting married now I'm not getting married. Just to help them out to get their careers going.

Relationships with other female cadets were valued, but the relationships with mentors carried a distinct value.

CADET: I like having the mentor because [having other female cadets in your class is] just not enough, like just having the other female support. Because they're also just as lost as I am. It's great to have each other. But having the mentor is I feel invaluable due only to the fact that she's done it. She's been through it. She's probably been through it actually worse than me due to the fact that Chief [NAME] kind of changed things up from less of a military craziness.

Most cadets connected well with their mentors.

CADET: Yeah, I've texted with [name], yeah, with [my mentor], I like her a lot.

Sometimes this resulted from the mentors selecting cadets that they thought they could connect with.

MENTOR: And I think I actually read her background history statement. I was like, "Oh, she seems cool. Maybe we have something in common." So I [asked], "Hey, I would like to be partnered up, or I would like to mentor her."

However, this was not always the case. Some cadets expressed a mismatch between themselves and their mentors.

CADET: And I think that the way that my mentor talked to me would work great for someone 12 years younger than me, but I was a different person 12 years ago. Oh, my God, I was different 12 years ago.

CADET: I'd rather have been matched with someone who knows how to talk to, that knows how to mentor an adult [rather] than [another] black person. You know what I mean?

CADET: I think I would rather [have had a different mentor], I mean, for me personally, and I'm an intellectual, I've had a full-time job for a very long time, I mean, I have such different values. There are so many different things that are important to me at this stage in my life.

Expectations for mentors: Cadets typically did not expect a substantial amount of contact with their mentors.

CADET: Probably once every two weeks or so, and it doesn't have to be long, doesn't have to be face to face, it could just be a quick email, just like, "How you doing? Everything good? You need anything?" Just very short, casual.

CADET: So, that's the one thing is for her to just kind of, if she hasn't heard from me, just be like, "Hey."

Still, some cadets expressed a sense that more contact might have been helpful.

CADET: I know it's through text message, FaceTime, phone calls. Honestly, I guess whatever works best between myself and my mentor. I'm not mistaken, it's two hours a month, so to speak, but honestly, I think that [we could] communicate more than that.

In contrast, mentors noted that they sometimes delayed contacting their mentees because they did not want to be overbearing or become a burden for cadets.

MENTOR: [My mentee] reached out to me yesterday. I was super excited, but I've been sitting here on pins and needles trying not to reach out, because I wanted to give them at least a week, send you a congratulatory email, "Woo hoo, you made it through week one," before I reached out. But I was like, I'm so glad you contacted me... But I'm waiting until after the end of close of business at 4:00 on Friday, tomorrow, before I say, "Okay, ladies, how'd we do?" So, just giving them some breathing room. I'm trying not to be a pest. I don't want it to be an additional burden to have this mentor. You've got this old lady who just keeps making them feel obligated to followup because [of my rank].

Cadets generally expressed a desire for mentors to support them, and providing help and encouragement was important. Having someone of higher rank providing these things was seen as meaningful.

CADET: So I mean, I know that she's there to help and encourage. Sometimes hearing from outsider is good. When I say outsider, I mean outside of our own [academy class]. So hearing from somebody else and hearing a separate perspective. I think it's beneficial, because sometimes we see things and it's not really what we see. It's like, no, like you're looking at it this way, but that's not really what it is. So I think that second voice is going to be key.

CADET: We're [not] on the same playing field, because she is a senior officer and I'm just brand new. But she doesn't make me feel like that. Which is awesome. I think that's huge too. Having someone because [being a cadet at] the academy is different; you are the lowest part on the pole during the academy.

Mentors indicated supporting cadets in a variety of ways. Sometimes it was advice or providing opportunities to the mentees. This could include letting cadets know that others had been where they were or working to instill confidence in the cadets.

MENTOR: And I have a lot of knowledge on that area. I want to see them be successful. And so you try to give them advice, just to make sure that their path is... because no one did that when I came through. I just had to figure it out for myself. And feel like if I can give a tips here and there, and they go on to have a successful career, then that's rewarding.

MENTOR: I give advice. I help out the new cadets. If they're struggling, because we've all been there.

MENTOR: I think it was the opportunities, advice, but I think one of the biggest things is instilling confidence.

MENTOR: …to keep them positively motivated about being there. To tell them, "Good job." To praise them. To direct them if they're having any issues to somebody that can help them if I can't. Just give them the perspective of somebody that's been there already and you will get through this kind of thing.

At times, cadets believed this helped them process their own doubts.

CADET: She mentored somebody in the previous class, and she gave me some words from that person that graduated. Like, "Hey, here's some words from her, that may help you for the academy. When you're thinking about why, just reflect back to those words." That was helpful. Just to have somebody that already went through it, the doubts she had, everything that she still made up. Just some words of encouragement.

Other times cadets discussed a desire that the relationship with their mentor continue after the academy.

CADET: I know I told her I would call her after the first week, let her know how everything went. I think that's good just to keep in touch with her, especially during big things. Like, "Hey, I finished the first week, these were, this is what happened. These are my concerns."
CADET: I mean, for me personally, I hope that most of us will still be able… because I know it'll go through the academy and through FTO period, and then it ends after that, but it would be nice to be able to still go to that person even if it's two years from now, if we need a question from them or something that we can still go to them and ask them that question. So it would be nice to be able to not necessarily be like, "Oh, we're best friends," but just to have that communication still open after the whole thing has been done with.
CADET: I mean, I think that she will always be someone that I look back on and [recognize that she] supported me. And I think [our relationship will] be ongoing, but maybe not, like a once in a while stay in touch.

Some mentors also discussed continuing relationships as well as developing female officers that would do the same for other cadets in the future.

MENTOR: I guess I don't like to use the word role model, but just something where they can have some kind of safe person to outreach to, maybe get advice from, and we can have a personal relationship, and they can carry that forward.

Instructors also saw themselves as a resource for cadets.

INSTRUCTOR: But along with that, we meet with [cadets] periodically throughout the academy and we talk to them. We get to know them, try to figure out what kind of person they are and basically build a relationship with them. And we are kind of like, the officer that I was talking to earlier, where he said, we're kind of their mentor in a sense. We are their professional guide.
INSTRUCTOR: [Cadets] come to [instructors] with any issues, anything at all. If they get pulled over or something, they ended up in the hospital, whatever the case, they contact you first and you deal with it. If it's something that's out of your hands, then you actually go to your supervisor.

Despite instructors' views about their roles, cadets indicated that there were several issues they might not want to talk to academy staff about. Sometimes this was a practical consideration.

CADET: If you get injured, you're really in a tough spot because you want to report your injury because you need to get treatment, but you also make yourself a target for essentially workplace discrimination.

Other times, cadets expressed that they might not want to talk to instructors because of the environment and a lack of willingness on the part of instructors to acknowledge that some issues in the academy were viewed by cadets as substantial problems.

CADET: [Cadets] wanted [instructors] to be like, "Okay, this is going to be hard for you, but I'm going to get you through it." And then what [cadets are] hearing is like, "Oh my god, this is really bad. But let me just try to steer them towards sticking it out anyway." And [cadets] are like, "No. What I'm telling you is egregiously bad."

CADET: Had I even stopped and said, I need to get some water or I have a question, I would have been berated… That was the atmosphere all day and everything about that to me is wrong.

Some mentors acknowledged similar concerns.

MENTOR: Because [cadets] can't talk to [instructors] because there are the repercussions from that and retaliation. And so, I think a lot of [the mentees] would talk about it when they felt a little more comfortable talking to us, like we weren't going to say anything.

This was also related to a perception that instructors often took no action when cadets raised concerns.

CADET: I think if someone tells you something that you know to be misconduct, you have to act on it. And it felt like they were being told things that probably at least at a base level needed to be looked into. And then, I don't know what… Nothing happened. And it's like, "How am I ever supposed to trust you if you don't act on that information?"

The communication issues noted between cadets and instructors were important in understanding why cadets felt more comfortable talking with mentors who made the cadets feel more at ease.

CADET: She sent me an email once so that I'd have her contact info. It's like her personal email address. That way it's just between the two of us and not on the department thing, but yeah.

CADET: [Without my mentor] there would have been no one else for me to call and say I had a problem because I didn't trust anyone. None of the ICS, no one to say, I have concerns about this and I just want to talk to someone and have my questions answered. I felt so threatened.

Mentors seemed aware of the need to make cadets feel comfortable. Often, they would note that their mentorship was personnel and for providing support; mentoring was not about reporting issues. However, managing conflict between obligations to mentees and to the organization could be challenging.

MENTOR: I'm there [to provide] support and encouragement. Understanding, because the training academy [is difficult], I do understand I make sure they know, I'm not here to run stuff up your chain. I'm not here to raise the flag for you.

MENTOR: We weren't to really direct them on what they should do. We can just provide them advice on maybe different outcomes of this route versus the outcome of taking this route and let them make their own decision. Again, because it was a voluntary program, we didn't want anything that we said to be perceived as an order. Navigating that was really tricky.

After establishing boundaries and developing a relationship, the mentoring support could address things that policies could not like interpreting rules.

MENTOR: And so, just having those… Her feeling comfortable enough to take a picture of her hair at the hairdresser and say, "Hey, is this a go?" That's fantastic because it gives her peace of mind. But it also shows that she's taking the initiative to address it prior to it being a problem.

MENTOR: Sure, one of them asked me a question about some policy things and she wasn't sure if she could continue to do… Well, she volunteers with alcohol and AA. We have a policy about getting around known felons when they're not family members. So she asked me a question about that, which I didn't know the answer to. So I directed her to somebody that would know it.

Some cadets noted that they perceived instructors as not being supportive of the mentoring program.

CADET: Which was, I think, another thing that might've ruffled feathers in the sense that I think in previous cadet classes, you had your IC and your IC was supposed to be your first point of contact for concerns, questions and things you were concerned with especially if you either wanted to stay or leave or talk things out. And now they weren't.

Some instructors clarified that they thought mentorship was important but that the academy was the wrong time to introduce an outside influence.

INSTRUCTOR: I think a mentoring group at this stage can be detrimental.

INSTRUCTOR: Mentoring is a great idea. Everybody should have one way down the line, that's where I want to be one day, or at least in that direction. But as a cadet, I think it's too much. And the potential is that the information that they're getting from someone 10, 15 years down the road doesn't really apply in the academy because the academy that they went through is not the academy that they are going through.

Instructors even noted that at times they believed that mentors were sending contradictory messages to mentees.

INSTRUCTOR: Then you have [mentors] downplaying the instructors, saying, "Well, you're not always going to get into a fight every day." Well, yes. We don't tell them. Could you potentially be in a fight every day? Sure. Are you really? No. It's just preparing them for that worst-case scenario. It felt like there was a lot of undermining with the last group, and we don't know what kind of training or conversation happened when they had that first group.

However, other instructors believed that the mentoring program was valuable.

INSTRUCTOR: This is where I think a mentorship program is awesome. You can come in, because here I am, a male that was just yelling at her. I can only hope that I was able to bring her back down and dial her in. But if not okay, if she does have another person, especially a female that she's probably going to feel more comfortable with, and I don't know what type of personal issue she may or may not have had with males or in other institutions in her past. There's your opportunity to maybe get a different perspective on it and then put it all together. As opposed to feeling like I got nobody.

Mentors noted that they were aware of potential conflicts and that their role in supporting cadets was distinct from the role of instructors. Further, at least some mentors made sure that mentees understood as well.

MENTOR: Now, by all means, if you tell me something that I believe is a violation of policy or something like that, then I will do my due diligence. But understand, if you have an issue, problem, something that's job-related, you need to take that to your IC for them to address.

MENTOR: I'm here to give you a morale boost, tips, tools, stuff like that, help you out with things, but I am not here for these professional check boxes that you need to do when it comes to your role as a cadet. So, I make it clear with mine that that's what it is, because I understand how there could be crossover, and I respect what [instructors] do.

Notwithstanding these efforts, there were circumstances where the lines between mentoring and chain of command were blurred. Instructors noted resentment about that, considering it a misuse of the mentoring program.

INSTRUCTOR: So, [the mentor] came over commander to commander and [said] this is a problem. And so, it started coming back down, [that an instructor] was going to get removed. So that was a pretty big black eye for the mentoring group when that happened.

INSTRUCTOR: The way that they framed it to the cadets was it's independent, it's outside of the chain of command, it doesn't affect, and so for me, the less I'm aware of it and the less that I know about it, the less I can... I won't be looking for that trying to explain something. If a cadet's having a hard time, I'm not going to be thinking, oh, I can go to their mentor and figure this out.

INSTRUCTOR: Some of it was misused. Some people would call their mentor and be like, "Oh, these officers were yelling at me because my backpack was in the wrong place." That got back to the commander, and commander got upset because that's not what the mentorship program should be. It shouldn't be the cadet calling their mentor and complaining that they got yelled at. It should be the mentor... The Academy is going to be tough with the 32 weeks. I wouldn't say, "Suck it up, buttercup," but for the most part, that's what it is.

Among the female cadets that left the academy, several indicated that their mentor had been an important part of their academy experience and was involved in their decision. After resigning, the mentors at times supported these cadets as they left by offering understanding and sensitivity that others may not have offered.

CADET: And had I stayed in, [my mentor] would have been probably the one thing that would've kept me, I trusted her that I could talk to her and she wouldn't be like, she wouldn't minimize it or judge and say, no, that's not a problem.

CADET: I said like, I still to this day wish that would have played out differently because I think that I could have done the job and all of these things were completely separate from the fact that you have this group of people manipulating and abusing your new hires. Because I talked to [my mentor] on the phone for a while that night and she said, I just really wish that you could have stayed in because I would have loved your perspective on all of this.

CADET: [My mentor and] and other female friends in the department who told me, "Before you decide to quit, call me and I'll talk you through it," and this and that. And then I had to tell them, "Hey, too late. I already did it." But it's what's best for me. And then everybody, at least the women, seemed understanding. It was other men that were like, "Well, why'd you do that?" And "You should've just stuck it out."

Mentors were aware that they might have a substantial role in cadets' decisions to resign, and some noted that they tried to let cadets know that they were available just in case.

MENTOR: And she would always call me and I would always make myself available. I don't care what time of day or night. And she did take me up on that. She had an issue in the cadet class so she called me one evening and I said, "Yeah, I'll call you." It's never a bother to me. I'm always available, because you never know, there could be a difference between them quitting or them staying.

Several cadets offered recommendations to the academy based on their experiences during the class. Cadets noted that the mentoring program was particularly important and recommended continuing it.

CADET: Especially with some folks that didn't understand that this was a game and manipulation. That I think that for those of us that really went in it with a servant's heart and a desire to serve that for us, having that safety net [i.e., a mentor] was invaluable.

CADET: I think [the mentorship program is] one of the few avenues that they have... Because I think through the process of the eight, nine months, [cadets] could [be] pitted against each other in so many ways, and there was infighting and there were so many insecurities...

Although some cadets, including those who appreciated the mentoring program, noted limitations in the program that could be addressed, and that there was more that should be done.

CADET: But [the mentoring program is] also the bare minimum. That like, "Oh, there are police officers looking out for younger ones." This has been going on for a long time, especially if you had family or friends in the department and putting together a formalized program one minor, tiny step in the right direction. But it was clumsy.

Regarding the program, cadets noted that some confusion about whether or not male cadets could request a mentor. Some suggested that several male cadets could have substantially benefited from mentoring as well.

CADET: I had heard that the black men and Latino men were also supposed to have a mentorship program. They were told that they were going to have a mentorship program and to check their emails and then nothing came to fruition. And that was hard on some of them who, I think, needed it and said they needed it and it never came.

MENTOR: I think mentorship needs to be mentorship across the board, not just for females. I think we need the mentorship program period for cadets if they want it, regardless of gender. So, I think that's something I'd like to look at in the future.

But other cadets noted that an opportunity for male cadets to be mentored was clearly articulated to cadets as well as instructors.

CADET: "Hey, we have [a mentoring] program, we're an offering it out to anyone who wants to be a part of it, but it's female officers that would be mentors." And she was very clear that like, this isn't just for the women here. Anyone that wants a mentor can have it.

CADET: Obviously none of the guys signed up. But, it wasn't even a side note offhand comment, it was this is for everyone.

CADET: I knew the instructors knew because [the lieutenant] had come to orientation, and [explained] the program we're doing.

Mentors who were supportive of continuing the mentoring program recommended continued evaluation.

MENTOR: I guess just the concerns were, we had 17 [in a previous class] and we graduated four. So, what are we missing, basically, just maybe something missing in there that you can't see. Maybe we're targeting people incorrectly on the recruiting end. Maybe they want to be social workers, and maybe they just weren't geared for this career in the first place. Or maybe there's something about the way that I mentor or we mentor; maybe we're missing something there. Does there need to be more personal interaction? Do we need more buy in? Maybe there's something we're not seeing or we're missing.

Other administrative issues unrelated to mentoring that cadets found unprofessional or problematic were noted.

CADET: A lot of the cadet have paperwork and instructions that are outdated for some reason. So [other cadets' paperwork says] you need to get this, this, and this. And then I'll have paperwork that says you need this, this and this. And they're like very similar, but you can tell they're different versions. One is from last year and mine is from this year. Or it'll have the wrong address, and mine will have the correct address because the place [cadets need to go to] has moved.

Finally, there were several recommendations related to underlying concerns such as sex, race, and imbalance of power.

CADET: They have to do literally the reading of what it means to fully understand systemic misogyny and how systemic misogyny, systemic sexism, how that can be acted out. The roots of policing and how it relates to white supremacy... It feels like they have never confronted their own history.
CADET: I think power dynamics is something that they're really need to look into because it's all of those things and then it's even worse because these weird power dynamics of the academy to begin with.

Some mentors reiterated similar ideas related to underlying dynamics and personnel at the academy. At times, this centered on race. Other times it was about gender.

MENTOR: [The academy] is not bad. Obviously, the training is really good, and the people out there know what they're doing. I think that there's no diversity out there at the Academy. Does that mean [current instructors] can't teach? No, it just means, I think, that we have a department of 1900 people. Are you telling me that no black officer can be an instructor, or there are no females who can be instructors? Just seems to be kind of a disconnect. We want these percentages [of female and black officers] higher, but then you go out to the academy that's all white males. Something's missing in there.
MENTOR: Now I'm not saying that a black cadet or a female cadet would feel more comfortable or they would get through the process if [there was more diversity] out there, maybe not.
MENTOR: There was one instructor out there who, in a lot of the female mentees' opinions, this was, was very chauvinistic. And he would say, "Hey girl," instead of their name, and he'd make comments about how they weren't physically able to do things and a lot of negativity.

Instructors noted that diversity discussions could be challenging but also indicated a need for more diverse academy classes.

INSTRUCTOR: As far as organizational goes, it can get political here in the Academy when you start talking about things like diversity.
INSTRUCTOR: Because it's already been said, we want more females out here. And I think that's absolutely necessary because, when you're trying to shape a cadet, you need to have

perspectives from every single angle. These cadets, most of them are males obviously, but they're going to be working with women on the street.

At least one mentor did see their role as advocating for diversity beyond participating in the mentoring program.

MENTOR: Not saying you want to be all activist and militant, but you have to be relevant. You have to have your voice heard. If not, you will just be... It'll be the same kind of pattern that I've seen all over the years.

However, instructors did not see issues related to the disparity in attrition as a function of the training academy itself. Instead, they largely saw it as a function of incorrect messaging in recruiting resulting in cadets who were not prepared for the academy or committed to a career in policing.

INSTRUCTOR: I don't think anything that we do here is going to lower the attrition rate. I think it starts outside of the academy and, but this goes against everything that the department is trying to do because what they're trying to do is get more female applicants. Well, how do you get more female applicants by telling them, "Hey, this is going to be very difficult for you and you're going to hear things that you don't want to hear. And you're going to have to look inward and figure out, hey, can you take somebody's life and still be okay the next day and be fine and be able to live your life normal. Or be put in a situation like that, are you going to be able to fight? Are You going to, without scaring them away?"

INSTRUCTOR: So back in the day, and by back in the day, not too long ago, maybe like two years ago, it was realistic, "Hey, this is what police work is. This is what the academy looks like. It's very, very hard. It's going to be very challenging. For the next eight months you are not going to have a life. If you're married with kids, sorry to say, but you're going to have to set them aside for those eight months so that way you can provide for them for the rest of your life and have a great retirement and everything. It's an obstacle you have to go through if you want this." And it was very clear that the academy was absolutely brutal. That you're going to get yelled at, and that you're going to have physical training, you're going to be out there in the heat, in Texas heat, you're going to get into fights.

INSTRUCTOR: But I just think it's important that we get more females. I just don't think that lying to them is going to help in any way, shape or form. Because if you're telling them that this is what it's going to be like, and then they get here and they get something different. Well, I didn't sign up for this shit, is what you're going to get.

Finally, some mentors noted that in their role they noticed other elements of the academy, including rules that should be re-evaluated. Some of these resulted in changes that have already occurred.

MENTOR: Something came up about [a cadet] failing academics, and now we're [at a] critical mass of how many people we've lost... So, I went to the chief and said, "Hey, can we have any conversations about why the people that fail out academically, why are we waiting a year [for them to reapply]?" I said, "We are losing all of that time and money." I said, "If you maybe get them back in the next class, they at least have a fresher memory... and [we] got with the commander of the academy. He was like, "Well, that's just what the rules are." I sent a memo to the chief, and I said, "Can we please reconsider this rule?" I said, they're not leaving because they couldn't cut it physically. They're not leaving because they couldn't cut it mentally. They're able to handle the stressors of the job. They're not leaving because some policy violation, criminal violation, or whatever. It's that they failed the test. They failed academically. So if we can get them to where they need to be, why can they not take them.

Conclusions

Despite not being able to complete the outcome evaluation of the women's mentoring program, the interviews conducted as part of the process evaluation provided insight into several key issues that practitioners and researchers should consider. While these considerations inform practitioners about hurdles that may inhibit the success of implementing programs related to academy training, they inform researchers about key elements that must be monitored to ensure fidelity when conducting evaluations of interventions or newly implemented protocols. In particular, three key concerns, important to both practitioners and researchers, arose. These included reasonable variation in the way mentors mentored, tension between mentors and instructors, and issues related to rank and departmental obligation.

Variation in mentoring styles and approaches was apparent. Mentors engaged cadets using different methods of communication including phone, text, email, and in-person visits. As well, mentors varied in the level of contact including both the frequency of contact and the length of contact. Finally, mentors varied in their beliefs about what types of support a mentor should provide. While some mentors relied almost exclusively on listening and providing positive messages to mentees, other mentors gave advice, provided opportunities, and even intervened on mentees' behalf. While having a mentor was almost exclusively viewed as a good thing, variation in these approaches to mentoring necessarily resulted in differential experiences for mentees. As well, variation in mentorship style might relate to some cadets who expressed that they did not connect well with their mentor.

From an implementation standpoint, this is a challenging issue. Overly standardizing an interpersonal experience like mentoring might remove some of the key elements that add value. Female cadets' expressed desires for relationships within the department, and friendships between cadets, while viewed as important, were considered wholly different than relationships with mentors. An unstructured program might best allow for the development of these relationships; however, it also increases the likelihood that some mentees will have better and some mentees will have worse experiences in the program. Addressing this concern might involve increased guidance to mentors while stopping short of actually defining rules for mentoring. As well, it may suggest that some form of feedback system to identify mentor and mentee pairs that are not working as well as intended, so any issues that arise might be addressed.

From a research standpoint, this issue relates to the need to work to standardize treatments when delivered by groups of individuals. This element is a substantial process, and, in police organizations where staff may be the individuals delivering treatment, this process can take a considerable amount of time and effort. In situations where preparation does not ensure fidelity, it is imperative that researchers develop measures of fidelity that can be incorporated into the analysis. Quantitative approaches all too often reduce a program like mentorship to a simple dichotomy – after all cadets either were or were not mentored. Yet the qualitative data herein demonstrate that something as complex as mentoring cannot be adequately measured this way. Rigorous measurements of fidelity can address this concern.

Tension between mentors and instructors was another issue that arose in the data. At times this could represent the impact of the mentoring program on operations like unscheduled meetings with cadets. More often, this related to philosophical differences and role confusion. Instructors saw themselves as mentors for cadets and may not have understood the rationale for external mentors. Behavioral elements may have exacerbated this issue; cadets were willing to share information with mentors that they did not feel comfortable sharing with instructors. This perception extended to some instructors who stated that mentoring cadets could be detrimental to the training process and result in undermining their authority.

From an implementation standpoint, this issue may have been related to inadequate preparation of the instructors. Attitudes about attrition suggesting it is primarily about cadets being unprepared or not having realistic expectations for the academy illustrates a lack of consensus within the department about the scope of the value of the program. Further, it illustrates an underlying issue related to potentially oppositional goals. While consensus building is a particularly daunting task in some circumstances, it is imperative that organizations work to inform staff about high-level goals and to build understanding about how individual processes relate to these goals. This process allows a context where consensus is possible, and individuals working in different roles can better relate to the challenges that crossover can create.

From a research standpoint, this issue relates to the need to develop buy-in from staff prior to attempting any implementation. Understanding individuals' initial positions and unique perspectives provides researchers insight into how to address implementation issues that result from personnel issues. Allowing involved department personnel the opportunity to participate in implementation design can be useful, as it creates the opportunity to build an understanding of interventions that might otherwise meet resistance. Recognizing that these elements of an evaluation can be very important to the overall outcome evaluation or may, as in this case, have value all their own.

The final concern is related to issues stemming from rank or command structure and the interpersonal of mentoring, which requires trust and may require confidentiality. While some mentors made it explicit to mentees that their role was not to formally address things the mentees shared, others did not. Sometimes this reflected concerns that advice given by a mentor might be perceived as an order given the mentors' ranks. Other times, it related to mentors acting on information that their mentees had shared with them. This elevated the mentees' concerns to formal issues about instructors or the academy that had to be resolved through formal channels. It also illustrated differences in perspectives between some instructors and some mentors. This likely exacerbated the issues noted about the tension between mentors and instructors.

From an implementation standpoint, this is an area where more direction is needed. Differences in style of and approach to mentoring are personal, and variation supports relationships between different people. In contrast, overarching rules about roles and responsibilities create necessary structures to manage issues like crossover between the obligations of mentors and instructors. Without defining explicit roles and responsibilities, variation in attitudes among individuals can result in similar circumstances being handled very differently. A particular concern raised by one mentee might be handled informally while a similar concern raised by another might result in official action. This is very important in a context where differential treatment may be perceived as bias, and particularly so given that a training academy exists within an organization with defined human resource rules about equal treatment.

From a research standpoint, this raises a variety of concerns. Among these are protecting the confidentiality or anonymity of participants. This concern can be a challenging issue when working on research projects within police departments. The extent to which information can be withheld when sworn staff may either be part of the data collection or present when it occurs. The implication of the first, assuring confidentiality, is clear. Researchers may not be able to guarantee confidentiality to participants when the information collected involves the department since departmental rules may override research agreements. The second, assuring anonymity, is also problematic. In some situations, rank staff may utilize their authority to insert themselves into the data collection process. While this may be well-intentioned, in situations such as interviews, it identifies a participant. Researchers have to work to address these issues to maintain ethical research practices. Negotiating these issues with a department in advance is a good practice. As well, researchers should consider the potential impact of utilizing the department or its resources to collect data given the implications. Finally, researchers should consider when and where things like interviews should occur. In some instances, the additional anonymity protections afforded by off-site locations might offset the convenience of using departmental facilities.

Notes

1. Data were not collected from the 142nd academy class because it was a modified class which ran on a shorten schedule. The 143rd academy class did not include a mentoring component and was excluded from data collection due to scheduling issues.
2. A 144th academy class began June 21, 2021.
3. Substantial revisions to the academy curriculum and training practices were implemented before the start of the 144th academy class to address recommendations made by three independent auditors.

References

Charmaz, K. (2014). *Constructing Grounded Theory*. London, UK: Sage.

Chen, G., Gully, S. M., & Eden, D. (2004). General self-efficacy and self-esteem: Toward theoretical and empirical distinction between correlated self-evaluations. *Journal of Organizational Behavior: The International Journal of Industrial, Occupational and Organizational Psychology and Behavior,25*(3), 375–395. https://doi-org/10.1002/job.251

Schwarzer, R., & Jerusalem, M. (2010). The general self-efficacy scale (GSE). *Anxiety, Stress, and Coping, 12*(1), 329–345.

Smith, J. (2004). Reflecting on the development of interpretative phenomenological analysis and its contribution to qualitative research in psychology. *Qualitative Research in Psychology, 1*, 39–54.

Smith, J., Lewis, K. L., Hawthorne, L., & Hodges, S. D. (2013). When trying hard isn't natural: Women's belonging with and motivation for male-dominated STEM fields as a function of effort expenditure concerns. *Personality and Social Psychology Bulletin, 39*(2), 131–143. https://doi.org/10.1177/0146167212468332

Smith, R. E., Schutz, R. W., Smoll, F. L., & Ptacek, J. T. (1995). Development and validation of a multidimensional measure of sport-specific psychological skills: The Athletic Coping Skills Inventory-28. *Journal of Sport and Exercise Psychology,17*(4), 379–398. https://doi.org/10.1123/jsep.17.4.379

Starks, H., & Brown-Trinidad, S. (2007). Choose your method: A comparison of phenomenology, discourse analysis, and grounded theory. *Qualitative Health Research,17*(10), 1372–1380. https://doi-org/10.1177/1049732307307031

10

Pracademic Insights from Police Research on Open Drug Scenes in Sweden

Mia-Maria Magnusson

Police Department of Stockholm Region, Sweden

Introduction

The Swedish Police

The Swedish police organization underwent a major reorganization in 2015, when 21 police authorities were combined into one. The reorganization was based on the idea of centralizing the police force, but also involved an effort to reduce the distance between local police departments and local communities and their citizens. The reorganization also involved a clear policy of employee driven development (Ju 2012:16).

National and international measures show high levels of public confidence in the Swedish police (GfK Verein, 2018; Kääriäinen, 2007). Sweden has not witnessed anything like the major Black Lives Matter campaign and the media attention directed at police misconduct in the United States. There may be several reasons why the police in Sweden are viewed as trustworthy and legitimate, such as culture, beliefs, political ideology, education, organizational structures, occupational culture, and history.

The Swedish police are nonetheless struggling with other issues, not least in relation to an increase in gun violence and open drug dealing, often in disadvantaged areas (Swedish Police authority, 2017; Gerell et al., 2021). In addition, there has been a decrease in the number of police officers, which in 2016 led the government to adopt a policy of making a massive investment in increasing police numbers by 2024. Today the police force has almost 34,000 employees, of which 21,000 are police officers while the rest are civilians, with the intention being to increase the total number of police employees to 40,000 by 2024 (Swedish Government, 2021). Making the Swedish police an attractive workplace has been made a priority, as well as increasing the number of applicants and students at the country's police education programs.

The Swedish police education program consists of two years of studies and six months of paid field training accompanied by instructors who are responsible for the trainees' conduct. The police education program is provided across five locations, all at universities. The program includes some standard university courses as part of the education provided, such as law, criminology, emergency care, and social science, since they are embedded inside the universities. The police program gives trainees higher education credits, and it is possible to study at the bachelor level at two of the police programs. The police programs conduct their work in close collaboration with their host universities, but the programs are still provided on the basis of a

DOI: 10.4324/9781003153009-13

contract with the Swedish Police. Entrance qualifications include a high school diploma, and approval on the basis of physical and psychological tests and interviews. The mean age of police students is around 27 years of age and many of the students have conducted university studies and some have university degrees. Although Sweden now has a single, unitary police authority, the police educations differ somewhat in the way they organize the police training program. There is a national syllabus regarding what should be included in the program, and in which subjects, but the specific contents of the program differ between the universities. It is gratifying to note, however, that several of the programs use literature on evidence-based policing (EBP) and translational criminology in their training of recruits.

In order to increase the number of police officers in Sweden, several initiatives have been undertaken in addition to increased recruitment to education. There is now a fast-track police training program for civilian police employees, whereby such employees can enter a shortened program, subject to passing a selection process, which provides them with a police diploma while at the same time allowing them to study in the context of their employment. This program has been initiated as a means of transforming civilian specialists into police officers, instead of providing further training to police officers to transform them into specialists, which would take longer. In addition to this internal fast track, it is also possible for external applicants with a university degree and equivalent work experience at another state agency to take the 18-month police education program.

There is no higher police degree education program in Sweden. There are training programs for specialists in some areas and police-chief training programs. Swedish police employees in more senior management positions have been able to apply to participate in the Cambridge police executive program at Cambridge University and just over 25 individuals have attended the course and a handful have completed the two-year diploma.

In many professions, exclusively practical or exclusively theoretical training programs are not possible. The police training program both in Sweden and elsewhere combines the theoretical and practical skills needed for the duties that await. This mix is not a recipe for success, but research is increasingly making its way into the Swedish police organization and police training.

Police Research in Sweden

In Sweden, there is no explicit field of police research and no structure for Swedish police research (Lindström & Sempert, 2018; Sarnecki, 2010). Most research on the police takes place at departments of criminology, social science or other disciplines at universities, sometimes in collaboration with police departments. A number of the five police programs employ researchers, and police research is conducted at some of the police education programs, which have associated researchers, but there is no national police research department either within the Swedish Police or at the police programs. The Swedish National Council for Crime Prevention (Brå) is a center for knowledge within the criminal justice system, working under the ministry of justice. Brå is responsible for Sweden's official criminal statistics and also conducts and initiates research on criminal justice, crime prevention, and criminal policy. The need for research is greater than the research produced by Brå (Sarnecki, 2010). Altogether there is little coherence in the field of police research in Sweden.

Most of the links between the police and research take the form of collaborations between police departments and universities for the purpose of evaluating police actions and methods and researching current issues of concern, such as shootings and investigation processes. Some researchers are employed by the police, while most are only placed there for a specific project. There are also collaborations between universities and the police such as that at Malmö

University, for example, with students of criminology and police departments engaging in exchanges focused on practice and theory in order to advance both organizations.

One positive recent development in Sweden is that the government has invested in a four-year " national research program on crime, segregation, and safe communities. Within the police, steps have been initiated to coordinate research at the national level, with the aim of structuring the research that is undertaken and handling the police's involvement in the governmental research " program moving forwards.

In 2010, in a report on the management of policing, Sarnecki proposed the use of EBP as a means of enhancing the cost-effectiveness of the Swedish police (Sarnecki, 2010). In 2016, the government made demands on the Swedish Police to be more evidence-based and to create structures for EBP. In the same year, the Stockholm police region signed a contract with Malmö University for two police employees to study for doctorates within the police. One was a civilian working as a controller with a focus on investigative efficiency and the other is the author of this text, who at the time was a police detective working with strategies focused on police practice in the field of drug enforcement.

Evidence-Based Policing (EBP)

There are many issues associated with the gap between policing and research (Magnusson, 2020a). Researchers often discuss the policing vs. research dichotomy in terms of the one being the other's nemesis (Bradley & Nixon, 2009) or, as formulated by Bertilsson et al. (2014), *"Another major obstacle can be that when groups with different kinds of education, background, and knowledge are to collaborate, there needs to be an exchange of knowledge between all parties involved before a collaborative research project can be properly designed"* (Bertilsson et al., 2014, p.166). The needs of research and those of policing have shown themselves to be difficult to combine. One example is the researcher's need to publish articles in peer-reviewed journals (Neyroud & Weisburd, 2014). Such texts may be seen as being indigestible among police officers and chiefs, and without translation or reworking, they will be ignored by practice.

Sherman advocates EBP as an approach in which experimental criminology and randomized controlled trials (RCTs) constitute the gold standard, but where the overall aim is to enhance police effectiveness and legitimacy via the use of research. Sherman's early ideas on EBP (Sherman, 1998) have been widely disseminated and have also influenced policing researchers to develop the ways of getting closer to the goal of basing police practices and policy on research. Lum and Koper (2017) have placed their emphasis on translating between research and practice and have built a research bank in which the results from policing research are located in a matrix (Lum, Koper, & Telep, 2011) in order to assist police departments in their search for research evidence. This matrix is one tool to help bridge the gap between research and practice.

The first step for a police authority is to search for tests that have been conducted by others in the field (Sherman, 2013). If there is no evidence to be found that may serve to guide practice, the next step is to conduct tests in their own departments, as in the "triple T" process (target, test, track) advocated by Sherman (2013). When knowledge and research do exist, the next problem is that this knowledge is not used to the extent it could be (Sherman, 2013).

Neyroud and Weisburd (2014) have argued that in order to enhance policing and public support, and to continue the process of innovation within policing, the police need to take ownership of police science. Placing science within police agencies is viewed as a way forward both for the implementation of research and to identify the scientific value of research (Neyroud & Weisburd, 2014). As has been argued by Martin and Mazerolle (2016), however, there is a need for a police leadership that demands and strives for the implementation of EBP. There must also be incentives for leaders to use and create evidence in their work in order to bring about change. The lack of studies and evidence in policing makes it hard for police chiefs to reform police authorities. The evidence-based ideology needs to be acknowledged at the top of the police organization in order to implement EBP thinking, strategies, and methods in the whole organization (Martin & Mazerolle, 2016).

EBP rests on a number of cornerstones. Research needs to be conducted in your field of interest; this research needs to be translated to fit practice; the implementation of the research in the real-world context of policing also needs to be mastered; and the organizational policy and command structure needs to be aware of and push for research. Much of the policing research that has been conducted lacks insight into the needs of policing practice (Neyroud & Weisburd, 2014), which constitutes a problem when it is police officers who will ultimately be required to execute the implementation of research findings (Mitchell & Huey, 2018). Officer motivation is also central if police officers are to assist in driving a transformation toward research-based practice (Magnusson, 2020a).

The issues of effectively steering the police toward EPB and the problems associated with the use of research in policing are transferrable to Sweden (Sarnecki, 2010). The ideas associated with EBP are present in Sweden, since the government used the term explicitly in 2016 in its instruction to the police authority. At the same time, however, no Swedish definition of the term is provided, and when the term *knowledge-based* is also added to the description of what the police should be basing their practice on, the issue becomes even more confused.

Swedish and International Drug Policing Research

In Sweden, police research is not a field of research in its own right, and most forms of police practice remain untested in the Swedish setting (Sarnecki, 2010). The field of policing research focused on drug crime is relatively limited even in the US and the UK, where far more policing research is conducted. Thus, the availability of research on the practice in question constitutes the first obstacle in relation to the policing of drug crime in Sweden. The police and other authorities in Sweden are looking for strategies to engage and fulfil the needs of neighborhoods with open drug markets, and also strategies focused on connected issues such as shootings and gang crime. There is little research to guide practice in this area, however, nonetheless, practice cannot wait for calmer or better times - the current lack of effective solutions means that the door is currently open.

It is difficult to determine which strategies should be chosen to tackle open drug scenes and their impact on various areas in Sweden, even if there is research on this issue from other countries. Some international research, for example, shows that repressive police responses may contain and decrease the problems associated with open drug markets (Frank & Bjerge, 2014). At the same time, however, research findings from a different setting show that the same strategy serves to increase the distance between abusers and treatment provision (McNeil et al., 2014). Another difficult question for police agencies is whom they should collaborate with in order to meet the needs of neighborhoods experiencing problems of this kind. Allowing healthcare alone to manage the locations of drug use and drug dealing has been shown to result in problematic trends in the form of an increase in the number of drug markets (Waal et al., 2014). Policing research shows that collaborations with a large number of actors are necessary to help reduce the level of undesirable problems associated with Open Drug Scenes (ODSs) and their effects on the surrounding communities (Connoly, 2012). Some research has also shown drug enforcement to result in increased levels of violence (Anderas & Wallman, 2009; Moeller & Hesse, 2013).

Research on violence and drug markets shows that violence is linked to the type of area in which a drug market is located, with low economic-status areas having more violent drug markets (Johnson, 2016). Levels of violence are also linked to the economic value of the substances sold. The more lucrative a given market, the more violence is required to protect market share (Friman, 2009). But violence may also be explained on the basis of an individual perspective, in which age (Reuter, 2009), personality traits, and substance abuse are variables of interest. Research has also found the relationships between dealers and users, and also their relations to the location of the drug market, to affect levels of violence, with local dealers and local users having more enduring relationships, which are characterized by lower levels of violence (Reuter & MacCoun, 1992). Another factor related to violence is the stability of the market, with established and well-known markets being more lucrative and therefore also worth fighting for, which in turn generates more violence (Reuter, 2009).

Depending on what might lie hidden beneath the surface, such as gang turfs, competition among criminal networks, and hierarchies, these factors may have consequences when police tactics are deployed (Lum, 2008; Moeller & Hesse, 2013). Finding out more about the nature of Swedish drug markets, in order to understand what the police are working with, would appear central to the development of interventions, strategies, and collaborations focused on counteracting drug trends.

The demands placed on the police by society and the government to tackle negative developments might present an opportunity for research to step in and participate in bringing about change. Sherman notes that situations involving this kind of pressure on police agencies are found repeatedly in police forces around the globe, and he argues that this pressure can be channeled to shift the focus onto research as a means of helping to "unfreeze" those practices that need to be altered in order for the police to become more effective (Sherman, 2015).

However, few researchers present a solution to the question of *how* the implementation, translation, institutionalization, and conversion of research might be accomplished. One solution to the problem of research evidence being underused and not implemented may be to focus on the practitioner perspective (Bradley & Nixon, 2009; Magnusson, 2020a;). Research questions need to be directed at the heart of police practice (Neyroud & Weisburd, 2014). Translational criminology focuses on how to bring the two worlds of research and policing closer to one another and how to develop an understanding between the two. The need for translation permeates encounters between research and police in all areas of policing. One way of addressing the need for translation between practice and research is by combining the knowledge from these two fields, and making use of individuals with the necessary skills in the areas of both policing research and policing practice. In the case at hand, this means combining research skills with practical knowledge of drug policing.

The Pracademic Solution to the Research-Practice Gap

In this chapter, the term pracademic is used to refer to this combination of being both a practitioner and an academic. This means having a double understanding of the context at hand. The term has been used by several researchers (see for example, Huey & Mitchell, 2016; Magnusson, 2020a; Posner, 2009; Sherman, 2013; Volpe & Chandler, 2001). In this case, the author is a police detective specialized in drug enforcement at the Stockholm police, and a PhD student in criminology at Malmö University. At the time of writing this chapter, the author is employed by the Department of Police Work at Malmö University.

The most challenging work for a pracademic is to translate the words, the understandings, the aims, routines, perspectives, and frustrations of police practice for academia, and the usefulness, methods, and explanations from academia in a way that can be used in practice. This translation is done all the time mostly without noticing by many individuals with the dual understanding. And sometimes this involves a great deal of effort.

This chapter will describe a method for information collection that serves to enhance knowledge at the strategic level in local police departments, and that at the same time collects research data on the locations of drug use and drug dealing in public spaces.

The ODS Study

Crime Concentration and Place-Based Policing

The use of science in policing has been helped by the development of technologies such as crime mapping (Chainey & Ratcliffe, 2014; Neyroud & Weisburd, 2014). Over recent years spatial data analysis has been used increasingly within policing, and crime data analysis has been enhanced by the use of geographic information systems (GIS) for example (Chainey & Ratcliffe, 2014). The research on ODSs has been influenced by EBP but also by the criminology of place, which promotes the use of place-focused policing strategies at micro geographic hot spots (Weisburd, 2015). Ideas have been adopted from researchers such as Brantingham and Brantingham (1993), and theories on crime patterns and crime concentration (Weisburd, 2015) have played a major role in focusing the study of the drug trade and drug use on open drug scenes and their multidimensional problems. Drug markets have previously been studied using this approach and these studies have found evidence of crime concentrations at drug hot spots (Weisburd & Mazerolle, 2000; Weisburd & Green, 1995).

The law of crime concentration, as described by Weisburd (2015), notes that there is stability in the problems associated with places, and identifies this as a good focus for research. This stability can also provide grounds for the police to identify such places in order to focus activities and prevention efforts on them. Established crime locations have many problems and therefore constitute a good focus for crime prevention resources (Weisburd, 2015). ODSs are a prevention-friendly environment for organizations because such locations may be viewed as places on which they can focus their work, resources, and collaborations. The issues associated with such locations are concrete and clear, and the problems are not new or strange to drug prevention organizations. And as has been found in research on drug market prevention, collaborations across several agencies are of fundamental importance (Corsaro & Brunson, 2013; Connoly, 2012), which was taken into consideration in the research design and process employed in the project on which this chapter is based.

ODSs might be seen as micro places, and learning about them and identifying what the police do at these locations may constitute a basis for developing new and better methods by following the steps of triple T (Sherman, 2013). This process also helps the local police departments to better understand the places in which they work and requires them to map and investigate the problems they are facing in a more systematic way.

Mapping ODSs

The research field in which this example is set is referred to in the Swedish context as research on open drug scenes. In an American setting, it would translate to open-air drug markets. The term open drug scene (ODS) has been used within the Swedish police and other public sector agencies for many decades. It has also been used in international research (Falk, 1981; Bless et al., 1995), but in the context of the research used as an example in this chapter, the term has been defined in a more specific way. Here the research is focused on places characterized by public drug use and drug dealing, and also on the effects that the open drug scene has on the surrounding area. The study area was Stockholm County, a region of almost 2.4 million inhabitants (Statistics Sweden, 2020). The aim was to expand the knowledge on open drug scenes in order to create better practices and tactics and also to inform the police and other agencies. The mapping process also had several other underlying objectives, however. The most obvious aims involved collecting data, establishing communication with local analysts, and producing a regional status report for the strategic level. Other objectives were to produce a focus on a concrete area of drug policy work connected to local places, enhancing knowledge on ODSs in local police departments, and to create a platform for the exchange of knowledge on ODSs with collaboration partners and among local police departments in the region. In addition, the research also had the objective of allowing police officers to participate in defining the location and the problems found in their areas in order to understand the problems for police practice associated with tackling ODSs. The officers were invited to contact and discuss the mapping with the author and to become engaged in the study.

The mapping of ODSs was based on experiences from police enforcement at these places, and also on knowledge of criminological theories, earlier empirical studies on ODSs, and literature reviews. All of these sources contributed to the selection and creation of the variables employed in the study. The research on open-air drug markets contained recurring themes or factors that the research has identified as both central and important. Among others, these include: transportation, access (Harocopos & Hough, 2005), substances sold (DEA, 1996; Friman, 2009), crime concentration (Weisburd, 2015; Brantingham & Brantingham, 1993), violence (Lum, 2008), community factors, and disorganization (McCord & Ratcliffe, 2007). Some of these are factors that I had myself witnessed as a drug detective.

Since the mapping was the first compilation of the ODS in the region, their age, how many years the locations have been places of open use and dealing of drugs, was an important factor. Then there were factors and ideas from practice that seemed sufficiently important to explore further. Some of these included openly smoking or injecting drugs, the police resources allocated to the specific area, the police actions currently being taken and those that had been taken previously, active collaborations, criminal networks in the area, proximity to schools, the presence of dealers on prescribed substitution medications, and the presence of female abusers or unaccompanied refugee minors. All of these factors were translated into questions about the drug markets and included in an online survey, the aim of which was to measure their prevalence and importance.

This dual approach to factors of interest produces a broader understanding than would be the case if only theory or practice were used. The inclusion of theoretical factors also contributed to expanding the understanding beyond the "street knowledge" of the officers responsible for answering the survey. The questions on some of the factors are easy to answer, such as those relating to transportation and access, while others demanded more effort, such as estimating the amount of resources allocated to the ODS locations. The survey also included a question on the greatest perceived obstacles in tackling the issues at the ODSs and questions regarding desirable collaborators who were absent at the ODS today. The survey was thus a means of attempting to reach the officers working at the ODS locations and to include their views, but also of attempting to encourage them to think about new partners who could be engaged in the work focused on ODSs.

Some of the variables in the survey measured disruption in the area associated with the ODS. These variables were combined into an index and used to analyze the impact of the ODSs in the neighborhood. The variables included items focused on whether the public avoided the place or whether the location was a hot spot for crime. If a location had five or more of seven variables, the location was classified as being severely disrupted, which constituted a means of comparing the locations scientifically (Magnusson, 2020b).

The web survey was sent to all 19 local police districts in Stockholm, and was returned via e-mail (Magnusson, 2020b). The survey was designed to be easy to complete and return, so that police officers could complete it correctly without having to devote too much time to it. The survey contained clear instructions and a number to call in case of any problems or uncertainties.

The next step in the method was to collect the geographic locations for the ODSs in order to compile them in GIS. The police officers who completed the survey also marked the locations in question on maps. The author undertook a PhD course in spatial data analysis at the Royal Institute of Technology in Stockholm (KTH). The locations were transferred to GIS and crime data were added to explore the overlap between violence, crime concentrations, and shootings at the ODSs. Data from citizen safety surveys were then added to explore links between perceived insecurity and ODSs. These maps were sent to the police departments in order to provide a visual presentation, but also a means of showing the benefits of using GIS for improved analysis.

The placement of the project at the regional strategic level of the police in Stockholm meant for example that it was possible to participate in the regional group for public-sector agency collaboration on drug policy and drug-related activities. The placement also provided access to several agencies with an interest in drug prevention and to their management at the strategic level. In the context of national policy in Sweden, evaluations of the drug work conducted in the regions take place every 4th year, and during each 4-year period every regional ANDT (Alcohol, Narcotics, Doping and Tobacco prevention) group in Sweden is required to monitor the work of the participating agencies and to develop strategies to meet the goals set by the government. The regional group in Stockholm decided to focus their work on ODSs, with the goal of reducing the number of ODSs in the region. In order to meet this goal, it was first essential to map and count the existing ODSs. This work was conducted by the police PhD student, the author by means of the survey described above. An annual mapping was then conducted to compare and monitor developments. During the first three years, the mapping was conducted by the author, who also wrote research articles on the basis of the data, and these data were also included in a folder describing ODS collaborations in the region created by the collaborating authorities involved in the ANDT project. The folder was made available to all agencies and organizations of interest and was used as a basis for lectures and conferences on the drugs topic, both within and outside the region. In the following year, the online survey included a question about the folder, whether it had been received by the local police department, whether it had been used and which of the strategies described, such as hot spot policing, had been employed. This constitutes a form of what Sherman labels tracking the police (Sherman, 2013).

The process of mapping is now based at the regional strategic group for management steering and analysis at the Stockholm region police as part of their analysis assignment. The sustainability of new scientific methods is important (Neyroud & Weisburd, 2014) and this method was implemented by the management division as a standard information collection method that is now repeated each year, with the results being compared to those from previous years.

Another product of the mapping work was the annual compilation of results from the survey, which were communicated with figures and tables in a language digestible by police officers and chiefs. The compilation of results was sent to all departments, together with maps and information and suggested further reading for interested officers. This product was produced in the form of a PowerPoint presentation and could also be used by the local departments as educational material within the police or as information for collaborating partners, such as the municipalities. The study was also reported in the form of a research article and published in a peer-reviewed setting. Using results as both research and police department information in this way may involve more work for the researcher, but it ensures that the outcome reaches both practitioners and researchers. Here the skills of the pracademic are used in an effective way to overcome the issues associated with the different needs of research and the police, as discussed by Neyroud & Weisburd (2014).

Being a practitioner also helps in gaining access to and understanding both the data and employees as a result of the individual's practical experience and network. In the case of mapping the region's ODSs, the survey was distributed from the regional chief's e-mail account to all local district chiefs in the form of an assignment and not a question. This resulted in all departments answering in time and reporting in their ODSs. Having the police chiefs on board is central to the research process.

Overall being a police PhD student means consistently bringing both practice and research to the table. When in class on courses during the PhD program, practice is present and is translated into the theories and methods explored. And conversely, when at work, meeting groups of officers and attending meetings focused on issues from practice, the theories and methods encountered on the PhD program are always present and being translated. When reading and conducting literature reviews in order to understand a new project or subject prior to a study, ideas and thoughts on issues of relevance to practice are compiled and communicated to police departments. Participation in courses, seminars, and webinars often results in ideas being raised in meetings at police departments. At the same time, experiences from practice are used in the context of courses in order to understand the theories and exemplify the abstract ideas or issues in terms of a concrete reality. The main contribution is that of combining the knowledge from both these worlds while at the same time recognizing when your understanding is not sufficient in either context.

In the current example, the researcher, together with a senior police researcher and the regional crime prevention coordinator, collaborated in the regional crime prevention project directed toward ODS. Together their network reached both municipal leaders and regional crime prevention strategists. A question on open drug dealing and drug use was suggested for inclusion in the municipal survey measuring levels of insecurity in the region and has been included in the surveys conducted since 2017. This made it possible to follow the way residents' opinions on the topic are associated with feelings of security (Magnusson, 2020b). The regional police department applied for funding for the police from the Swedish National Council for Crime Prevention (Brå), in order to conduct a scientific evaluation of practice at ODSs. The police were awarded the funding and used it to procure an evaluation of police practice over a three-year period from a research center with expertise in drug and alcohol research (Stockholm Prevents Alcohol and Drug Problems [STAD]). This was done in order to test practice, thus covering the third T of Sherman's triple T (Sherman, 2013). STAD is now conducting research on the strategies employed at two different ODSs. In this case, the police commissioned external researchers (STAD) to evaluate police practice at ODSs in order to see which methods, collaborations, and tactics are effective and which are not. The evaluation was based outside the police due to a lack of resources and knowledge on rigorous evaluation methods for drug prevention within the police organization.

Analysis

Results of the Mapping and How They Were Used

Each year about 50 ODSs were identified and mapped in the region. Most of these were recurrent, established locations for drug dealing and disorder. Many were located in local shopping centers in communities close to public transportation nodes. The index comprised of variables measuring effects in the neighborhood divided the ODSs into groups with more and less severe problems respectively, with many of the areas experiencing severe disruption (Magnusson, 2020b).

The visual presentation in ArcGIS showed the links between the ODSs and public transportation in Stockholm (Magnusson, 2020b). This information could then be used in several ways. Compared to the findings of a US study, where open-air drug markets were located on streets and accessed by car (Harocopos & Hough, 2005) the ODSs in Stockholm were strongly linked to public transportation. In Stockholm, many of the commuter train stations and subway stations are part of ODS areas, and the selling and use of drugs takes place both inside and outside these stations. This information was used in communications with municipal representatives. One way to use this information is in collaboration with the local transport provider in Stockholm and its security guards. Another is to relocate police stations and security closer to these areas and to take this factor into consideration when building new stations and planning the areas around stations, by including control mechanisms nearby or at the scene. In this way, city planning officers and architects can build better, safer places.

The age variable relating to the ODSs showed that most of them had been established at least five years earlier (Magnusson, 2020b). This suggests that these sites are suitable for crime prevention on the basis of Weisburd's (2015) reasoning on the benefits of preventing established and concentrated problems. The locations of the ODSs and the problems associated with them are stable, and it would thus appear smart to focus resources on these places.

The age variable was also combined with the disruption index to explore whether there was any correlation between the age of the ODS and disruption. This would help to understand whether the degree to which the locations had become established, and their stability over time, led to their producing greater levels of problems, or whether some locations were associated with more disruption due to other factors. The oldest ODSs had a higher level of disruptive problems, but there was no correlation between age and levels of disruption at other levels of the age variable.

The clientele at the ODSs were also analyzed. In this analysis, it became clear that some ODSs were linked to criminal networks in the areas surrounding them (Magnusson, 2020b). This may constitute one of several signs of the presence of a hierarchal structure at an ODS. Understanding this link makes it possible to make informed choices with regard to police tactics, thus avoiding the risk of these tactics resulting in excessive violence. Another important factor in this analysis was the substances sold at the ODSs. The substances varied but there was a correlation between the presence of a criminal network and the substances cannabis, cocaine, and tramadol (Magnusson, 2020b). This might say something about the lucrativeness of different substances at open drug markets. At the same time, it also provides information for the police regarding the level of market share that needs to be protected by the dealers at a given ODS and also how the sales are conducted. This makes a difference to the measures needed in the work to combat an ODS. The greater the level of risk linked to the drug sales, the more precautions those involved in the trade will take, and the harder it becomes for police to witness and prosecute offences.

The variables regarding the actions currently being taken by local police departments and resource allocation showed that in 2017, many of the worst ODSs were those that were assigned the lowest levels of resources. This was communicated to chiefs in the region and the surveys between 2018 and 2019 showed that resource allocation had shifted a great deal, with more resources being allocated overall, and with the biggest increases in resources being allocated to the ODSs with the highest numbers of shootings and where criminal networks were present. By including questions on the actions currently being taken by the police at the ODS locations and on the resources allocated to the area by the local police department, it also became possible to compare the levels of assigned departmental resources and of problems and to communicate this to senior officers at the regional level.

The question on which collaborating partners were lacking in the areas concerned constituted the basis for compiling a list of possible collaborators, which was communicated to all participating departments to provide both information and stimulation.

The first mapping showed that there were different types of ODS that shared a number of characteristics. A typology of three types of ODS was developed. Some of the ODSs were characterized by the presence of criminal networks and the occurrence of shootings, while one type was different from the other two in being located in a city business area away from residential areas and in a more anonymous setting (Magnusson, 2020b). The typology helped to identify and select policing methods and which actors should be engaged in collaborations. The information produced by the typology may provide a basis for crime prevention coordinators to make important choices. Responsibility for the locations containing an ODS is shared among different actors, but these different agencies and organizations have different tools that may be used to attempt to reduce the problems at these locations. The three types of ODSs suggested the use of different sets of evidence-based interventions that have been studied in Sweden, such as hot spot policing, GVI and MUMIN (a drug abuse rehabilitation intervention used and studied in Stockholm).

Additional measures from the municipal survey on levels of public insecurity showed that areas with more ODSs were characterized by higher levels of insecurity. The areas with ODSs also showed higher levels of public distress due to drug dealing and drug use in the area (Magnusson, 2020b). This confirmed the picture provided by the police mapping of troubled areas, but also added the views of citizens on insecurity, and also on whether they avoided these locations, for example. Speaking the same language as municipal representatives in relation to the issue of insecurity provided the basis for a shared understanding of the effects of ODSs and of the need for a joint focus on strategies and collaborations.

Data on crime types showed the presence of crime concentrations in the ODSs. Hot spots of outdoor violence coincided geographically with 65 percent of ODSs in 2017 (Magnusson, 2020b). The analysis of crime concentrations was also complemented with the addition of buffer zones and by exploring five crime types in this way, showing for example that 30 percent of all outdoor assaults and 22 percent of all homicides took place within ODS buffer zones despite these areas only accounting for 0.29 percent of the regional land area (Magnusson, 2020b). There was also an overlap between shootings and the ODSs. This concentration of problems led regional chiefs to take steps toward focusing on the places where insecurity, violence, and shootings coincided, i.e. the ODSs (Radio interview with Stockholm's regional chief of police 23/02/21). Cost-effectiveness is one of the goals of Sherman's EBP (1998), and the focus on places, resources, and assistance from other agencies at micro places constitutes one of the results of the research presented here. Another will be continued research focused on finding the right methods of engaging with the three different types of ODS. The ODS-evaluation from STAD, focused on two different ODSs, will provide a starting point for this research.

The locations and their problems were communicated to all police departments, and lectures were held for all local police departments, the regional operational executives, and the regional intelligence department. Several of the local police departments used the information on these locations in their collaborations with the municipalities in order to provide a focus for crime prevention strategies.

Conducting the mapping as a means of helping local police districts to better understand their local drug markets, and at the same time providing the strategic level with a method for compiling the regional perspective and conducting follow-ups generated a continued dialogue between these two levels. In the new police organization in Sweden, all local police departments are responsible for describing their own community problems, and for prioritizing and engaging in activities to counteract their local problems (Ju 2012:16). These descriptions, along with priorities and planned actions, are shared at the regional and national levels to produce a picture of the current regional and national situation. However, depending on how well analyzes are conducted at the local level, the problems may be interpreted in many different ways, depending on the analytical tools, knowledge, resources, etc. employed. The new structure of the Swedish police organization would benefit from having more a scientific approach to mapping and analysis, and an enhanced understanding of their local problems such as ODSs. This would also improve the understanding of the current crime situation at the aggregate level. One way of generating better analysis may be to develop methods for data collection, mapping, and educating local police departments, such as those employed in this project, in order to improve their understanding of their local situation. The typology is perhaps the simplest example of this approach. It uses the information provided by police officers in a survey, in the form of a few selected variables, and translates this information into a format that facilitates the choice of prevention focus. The choice to include shootings as a distinguishing characteristic was made based on the knowledge that violent drug markets in other countries have experienced increases in violence following police enforcement efforts (Moeller & Hesse, 2013).

Pracademic Facilitation and Implications

The pracademic contribution can be summed as being an in-house resource for police practice, with access to crime data and a connection with employees and departments, and also with knowledge of police structures and the police organization, together with its data systems and data problems, and with this being combined with a dual understanding based on the interaction between higher education and policing knowledge. This provides assistance to research projects in gaining time and in producing effective research focused on questions that meet the needs of police practice, while at the same time identifying the level of readiness to implement research findings and facilitating the widespread dissemination of these findings.

There are a large number of benefits associated with the use of pracademic skills in policing and research (Huey & Michell, 2016). There are also problems associated with this role, however. Much is dependent on individuals. The police need a structure for pracademic or translational organs located between research and practice that have the mandate required to have an effect. In some divisions, it may be difficult to present negative findings on current police practice or policies or even on legislation that is ineffective. This needs to be counteracted by means of an external research affiliated to a university or similar.

Pracademic knowledge may also vary from person to person (Magnusson, 2020a), and the overall level of influence will be rather small if the number of such individuals is small. Police organizations need to have several research initiatives in place in order to have a wider impact within the organization, and these need to be located at a strategic level with a sufficient mandate or status to ensure that results will be used to direct police departments and formulate policy.

If a pracademic is too focused on practice and becomes too involved with practitioners, it might be argued that biased research can take place, since one may become blinkered and ideas may become fixed. Individuals in this situation may also be influenced by police chiefs with regard to what should be studied and what evidence should be produced. Quality control (Sherman, 2013) by senior researchers and senior police chiefs is needed in order for the term pracademic to be associated with reliable and valid research, and to avoid it becoming associated with less academic or lower standard research. The research standards and structure used in relation to policing research are fundamental to the production of valid evidence (Neyroud & Weisburd, 2014).

Concluding Recommendations

The mapping of ODSs resulted in a research paper, a folder for use in collaborations on ODSs that was sponsored by several different agencies and organizations, lectures both within and outside the police organization and academia, presentations at conferences on drug prevention, criminology, and in municipal settings, universities, etc., and the research has also been used as a reference in governmental reports, Brå-reports and by the media. The ODSs are now included in the national police drug policy and the term is referred to by the government as a drug enforcement issue.

The steps required for the Swedish police to increase internal police research do not seem impossible. The police education programs are situated at universities; the police education program is relatively long and is becoming increasingly science-based (and inclusive of literature on EPB); the new police organization is based on employee-driven development; there is government funding for a research program on criminality; there are demands on the police to become more effective in tackling gangs and shootings; there is an ongoing, previously unequalled investment to increase the number of police employees; and the coordination of research within the police has only just started. There are nonetheless a number of recommendations that might help to keep moving in the right direction, both in Sweden and elsewhere.

Create Learning by Doing

Educating while at the same time conducting research may be a goal that is beyond reach, but formulating research designs that lead to research that enhances knowledge on various topics does not seem impossible. How can we construct experimental processes that produce learning at police departments? But also: What do we want them to learn? One development that is needed in Swedish policing is for police chiefs to identify steering goals that are not only based on numbers of cleared offences or seizures (Sarnecki, 2010). In the context of enforcement at ODSs, goals need to be set to help departments focus on the right things. If counting numbers is the only language spoken by police chiefs, then they should count things that are important for the development of policing measures. How many guns did they take off the streets? How many people did this department help to leave gangs? How many informants has the group developed? How many schools have they visited, and how many names do they know among 9th graders? How many meetings have they had with social services that have informed their practice? If new actions are taken at ODSs, be sure to begin by at least planning for the conduct of before-and-after measurements. It might be possible to use some of the 50 ODSs as a control group when testing new policing initiatives.

Urgently Promote the Use of EBP

Identifying issues, groups or departments where change or assistance is required, and where there is significant frustration or motivation, constitutes one way of moving forward toward EBP. The readiness of departments to implement measures, or even to open up to change, is crucial (Magnusson, 2020a). Today in Sweden, the continued increase in gun violence is troubling (Sturup et al., 2019) and is a major concern for police departments and the strategic level. Finding ways to decrease or even contain the spread of violent places is essential, and here we have a door that is open to researchers. As discussed by Sherman (2015), outside demands or pressures may help to open up or "unfreeze" practice, providing opportunities for new ideas to enter and perhaps transform police agencies (Sherman, 2015). As Sherman (2015) also notes, however, there is a risk that unrealistic expectations may be placed on research and EBP. The police may either give research too much to resolve or may want results to come too fast. Here the need for translators as a link between research and practice is unmistakable. Knowing how much time research takes, and what questions research can answer, constitutes a central role for translational functions or individuals inside the police organization.

There is no way to find solutions to the complex situations surrounding ODSs simply by increasing the number of officers or trying new strategies if these are not tested sufficiently well to show evidence of effects. It is important not only to try new tactics, but also to include follow-ups and use control groups to conduct rigorous evaluations (Sherman, 2015). To do this, more resources need to be made available to police department researchers or police research groups – this needs to be seen as the only way forward and prioritized in order to produce the necessary evidence and then use it to combat the violence and insecurity in the neighborhoods in question.

Create Structure and Blueprints

In order to transform frustration into motivation and a willingness to try something new, openness and drive are needed. As Sherman (2015) and Neyroud (2017) have emphasized, however, research standards must prevail. Counteracting the effects of unfocused energy may be facilitated by blueprints on how to engage in and start research projects. A research network or a department that may be contacted for ideas and guidance constitutes another structural component that may improve developments in this area.

Structure may also assist in providing information on the use of partnerships, in writing contracts with academia, and in compiling the research that is taking place within the organization so that it can be disseminated while at the same time ensuring that several similar projects are not being conducted at different departments. The same is true in relation to procedures on how to conduct in-house evaluations, how to gather existing evidence and make it easy to access, and on scientific guidance and research design.

In the case of education, the training of police officers provides another possible situation in which the translation process may be developed. The transition from practice to education of teachers of policing, and police employees who work as educators on police training programs are an issue at many academies (Eckblad, 2019). Transitioning police officers to become educators on practical components at police programs, and guidance and translation into the language of learning are needed. There are also problems associated with mastering the role of being both a teacher and police officer (Eckblad, 2019). These are another set of pracademics where there is a need for translation. Recruits cannot be taught and prepared for the reality of policing by teachers from academia alone as a result of credibility issues and a lack of skills and up-to-date experience of police practice. A framework for the participation of police practitioners in the education of recruits is necessary for a smooth transition to the schedules, teaching perspectives, and behavior required by universities.

Offer Police Employees Higher Education Careers Within the Organization

One way for police forces to take ownership of science (Neyroud & Weisburd, 2014), while at the same time improving the scientific quality of police research, is to offer police employees with an academic background and diplomas and the chance to continue their academic path as they also continue their police careers. Providing the opportunity to engage in masters, PhD or postdoctoral studies, or allowing time for on-the-job research would constitute one way of enabling those officers and civilians in many police forces around the world who already have an education to contribute. Another would be to fund police research and police PhD programs at police educations, since these are already situated at universities, thus making it possible to have a career in research within the Swedish police. The benefits for police agencies could be massive if these opportunities were used in the right way.

Start the Process of Dissemination: Bottom Up, Top Down, Center Out

Demands regarding the effectiveness of police agencies also raise questions about professionalism. Hough et al. (2018) discuss professionalism as a regulator to assist in producing structure and accountability among members. There is a growing urge to professionalize policing in order to eliminate corruption and enhance the quality of conduct and investigations by means of education. The regulating structure within the Swedish police remains hierarchical, while Hough et al. (2018) argue that the EBP movement requires a different form of structure. They also raise the question of whether evidence-based or knowledge-based policing might challenge or even replace the hierarchal structures that exist today (Hough et al., 2018).) Another way of looking at this issue is through the lens of procedural justice. This perspective views trust in the police as coming from the way in which the police behave, and the public's views on how policing is conducted constitute a key issue (Tyler & Meares, 2006). Regardless of perspective, the police profession would benefit from an expansion in the number of highly educated police officers employed in a translational role inside police agencies.

The frontline officer in Sweden has a great deal of autonomy and with it responsibility, having tough decisions to make as a person in authority but still being placed in a clear hierarchal chain. Since much of police practice has no evidence-based methods to follow, changing too quickly might be dangerous. A slow transformation is more likely, and there is a possibility that some parts of the organization will not be transformed or become evidence-based at all, but will continue to rely on experiences. One way of increasing the professionality of police officers is by increasing the amount and the standard of research employed in police practice, but also in police education.

In order to encourage police organizations to adopt and change in accordance with research findings, the EBP perspective and police research must be introduced and used throughout the police training program (Sherman 2015; Weisburd & Neyroud, 2011). The open minds of new recruits and the younger generation may help rebut the advocates of opinion, craft, and intuition that remain in many departments. Newly educated officers may bring new ideas and openness to research from a grassroots perspective.

Practitioners and street-level officers may also become a major and powerful force if they have sufficient motivation. Engaging officers in the issues of where experiments should be conducted, and what tactics should be evaluated, will empower them to assist in producing change. The translation process between police practice and research would be helped if individuals with links to street-level officers were located at strategic levels in order to facilitate the formulation of policy using research based on insights that are closely linked to practice.

As Sherman (2015) has argued, in order to realize the use of EBP, change needs to be implemented in a way that brings together former skeptics with those accustomed to research. This shift of organizational perspective may be driven by good examples of the benefits research provides for practice, and it needs to come from both the top and the bottom of the policing structure. As argued by Martin and Mazerolle (2016), budgets need to include research and incentives for police leaders and police officers to drive this change and to disseminate the use of EBP in police forces from above.

EBP needs to find its way into policy and become a part of the strategies implemented from above. Pressure from the highest level on the use of research as a part of the organization's mission is central to the dissemination of EBP within the Swedish police organization. The education of recruits in the EBP perspective may enhance the acceptance of, and faith in, the use of EBP as a part of the work of the organization. At the center of the organization, at the strategic level, pracademics and research projects would serve as a link between the EBP movement among new police students and practitioners and the evidence-based strategies and demands being made from the top, both changing the hierarchal structure and bringing about a shift to the evidence-based perspective.

References

Anderas, P., & Wallman, J. (2009). Illicit Markets and Violence: What Is the Relationship? *Crime, Law and Social Change, 52*(3), 225–229. https://doi.org/10.1007/s10611-009-9200-6

Bertilsson, J., Fredriksson, P., Piledahl, L., Macnusson, M., & Fransson, P. (2014). Opportunities and Challenges of Research Collaboration between Police Authoriteis and University Organizations. In F. Lemieux., G. D. Heyer., & D. K. Das (Eds.), *Economic Development, Crime, and Policing: Global Perspectives* (pp. 163–180). New York, NY: Taylor & Francis Group, LLC.

Bless, R., Korf, D. J., & Freeman, M. (1995). Open drug scenes: a cross-national comparison and urban strategies. *European Addiction Research, 1*, 128–138. https://doi.org/10.1159/000259053

Bradley, D., & Nixon, C. (2009). Ending the 'dialogue of the deaf': Evidence and policing policies and practices. An Australian case study. *Police Practice and Research: An International Journal, 10*(5-6), 423–435. https://doi.org/10.1080/15614260903378384

Brantingham, P. L., & Brantingham, P. J. (1993). Environment, routine and situation: Toward a pattern theory of crime. *Advances in criminological theory, 5*(2), 259–294.

Chainey, S., & Ratcliffe, J. (2013). *GIS and crime mapping*. Chichester, West Sussex: John Wiley & Sons.

Connoly, J. (2012). *A better city for Aall: A partnership approach to address public substance misuse and perceived anti-social behaviour in Dublin City Centre*. Dublin: Strategic Response Group.

Corsaro, N., & Brunson, R. K. (2013). Are suppression and deterrence mechanisms enough? Examining the "pulling levers" drug market intervention strategy in Peoria, Illinois, USA. *International Journal of Drug Policy, 24*(2), 115–121. https://doi.org/10.1016/j.drugpo.2012.12.006

DEA Publications (1996). *Methamphetamine situation in the Unites States*. Springfield, Virginia: US Drug Enforcement Administration.

Eckblad, K. (2019). Instruktøren som veileder–i spennet mellom rollene som pedagog og politi. *Uniped, 43*(01), 33–44.

Falk, P. (1981). Auflösung einer öffenen Drogenszene. *Kriminalistik, 5*, 256–259.

Frank, V. A., & Bjerge, B. (2014). From zero tolerance to non-enforcement: Creating a new space for drug policing in Copenhagen, Denmark. *Contemporary Drug Problems, 41*(2), 261–291. https://doi.org/10.1177/009145091404100206

Friman, H. R. (2009). Drug markets and the selective use of violence. *Crime, law and social change, 52*(3), 285–295. https://doi-org.mutex.gmu.edu/10.1007/s10611-009-9202-4

Gerell, M., Sturup, J., Magnusson, M. M., Nilvall, K., Khoshnood, A., & Rostami, A. (2021). Open drug markets, vulnerable neighbourhoods and gun violence in two Swedish cities. *Journal of Policing, Intelligence and Counter Terrorism*, 1–22. https://doi.org/10.1080/18335330.2021.1889019

GfK Verein. (2018). Trust in professions 2018 A GfK Verein Study. Accessed by: https://www.nim.org/sites/default/files/medien/135/dokumente/2018_-_trust_in_professions_-_englisch.pdf

Harocopos, A., & Hough, M. (2005). Drug dealing in open-air markets. Washington, DC: US Department of Justice. *COPS*, 31,7–37. Retrieved from Center for problem-oriented policing.

Hough, M., Stanko, B., Agnew-Pauley, W., Belur, J., Brown, J., Gamblin, D., … & Tompson, L. (2018). *Developing an evidence based police degree-holder entry program. Project Report*. Mayor of London Office for Policing and Crime.

Huey, L., & Mitchell, R. J. (2016). Unearthing Hidden Keys: Why Pracademics Are an Invaluable (If Underutilized) Resource in Policing Research. *Policing: A Journal of Policy and Practice, 10*(3), 300-307. https://doi.org/10.1093/police/paw029

Johnson, L. T. (2016). Drug Markets, Travel Distance, and Violence: Testing a Typology. *Crime and Delinquency, 62*(11), 1465-1487. https://doi.org/10.1177/0011128714568302

Ju 2012:16. *Polismyndighetens styrmodell Rapport (Govermental inquiry. Report on the Police authority's steering model)*: Ju2012:16/2014. Genomförandekommitén för nya Polismyndigheten (Commity of execution of the new police authority).

Kääriäinen, J. T. (2007). Trust in the police in 16 European countries: A multilevel analysis. *European Journal of Criminology, 4*(4), 409–435. https://doi.org/10.1177/1477370807080720

Lindström, P., & Sempert, U. (2018). *Kriminologi och poliskunskap: Mötet mellan forskning och praktik.* Studentlitteratur AB.

Lum, C. (2008). The Geography of Drug Activity and Violence: Analyzing Spatial Relationships of Non-Homogenous Crime Event Types. *Substance Use & Misuse, 43*(2), 179-201. https://doi.org/10.1080/10826080701690573

Lum, C., Koper, C. S., & Telep, C. W. (2011). The evidence-based policing matrix. *Journal of Experimental Criminology, 7*(1), 3–26. https://doi.org/10.1007/s11292-010-9108-2

Lum, C., & Koper, C. S. (2017). *Evidence-based policing : Translating research into practice* (1st ed.). Oxford University Press.

Magnusson, M. M. (2020a). Bridging the gaps by including the police officer perspective? A study of the design and implementation of an RCT in police practice and the impact of pracademic knowledge. *Policing: A Journal of Policy and Practice, 14*(2), 438–455. https://doi.org/10.1093/police/pay022

Magnusson, M. M. (2020b). Mapping Open Drug Scenes (ODS). In Ceccato, V., & Nalla, M. K. (Red). *Crime and fear in public places: Towards safe, inclusive and sustainable cities* (pp.305–325). Taylor & Francis.

Martin, P., & Mazerolle, L. (2016). Police leadership in fostering evidence-based agency reform. *Policing: A journal of policy and practice, 10*(1), 34–43. https://doi.org/10.1093/police/pav031

McCord, E. S., & Ratcliffe, J. H. (2007). A micro-spatial analysis of the demographic and criminogenic environment of drug markets in Philadelphia. *Australian & New Zealand Journal of Criminology, 40*(1), 43–63. https://doi-org.mutex.gmu.edu/10.1375/acri.40.1.43

McNeil, R., Shannon, K., Shaver, L., Kerr, T., & Small, W. (2014). Negotiating place and gendered violence in Canada's largest open drug scene. *International Journal of Drug Policy, 25*(3), 608–615. https://doi.org/10.1016/j.drugpo.2013.11.006

Mitchell, R., & Huey, L. (2018). *Evidence based policing : An introduction* (1st ed.). Policy Press.

Moeller, J., & Hesse, M. (2013). Drug market disruption and systemic violence: Cannabis markets in Copenhagen. *European Journal of Criminology, 10*(2), 206-221. https://doi.org/10.1177/1477370812467568

Neyroud, P. W. (2017). Learning to Field Test in Policing: Using an analysis of completed randomised controlled trials involving the police to develop a grounded theory on the factors contributing to high levels of treatment integrity in Police Field Experiments. (Doctoral thesis). https://doi.org/10.17863/CAM.14377

Neyroud, P. & Weisburd, D. (2014). Transforming the police through science: the challenge of ownership. *Policing: A Journal of Policy and Practice, 8*(4), 287-293. https://doi.org/10.1093/police/pau048

Posner, P. L. (2009). The pracademic: An agenda for re-engaging practitioners and academics. *Public Budgeting & Finance, 29*(1), 12–26. https://doi.org/10.1111/j.1540-5850.2009.00921.x

Reuter, P. (2009). Systemic Violence in Drug Markets. *Crime, Law and Social Changes,* 52, 275-284.

Reuter, P., & MacCoun, R. (1992). Street Drug Markets in Inner-City Neighborhoods: Matching Policy to Reality. In J. Steinberg., D. Lyon., & M. Vaiana. (Eds.), *Urban America: Policy Choices for Los Angeles and the Nation*. Santa Monica, CA: RAND.

Sarnecki, J. (2010). *Polisens prestationer– en ESO-rapport om resultatstyrning och effektivitet. (Police performance– an ESO report on management by results and effectiveness)*. Rapport till Expertgruppen för studier i offentlig ekonomi 2010:3. Elanders Sverige: Stockholm.

Sherman, L.W. (1998), '*Evidence-based policing*', Ideas in American policing, police foundation, Washington DC.

Sherman, L. (2013). The Rise of Evidence-Based Policing: Targeting, Testing, and Tracking. *Crime and Justice,* 42, 377-343. https://doi.org/10.1086/670819

Sherman, L. W. (2015). A tipping point for "Totally Evidenced Policing": Ten ideas for building an evidence-based police agency. *International Criminal Justice Review, 25*(1), 11-29. https://doi.org/10.1177/1057567715574372

Statistics Sweden (2020). Tables of population per county. Accessed through; http://www.statistikdatabasen.scb.se/2021-03-15..

Sturup, J., Rostami, A., Mondani, H., Gerell, M., Sarnecki, J., & Edling, C. (2019). Increased gun violence among young males in Sweden: A descriptive national survey and international comparison. *European Journal on Criminal Policy and Research,* 25, 365–378. https://doi-org.mutex.gmu.edu/10.1007/s10610-018-9387-0

Swedish Government (2021). *Ny statistisk visar på rekordnivåer av antalet polisanställda.* Article on Swedish government website 26/1 2021. Accessed at: https://www.regeringen.se/artiklar/2021/01/ny-statistik-visar-pa-rekordnivaer-av-antalet-polisanstallda/

Swedish Police Authority (2017). *Utsatta områden [Disadvantaged areas].* Stockholm: Swedish National Police.

Tyler, T. R., & Meares T.L. (2006). Procedural justice policing. In police innovation. In Weisburd, D., & Braga, A. A. (Ed.), *Police Innovation: Contrasting Perspectives.* New York: Cambridge University Press.

Volpe, M. R., & Chandler, D. (2001). Resolving and managing conflicts in academic communities: the emerging role of the "pracademic". *Negotiation Journal, 17*(3), 245–255.

Waal, H., Clausen, T., Gjersing, L., & Gossop, M. (2014). Open drug scenes: responses of five European cities. *BMC Public Health, 14*(1), 1–12. https://doi.org/10.1186/1471-2458-14-853

Weisburd, D. (2015). The law of crime concentration and the criminology of place. *Criminology, 53*(2), 133–157. https://doi.org/10.1111/1745-9125.12070

Weisburd, D., & Green, L. (1995). Policing drug hot spots: The Jersey City drug market analysis experiment. *Justice Quarterly, 12*(4), 711-735. https://doi.org/10.1080/07418829500096261

Weisburd, D., & Mazerolle, L. G. (2000). Crime and Disorder in Drug Hot Spots: Implications for Theory and Practice in Policing. *Police Quarterly, 3*(3), 331-349. https://doi.org.10.1177/1098611100003003006

PART IV

International Perspectives on Translational Criminology in Policing

11

The Proclivity to Rely on Professional Experience and Evidence-Based Policing

Findings from a Survey of High-Ranking Officers in the Israel Police

Tal Jonathan-Zamir

THE HEBREW UNIVERSITY OF JERUSALEM

David Weisburd

THE HEBREW UNIVERSITY OF JERUSALEM
GEORGE MASON UNIVERSITY

Michal Dayan and Maia Zisso

THE ISRAEL POLICE

In his seminal address to the Police Foundation in 1998, Lawrence Sherman called for "Evidence-Based Policing" (EBP), or use of the best available scientific evidence to guide police practice (Sherman, 1998). He argued that police agencies should base their decisions about policies, strategies, and tactics on rigorous scientific evaluations and on analytic knowledge generated within the agency. Since then, this philosophy has been drawing much attention among police researchers and practitioners (e.g., Greene, 2014; Neyroud & Weisburd, 2014; Sherman, 2015; Sparrow, 2011; Willis & Mastrofski, 2014).

One important issue that has been occupying advocates of EBP concerns potential barriers to its successful implementation. These may include political or public pressure on the agency to adopt (or neglect) particular policies or practices, irrespective of scientific evidence. Police agencies face budget and time constraints, which may inhibit their ability to stay informed about the latest research evidence, invest in research, and implement policies and practices that were found to be effective. Sufficient scientific evidence about "what works" is often lacking, but even if available, police may face difficulties in accessing and comprehending academic publications or drawing concrete, practical conclusions from data or knowledge generated elsewhere. Practitioners may not view the topics scholars focus on as central, but even if the interests of academics and practitioners align, scientific answers are often not provided within the timeframe required for real-world decision making. Finally, police leaders may be concerned that research could expose them or the agency to unnecessary criticism (e.g., Fleming & Rhodes, 2018; Lum & Koper, 2017; Lum, Telep, Koper, & Grieco, 2012; Weisburd & Neyroud, 2011).

Scholars have also known for decades that experience, or "craft," plays a key role in police decision making in the field (e.g., Bayley & Bittner, 1984; Muir, 1977; Wilson, 1978), and this

DOI: 10.4324/9781003153009-15

has often been treated by proponents of EBP as a major obstacle to evidence-based reforms (Willis, 2013). They have, thus, tried to rationally argue for the benefits of scientific evidence over arbitrary experiences and unsystematic reasoning (e.g., Lum, 2009; Sherman, 1984, 1998) but in doing so, have paid little attention to the psychological mechanisms (that are not necessarily influenced by rational arguments) pushing practitioners to place substantial weight on professional experience when making decisions. In this chapter, we illuminate these psychological processes and illustrate the extent to which police prefer experience to science as a basis for decision making, even when they are convinced of the value of EBP.

Drawing in large part on theory and research in psychology, we review, more generally, the tendency of practitioners to prefer experience to research as the basis for decision making, its roots, and potential implications. We then present findings from a "receptivity to research" survey carried out among high-ranking officers in the Israel Police (IP). In line with our hypotheses, we find broad support for the philosophy of EBP, coupled with an apparently contradictory preference for relying on professional experience when making decisions. The two formed different (yet correlated) constructs. We also find that the tendency to favor experience over science is an overarching trait, not associated with any particular personal-level characteristics. We conclude by discussing the potential implications of this broad, psychological tendency for the implementation of EBP.

Practitioners' Proclivity to Base Decisions on Professional Experience

There is broad agreement that practitioners display a preference for basing professional decision making on experience and intuition, even when scientific evidence is available and its value is recognized. This tendency was identified in diverse fields such as medicine (e.g., Swennen et al., 2013), psychiatry (Hannes, Pieters, Goedhuys, & Aertgeerts, 2010), nursing (Mills, Field, & Cant, 2009), physical therapy (Schreiber & Stern, 2005), occupational therapy (Thomas & Law, 2013), psychology (e.g., Steward, Stirman, & Chambless, 2012), and human resources (e.g., Highhouse, 2008). Not surprisingly, this inclination was also identified in studies in policing, where the balance between experience and scientific knowledge has been compared.

For example, Telep and Lum (2014) surveyed officers from three police agencies in the United States and concluded that:

> Respondents. . . overwhelmingly believed that collaboration with researchers is necessary for a police agency to improve its ability to reduce crime. . . officers generally recognize the importance of research evidence to help make their department better at fighting crime. (p. 19)

At the same time, they found that the most common response to a question about the appropriate balance between the use of scientific research and personal experience was 25%:75%, respectively. Their findings were replicated in a sample of chiefs and sheriffs from Oregon (Telep & Winegar, 2015), and resemble those of surveys, interviews, and focus groups from the United Kingdom (Fleming & Rhodes, 2018; Hunter, Wigzell, May, & McSweeney, 2015; Palmer, 2011).

The explanations offered in the policing literature for such findings were often based on rational reasoning. Willis and Mastrofski (2014), for example, argue that police would "continue to rely on experience, not science, to direct their practices" because "science does not solve 'their' most pressing problem" (p. 322). Indeed, in numerous areas (such as police recruitment and training, use of force, and perceived police legitimacy), criminology research has yet to produce a body of knowledge that enables prediction with high probability and sufficient strength to generate guidance for both what police should be doing and how they should be doing it (President's Task Force on 21st Century Policing, 2015; Telep, 2016; Weisburd & Majmundar, 2018). Lum and Koper (2017) claim that police persistently argue for the value of their "craft" to avoid forces such as technology or scientific knowledge from limiting their discretion and autonomy. These explanations provide valuable insight but overlook the generality of the phenomenon: The inclination to prefer experience to research as the basis for decision making is not unique to policing, and develops from familiar psychological mechanisms, which we will review later.

One explanation is offered by Ruscio (2010). He explains that since personal experience produces knowledge that is acquired firsthand, it is often more emotionally resonant than the colorless scientific evidence reported in the literature, and consequently more vivid. Vivid information is more easily retrieved from memory. In turn, the availability heuristic (Tversky & Kahneman, 1973) leads one to believe that an experience that is easily recalled represents an occurrence that is frequent or highly likely. Thus, the vivid personal experience, which quickly came to mind, appears particularly relevant.

Giluk and Rynes (2012) argue that the tendency to trust personal experience stems from a combination of individuals' preference for "anecdotal evidence"—evidence in the form of "stories" (p. 140)—coupled with a strong need to believe in one's own stories. They explain that people use stories to make sense of the world (Mink, 1978), and that specific cases tend to influence people more than abstract probabilities (Kahneman & Tversky, 1973). They further propose that personal experience is a particular type of "story," "one of the most powerful stories of all in terms of its ability to produce resistance to contradictory research evidence" (p. 141). The first reason for this is that individuals have the need to view themselves favorably, and therefore think and behave in ways that maintain their positive self-image (e.g., Epstein, 1973). Research evidence that suggests to practitioners that their knowledge is incorrect, or their methods are flawed, challenges their self-esteem. Second, people seek consistency between their attitudes and behavior to avoid cognitive dissonance (Festinger, 1957). This inhibits their ability to question the effectiveness of their practice.

Grove and Meehl (1996) discuss impressionistic versus mechanical prediction and list several sociopsychological factors that, in their view, help to explain the frequent preference for subjective prediction in various professional settings. First, practitioners may be concerned that "technology" (or science) would make them unnecessary to the point of unemployment. In the context of policing, officers may fear that in an evidence-driven department, officers who are experts in scientific evidence would advance, whereas those who are not would be left behind. Mechanical prediction may threaten practitioners' self-esteem. They may also be attached to a particular "theory" about how the world works and threats to this "theory" may arouse cognitive dissonance. Professionals may believe that "technical" methods would lead to cold, detached, un-empathic treatment, and consequently may be dehumanizing to their clients; they may feel resentment to the idea that computers (or science more generally) can outdo human cognitive performance; or they may resist mechanical prediction due to poor education.

Finally, Highhouse (2008) offers an explanation based on the need to feel optimistic about the outcome of a decision. He builds on Einhorn (1986), who differentiates between the intuitive and analytical approaches to human prediction. The intuitive (or experience-based) approach reflects a deterministic view of the world, in which the idea that the future is inherently probabilistic is rejected. Accordingly, potential errors in predicting the outcome of a decision remain abstract and ambiguous. The analytical (or research-based) approach accepts uncertainty as inevitable and, thus, error is recognized and becomes an inherent part of the prediction. In turn, ambiguity about the likelihood of an outcome enables more optimism than a known, low probability of success (Kuhn, 1997). In other words, experience-based solutions with an unknown chance of success are attractive because they allow one to be more optimistic about the outcome, compared with a research-based solution with a known probability of failure.

In sum, the psychology literature suggests that the proclivity to rely on professional experience and common sense when making decisions, even when recognizing and valuing science, is rooted in various emotional needs and cognitive biases and heuristics, which influence everyone, including highly experienced professionals. Personal experience is vivid, easily retrieved from memory, and consequently appears particularly relevant. It makes sense because it is a "story" rather than "data," and people have a strong need to believe in these stories to preserve their favorable self-image and avoid dissonance between what they believe and what they do. For similar reasons, they are concerned that "technical" or "statistical" solutions would take over, making them inferior or unnecessary and/or their work impersonal and detached. Finally, practitioners are inclined to solutions that enable them to feel optimistic about the outcomes of their decisions.

Experience-Based Decision Making in the Context of Evidence-Based Policy

As noted earlier, the inclination to base decision making on personal experience and intuition has been treated by some proponents of evidence-based policy as a major obstacle to its successful implementation. In this section, we elaborate on their arguments, but also on arguments in favor of experience-based decision making and demonstrate that scholars are of two minds about if (and how) experience should be used when making professional decisions.

On the one hand, Ruscio (2010), for example, claims that "(t)o grant center stage to one's personal experience. . . can be to devalue the more informative collective experience of many other clinicians who have worked with a much larger and broader sample. . . " (p. 301). He explains that generalizing from personal experience violates the principles of scientific reasoning: It is unclear what the sample of one's experiences represents and how much or what type of "data" is missing due to memory limitations and biases, "conditions" of treatment are not "assigned" randomly, the reliability and validity of the outcomes as recalled from memory are questionable, and the "analysis" is vulnerable to illusory correlations, while real relationships that are subtle or counterintuitive may go unnoticed. In the context of policing, Lum and Koper (2017) argue that experience can often be overvalued, and given the high levels of discretion that characterize the profession, it can impede receptivity to outside knowledge and change. This becomes particularly problematic when research evidence contradicts conventional wisdom. Other proponents of EBP make similar claims (e.g., Lum, 2009; Sherman, 1984, 1998).

On the other hand, some argue for the importance of "expertise-based intuition," developed through extensive practice and experience. Salas, Rosen, and Diaz Granados (2010) clarify the distinction between two information-processing systems: An "intuitive" system, that is, "fast, holistic, and does not require conscious cognitive effort," and a "conscious deliberative" system, that is, "slower, analytic, and cognitively effortful" (p. 945). Their review of the literature suggests that there are conditions under which the intuitive system is more likely to be accurate: Among more experienced practitioners (as long as this experience was accompanied by feedback), when the present situation falls within the experience domain of the decision maker, when the task is complex (e.g., the definition of "success" is ambiguous), and when the environment is characterized by stressors such as time pressure. It is important to note that one's tendency to rely on either of the two systems has been treated by researchers as an individual difference variable: people prefer to process information using cognitive reasoning or intuitive impressions and feelings. We have no reason to suspect, however, that police officers' sociodemographic and other individual-level characteristics typically measured in police surveys would be associated with this preference.

In the context of policing, Willis (2013) echoes early arguments by Bayley and Bittner (1984) about the importance of the policing "craft." He argues that unlike strict scientific evidence, the policing craft enables creativity and flexibility in matching responses both to the particulars of the situation, and to the skills and personal traits of the responding officer, such as level of experience and verbal facility. In addition, police are often expected to accomplish numerous goals beyond crime control (which has traditionally been the focus of scientific inquiry), such as responsiveness to the victim, ensuring safety at the scene, preventing escalation, and, more broadly, equity, legitimacy, liberty, and other public values. Science is often silent about the best way to achieve such outcomes, and consequently there is no substitute for officers' professional experience (also see Willis & Mastrofski, 2014).

We return to the debate on the roles professional experience and scientific evidence should play in police decision making, and link it to our findings and their implications, in the "Discussion" section. At this juncture, as already noted, the main point we take from the literature is that earlier findings revealing police officers' proclivity to view science favorably, but nevertheless prefer experience as the basis for decision making, are not unique to policing, which is not surprising given that this inclination develops from familiar, deep-rooted psychological mechanisms. Accordingly, we put forward the following hypotheses:

Hypothesis 1: Police officers in our sample would show broad support for EBP.

Hypothesis 2: At the same time, despite this support, officers would display a preference for basing decision making on professional experience rather than scientific evidence (e.g., Telep & Lum, 2014).

Hypothesis 3: Support for EBP and the inclination to rely on experience would form two separate constructs (which may nevertheless be correlated).

Hypothesis 4: The tendency to prefer experience over science as the basis for decision making would not be associated with officers' personal-level characteristics.

Method

Study Context

The present study was carried out in the IP, Israel's national and only police agency.[1] Due to the circumstances of its establishment (in a time of war, on the basis of the British Mandate Police, a colonial military police force), and the major role this agency has played in leading internal security efforts, the IP is often considered a relatively centralized, quasimilitary agency in organization, culture, and procedures (see review by Jonathan-Zamir & Harpaz, 2018). At the same time, there are strong similarities between the IP and many Western, democratic police agencies. Israeli police officers are constrained by law from abusing their authority and are obligated to provide equal treatment to all. The day-to-day duties and operations of the local police stations resemble those of local police agencies in the United States or Europe: They are responsible for all local crime, disorder, and traffic problems, and their patrol and traffic officers handle most interactions with citizens (e.g., Weisburd, Jonathan, & Perry, 2009). Finally, the IP has been influenced over the years by international trends in policing, such as community policing, hot spots policing, and problem-oriented policing (see review by Jonathan-Zamir, Weisburd, & Hasisi, 2015).

Importantly, the Acting Commissioner of the IP at the time of the study (Inspector General Roni Alsheikh) was very much committed to the idea of EBP. Based on the principles of problem-oriented policing (e.g., Goldstein, 1979), situational crime prevention (e.g., Clarke, 1980), community-oriented policing (e.g., Skolnick & Bayley, 1988), and public legitimacy as the basis for legal compliance (e.g., Tyler, 2009), he introduced a broad strategic plan oriented toward addressing the problems troubling the public (see reviews by Casey, 2017; Zisso, 2017).[2] His approach led to the development of a computerized system guiding the day-to-day operation of the local stations. This system, which translates the principles of the strategy into action, allows local station commanders to identify the salient problems in their area (based, in large part, on the priorities of the local community[3]) and track their accomplishments in addressing these problems (Laufman-Gavri & Hasisi, 2017). In sum, our study took place in a period where the philosophy of EBP was highly valued by the top leaders of the agency, and, through an innovative management system, influenced the day-to-day decision making of the local station commanders. These circumstances further strengthened our hypothesis that officers in our sample would support and value the philosophy of EBP.

Participants

The study population includes all IP nonadministrative top commanders at the rank of Superintendent or above (excluding the Commissioner), such as the commanders of the districts, subdistricts, and local stations; "Operations" and "Investigations" commanding officers at the district and subdistrict levels; and the top commanders of the five national divisions: "Patrol," "Intelligence," "Investigations," "Operations and Security," and "Traffic" ($N = 420$). This population was chosen because the officers' position as top field commanders allowed them to play a major role in implementing evidence-based policy in real-world street policing. All officers who met our inclusion criteria were approached and invited to participate in the study (see below). Of this population, 227 agreed (response rate of 54%). This response rate is considered high for anonymous, self-administered web-based surveys (Nix, Pickett, Baek, & Alpert, 2017). Ten respondents were excluded from the final sample either because, despite their position, their rank was not within our inclusion criteria (6) or because their rank was not specified (4). This resulted in a final sample of 217 officers. The characteristics of these officers are described in the middle column of Table 11.1.

As can be seen in Table 11.1, officers in our sample are at least 30 years old, with higher education (86% hold a master's degree), and a minimum of 7 years of policing experience. These characteristics are not surprising given that our population was defined as the top command of the force: higher education and experience are necessary steps in promotion. Notably, Telep (2017) found a relationship between master level education and increased receptivity to research, which again strengthened our hypothesis that these officers would show broad support for EBP.

Most officers hold one of the two lower ranks in our inclusion criteria—Superintendent or Chief Superintendent—and their background is primarily in the Operations or Investigations and Intelligence Divisions. Almost all are majority Jewish men, who were born in Israel. This socio-demographic profile is not unique to Israeli policing and characterizes traditional recruitment patterns in police agencies (e.g., Loftus, 2010). Telep and Winegar (2015), for example, found in their sample of chiefs and sheriffs from Oregon, that nearly 87% were White, non-Hispanic males.

In the right column of Table 11.1, we report the individual-level characteristics of the study population, as were made available to us at the aggregated level. These figures suggest that our sample closely mirrors the population from which it was drawn in terms of sex, age, and years of experience. The top two ranks of the population are somewhat underrepresented in our sample, while the lower

TABLE 11.1 Personal-Level Characteristics of the Sample and Population

Variable	Sample (N = 217)	Population (N = 420)
Sex	Male: 95.3% Female: 4.7% *n* valid = 214	Male: 94.9% Female: 5.1%
Age (years)	*M* = 46.40; *SD* = 5.00; Minimum = 30; Maximum = 61 *n* valid = 207	*M* = 46.22; *SD* = 5.50
Experience in the Israel Police (years)	*M* = 22.82; *SD* = 5.21; Minimum = 7; Maximum = 44 *n* valid = 210	*M* = 23.81; *SD* = 5.49
Rank (low to high)	Superintendent: 34.1% Chief Superintendent: 43.8% Commander: 17.5% Brigadier General: 4.1% Major General: 0.5% N valid = 217	Superintendent: 32.0% Chief Superintendent: 38.5% Commander: 18.4% Brigadier General: 7.0% Major General: 3.9%

Main professional background	Operations Division: 49.1%
	Investigations and Intelligence
	  Division: 38.8%
	Border Guard: 3.3%
	Other: 8.9%
	n valid: 214
		Operations Division: 28.1%
		Investigations and Intelligence
		  Division: 29.5%
		Border Guard: 3.9%
		Command: 31.5%
		Other: 6.9%

Education (low to high)	Higher education beyond high school: 1.4% Bachelor's degree: 11.2% Master's degree: 86% Doctorate: 1.4% *n* valid = 214	
County of origin	Israel: 91.1% Other: 8.9% *n* valid = 213	
Ethnicity	Jewish: 96.3% Druze: 3.7% *n* valid = 214	
Level of religiosity (low to high)	Secular: 61.2% Traditional: 33.6% Religious: 4.7% Ultra-orthodox: 0.5% *n* valid = 214	

two are slightly overrepresented. With regard to main professional background, the IP measures this variable using an additional category that was not included in our survey: "Command." Discussions with IP representatives clarified that these officers primarily belong to either the Operations or Investigations and Intelligence Division. In other words, 87.9% of our sample and 89.1% of the study population belong to one of these two divisions. In sum, the data reported in Table 11.1 suggest that the findings described represent the views of the top field commanders of the IP, although more so the lower two than the top two ranks in this population of officers.

The Survey Instrument

The questionnaire was designed by the research team based on similar surveys carried out in the United States, and the "receptivity to research" literature more generally (e.g., Lum et al., 2012; Telep & Lum, 2014; Telep & Winegar, 2015). In line with this literature, and to ensure its content validity, the survey captured the following themes: exposure to research evidence and obstacles to exposure, the perceived relevance of research evidence and barriers to applying the philosophy in real-world policing, how research evidence is used by the agency and officers' views on its use, willingness to cooperate with research initiatives, and ideas for future research in the agency. Most items were statements, which the officers were asked to rank according to their agreement, on a scale ranging from 1 (*strongly disagree*) to 5 (*strongly agree*). For some items, the officers were asked to rank-order several options according to priority (the way they wish to be exposed to research evidence and the factors that ought to be considered when making decisions). Finally, an open-ended question asked respondents to propose topics for future research. The internal consistency and discriminant validity of the scales used in the present analysis are reflected in the factor analysis and Cronbach's alpha levels reported in the findings section below.

Procedure

The survey was carried out online, using the internal web of the IP. A high-ranking figure in the Planning and Organization Department of the IP (with no commanding authority over the study population) sent an email to all officers who met our inclusion criteria, in which she explained the study and its importance and asked for their cooperation. Officers who concurred clicked on a link that opened the questionnaire. It began with a consent script detailing the identity of the researchers, the purpose of the study, and its expected contribution to the IP. Officers were assured that their participation was voluntary, the survey was anonymous, and their answers would be used for research purposes only. Emails requesting participation were initially sent on November 1, 2017. Reminder emails were sent three more times during the month of the survey.[4]

Analytic Strategy

Our hypotheses directed us to the two sets of survey items used in the present article: nine questions that measure general attitudes toward EBP and two questions that directly ask about the relative roles that personal experience and scientific evidence should play in professional decision making. We begin by examining the distribution of these items. Next, we use factor analysis to determine whether these two sets of questions indeed form two different constructs. We create scales based on the two factors, and, using an ordinary least squares (OLS) regression model, predict resistance to EBP (dependent variable [DV]) using officers' proclivity to base decision making on experience (independent variable [IV]), while controlling for personal-level characteristics. Finally, we compare the personal-level characteristics of officers who display particularly high proclivity to base decision making on experience, to all other officers.

Results

In Table 11.2, we present the distribution of the nine items that measure officers' broad views on the relevance of scientific evidence to their work. For all statements, agreement indicates resistance to EBP. As can be seen in Table 11.2, responses suggest broad support for this philosophy: More than 60% disagree with most statements, whereas only 7–16% agree. For example, 65.6% disagree that "In the world of policing, research should be viewed as a luxury rather than a necessity," compared with 11.6% who agree. A majority of 63.3% disagree that "Most policing studies are not relevant to my work" (9.3% agree), and 62.7% disagree that "Policing studies are often not about the core of police work," compared with only 16.3% who agreed.

TABLE 11.2 Officers' Views on the Relevance of Scientific Research to Real-World Policing

Descriptive statistics	Studies carried out in other police forces around the world are not relevant to the IP	Policing studies are often not about the core of police work	Policing studies are good in providing general knowledge, but are not helpful in providing real-world solutions	Studies about policing carried out in the academia are disconnected from reality	I have no trust in a policing study carried out by someone who never sat in a police car	Most policing studies are not relevant to my work	In the policing world, by the time studies provide results the topic is no longer relevant	The "hot" topics in the IP change too quickly for it to be worthwhile to study them	In the world of policing, research should be viewed as a luxury rather than a necessity
Disagree (responses 1 + 2)	69%	62.7%	54.9%	51.4%	57%	63.3%	64.3%	74.3%	65.6%
Agree (responses 4 + 5)	7.4%	16.3%	11.8%	14%	16.2%	9.3%	11.7%	8%	11.6%
M	2.21	2.48	2.49	2.60	2.52	2.37	2.39	2.23	2.31
SD	0.90	0.91	0.87	0.87	0.99	0.84	0.89	0.82	0.90
Range	1–5	1–5	1–5	1–5	1–5	1–5	1–5	1–5	1–5
n valid	216	215	213	214	216	215	213	214	215

Note: IP = Israel Police.

At the same time, a different picture emerges when officers are requested to rank-order the factors that, in their view, should be considered when making professional decisions. The officers were asked, "When making decisions about courses of action at the organization level, what should, in your view, be considered?" They were then presented with five options: the personal experience of the top command, the common sense of the top command, data/studies from within the IP, studies carried out in Israel by a figure external to the IP, and studies carried out abroad.[5] This question was again asked about decisions at the unit level, where a sixth option was added: data/studies from within the unit. Respondents were requested to rank-order these possible considerations by assigning the value of "1" to the most important consideration, and the value of "5" (or "6") to the factor that, in their view, should have the least effect on decision making. In Table 11.3, we report the most common response to each consideration and the percentage of officers who gave that response.[6]

As can be seen in Table 11.3, the value assigned most frequently to the "personal experience of the top command" consideration was "1," indicating that it should be the primary factor affecting decisions at both levels (49.7%; 54.1%). Officers also show consistency in the value they assigned research evidence: In their view, it should come after the personal experience and common sense of the top command, and the further from the decision-making unit the study originates, the less influence it should have on decisions. More than 70% of the officers in our sample expressed the view that studies carried out abroad should be assigned the least weight when making decisions.

The findings reported in Tables 11.2 and 11.3 suggest that, in line with our hypotheses, officers in our sample hold favorable views toward EBP overall, but nevertheless believe that decisions should be guided primarily by their professional experience, followed by their common sense. Only then should research evidence be considered, and the further its origin from the unit/agency, the less influence it should have. In Table 11.4, we present a factor analysis revealing that the survey items reported in Tables 11.2 and 11.3 indeed load onto two separate factors (for the items reported in Table 11.3, we only include those in which the most common response reflects the views of at least 50% of the officers).

TABLE 11.3 Officers Views on the Factors that Should Affect Decision Making at the Organization and Unit Levels

Considerations	When making decision about courses of action at the organization level, what should, in your view, be considered?	When making decision about courses of action at the unit level, what should, in your view, be considered?
The personal experience of the top command of the agency/unit.	1 (49.7%; n valid = 197)	1 (54.1%; n valid = 207)
The common sense of the top command of the agency/unit.	2 (28.9%; n valid = 197)	2 (36.1%; n valid = 202)
Data/studies from within the unit.	N/A	3 (38.2%; n valid = 204)
Data/studies from within the IP.	3 (34.2%; n valid = 199)	4 (50.2%; n valid = 203)
Studies carried out in Israel by a figure external to the organization.	4 (50.3%; n valid = 195)	5 (65.7%; n valid = 198)
Studies carried out abroad.	5 (71.1%; n valid = 194)	6 (81.8%; n valid = 198)

Note: The figures in the middle and right columns represent officers' priorities about the effect each consideration (left column) should have on decision making, where 1 = *the most effect* and 5/6 = *the least effect*. We report the most common response for each consideration, and, in parentheses, the percentage of officers who gave that response. IP = Israel Police.

TABLE 11.4 Principal Components Analysis Differentiating Broad View of Evidence-Based Policing from the Proclivity to Rely on Professional Experience

Item	F. 1	F. 2
1. Studies carried out in other police forces around the world are not relevant to the IP.	0.67	
2. Policing studies are often not about the core of police work.	0.75	
3. Policing studies are good in providing general knowledge, but are not helpful in providing real-world solutions.	0.68	
4. Studies about policing carried out in the academia are disconnected from reality.	0.78	
5. I have no trust in a policing study carried out by someone who never sat in a police car.	0.65	
6. Most policing studies are not relevant to my work.	0.60	
7. In the policing world, by the time studies provide results the topic is no longer relevant.	0.71	
8. The "hot" topics in the IP change too quickly for it to be worthwhile to study them.	0.70	
9. In the world of policing, research should be viewed as a luxury rather than a necessity.	0.69	
10. When making decisions at the organization level, what should be the role of the personal experience of the top command?		−0.83
11. When making decisions at the organization level, what should be the role of studies carried out in Israel by an external figure?		0.78
12. When making decisions at the organization level, what should be the role of studies carried out abroad?		0.73
13. When making decisions at the unit level, what should be the role of the personal experience of the top command?		−0.90
14. When making decisions at the unit level, what should be the role of studies carried out in the IP?		0.58
15. When making decisions at the unit level, what should be the role of studies carried out in Israel by an external figure?		0.71
16. When making decisions at the unit level, what should be the role of studies carried out abroad?		0.64
Eigenvalues	5.38	3.07
Variance explained (%)	33.64	19.17

Note: Varimax rotation with Kaiser Normalization; Kaiser–Meyer–Olkin measure of sampling adequacy = .78; only factor loadings > .40 are displayed. IP = Israel Police.

The next step was to examine whether the tendency to base professional decision making on personal experience and broad views about the relevance of scientific evidence are nevertheless correlated. We have thus constructed two indices: "Resistance to EBP" (average of Items 1–9 in Table 11.4; Cronbach's α = .86; M = 2.40, SD = .60; Range: 1.00–4.11; N valid = 206), and "Preference for experience over research" (average of Items 10–16 in Table 11.4; Items 10 and 13 were recoded so that higher scores reflect stronger preference for experience over research; Cronbach's α = .87; M = 4.30, SD = .83; Range: 1.71–5.00; N valid = 191). In Table 11.5, we present an OLS regression model predicting broad resistance to EBP using officers' preference for experience over science and personal-level characteristics. The variables "age," "years of service in the IP," and "rank" are all indicators of policing experience, and therefore only "years of service" was included. The values of the variance inflation factors (VIF) were smaller than 1.15, indicating that multicollinearity is not a problem in our data (O'Brien, 2007). The model is statistically significant (p = .01), but explains only a small percentage (6.9%) of the variance in officers' resistance to EBP. A previous study assessing the predictors of police receptivity to research reported similar R square values (Telep, 2017). Clearly, more work is needed to identify

TABLE 11.5 OLS Regression Model Predicting Officers' Resistance to Evidence-Based Policing

Variable	b	SE	β	95% confidence interval	
				Upper limit	Lower limit
Preference for experience over research	2.4★★★	0.06	0.32	0.13	0.34
Years of service	0.01	0.01	0.08	−0.01	0.03
Background: Investigations (vs. operations)	0.05	0.10	0.04	−0.15	0.24
Background: Other (vs. operations)	0.04	0.15	0.02	−0.25	0.34
Female (vs. male)	−0.08	0.22	−0.03	−0.50	0.35
Education	−0.05	0.11	−0.03	−0.28	0.18
Born abroad	0.11	0.17	0.05	−0.22	0.44
Ethnicity: Druze (vs. Jewish)	0.28	0.24	0.09	−0.19	0.75
Level of religiosity	−0.08	0.08	−0.07	−0.23	0.08
R^2 (Adjusted R^2)		0.12 (.07)★★			
N		176			

Note: OLS = ordinary least squares.

★★ $p \leq .01$.

★★★ $p \leq .001$.

the factors that influence these views. Nevertheless, as can be seen in Table 11.5, preference for personal experience over scientific evidence is positively associated with resistance to EBP.

The final step in our analysis was to examine whether the proclivity to base decision making on experience is related to one or more personal-level characteristics. In Table 11.6, we compare the characteristics of officers with a particularly strong preference for basing decisions on experience, to all other officers. They were identified using a natural breaking point in the distribution of the "Preference for experience over research" index: Nearly one-third (31.4%) of the officers had the highest score possible: 5 (the other 68.6% were spread across all other scores; 0.5%–10.5% in each score). As can be seen in Table 11.6, these officers are very similar in their personal-level characteristics to all other officers. No statistically significant differences between the groups were found, suggesting that the proclivity to base decision making on professional experience is not associated with any particular sociodemographic or other personal-level characteristic in our data.

Discussion

Evidence-based policing has become a major topic of interest in the policing literature in recent years. In seeking ways to foster its implementation, scholars sought to convince police of its benefits and worked diligently to make research evidence clear, accessible, and relevant to practitioners (e.g., Lum & Koper, 2017). Indeed, studies show that police often express both familiarity with and support for EBP (e.g., Telep, 2017; Telep & Lum, 2014; Telep & Winegar, 2015). At the same time, these studies also reveal that officers believe that their professional decisions should be based primarily on experience, not research. These confusing findings are intriguing, but to date policing scholars have made little effort to consider them in the broader context of other professions, understand their psychological basis, or think through their implications for implementing EBP. In the present study, we set out to illuminate this phenomenon, both theoretically (using the psychology literature) and empirically (with a sample of high-ranking officers from the IP), and consider its implications.

TABLE 11.6 Personal-Level Characteristics of Officers with Strong Preference for Experience over Research and all Other Officers

Variable	Strong preference (n = 60)	All other (n = 131)
Sex	Male: 93.3% Female: 6.7%	Male: 96.9% Female: 3.1% χ^2 (1, n = 190) = 1.31, p > 0.05
Age	M = 46.36; SD = 5.24; Minimum = 30; Maximum = 56	M = 46.44; SD = 4.85; Minimum = 30; Maximum = 58 t (182) = .11, p > 0.05
Experience in the Israel Police (years)	M = 22.52; SD = 5.50; Minimum = 7; Maximum = 33	M = 22.99; SD = 5.10; Minimum = 11; Maximum = 44 t (184) = .58, p > 0.05
Rank (low to high)	Superintendent: 25% Chief Superintendent: 53.3% Commander: 18.3% Brigadier General: 3.3%	Superintendent: 37.4% Chief Superintendent: 41.2% Commander: 17.6% Brigadier General: 3.8% χ^2 (3, n = 191) = 3.27, p > 0.05
Main professional background	Operations Division: 50% Investigations and Intelligence Division: 36.7% Border Guard: 3.3% Other: 10.0%	Operations Division: 51.2% Investigations and Intelligence Division: 38.8% Border Guard: 2.3% Other: 7.8% χ^2 (3, n = 189) = 0.46, p > 0.05
Education (low to high)	Higher education beyond high school: 3.3% Bachelor's degree: 8.3% Master's degree: 86.7% Doctorate: 1.7%	Higher education beyond high school: 0.8% Bachelor's degree: 13.1% Master's degree: 84.6% Doctorate: 1.5% χ^2 (3, n = 190) = 2.53, p > 0.05
County of origin	Israel: 96.7% Other: 3.3%	Israel: 89.1% Other: 10.9% χ^2 (1, n = 189) = 2.99, p > 0.05
Ethnicity	Jewish: 98.3% Druze: 1.7%	Jewish: 95.4% Druze: 4.6% χ^2 (1, n = 189) = 0.97, p > 0.05
Level of religiosity (low to high)	Secular: 65% Traditional: 30.0% Religious: 5.0% Ultra-orthodox: 0%	Secular: 62.0% Traditional: 32.6% Religious: 4.7% Ultra-orthodox: 0.8% χ^2 (3, n = 189) = 0.62, p > 0.05

Note: IP = Israel Police.

In line with the literature, we find that the top field commanders of the IP display the proclivity to base decision making on experience, but also hold favorable attitudes toward EBP overall. Not surprisingly, the two were found to be correlated, but nevertheless distinct constructs. We suspect that this is due to the fact that while general views of EBP may have been influenced by external forces (higher education, the approach of the acting commissioner[7]), the inclination to rely on experience, which is psychological in nature, was not affected in a similar way or to the same extent. This suggests that attempts to "convince" police of the benefits of science are of limited value. Logical reasoning may improve understanding of and support for EBP, but it is unlikely to tap deep-rooted psychological inclinations. Furthermore, we find that the proclivity to prefer experience to science does not characterize a particular "profile" of officers, at least not among highly educated, experienced commanders.

The limitations of these findings should be acknowledged. First, we recognize that in a more heterogeneous sample, a profile characterizing officers with particularly strong preference for experience-based decision making may have emerged (see Telep, 2017). More generally, we are aware of the specific characteristics of our context and are clearly not suggesting that these findings necessarily represent the situation in other countries, police agencies, or policing contexts. We strongly encourage future replications. At the same time, our findings are very much in line with the theoretical arguments and earlier studies reviewed above.

To the extent that the findings reported here are not unique, a major question becomes: In seeking ways to implement EBP, how should we treat officers' inclination to place substantial value on their professional experience? Perhaps the first issue to address is pragmatic: Is it possible to "make" officers place less weight on experience and more on science when making decisions? The literature reviewed above suggests that the proclivity to rely on experience develops, in large part, from deep-rooted psychological mechanisms that are not necessarily rational or easily susceptible to change. This conclusion leads to at least two important policy implications. First, it suggests that valuing EBP is not enough. Police need a structure encouraging them to make decisions in a systematic way. An example of this is the SARA model, which organizes the philosophy of problem-oriented policing into four clear steps (scanning—identifying a problem, analysis—collecting data on the problem, response—designing an appropriate response, assessment—evaluating the response; Eck & Spelman, 1987).

Second, if we accept that the tendency to rely on experience is "a fact of life," it will likely be more useful to invest in strengthening (rather than suppressing), the intuition/experience-based processing system, by making the content of officers' experience more reliable and consistent with scientific evidence. This proposition is in line with Lum and Koper's (2017) argument that police "experience," or "craft," are not magical or immutable. They develop from daily tasks, policies, procedures, organizational structures, and rules. If these change, the content of one's experiences change. Hence, science can be made part of the "experience" and "intuition."

Accordingly, we propose that given the psychological significance of knowledge that is acquired firsthand (Ruscio, 2010), police training and other reform initiatives should center on officers fully experiencing EBP. This would involve gaining direct, personal experience both in the process of scientific reasoning, and in the implementation of policing practices that were found to be effective. These experiences should involve officers' intellect, feelings, and senses. Furthermore, training staff should recognize and appreciate officers' past experiences, use these experiences to construct meaning, and lead a process of reflection and integration, as expressed in the "experience-based learning" approach (e.g., Andresen, Boud, & Cohen, 2000) and in the idea of "intuitive expertise" in organizations (Hodgkinson, Sadler-Smith, Burke, Claxton, & Sparrow, 2009). Future studies could begin testing this proposition by comparing the tendency to rely on experience/science, and the proclivity to use practices that were found to be effective (e.g., hot spots policing; see Weisburd & Majmundar, 2018), across officers who vary in the degree to which they were trained using the principles of experiential learning.

The second question to consider is normative: Is the proclivity to rely on experience "good" or "bad?" Should there be a place for experience and intuition in evidence-based policy? As reviewed earlier, scholars are of two minds (Rousseau & Gunia, 2016). Our study was not designed to contribute to this important, normative question. We do argue, however, that given the intrinsic nature of the inclination to rely on experience, it would be useful for policing scholars to begin viewing scientific evidence and professional experience not as conflicting viewpoints, but as elements that have to be combined for successful policing, because it would open the door for considering exactly what their roles should be. Such attempts have already begun in other fields, such as critical care medicine (Tonelli et al., 2012).

One proposition (which entails clear policy implications) is to differentiate between levels of decision making when considering the optimal information-processing system. It may be that tactical decisions at the street-level, in complex situations under varying degrees of stress and time pressure, should be made based on patrol officers' experience and intuition. Assuming that this "intuition" developed from evidence-based education, on the job experiences and feedback, and that the officers exercise "intuitive expertise" (Hodgkinson et al., 2009), the benefits of the fast, holistic, and relatively effortless processing system should outweigh its limitations in this context. At the same time, strategic decisions at the agency or unit level should be made based on the best available evidence, including the broad academic literature and in-house assessments (Sherman, 1998). Decision making at this level could, and therefore should, allow for slower, analytic, and cognitively effortful processes. Future inquiries could test this model by comparing the accuracy of predictions made in various situations (e.g., emergency conditions, ordinary patrol or traffic encounters, long-term strategic decision making) using different information-processing methods.

Conclusion

Recent discussions about the implementation of EBP have paid little attention to the fact that, similar to other professionals, police officers are psychologically inclined to rely on their professional experience, not research evidence, when making decisions, even when they are aware of and value scientific evidence. In the present study, we have illuminated this proclivity by providing theoretical foundations based on the psychology literature and empirical evidence from a survey of top Israeli police commanders. We conclude that initiatives to implement EBP in police agencies cannot assume that the process of adopting EBP is fully rational, that is, if we just convince police of the benefits of science, produce sound, relevant scientific evidence, and make it accessible, officers would embrace EBP. Our findings suggest that police officers often do view EBP favorably but are nevertheless influenced by deep-rooted psychological processes that are not necessarily rational. We, therefore, argue that attempts to implement EBP should be fully aware of practitioners' psychological inclination to trust experience over science, and, instead of trying to suppress it, EBP initiatives should build on it and "import" scientifically sound practices into the experience. We also propose that policing scholars should begin treating scientific evidence and professional experience as necessary components in successful policing and encourage future inquiries on how the two can best be combined.

Acknowledgements

The authors would like to thank the various figures in Planning and Organization Department of the Israel Police who have supported and assisted with the present study. We are also grateful to Prof. Stephen D. Mastrofski, Prof. Cynthia Lum, and the anonymous reviewers for their constructive feedback on earlier versions of this paper. Correspondence concerning this article should be addressed to Tal Jonathan-Zamir, Institute of Criminology, Faculty of Law, The Hebrew University of Jerusalem, Mt. Scopus, Jerusalem 91905, Israel; e-mail: tal.jonathan@mail.huji.ac.il.

Notes

1. Nearly 31,000 officers are employed by the Israel Police (IP). Its geographical structure mirrors its hierarchy of command: the country is divided into districts, subdistricts, and about 80 police stations that serve local communities, all supervised by the Commissioner who is appointed by the government every 3–4 years.

2. This program is called "Emun," which in Hebrew means "trust" and as an acronym stands for prevention strategies and focused management.
3. The issues troubling local citizens are measured using an annual, large-scale survey of roughly 26,000 citizens from all stations, clustered at the station level.
4. The survey instrument and procedure were reviewed and approved by the Human Research Ethics Committee of the Institute of Criminology, Faculty of Law, The Hebrew University of Jerusalem.
5. By asking about the "top command," the question was indirectly asking officers about themselves (as noted earlier, the study population was defined as the top field commanders of the agency). We chose to use an indirect question in this context so as to allow honest responses without the self-presentation of arrogance ("my personal experience should be the most important factor affecting decision-making").
6. For example, when presented with the question "When making decision about courses of action at the organization level, what should, in your view, be considered?," and the option "The personal experience of the top command of the agency/unit," 49.7% of respondents gave the response of "1," indicating that, in their view, personal experience should have the most effect on decision making. The ranks of "2," "3," "4," and "5" were assigned to the personal experience consideration by 16.2%, 15.7%, 12.2%, and 6.1% of the officers, respectively. In Table 3, we only report the most common response to each consideration, which, in this case, was "1."
7. This proposition is supported by institutional theory (Crank, 2003), which would predict that because advocating for EBP has become fashionable, these officers would express much support for the philosophy on the surface, but would not actually give science more weight in their decision-making process (for a similar example with COMPSTAT, an organizational management tool introduced in the New York Police Department [NYPD] in the early 1990s, see Willis et al., 2007).

References

Andresen, L., Boud, D., & Cohen, R. (2000). Experience-based learning. In G. Foley (Ed.), *Understanding adult education and training* (2nd ed., pp. 225–239). Sydney, Australia: Allen & Unwin.

Bayley, D. H., & Bittner, E. (1984). Learning the skills of policing. *Law & Contemporary Problems, 47,* 35–59.

Casey, Y. (2017). "Classic policing": The empirical basis for the "Emun" reform in the Israel Police. In M. Ziso (Ed.), *The essence of research* (pp. 13–39). Jerusalem: The Israel Police, Planning and Organization Department, Strategic Division. (In Hebrew)

Clarke, R. V. (1980). "Situational" crime prevention: Theory and practice. *British Journal of Criminology, 20,* 136–147.

Crank, J. P. (2003). Institutional theory of police: A review of the state of the art. *Policing: An International Journal of Police Strategies & Management, 26,* 186–207.

Eck, J. E., & Spelman, W. (1987). *Problem-solving: Problem-oriented policing in Newport News.* Washington, DC: Police Executive Research Forum.

Einhorn, H. J. (1986). Accepting error to make less error. *Journal of Personality Assessment, 50,* 387–395.

Epstein, S. (1973). The self-concept revisited: Or a theory of a theory. *American Psychologist, 28,* 404–416.

Festinger, L. (1957). *A theory of cognitive dissonance.* Evanston, IL: Row Peterson.

Fleming, J., & Rhodes, R. (2018). Can experience be evidence? Craft knowledge and evidence-based policing. *Policy & Politics, 46*(1), 3–26.

Giluk, T. L., & Rynes, S. L. (2012). Research findings practitioners resist: Lessons for management academics from evidence-based medicine. In D. M. Rousseau (Ed.), *The Oxford hand-book of evidence-based management* (pp. 130–164). New York, NY: Oxford University Press.

Goldstein, H. (1979). Improving policing: A problem-oriented approach. *Crime & Delinquency, 25,* 236–258.

Greene, J. (2014). New directions in policing: Balancing prediction and meaning in police research. *Justice Quarterly, 31,* 193–228.

Grove, W. M., & Meehl, P. E. (1996). Comparative efficiency of informal (subjective, impressionistic) and formal (mechanical, algorithmic) prediction procedures: The clinical–statistical controversy. *Psychology, Public Policy, and Law, 2,* 293–323.

Hannes, K., Pieters, G., Goedhuys, J., & Aertgeerts, B. (2010). Exploring barriers to the implementation of evidence-based practice in psychiatry to inform health policy: A focus group based study. *Community Mental Health Journal, 46,* 423–432.

Highhouse, S. (2008). Stubborn reliance on intuition and subjectivity in employee selection. *Industrial and Organizational Psychology, 1*, 333–342.

Hodgkinson, G. P., Sadler-Smith, E., Burke, L. A., Claxton, G., & Sparrow, P. R. (2009). Intuition in organizations: Implications for strategic management. *Long Range Planning, 42*, 277–297.

Hunter, G., Wigzell, A., May, T., & McSweeney, T. (2015). *An evaluation of the "What Works Centre for Crime Reduction": Year 1: Baseline.* London, England: Institute for Criminal Policy Research.

Jonathan-Zamir, T., & Harpaz, A. (2018). Predicting support for procedurally just treatment: The case of the Israel National Police. *Criminal Justice and Behavior, 45*, 840–862.

Jonathan-Zamir, T., Weisburd, D., & Hasisi, B. (2015). Editors introduction. In T. Jonathan-Zamir, D. Weisburd, & B. Hasisi (Eds.), *Policing in Israel: Studying crime control, community and counterterrorism* (pp. 1–6). Boca Raton, FL: CRC Press.

Kahneman, D., & Tversky, A. (1973). On the psychology of prediction. *Psychological Review, 80*, 237–251.

Kuhn, K. (1997). Communicating uncertainty: Framing effects on responses to vague probabilities. *Organizational Behavior and Human Decision Processes, 71*, 55–83.

Laufman-Gavri, L., & Hasisi, B. (2017, November 15). *"Let my station go": Reforming police practices in Israel.* Paper presented at the Annual Meeting of the American Society of Criminology, Philadelphia, PA.

Loftus, B. (2010). Police occupational culture: Classic themes, altered times. *Policing & Society, 20*(1), 1–20.

Lum, C. (2009). Translating police research into practice. *Ideas in American Policing, 11*, 1–15.

Lum, C., & Koper, C. S. (2017). *Evidence-based policing: Translating research into practice.* Oxford, UK: Oxford University Press.

Lum, C., Telep, C. W., Koper, C., & Grieco, J. (2012). Receptivity to research in policing. *Justice Research and Policy, 14*, 61–95.

Mills, J., Field, J., & Cant, R. (2009). The place of knowledge and evidence in the context of Australian general practice nursing. *Worldviews on Evidence-based Nursing, 6*, 219–228.

Mink, L. O. (1978). Narrative form as a cognitive instrument. In R. H. Canary, & H. Kozicki (Eds.), *The writing of history: Literary form and historical understanding* (pp. 129–149). Madison: University of Wisconsin Press.

Muir, W. K. (1977). *Police: Streetcorner politicians.* Chicago, IL: University of Chicago Press.

Neyroud, P., & Weisburd, D. (2014). Transforming the police through science: The challenge of ownership. *Policing: A Journal of Policy and Practice, 8*, 287–293.

Nix, J., Pickett, J. T., Baek, H., & Alpert, G. P. (2017). Police research, officer surveys, and response rates. *Policing & Society.* Advance online publication. doi:10.1080/10439463.2017.1394300

O'Brien, R. M. (2007). A caution regarding rules of thumb for variance inflation factors. *Quality & Quantity, 41*, 673–690.

Palmer, I. (2011). Is the United Kingdom police service receptive to evidence-based policing? *Testing attitudes towards experimentation (Master's thesis, Cambridge University, UK).* Retrieved from http://library.college.police.uk/docs/theses/Palmer-evidence-based-policing-2011.pdf

President's Task Force on 21st Century Policing. (2015). *Final report.* Washington, DC: U.S. Department of Justice.

Rousseau, D. M., & Gunia, B. C. (2016). Evidence-based practice: The psychology of evidence-based policing implementation. *Annual Review of Psychology, 67*, 667–692.

Ruscio, J. (2010). Irrational beliefs stemming from judgment errors: Cognitive limitations, biases, and experiential learning. In D. David, S. J. Lynn, & A. Ellis (Eds.), *Rational and irrational beliefs: Research, theory, and clinical practice* (pp. 291–312). New York, NY: Oxford University Press.

Salas, E., Rosen, M. A., & Diaz Granados, D. (2010). Expertise-based intuition and decision making in organizations. *Journal of Management, 36*, 941–973.

Schreiber, J., & Stern, P. (2005). A review of the literature on evidence-based practice in physical therapy. *The Internet Journal of Allied Health Sciences and Practice, 3*, 2–10.

Sherman, L. W. (1984). Experiments in police discretion: Scientific boon or dangerous knowledge? *Law and Contemporary Problems, 47*, 61–81.

Sherman, L. W. (1998). Evidence-based policing. *Ideas in American Policing, 2*, 1–15.

Sherman, L. W. (2015). A tipping point for "totally evidenced policing": Ten ideas for building an evidence-based police agency. *International Criminal Justice Review, 25*(1), 11–29.

Skolnick, J. H., & Bayley, D. H. (1988). Theme and variation in community policing. *Crime and Justice, 10*, 1–37.

Sparrow, M. K. (2011). *Governing science: New perspectives in policing*. Washington, DC: Department of Justice, National Institute of Justice.

Steward, R. E., Stirman, S. W., & Chambless, D. L. (2012). A qualitative investigation of practicing psychologists' attitudes toward research-informed practice: Implications for dissemination strategies. *Professional Psychology: Research and Practice*, *43*, 100–109.

Swennen, M. H., van der Heijden, G. J., Boeije, H. R., van Rheenen, N., Verheul, F. J., van der Graaf, Y., & Kalkman, C. J. (2013). Doctors' perceptions and use of evidence-based medicine: A systematic review and thematic synthesis of qualitative studies. *Academic Medicine*, *88*, 1384–1396.

Telep, C. W. (2016). Expanding the scope of evidence-based policing. *Criminology & Public Policy*, *15*(1), 243–252.

Telep, C. W. (2017). Police officer receptivity to research and evidence-based policing: Examining variability within and across agencies. *Crime & Delinquency*, *63*, 976–999.

Telep, C. W., & Lum, C. (2014). The receptivity of officers to empirical research and evidence-based policing: An examination of survey data from three agencies. *Police Quarterly*, *17*, 359–385.

Telep, C. W., & Winegar, S. (2015). Police executive receptivity to research: A survey of chiefs and sheriffs in Oregon. *Policing: A Journal of Policy and Practice*, *10*, 241–249.

Thomas, A., & Law, M. (2013). Research utilization and evidence-based practice in occupational therapy: A scoping study. *American Journal of Occupational Therapy*, *67*(4), e55–e65.

Tonelli, M. R., Curtis, J. R., Guntupalli, K. K., Rubenfeld, G. D., Arroliga, A. C., Brochard, L., & Mancebo, J. (2012). An official multi-society statement: The role of clinical research results in the practice of critical care medicine. *American Journal of Respiratory and Critical Care Medicine*, *185*, 1117–1124.

Tversky, A., & Kahneman, D. (1973). Availability: A heuristic for judging frequency and probability. *Cognitive Psychology*, *5*, 207–232.

Tyler, T. R. (2009). Legitimacy and criminal justice: The benefits of self-regulation. *Ohio State Journal of Criminal Law*, *7*, 307–359.

Weisburd, D., Jonathan, T., & Perry, S. (2009). The Israeli model for policing terrorism: Goals, strategies, and open questions. *Criminal Justice and Behavior*, *36*, 1259–1278.

Weisburd, D., & Majmundar, K. (Eds.) (2018). *Proactive policing: Effects on crime and communities*. Washington, DC: National Academies Press.

Weisburd, D., & Neyroud, P. (2011, January). *Police science: Toward a new paradigm* (New Perspectives in Policing). Retrieved from https://www.ncjrs.gov/pdffiles1/nij/228922.pdf

Willis, J. J. (2013). Improving police: What's craft got to do with it? *Ideas in American Policing*, *16*, 1–13.

Willis, J. J., & Mastrofski, S. D. (2014). Pulling together: Integrating craft and science. *Policing: A Journal of Policy and Practice*, *8*, 321–329.

Willis, J. J., Mastrofski, S. D., & Weisburd, D. (2007). Making sense of COMPSTAT: A theory-based analysis of organizational change in three police departments. *Law & Society Review*, *41*(1), 147–188.

Wilson, J. Q. (1978). *Varieties of police behavior: The management of law and order in eight communities*. Cambridge, MA: Harvard University Press.

Zisso, M. (2017). "High policing": The empirical basis for the "Emun" reform in the Israel Police. In M. Zisso (Ed.), *The essence of research* (pp. 41–58). Jerusalem: The Israel Police, Planning and Organization Department, Strategic Division. (In Hebrew)

12

From Cincinnati to Glasgow

A Case Study of International Policy Transfer of a Violence Reduction Program

William Graham

ABERTAY UNIVERSITY, DUNDEE, SCOTLAND, UNITED KINGDOM

Introduction

In 2008, faced with the ongoing problems of gang/group-related violence in the West of Scotland and in the city of Glasgow in particular, the Scottish Violence Reduction Unit (VRU) launched a new program, the Glasgow Community Initiative to Reduce Violence (hereinafter known as 'Glasgow CIRV').[1] This program had its origins in the American city of Cincinnati, Ohio and its Cincinnati Initiative to Reduce Violence (referred to hereinafter as 'CIRV' to differentiate between the two initiatives). 'CIRV' had been established in 2007 to address Cincinnati's gang/group violence problem and the associated homicides that had reached a 'trigger point' for city authorities (see Engel, 2013, in Deuchar, 2013). The situation in Cincinnati had become increasingly violent and the use of firearms increased, with a resultant rise in homicides and the targeting of police officers. Illegal guns started to flood the city, and by 2006, the homicide rate in Cincinnati reached an all-time high of 88 homicides per year with an average of 35 shootings a month, while violence in the predominantly minority communities continued to rise (Engel, 2013, in Deuchar, 2013).

The creation of 'CIRV' had drawn heavily on the concept of the 'focused deterrence strategy' (FDS) developed in the mid-1990s as part of 'Boston Operation Ceasefire,' also referred to as 'The Boston Gun Project,' to tackle homicides associated with gangs/groups involved in drugs supply and acquisitive crime (Kennedy, 1997; Braga *et al.*, 1999, 2001). The concept of 'FDS,' which involves a proactive, problem-orientated policing approach, was subsequently adopted and used in many violence reduction programs and initiatives across the United States, including Oakland and Los Angeles, Cleveland, Detroit, and Minneapolis (National Network for Safer Communities, 2014), but it was the Cincinnati example that largely informed 'Glasgow CIRV,' hence the focus here.

The problem common to both Cincinnati and Glasgow was persistent cross-generational gang or group-related violence, involving high levels of offending and victimization among relatively low numbers of individuals. This issue reflected social norms and group dynamics, which was seen to demand new social control mechanisms, or levers, both formal and informal, in order to prevent/deter cycles of offending and re-offending. It was also recognized that some gang and group members wanted to desist from offending (Kennedy, 1997). Although the gang cultures of America and Scotland were seen to differ (guns were more prevalent in America;

DOI: 10.4324/9781003153009-16

while knives, bottles, and sticks were the common weapons used in Scotland; alcohol misuse was a significant factor in Glasgow, unlike in the United States, where, in comparison, ethnicity was a factor); the VRU nonetheless recognized that common socio-economic factors (both are post-industrial cities, experiencing economic decline, high levels of unemployment and rising violent crime, with large urban youth populations experiencing deprivation and involved in territorial issues/turf wars), underpinned gang/group violence, meaning similar deterrence approaches to those undertaken in the United States, could potentially work in Glasgow.

The experiences of Cincinnati thus became a focus for Glasgow's fact-finding endeavors in seeking to develop an appropriate model to capitalize on the apparent success of such strategies in America, using elements of FDS to reduce gang-related violence, initially in one part of the city ('Glasgow CIRV' Six Month Report, 2009).

During this period, the author was a senior police officer and Deputy Project Manager of 'Glasgow CIRV', a position held for over two years until retirement from the police in 2010. He then embarked on doctoral research to explore this policy transfer from Cincinnati to Glasgow from an empirical and theoretical perspective, hence the focus of this chapter. The focus of the research was to understand the policy transfer process and mechanisms that underpinned it, as well as the outcomes, by applying and evaluating policy transfer models. The following sections discuss the situation in Glasgow, before summarizing the significant aspects of the policy transfer, and highlighting and discussing the key finding of the research – a back-flow of policy transfer (see Graham, 2016; Graham & Robertson, 2021), which does not appear to be documented elsewhere.

Glasgow and Its Gangs

Glasgow is Scotland's largest city, situated on the River Clyde in the west of the country, and was first established as a religious center in the 6th century. Following the Industrial Revolution of the 18th and 19th centuries, the population and economy of Glasgow grew exponentially, and it became 'the Second City of the (British) Empire' and one of the world's most important centers of heavy industry, especially in shipbuilding and engineering (Craig, 2010). In 1939, the population of the city of Glasgow peaked at 1,128,473, which led to significant urban renewal projects to reduce the inner-city population. The next few years saw a large-scale relocation of people to the peripheral suburbs of Pollok and Castlemilk in the south of the city, Drumchapel in the west, and Easterhouse in the northeast of the city, and also to new towns being built outside the city. This had the effect of massively reducing the population to its current level of 626,410, with the Greater Glasgow conurbation having a population of approximately 2,500,000 people (National Records of Scotland, 2018).

The east end of Glasgow, the area where 'Glasgow CIRV' first operated, contains the suburb of Easterhouse and includes some of the most socially and economically deprived areas in the UK (SIMD, 2020). Easterhouse, especially, has suffered from a long history of social problems, which have arisen due to the failure of city authorities to provide basic civic amenities when the housing scheme (or housing estate) was first built. In areas to the north of Glasgow, for example, Springburn and Maryhill, unemployment levels and drug abuse are among the highest in Scotland (Deuchar, 2009). Housing regeneration has made a difference, with old tenement buildings demolished or refurbished. However, social and economic deprivation still exits at high levels, which, in parallel with American cities like Cincinnati, has led to social problems and high levels of crime and delinquency (Deuchar, 2009).

Various researchers have discussed the fact that Glasgow has suffered for generations from a 'gang problem' along with the associated violence and territorialism issues (see Patrick, 1973;

Davies, 2007 and 2013; Deuchar, 2009, 2010; Deuchar & Holligan, 2010; Kintrea *et al.*, 2010). The gangs in Glasgow, especially those in the east end where 'Glasgow CIRV' was implemented, comprised young males typically in their teens, aged 12 years of age and up to their mid-20s. The issue of territoriality, or as Suttles (1972) describes it, 'defended territory,' can lead to regular large-scale fights and instances of violence, including serious assaults and murders (homicides) (see Kintrea *et al.*, 2010). For example, a senior police officer involved in violence reduction commented that gang violence had always been a part of life in Glasgow, with generations of family members being part of the gang culture and structure:

> Gang violence in Glasgow .... was almost a cultural norm.... that's what happens, that's what we do, and that's how it is. .... your dad was a gang fighter, so you'll be a gang fighter.
>
> (Senior Police Officer Interview)

Glasgow has long had a violent image and reputation, with Leyland (2006) stating that the homicide rate in Glasgow was approximately three times higher than the rest of Scotland. The official picture of the violence in Glasgow has also been a common theme in the media with reports that homicides (murders) are commonplace. It was these comparatively high levels of violence that led to the creation of the VRU in 2004, at first in the west of Scotland in the Strathclyde Police area and then, to cover the whole of Scotland, in an effort to tackle the perceived violence problems in the country, including gang violence, especially in the Glasgow area.

In contrast to Glasgow, Cincinnati had a different gang structure, which was commented on by a 'CIRV' official, who stated that they did not have formal structures with a 'king pin.' It appeared that initially the Cincinnati Police Department was skeptical that the gangs actually existed, and they believed that the gangs were more loosely connected and came together to commit crime:

> I guess like many cities, Cincinnati Police Department was in denial around the gang issue and I think a lot of that resulted from the formal definition of gangs. We did not have those well-formed gangs operating with the hierarchy, with a kingpin, these were more the loose-knit gangs, so once we started looking at the problem from that perspective, we could see that the gang problem evolved into these loose-knit crews, posses, whatever they call themselves, they hang together and commit crime.
>
> (CIRV Official Interview)

The Cincinnati Police Department engaged in an intelligence gathering exercise that analyzed the gang networks that existed in the city and demonstrated the level of interaction, and the number of gangs in Cincinnati, an exercise that 'Glasgow CIRV' also carried out later. A network analysis carried out by police and University of Cincinnati personnel established that the gangs/group networks are extensive in nature and show the levels of interaction, both in collaboration and in conflict, that exist between the gangs.

The doctoral research (which this chapter is based on), suggested that there were various reasons why Glasgow looked to adopt a new way to reduce and/or prevent gang-related violence. These included the issues of territorialism and violence and the impact on resources of city agencies, the media image of the city and the fear of crime experienced by the public. However, 'Glasgow CIRV' was established as the result of what appeared to be a gradual realization that a new approach was required to deal with the gang violence issue in the city, that will be discussed later in this chapter. This contrasts to the reasons why Cincinnati adopted the new approach for them when they reached a 'trigger point' in homicide and shootings and a realization that something drastic had to be done.

The Policy Transfer Process

Policy transfer research has, until relatively recently, been more significant in the areas of political science, especially studies in comparative politics and international relations between differing states (Stone, 1999; Dolowitz & Marsh, 2000). It now encompasses a variety of policy spheres, including welfare policy (Peck & Theodore, 2010), education (Bache & Taylor, 2003), police reform (Robertson, 2005), and transport (Marsden & Stead, 2011). Although a lack of empirical research has been noted in the field of criminal justice policy transfer (Jones and Newburn in Newburn and Sparks, 2004), key studies have been conducted on issues such as private prisons, Zero Tolerance Policing, 'Three Strikes' and mandatory sentencing (Jones & Newburn, 2007), electronic monitoring, and the role of the 'Drugs Czar' (Newburn, 2002). This chapter contributes to the evidence base, with a focus on one case of international criminal justice policy – the transfer of a violence reduction initiative from America to Scotland.

In using policy transfer models there are two key aspects of research that need to be considered: the so-called 'orthodox' view and the 'non-orthodox' also known as the social constructionist perspective. The orthodox view is best illustrated by the work of Dolowitz and Marsh (1996, 2000), who argue that policy makers have a range of options to incorporate lessons into a system or organization, which they categorized into four options: *copying, emulation, hybridization and synthesis,* and *inspiration*.

1. *Copying* is when a policy, program or institution is adopted in its entirety by the borrower without any amendment to or adaptation of the originating policy.
2. *Emulation* is when a policy, program or institution is not copied, but provides best practice to adopting actors, with changes and adaptations made to take into account the borrowing environment.
3. For *hybridization/synthesis,* Dolowitz and Marsh (1996, 2000) combined the two separate categories discussed by Rose (1993) in 'lesson-drawing,' whereby elements found in two or more countries are used to develop best practices to suit the adopter.
4. *Inspiration* is the study of familiar problems in unfamiliar settings that can inspire or expand ideas and fresh thinking about what is possible (see also Evans, 2009a).

The Dolowitz and Marsh model has been subject to criticism over the years, for example, by Evans and Davies (1999), who argue that the study of policy transfer has a multi-disciplinary character and that researchers do not have a unified theoretical or methodological discourse, from which they can learn lessons and develop hypotheses. Evans (2009b) developed this critique by focusing on four main deficits: First, it cannot be distinguished from normal forms of policy-making, as well as rational approaches to policy-making (see James & Lodge, 2003), and has no distinct form of enquiry. Second, policy transfer analysts fail to advance an explanatory theory of policy (James & Lodge, 2003). Third, it is claimed policy transfer analysts have failed to provide rigorous empirical tools for evaluating whether policy transfer has occurred or not. Finally, Evans (2006) maintains that policy transfer analysts fail to make research relevant to the real world of practice.

More recently, 'orthodox' policy transfer approaches have also been critiqued by critical human geographers and policy scholars, including Peck and Theodore (2010), Peck (2011), and McCann and Ward (2012), who examine the difference between the 'rational-formalist tradition of work on policy transfer, rooted in orthodox political science, and the social-constructionist approaches to policy mobility and mutation' (Peck, 2011, p. 774). Peck (2011) argues that the concept of 'policy mobilities' is better suited to explain the wandering and mobile nature of public policies across the world due to, for example, the increased globalization of communications. Peck and Theodore (2010) propose five key features of the 'mobilities' approach (pp. 169–170):

1. Policy formation and transformation are socially-constructed processes, best seen as a 'field of adaptive connections, deeply structured by enduring power relations and shifting ideological alignments'; policy transfer processes are rarely just about transferring policy knowledge and technology from one place to another, as there are intrinsic politics in play.
2. Those involved in policy transfers are not 'lone actors,' but are heavily involved in epistemic communities (Haas, 1992), involving consultants, advocates, evaluators, gurus, and critics.
3. Mobile policies rarely travel as 'complete' packages, but instead are transferred in a piecemeal fashion and often transformed in the process. They arrive at their destination, not as copies, but as 'policies already-in-transformation.'
4. Policy transfer is not a linear process of replication or simple emulation, but a complex process of non-linear reproduction and that 'policies will mutate and morph' during their journeys.
5. Given the 'spatiality' of policy making, policies should not be seen as traveling across an inert landscape, but rather in terms of a 'three-dimensional mosaic of increasingly reflexive forms of governance, shaped by multi-directional forms of cross-scalar and interlocal policy mobility' (Peck & Theodore, 2010, p. 170). In other words, policies do not transfer intact across boundaries, but evolve through mobility, transforming the landscape and remaking the relational connections between policy-making sites.

While conceding that orthodox policy transfer literature can illuminate policy actors, institutions and practices involved in international policy transfer, human geographers also contend that the literature is limited in three key ways: First, it does not look at the concept of 'agency,' and is focused on a limited set of actors. Second, the conceptualization of policy process is overly rationalistic as 'there is a tendency for good policies to drive out bad,' in a process of optimizing diffusion (Peck & Theodore, 2010, p. 169). Finally, there is a tendency to make assumptions that models are fully formed and ready for transfer, which does not take into account social, spatial, and economic issues (Peck & Theodore, 2010; Peck, 2011).

Marsh and Evans (2012) have addressed some of the concerns raised. For example, they disagree policy transfer researchers ignore agency by focusing all their attention on a limited set of actors; argue lots of research is not just focused on nation states; suggest policy transfer does not ignore transformational issues; and argue research in this field is also focused on processes and not just on outcomes. Finally, they contend that all policy transfers are complex.

A key aspect of the social-constructionist critique of orthodox policy transfer relates to the use of the term 'policy transfer,' which does imply a one-dimensional, linearity of approach. This was found to be a limitation of orthodox policy transfer modeling when it came to accounting for a key finding of this research – the concept of policy transfer 'backflow.' In contrast, the terms 'policy mobilities' and 'policy mutations,' discussed by Peck (2011), offer a useful way of conceptualizing and understanding the transfer process investigated in this research, impacted not only by the social, spatial, and economic reality of the host city, but also by Scotland's legal and criminal justice framework. However, this also does not allow for the possibility of 'backflow,' as discussed later.

It's Not Working!

One of the key issues in the policy transfer process is the case of voluntary transfer, when it becomes apparent to key actors that there is some dissatisfaction or problem with the status quo. When any policy, program or institution is no longer effective, or is perceived to be ineffective by the key actors, then it becomes apparent that there is a need for a new approach to be implemented (Dolowitz & Marsh, 1996; Rose, 1993).

This research indicated that one of the main reasons why Glasgow developed the policy transfer of 'CIRV' from Cincinnati was that there was a distinct dissatisfaction with past programs and initiatives and problems with the status quo on how to tackle the issues. What had been done and what was being done, by various agencies, was no longer effective or was perceived to be ineffective by many of the key interviewees. There was a general feeling in Glasgow's statutory and voluntary agencies that these issues of 'the fear of crime,' territoriality and gang violence were having a serious impact on the daily lives and future of the public, including the young people involved in the violence. It was also realized that past attempts to tackle the problems, by all of the agencies involved, were not working, as commented on by the Director of the VRU:

> There was an assumption about it. That's what we did and that's all you could do, you couldn't do anything else.... I've often said it, we pick up the ones who are injured and call them victims and we catch the ones who are fighting and assaulted and we call them accused, but that's quite a random outcome, and we only caught the feckless and the stupid so it was, and we kept doing it....We never seemed to tackle it.
>
> (Glasgow VRU Director Interview)

These comments suggest that the police were not selective in who they arrested when they turned up at gang fights. They would deal with those who were injured and 'label' them as victims and arrest those they caught and 'label' them as accused and pass them on to prosecutors, but this was not having any long-term impact on the problems. The Director further commented that even when murders occurred it seemed that there was almost an acceptance of the fact that murders were commonplace.

The Glasgow VRU Director further discussed the cultural acceptance of violence in Glasgow in recalling a meeting in London with the UK Government Home Secretary and others that had been instigated in response to a series of homicides in London. The Director listened at the meeting and realized that the public in Glasgow seemed to accept the levels of violence. Glasgow had witnessed three men murdered in the course of a weekend, all under 19 years of age, yet nobody seemed to care. It was almost as if the social and economic factors in the city, high levels of social deprivation in relation to alcohol and drugs misuse and unemployment, determined that these young men would die anyway of either alcoholism or a drugs overdose. There almost seemed to be a perverse pride in the fact that Glasgow had this image of being 'tough' and even professionals perpetuated this image (Glasgow VRU Director Interview).

The view of cultural acceptance and perverse pride in Glasgow's image of being tough by certain professionals was corroborated by a youth worker, who mentioned this in relation to the public perception of violence in Easterhouse:

> They accepted that was the norm and that was as it is. And some people were a bit downtrodden by the perception of Easterhouse and, unfortunately, some people wore it a bit like a badge of honor and took a perverse pride out of the notoriety.
>
> (Glasgow Youth Worker Interview)

Any attempt to tackle the problems proved to be unsustainable. It was clear that the city agencies had been engaged in trying to tackle the problem for many years and that the approaches adopted were not working. For example, a Housing official commented that short-term projects were favored in the past and tended to focus on small geographical areas:

> We have been trying to deal with the issues of gang violence in Glasgow for many, many years and in GHA (Glasgow Housing Association) we recognized that the approach taken simply wasn't working as the problem just went from generation to generation. What was tried in the past, was short-term projects. We would have a, have an impact on a relatively small area. Therefore, the problem was just moved elsewhere. So what we required was a joined-up approach to the issues.
>
> (Glasgow Housing Officer Interview)

The issue of the potential displacement of crime, as a result of the 'short term projects,' has been discussed in the past in relation to the use of dispersal zones to tackle crime in a particular area. This power to create a dispersal zone was used in the Parkhead area of Glasgow in 2009 for a period of four months in an effort to combat a rise in serious crime by one gang, in particular, the Parkhead Rebels. Clarke (1995) comments that displacement can have an effect on target, time, or place, however, an evaluation of the Dispersal Zone in Parkhead (McMillan & Roberston, 2012) found that police reported little evidence of dispersal in this instance, possibly due to the large geographical area of the dispersal zone.

Other interviewees supported the view that what had been tried in the past was not working, with the Education Director commenting that there was recognition that something had to be done differently, especially for young people involved in the gang violence (Glasgow Education Director Interview).

The recognition that past programs had been ineffectual was a subject of comment by a Scottish Government civil servant, who noted that what had been tried in the past in relation to gang violence, had not delivered the required results:

> ......There was recognition that, as we began to focus in, not just on violence, but then on gang violence, whatever it was, generally around violence wasn't quite delivering the results that we needed.
>
> (Government Civil Servant Interview)

Various interviewees, including the Social Work Manager, were of the view that the previous approaches to tackle gang violence had been ineffectual and 'piecemeal.' A single agency, on its own, could not solve the problem and there had been a lack of strategic thinking in the past. Police officers also commented on the failure of past approaches and the continuing violence issues. One officer stated that 'it was clear it hadn't worked because the gang violence was still there' (Glasgow Police Task Force Commander Interview), while another officer stated:

> There was a huge recognition that it hadn't worked and that was quite simply because the gang violence and culture was still continuing and it didn't seem to matter what we did.
>
> (Glasgow Police Area Commander Interview)

This research established that there had been a growing recognition and realization among city agencies and the Scottish government that what had been tried in the past was not working and was ineffectual. There was dissatisfaction with past initiatives that had been short-term and localized, and it was recognized that the status quo was not an option; therefore, the circumstances and timing led to the voluntary transfer of the CIRV model from Cincinnati.

Policy Transfer Mechanisms

Processes

As noted above, 'Glasgow CIRV' was developed to try to address the city's long-standing gang violence problem. It stemmed from a growing recognition and realization among city agencies and the Scottish Government that small-scale, short-term strategies generally proved ineffectual in the longer term, as identified in interviews with a housing officer and senior police officer:

> We have been trying to deal with the issues of gang violence in Glasgow for many, many years, and …. we recognized that the approach taken simply wasn't working as the problem just went from generation to generation.
>
> (Glasgow Housing Officer Interview)

> There was a huge recognition that it hadn't worked and that was quite simply because the gang violence and culture was still continuing…. it didn't seem to matter what we did.
>
> (Glasgow Police Commander Interview)

Dissatisfaction with past initiatives and consistent rises in levels of violent crime resulted in a proposal to adopt this new violence reduction initiative in Glasgow. This occurred after senior officials from the police and city council visited America on a fact-finding mission and learned about the Boston Operation Ceasefire project and its iteration in Cincinnati – 'CIRV.' On returning to Glasgow, the VRU Director presented the idea of adopting the 'Cincinnati approach' to senior police management in Glasgow, and it was approved for implementation in the East End of the city, which had been identified as the worst area for gang violence and associated problems:

> What really appealed to us about (US) CIRV, is it was really a partnership approach to things. It was something that we had perhaps tried in different small parts but we hadn't done it in the way that they had.
>
> (Police Executive Officer Interview)

The multi-agency approach prevalent in UK crime prevention strategies meant that consensus was sought with key agencies and actors in Glasgow to establish and develop the 'Glasgow CIRV' model, based on 'CIRV.' Meetings were held with key actors and service providers previously identified, as well as members of the Crown Office and Procurator Fiscals Service (COPFS) and the Scottish Children's Reporter Administration (SCRA).[2,3] The participation of the Community Planning Partnership was also required as this was seen as vital to the long-term sustainability of the project.[4]

> I was completely bowled over by it. I couldn't actually understand why we were only just finding out about it given that they had been operating it for the best part of 2 years at the time. (….) my first impressions were that the couple of multi-agency meetings that I went to were extremely well organized…..and I thought that was real commitment to trying to get the barriers down and making it work.
>
> (Glasgow Social Work Manager Interview)

> It is not just about doing something. It is about what change has it made? So in many ways, that's where the development into 'CIRV' in Cincinnati interested me because it appeared that it offered young people a route out of something. Whether it is into further education or whether it is into employment or real jobs, real people or real opportunities and actually changing a systemic culture. I think that's what's around for some of our kids in Glasgow

schools, those second and third generation lack of ambition, poverty of aspirations. And I think those are things that we needed to try and break that cycle.

(Glasgow Education Officer Interview)

However, not everyone involved was initially supportive of the proposal, even having observed first-hand how it worked in America:

> I hadn't really seen anything that I thought was particularly innovative or that interesting….For me, the gang culture in America was entirely different, and of a nature that beggared belief, where murder (homicide), weapons, like firearms, was actually commonplace. It was also very racial with black and Mexican gangs and membership at an entirely different level from what it would be in Glasgow, Scotland. ……. I never saw much there that I thought was transferrable.

(Community Safety Officer Interview)

Nonetheless, even given the negative views of this official, there was wide enough support across the multi-agency partners for the project to go ahead. The VRU was given the task of creating community 'buy in' and focus groups were held with community members in the east end of the city. Key actors (academic and policing) from Boston and Cincinnati were invited to Glasgow to provide insight into their experiences. Subsequently, £1.6 million of funding was secured from the Scottish Government for 'Glasgow CIRV' to run for a 3-year period, after which it was expected to be extended across the city, with financial responsibility and oversight being assumed by the city council.

Mechanisms

As already mentioned earlier in this chapter, the aim of 'CIRV' was to reduce the incidence of rising gang-related homicides in Cincinnati (Engel, 2013, in Deuchar, 2013). To this end, 'CIRV' adopted the FDS developed in Boston in 1995 (Kennedy, 1997) and created a multi-agency team to focus on rival gangs/groups engaged in the drugs market and who's feuding often resulted in shootings and homicides. In Cincinnati, police intelligence and probation records provided lists of gang members who were required to engage with 'CIRV' by attending a series of 'Call-In' sessions held in a courtroom, where they listened to various messages delivered by law enforcement, community members, and service providers (see Engel *et al.*, 2008, 2010). The key messages were, that the violence had to stop, the community had had enough, and that there was support available for those who wanted to change their lives by engaging with the initiative. 'CIRV' was praised for contributing to a 34% reduction in homicides in Cincinnati over the following 2 years (see Engel *et al.*, 2010, 2013).

Taking inspiration from the success of the Cincinnati initiative, 'Glasgow CIRV,' in seeking to address its gang violence problems, initially sought to *copy* 'CIRV,' although as previously mentioned, not all parties were initially convinced this was possible for various reasons:

> I was a bit concerned about how transferable some of it was into a Scottish context and whether or not they were going to try and straight lift the model or adapting it for context.

(Glasgow Education Officer Interview)

Such concerns highlight the importance of contextualizing the project taking into account the local environment. For example, it quickly became clear that there were legal restraints that made a direct *copy* impossible, and some adaptations had to be made. As a result, rather than *copying* 'CIRV,' a process of *emulation* (Dolowitz & Marsh, 1996, 2000) occurred, with certain aspects of 'CIRV' fully adopted, such as the management structure, whereas other key aspects had to be adapted.

> It wasn't a lift and lay. It was a 'tartanization'.... It was about.... unpacking it line by line. .... "Would A transfer to here? No. What do we need to do to A to make it transfer? If we tweak this or that, what's our hybrid version of that? That's us sorted A, now let's move on to B". It was very much unpicking it like a jigsaw and then rebuild it.... An adaptation, but guided by their experience, footprint, understanding, and their knowledge.
>
> (Glasgow CIRV Official Interview)

One key change that had to be made related to the compulsory nature of the American 'Call-Ins,' which could not be replicated in Scotland for legal reasons. In Cincinnati, probation powers were used as a mechanism to compel targeted offenders to take part, but this was not possible in Scotland, where it was initially proposed instead to use 'bail' mechanisms to compel gang members to attend 'Call-In' sessions. However, senior law officials in Scotland argued that, as bail powers are only applicable in the pre-trial period; their use could later prejudice a fair trial. It was determined that if a person agreed to attend a session linked to the gangs' project, then it might be construed that they were linked to gangs and violence. Therefore, to overcome the legal differences and constraints, 'Glasgow CIRV' embarked on a program of *inviting* gang members to attend *voluntarily*, what became known as 'Self-Referral Sessions' (in contrast to the compulsory US 'Call-Ins'):

> We couldn't force people in and we had to engage far more.... and convince people in hearts and minds. We had to do it on a much broader range of people.
>
> (Senior Police Officer Interview)

This was a significant difference from the approach used in the US and an example of the 'borrower' (Dolowitz & Marsh, 1996) having to adapt their approach to suit the local (in this case legal) context.

Self-Referral/Call-in Sessions

The first Self-Referral Sessions took place at Glasgow Sheriff Court on 24 October 2008, following the same structure as the US Call-Ins, but with the messages delivered to gang members in attendance taking into account the local context. The focus of the sessions was to demonstrate the expectations of the community, the availability of services for those wishing to engage, and the consequences for individuals and gangs should the violence continue. The session speakers followed a similar pattern as 'CIRV' to ensure communication of the 'Glasgow CIRV' key messages to those attending:

- There is a new law enforcement strategy (in place). For any subsequent act of violence, every member of the group will be pursued to the fullest extent of the law.
- The community has had enough. Stop the violence. Stop the killing.
- There is help available. There are ways out. ('Glasgow CIRV' Self-Referral Session Practice Note, 2010)

When seeking to *copy* the model developed by 'CIRV,' it was the intention of the 'Glasgow CIRV' team to invite members of different gangs to the session to attempt to 'widen the net' and publicize key messages to as many young people as possible. However, bringing so many 'opposing factions' together, could potentially compromised safety and security in the courtroom. This was offset at the Self-Referral Sessions by the Police presenting an 'image of strength' to the gang members, which resulted in the involvement of a range of officers from different services, including police court officers, Gangs Task Force, Mounted and Dog Branch officers, and even the police helicopter being present in and around the court building (Donnelly & Tombs, 2008).

Similar to 'CIRV,' the use of the courtroom was intended to provide gravitas to the occasion, especially with the Sheriff (Judge), in full judicial regalia, outlining the conduct expected of those in attendance in the courtroom. Guests were invited from a variety of statutory and voluntary agencies, representing those providing assistance to gang members to 'change their lives,' also in attendance were members of the community who could 'testify to the damage caused to them and the places they lived in' ('Glasgow CIRV' Self-Referral Session Practice Note, 2010: 4). The impact could be emotional:

> When we went along to the 'Call-In' session …. I was just quite staggered with that. You could see the immediate impact on young people and adults. It wasn't something that you went away thinking that, they must have felt this, or how did they feel? You could actually visibly see the impact on them.
>
> (Glasgow Social Work Officer Interview)

There were two sessions on the first day the initiative ran in Glasgow. The first was for young people aged 16 and under from high schools in the east end of the city, who had been identified by police intelligence and local head teachers as being gang members and who could potentially benefit from attending. As gang membership in Glasgow is generational, one of the aims of 'Glasgow CIRV' was to engage younger people in an effort to try to prevent them from becoming involved in gangs and violence, to try to 'break the links' with gangs that their older brothers, fathers, and uncles may have been actively involved with. A total of 95 young people attended on the day, including some aged 16–17 who were subject to a Supervision Order imposed by the Children's Hearing System.[5]

The second session, in the afternoon, was for adults aged 16 and over and included some prisoners from the local Young Offenders' Institute, who had been invited to attend and were brought to the court under guard. A stronger message was delivered to the 40 older males who attended this session, to reflect their age and gang involvement ('Glasgow CIRV' Self-Referral Practice Note,2010b.

Over the 3-year period that 'Glasgow CIRV' operated, there were a total of ten 'Self-Referral Sessions' held, with over 400 people attending out of approximately 700 invitees. The format and speakers originally mirrored the US Call-Ins, with speakers drawn from the local areas affected by the gang violence to reflect the Scottish context. The speakers included senior police officers who explained that if gangs did not stop the violence, then the law enforcement agencies would use all legal means available to prosecute them. Doctors also pointed out the futility and dangers of violence, and a mother of a victim of gang violence spoke passionately about the effect on her and the family. Ex-offenders also spoke of the waste of life due to the life of crime, and service providers highlighted the opportunities available should they engage with the program. This format evolved in subsequent sessions with some speakers being replaced with others. For example, the use of religious speakers in Glasgow was found to be ineffective, as opposed to the profound effect of such speakers on those attending 'Call In' sessions in Cincinnati, and therefore these speakers were not used again in Glasgow. Therefore, given the changes that were necessary in order for the project to fit the local context, it can be argued that 'Glasgow CIRV' used a process of *emulation,* as discussed by Dolowitz and Marsh (1996), adapting the 'CIRV' model as necessary.

Case Management

The case management process developed by 'Glasgow CIRV,' was distinctly different from that operated by 'CIRV.' In Cincinnati, case management was provided by an external partner, a non-profit organization 'Cincinnati Works,' which only dealt with adult 'clients' and focused on employability, reflecting the perceived needs of the target population (adult gang members involved in serious violence). In contrast, in Glasgow, the target audience encompassed a wider range of young people, who were nonetheless involved in gangs, who had not necessarily come to the attention of the criminal justice system agencies but wished to engage with the initiative. The prevention element of engaging with such people was an important difference from CIRV in Cincinnati, which only dealt with those already in the criminal justice system. The in-house 'Glasgow CIRV' Case Management team identified their needs, allocated appropriate services and mentors, and monitored their progress. By signing a pledge that they would cease their violent offending behavior, they were able to access a range of services offered under the 'whole systems approach' ('Glasgow CIRV' Case Management Practice Note, 2010a), where the focus was not just on employability, but included life-skills, well-being and health, personal development and skills, and anti-violence and knife awareness courses. This clearly reflected the 'public health approach' (Krug *et al.*, 2002) adopted by the VRU in Scotland, which treats violence as a social malaise and seeks to address the key risk factors that may increase the likelihood of violent behavior.

These different approaches were deemed successful, as evidenced by the evaluations conducted both on Cincinnati (Engel *et al.*, 2008, 2011) and 'Glasgow CIRV' that saw an average 46% reduction in violent offending by those gang members who have engaged with the program and a 34% reduction in all other types of crimes and offences. Involvement in gang fighting in the area also reduced by an average of around 73%, and weapon possession by 85%. Violent offending reduced by 56% (and other types of offending by 34%) among those clients who were subject to 'Glasgow CIRV's' most intensive personal development and employability programs (see Williams *et al.*, 2014; Graham & Robertson, 2021; Glasgow CIRV 2nd Year Report, 2010c).

However, this research identified a switch in these approaches in 2009 whereby, following a change in management at 'Glasgow CIRV,' it was proposed that Cincinnati's 'one-stop-shop' approach should be adopted in Glasgow, while, at more or less the same time, Cincinnati decided to restructure their service provision along the lines of Glasgow's 'whole systems' approach (from the interview with Professor Engel, 2012). This development appears to be the direct result of discussion and knowledge sharing between members of the epistemic network (discussed further later) that developed and grew from the planning and implementation of Glasgow 'CIRV,' although it was not seen as significant at the time. This finding forms the basis of a seemingly original insight into the policy transfer process – a 'back flow' – discussed further later.

Outcomes

This section will address the outcomes of this violence reduction policy transfer, in order to assess the applicability of transfer models, and reflect on their value in relation to understanding policy transfer more generally. The Dolowitz and Marsh model of policy transfer was used as a framework for this analysis owing to its flexibility as a tool for framing both the empirical and theoretical analyses. It was also useful in analyzing the results of the policy transfer, in terms of whether it could be considered a successful transfer.

According to Dolowitz and Marsh (1996, 2000), not all policy transfers are successful, the measure of which may be interpreted in different ways, for example, was it seen as a success by the key actors involved and/or did it meet its intended aims? 'Glasgow CIRV' was seen as a success, insofar as it appears to have met the aim of engaging young people and diverting them away from violent crime (Williams et al., 2014).

From a more technical and theoretical perspective, policy failure relates to cases that are uninformed, incomplete or inappropriate, none of which apply in the case of 'Glasgow CIRV.' Using such terms of reference, the transfer can be considered a success, as it was informed, complete, and appropriate for the city, even if the longer-term aim of sustainability was not achieved in Glasgow ('Glasgow CIRV' ceased to operate in 2011).

Backflow of Policy Transfer

In analyzing this case of policy transfer, it became clear that an important outcome, from both an empirical and theoretical perspective, warranted further consideration. As mentioned above, as a result of an exchange of ideas on mechanisms, specifically the case management structure/service, the originator of the initiative, and hence the donor in this case of policy transfer, 'CIRV,' appears to have 'learned lessons' from the transfer recipient, 'Glasgow CIRV,' and changed a key mechanism of their original project. In this way, 'CIRV' subsequently emulated 'Glasgow CIRV' and the research identified a 'backflow of policy transfer' (see Figure 12.1), thus, named because it demonstrates how aspects of adapted policies, mechanisms, or approaches may 'flow back' to the originating source (the donor) from the original borrower (the recipient) of the policy, program or approach.

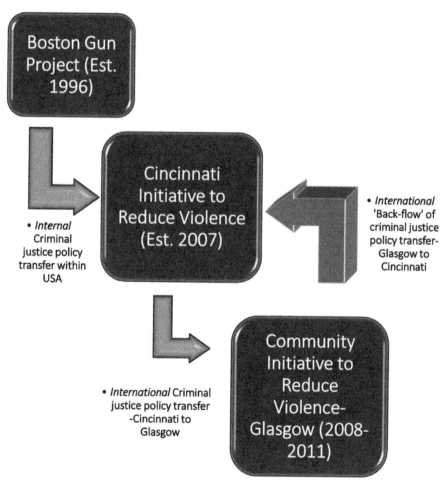

FIGURE 12.1   Backflow of policy transfer

Source: Graham (2016)

As mentioned above, a change in the management of 'Glasgow CIRV,' early in 2009, with a new project manager being recruited from the police, prompted a site visit to Cincinnati by members of the 'Glasgow CIRV' project team. After this site visit, some recommendations emerged as part of a review process in 'Glasgow CIRV' that it could be argued had limited impact and success. For example, the intention of a robust enforcement capability was not possible, due to the differences between US Law and Scots Law. Other measures included developing the 'moral voice of the community,' which was successfully engaged in 'CIRV,' but not in Glasgow. As a result of the *different* context/environment in Glasgow, it proved to be difficult to engage with community members to allow their voices to be heard, as opposed to the success of this approach in 'CIRV,' which was particularly strong in engaging local communities. 'CIRV' had dedicated local members of the communities who were fully engaged and assisted by the 'CIRV' Community Team lead, and regularly took part in local activities, spreading the 'CIRV' messages. This was not the case in 'Glasgow CIRV,' where difficulties in identifying and engaging key community members resulted in a distinct lack of community support. Furthermore, diversionary schemes were identified for young people under 16 for improvement and the establishment of a mentoring scheme for 'Glasgow CIRV,' but these failed to develop significantly. However, the new 'Glasgow CIRV' manager was impressed by the one-stop-shop approach offered by 'Cincinnati Works' and began developing a similar model for 'Glasgow CIRV,' a 'Glasgow CIRV Academy' model.

Paradoxically, this research has determined that following the 'Glasgow CIRV' site visit to Cincinnati, the 'CIRV' team discussed the 'whole systems' approach that 'Glasgow CIRV' had developed, of looking at the individual needs of the person and addressing those needs by offering courses and assistance as required: It was felt in Cincinnati that the current service provider, 'Cincinnati Works,' could not sustain a 'whole systems' approach to services, as it was more focused on employment provision for adults. Thereafter, 'CIRV' restructured their service provision to mirror that operated by 'Glasgow CIRV' at that time and offer more services to take into account the social and health needs of individuals and not just employability issues, by employing a new service provider, 'Taberham House.'

This change in focus and direction was developed as a direct result of the visit of the 'Glasgow CIRV' team members and by learning from their experiences, an example of information and practices being shared by epistemic networks (Haas, 1992). This development and change of operation indicate that 'CIRV,' the originator of the project in Cincinnati and the policy transfer to 'Glasgow CIRV,' learned from the recipient of the original policy transfer, Glasgow CIRV. Figure 12.1 illustrates this flow of ideas and working practices, first internally within the US, from Boston to Cincinnati. This was followed by the instance of international criminal justice policy transfer, where the information and learning from best practice flowed from Cincinnati ('CIRV') to Glasgow ('Glasgow CIRV') in 2008. Thereafter, there was a further exchange of working practices and ideas back to Cincinnati from Glasgow in 2009, which led to 'CIRV' changing their services to mirror those in 'Glasgow CIRV.'

The author has termed this transfer of policy as a *'back-flow of policy transfer,'* as it indicates that adapted policies and programs, or parts thereof, can flow back to the originating source from the original 'borrower' of the policy or program, in this case 'CIRV' to 'Glasgow CIRV' and back to 'CIRV,' leading to developments in 'CIRV' to improve services. It does not appear that this phenomenon has been documented before in the field of international criminal justice policy transfer in the studies that have been analyzed, for example, private prisons, electronic tagging, Zero Tolerance Policing, 'Three Strikes and You're Out,' and the 'broken windows' approach (Newburn & Sparks, 2004; Jones & Newburn, 2007).

The perceived growing trend of the UK importing policies from America has been discussed by Newburn (2002), Newburn and Sparks (2004), and Jones and Newburn (2007), in relation to the convergence of UK and US crime control policy. It has been the 'normal' practice, in the past that ideas and best practices generally flow from the US to the UK, as in this instance; the CIRV approach initially flowed from the US (Cincinnati) to Scotland (Glasgow). However, the process has in fact been partly reversed and subsequent working practices, in terms of the model of how to deal with and manage clients, flowed back to the US from the UK. As such, this is a key finding of the research and it adds to the existing academic knowledge base. This aspect indicates that policy transfer in the criminal justice field can, in fact flow both ways. This finding may have an impact on the study of criminal justice policies by proposing an extension to the Dolowitz and Marsh model of policy transfer beyond its linear and finite scope, by showing that transfer can be cyclical in nature and not be restricted to 'one-way traffic.'

Conclusion

In conclusion, this research suggests that policy transfer models, whether they be orthodox (e.g. Dolowitz and Marsh, 1996), or non-orthodox (e.g. McCann & Ward, 2012; Peck, 2011; Peck & Theodore, 2010), are useful in different ways when analyzing cases of policy transfer from a theoretical perspective, with orthodox approaches also offering a useful practical framework for planning and conducting empirical research. It was found that no single model was able to accommodate the 'backflow' identified from the case study; however, there was more scope for this in the non-orthodox approaches, underpinned by mobility and mutation, than orthodox approaches, underpinned by 'linearity.'

Policy transfers are often complex and can have both intended and unintended outcomes – as revealed by the 'backflow' finding here. This raises the question of when the process of policy transfer ends, which is not easy to answer and perhaps warrants further research. In terms of relevancy to the 'real world' of policing and violence reduction, this research suggests there is scope for policy transfer in similar socio-economic and crime contexts, even when the characteristics of crime patterns are different, provided the nature of the target population and their offending behavior is understood and used to modify policies accordingly so that they are fit for purpose. Adaptability and flexibility are, therefore, key, meaning policies are likely always to evolve through mobility, as highlighted by non-orthodox transfer theorists.

This case study also highlighted the key role of the police in policy transfer, which was significant. The key responsibility of the police has been, and is primarily, as a law enforcement agency. However, their search for knowledge and sharing of ideas, approaches and experiences was the catalyst for this policy transfer, highlighting the dual role played by the police in this instance, as both law enforcers and policy entrepreneurs. In this respect, it is interesting to note that similar initiatives to gang/group-related violence have subsequently been adopted through further processes of emulation in several cities in the United Kingdom, indicating ongoing policy transfer by new epistemic networks, worthy of further research.

Notes

1. The VRU is a police-led agency established in 2005 by the police and Scottish government to investigate and coordinate violence reduction initiatives across Scotland http://www.svru.co.uk
2. The Crown Office and Procurator Fiscal Service (COPFS) is the prosecuting agency in Scotland. The police report all cases to COPFS for consideration of prosecution or not.
3. The Scottish Children's Reporter Administration (SCRA) is responsible for the operation of the Children's Hearing System and the reporting of young people who have committed crimes and/or are in need of care and welfare.

4. The Community Planning Partnerships (CPPs) were established by the Scottish Government as part of the Local Government (Scotland) Act 2004 that placed a legal obligation on agencies to work in partnership established in February 2004 to bring together the key public, private and voluntary agencies to deliver better and more co-ordinated services in the city.
5. This supervision order had the effect of treating the relevant young people as 'children' and under the care of the Children's Hearing System (SCRA).

References

Bache, I., & Taylor, A. (2003). The politics of policy resistance: Reconstructing higher education in Kosovo. *Journal of Public Policy 23*(3), 279–300. doi: 10.1017/S0143814X03003131

Braga, A. A., Kennedy, D., & Piehl, A. (1999). *Problem-Oriented Policing and Youth Violence: An Evaluation of the Boston Gun Project.* (Unpublished Report). Washington, DC: National Institute of Justice

Braga, A. A., Kennedy, D. M., Waring, E. J., & Piehl, A. M. (2001). Problem-oriented policing, deterrence, and youth violence: An evaluation of Boston's operation ceasefire. *Journal of Research in Crime and Delinquency, 38*(3), 195–225. https://doi-org.mutex.gmu.edu/10.1177/0022427801038003001

Clarke, R.V.G. (1995). 'Situational Crime Prevention', in Tonry, M. and Farrington, D. (eds.) *Building Safer Communities*, Chicago: Chicago University Press.

Craig, C. (2010) *The Tears That Made The Clyde.* Glendaruel. Argyle Publishing.

Davies, A. (2007). Glasgow's 'reign of terror': Street gangs, racketeering and intimidation in the 1920s' and 1930s'. *Contemporary British History, 21*(4), 4405–4427. https://doi.org/10.1080/13619460601060413

Davies, A. (2013). *City of Gangs; Glasgow and the Rise of the British Gangster.* London: Hodder and Staughton.

Deuchar, R. (2009). *Gangs, Marginalised Youth and Social Capital.* Stoke-on-Trent: Trentham Press.

Deuchar, R. (2013). *Policing Youth Violence, Transatlantic Connections.* London: Trentham

Deuchar, R. (2010). 'Its just pure harassment... As If It's a Crime to Walk in the Street': Anti-social Behaviour, Youth Justice and Citizenship — The Reality for young men in the east end of Glasgow. *Youth Justice, 10*(3), 258–274. https://doi-org.mutex.gmu.edu/10.1177/1473225410381686

Deuchar, R., & Holligan, C. (2010). Gangs, sectarianism and social capital: A qualitative study of young people in Scotland. *Sociology, 44*(1), 13–30. https://doi-org.mutex.gmu.edu/10.1177/0038038509351617

Dolowitz, D., & Marsh, D. (1996). Who learns what from whom? A review of the policy transfer literature. *Political Studies, 44*(2), 343–357. https://doi.org/10.1111/j.1467-9248.1996.tb00334.x

Dolowitz, D., & Marsh, D. (2000). Learning from abroad: The role of policy transfer in contemporary policy-making. *Governance, 13*(1), 5–24. https://doi-org.mutex.gmu.edu/10.1111/0952-1895.00121

Donnelly, P. D., & Tombs, J. (2008). An unusual day in court. *British Medical Journal, 337*, a2959. https://doi.org/10.1136/bmj.a2959

Engel, R., Baker, S. G., Tillyer, M. S., Eck, J. E., & Dunham, J. (2008). *Implementation of the Cincinnati Initiative to Reduce Violence (CIRV): Year 1 Report.* Cincinnati, OH: CIRV.

Engel, R., Corsaro, N., & Tillyer, M. S. (2010). *Evaluation of the Cincinnati Initiative to Reduce Violence (CIRV).* Cincinnati, OH: University of Cincinnati Policing Institute for the City of Cincinnati and the Ohio Office of Criminal Justice Services (OCJS).

Engel, R., Tillyer, S. M., & Corsaro, N. (2013). Reducing gang violence using focused deterrence: Evaluating the Cincinnati Initiative to Reduce Violence (CIRV). *Justice Quarterly, 30*(3), 403–439. https://doi.org/10.1080/07418825.2011.619559

Evans, M. (2006). At the interface between theory and practice – Policy transfer and lesson drawing: Learning from comparative public policy: A practical guide Richard Rose. *Public Administration, 84*(2), 479–515. https://doi-org.mutex.gmu.edu/10.1111/j.1467-9299.2006.00013.x

Evans, M. (2009a). Policy studies in critical perspective. *Policy Studies, 30*(3): 243–268. https://doi.org/10.1080/01442870902863828

Evans, M. (2009b). New directions in the study of policy transfer. *Policy Studies, 30*(3), 237–241. https://doi.org/10.1080/01442870902863810

Evans, M., & Davies, J. (1999). Understanding policy transfer: A multi-level, multi-disciplinary perspective. *Public Administration, 77*(2), 361–385. https://doi-org.mutex.gmu.edu/10.1111/1467-9299.00158

Glasgow Community Initiative to Reduce Violence (CIRV). (2009). Six month report. Available at: http://www.svru.co.uk/resources

Glasgow Community Initiative to Reduce Violence (CIRV). (2010a). Case management practice note. Available at: http://www.svru.co.uk/resources

Glasgow Community Initiative to Reduce Violence (CIRV). (2010b). Self-referral session practice note. Available at: http://www.svru.co.uk/resources/

Glasgow Community Initiative to Reduce Violence (CIRV). (2010c). 2nd Year report. Available at http://www.svru.co.uk/resources/

Graham, W. (2016). Global concepts, local contexts: A case study of international criminal justice policy transfer. PhD Thesis, Glasgow Caledonian University, Glasgow, In: British Library. Available at: http://ethos.bl.uk/OrderDetails.do?did=1&uin=uk.bl.ethos.726773

Graham, W., & Robertson, A. (2021). Exploring criminal justice policy transfer models and mobilities using a case study of violence reduction. *Criminology and Criminal Justice.* Available at: https://doi.org/10.1177/1748895821991607

Haas, P. M. (1992). Introduction: Epistemic communities and international policy coordination. *International Organization, 46*(1), 1–35. https://doi.org/10.1017/S0020818300001442

James, O., & Lodge, M. (2003). The limitations of 'policy transfer' and 'lesson drawing' for public policy research. *Political Studies Review, 1*(2), 179–193. https://doi.org/10.1111/1478-9299.t01-1-00003

Jones, T., & Newburn, T. (2007). *Policy Transfer and Criminal Justice: Exploring US Influence over British Crime Control Policy.* Maidenhead: Open University Press.

Kennedy, D. M. (1997). Pulling levers: Chronic offenders, high-crime settings and a theory of prevention. *Valparaiso University Law Review, 31*, 449–484.

Kintrea, K., Bannister, J., & Pickering, J. (2010). Territoriality and disadvantage among young people: An exploratory study of six British neighbourhoods. *Journal of Housing and the Built Environment, 25*, 447–465. https://doi-org.mutex.gmu.edu/10.1007/s10901-010-9195-4

Krug, E., Dahlberg, L. L., Mercy J.A., et al. (2002). World Report on Violence and Health. Geneva: World Health Organization. *The Lancet (British Edition), 2002-10-05*, Vol. 360 (9339). p. 1083–1088

Leyland, A. H. (2006). Homicides involving knives and other sharp objects in Scotland, 1981–2003. *Journal of Public Health, 8*(2), 145–147. https://doi.org/10.1093/pubmed/fdl004

Marsden, G., & Stead, D. (2011). Policy transfer and learning in the field of transport: A review of concepts and evidence. *Transport Policy, 18*(3), 492–500. https://doi.org/10.1016/j.tranpol.2010.10.007

Marsh, D., & Evans, M. (2012). Policy transfer: Into the future, learning from the past. *Policy Studies, 33*(6), 587–591. https://doi.org/10.1080/01442872.2012.736796

McCann, E., & Ward, K. (2012). Policy assemblages, mobilities and mutations: Toward a multidisciplinary conversation. *Political Studies Review, 10*(3), 325–332. https://doi.org/10.1111/j.1478-9302.2012.00276.x

McMillan, L., & Roberston, A. (2012). Evaluation of the Use of Dispersal Powers in the East End of Glasgow: Full Report. Available at https://researchonline.gcu.ac.uk/en/publications/evaluation-of-the-use-of-dispersal-powers-in-the-east-end-of-glas

National Network for Safer Communities. (2014). Available at https://nnscommunities.org/impact/cities/ on September 24 2021

National Records of Scotland. (2018). Available at https://www.nrscotland.gov.uk/files/statistics/council-area-data-sheets/glasgow-city-council-profile.html. on September 24 2021

Newburn, T. (2002). Atlantic crossings: 'Policy transfer' and crime control in the US and Britain. *Punishment and Society, 4*(2), 165–194. https://doi-org.mutex.gmu.edu/10.1177/14624740222228536

Newburn, T., & Sparks, R. (2004). *Criminal Justice and Political Cultures: National and International Dimensions of Crime Control.* Devon: Willan

Patrick, J. (1973). *A Glasgow Gang Observed.* Glasgow: Neil Wilson Publishing.

Peck, J. (2011). Geographies of policy: From transfer-diffusion to mobility-mutation. *Progress in Human Geography, 35*(6), 773–797. https://doi.org/10.1177/0309132510394010

Peck, J., & Theodore, N. (2010). Mobilizing policy: Models, methods and mutations. *Geoforum, 41*(2), 169–174. https://doi.org/10.1016/j.geoforum.2010.01.002

Robertson, A. (2005). Criminal justice policy transfer to post-Soviet states: Two case studies of police reform in Russia and Ukraine. *European Journal on Criminal Policy and Research, 11*(1), 1–28. https://doi-org.mutex.gmu.edu/10.1007/s10610-005-2290-5

Rose, R. (1993). *Lesson-Drawing in Public Policy: A Guide to Learning Across Time and Space.* Chatham, New Jersey: Chatham House.

Scottish Index of Multiple Deprivation (SIMD). (2020). https://www.gov.scot/collections/scottishindex-of-multiple-deprivation-2020

Stone, D. (1999). Learning lessons and transferring policy across time, space and disciplines. *Politics, 19*(1), 51–59. https://doi-org.mutex.gmu.edu/10.1111/1467-9256.00086

Suttles, G. (1972). *The Social Construction of Communities.* Chicago, IL: University of Chicago Press.

Williams, D. J., Currie, D., Linden, W., & Donnelly, P. D. (2014). Addressing gang-related violence in Glasgow: A preliminary pragmatic quasi-experimental evaluation of the Community Initiative to Reduce Violence (CIRV). *Aggression and Violence Behaviour, 19*(6), 686–691. https://doi.org/10.1016/j.avb.2014.09.011

13

Translational Criminology in the Antipodes

A Tale of Trials, Tribulations, and (Sometimes) Triumph

Lorraine Mazerolle, Sarah Bennett, and Peter Martin

School of Social Science, University of Queensland, Australia

Michael Newman and Debbie Platz

Queensland Police Service and University of Queensland, Australia

Introduction

Starting in the 1990s, "translational research" was the terminology used in the medical field to describe the process of "…taking discovery-based research through the steps of applying it to clinical research and patient-oriented care" (Felege, Hahn, & Hunter, 2016, p. 2). More specifically, the translational process in our field of criminology is described as "…knowledge creation through scientific research and its subsequent use to inform policy and practice in criminal justice" (Pesta, Blomberg, Ramos, & Ranson, 2019; see also Laub & Frisch, 2016). The medical "bench to bedside" movement - or what Mazerolle et al. (2017) term in criminal justice research to be "Bench to Curbside" – aims to strategically and holistically move basic science research to create new, evidence-based approaches to a wide range of problems in society: disease, crime, homelessness.

Translational research is neither a linear nor easy process, as most of the commentaries on the challenges of translational work attest (Laub & Frisch, 2016; Lum & Koper, 2017; Sampson, Winship & Knight, 2013; Sullivan, 2013). Laub and Frisch (2016) observe that "researchers often do not acknowledge the professional expertise of policy makers as legitimate or relevant to scientific research [and] conversely policy makers may not see criminological research as objective or relevant to specific policy questions" (Laub & Frisch, 2016, p. 54). Lum et al. (2012) report that much of the difficulties arise in policing because the researchers and practitioners have "…different expectations and worldviews that result in divergent interpretations of knowledge and different philosophies about the role and meaning of science in policing" (Lum et al., 2012, p. 62).

This chapter explores the experiences of translational criminology in policing across the Antipodes: Australia and New Zealand. In the context of research translation on a global scale, we explore the down-under story of criminological science and randomized controlled trials (RCTs) recounting the tribulations, describing some disappointments, and highlighting the triumphs in our Australian translational policing journey. We begin with some background context about policing and policing research historically in Australia. We then identify four

DOI: 10.4324/9781003153009-17

key ingredients needed for success in translational research: first, starting from a strong the-oretical basis; second, forging strong partnerships with movers (not shakers) and with people within policing who not only share the vision of evidence-based policing (EBP) but see its organizational potential; third, finding an authorizing environment that ideally co-funds and creates opportunities to test (and even fail); and fourth, fostering a dissemination program that is both diverse and inclusive in its delivery. We draw primarily from our experiences with the Queensland Community Engagement Trial (QCET), comparing and contrasting QCET with a range of other field projects, to bring together some insights about translational criminology in policing in Australia and New Zealand.

Background Context

Twenty years ago, the primary focus of policing research in Australia and New Zealand was to highlight problems around police process and powers (see Dixon, 1999; Westling & Waye, 1998), police brutality (see Blagg & Wilkie, 1997; Cunneen, 1990; Prenzler, 1997), police cul-ture (Chan, 1996a) and lack of police ethics (see Darvall-Stevens, 1994; Lewis & Prenzler, 1999; Prenzler & Mackay, 1995; Small & Watson, 1999). Conflict theory drove much of the policing scholarship in Australia (see Broadhurst, 1997; Chan, 1996b) which was largely driven by a series of high-profile royal commissions into police corruption (see Finnane, 1990). At the same time, during the period immediately prior to the turn of the century, most criminology taught at the tertiary level education in Australia was embedded in disciplines such as history, sociology, and political science (for an exception, see Wortley & Wimshurst, 2000). The end result was that policing scholars in Australia rarely worked on projects in partnership with academics and, as Rojek, Martin, and Alpert (2015) suggest, "...police agencies and police practitioners were closed to the outsider's inputs and views" (2015: 64).

Fast forward to 2020 and the policing research landscape across the Antipodes is completely transformed. Most universities across Australia have criminology and criminal justice depart-ments with high enrollments in undergraduate degree programs that include at least one ded-icated course in policing. Indeed, at the University of Queensland, enrollments of students into criminology outstrip enrollments into sociology and anthropology with dedicated polic-ing courses and coverage of policing topics embedded in several courses. Unlike in the 1990s, police agencies across Australia and New Zealand now have robust research committees that are inundated with students and academic requests to conduct research on a large volume of diverse research projects that are subsequently undertaken in collaborative ways between policing schol-ars and practitioner partners (Cherney, Antrobus, Bennett, Murphy, & Newman, 2019).

Another example of a significantly altered policing landscape is the success of the Australia and New Zealand Society of Evidence Based Policing (ANZSEBP). The society was formed in 2013 and now has 3,184 members and hosts an annual conference that includes both policing scholars and practitioners reporting on collaborative research projects. Peter Martin – Assistant Commissioner of Metropolitan North Operations at the time ANZSEBP was formed – was voted in as the inaugural President of the Society, with Mazerolle, Bennett, and Platz serving on the Executive committee since formation and Newman serving as the ANZSEBP secretary and journal editor.

The collaborative style of academic-practitioner research that characterizes the work of ANZSEBP members, was described a decade ago by Martin Innes (2010). Consistent with Innes' (2010) ideas, we argue that policing scholarship in Australia and New Zealand is now primarily – but not always – done with police and academics working together, not academ-ics working "on" or writing "about" police without deep engagement "with" police (yet see

Bradley & Nixon, 2009). Innes (2010) identified the four different ways in which police research is conducted with the last form – "with the police" – being what Australian policing research has largely evolved toward in the last two decades:

> **Research by the police**: Significant amounts of research are now conducted internally within policing organizations in support of operational decision making and strategic planning, with no direct input from academics. Most agencies employ a cadre of crime and performance analysts to process data and generate intelligence on prolific offenders, crime series, and hotspots and to gauge the impact of the organization in relation to these.
>
> **Research on the police:** It is probably the orthodox mode, where research is done by academics on policing, and the police aren't really involved in the conduct or design of the research itself. Rather they are the topic that is researched.
>
> **Research for the police:** It involves a police organization commissioning work on a specific topic from individuals specializing in the conduct of research, the research design, data collection, and analysis being managed by the external professional researcher.
>
> **Research with the police:** This is a more collaborative and co-productive endeavor that seeks to find a way for researchers and police staff to work together to address a particular issue or problem.
>
> (Innes, 2010, p. 128)

Australian policing scholarship opportunities arise from the way Australian policing is structured. Australian policing comprises just seven state/territory-based police services and the Australian Federal Police (AFP). Each state/territory jurisdiction in Australia is responsible for funding, recruiting, training, and maintaining its own police service. The AFP provides domestic policing services to Australia's territories and also has broad national and international policing responsibilities including jurisdiction over what is defined as "commonwealth" crimes such as human trafficking, smuggling, terrorism, child exploitation, and telecommunication crimes. The small number of large agencies offers policing scholars in Australia the opportunity to work with large agencies yet, at the same time, choose agencies to work with that are receptive to collaborative research engagement. In the experience of the authors of this chapter, there are shifts over time between which agencies are more or less receptive to high-quality scientific inquiry.

The other factor that distinguishes policing scholarship in Australia is the fact that public support for police in Australia is generally quite high: 76% of people agree that police treat people fairly and equally, 87% believe that police perform their job professionally and 75% of people perceive the police as honest (Australian Government Productivity Commission, 2018). Murphy et al. (2010) also show that over 90% of Australians are willing to comply with police directives: much higher levels of cooperation than is found in the US and UK. Australian police officers have relatively high levels of education prior to their recruitment and are more representative of the communities they serve than 30 years ago (McLeod & Herrington, 2017). Deployment of ethnic liaison officers into ethnically diverse communities aims to improve relationships with those communities (Cherney & Chui, 2009). This level of underlying public support for police offers both opportunities and barriers for police scholars. On the one hand, police leaders are sometimes reluctant to engage in research on topics where public support is volatile. On the other hand, there are a myriad of examples where academics in Australia have been very valuable to police reform efforts on highly politicized crime topics such as in the areas of domestic violence, youth violence, and policing mental health.

Our chapter starts from the premise that the historical context of Australian criminology and policing is significant in the way that EBP has shaped the translation of research into policy and practice. In this chapter, we will draw on our experience with the first-ever randomized experiment conducted with the Queensland Police Service (QPS) to explicate a translational experience in Australia. Specifically, we will discuss the QCET along with a series of experiments undertaken since QCET to describe the translational journey of the Antipodes. We focus on four key themes: first, how translation in Australian policing research has worked best when the research has started from a strong theoretical basis; second, how the QCET experience was built from a long-term partnership with a senior police leader – Peter Martin – who not only shared the translational vision of academics Mazerolle and Bennett but also saw, from the outset, its organizational potential; third, we explore how the authorizing environment co-funded and created new and unique opportunities for both police and academics; and fourth, we examine how the police fostered a dissemination program that fostered police demand for high-quality and policy-relevant research.

Theory Guiding Translation

With some notable exceptions (see for example Braga, 2008; Brunson, 2015; Buerger & Mazerolle, 1998; Nagin, Solow, & Lum, 2015; Sherman et al., 2015; Weisburd, 2015; Wilson & Kelling, 2017), one of the long-term deficits of much policing research throughout the world is the lack of theoretical engagement. Research about policing often focuses on effectiveness questions without asking the harder theoretical questions about the meaning of a particular police approach, why and how the approach might (or might not) work, and situating policing practices in a broader theory of social control. Similarly, research on police organizations (how they work, what works, questions about culture) often fails to situate the research within broader organizational theories stemming from organizational psychology or business theories (for exceptions, see Hassell, Zhao, & Maguire, 2003; King, 2009). Prior to the turn of the century in Australia, police research rarely focused on the theories underpinning police effectiveness and was distinctive in the near universal focus on the negative aspects of policing using critical criminological perspectives to explore police and police powers as discriminatory agents of social control.

Arguably, it wasn't until the UK-based paper by Pawson and Tilley (1994) on the scientific realist approach to evaluation found its way down under, that policing scholars in Australia started asking questions about the theoretical mechanisms that might be at work in driving police effectiveness. Indeed, it is our view that Australian criminological scholarship in general and policing scholarship, in particular, has been much more influenced over the years by British research than North American research. Pawson and Tilley (1994) countered the quantitative method-driven nature of evaluation research and, therefore, the realist approach resonated with a largely qualitative method skilled Australian-based policing scholars who universally opposed the positivist, experimental black-box approach for evaluating policing practice. Yet, the central argument that emerged from the Pawson and Tilley (1994) paper is the importance of understanding the mechanisms and contexts in which policing interventions operate. This call to understand the theory of change is arguably core to the success of policing scholars in the translational process.

One theory of policing that has dominated the academic and practitioner discourse since the early 2000s is legitimacy policing and procedural justice. Led by the now Yale University based scholar Tom Tyler, citations to Tyler started to rise exponentially in 2001. In 1990, there were just 300 citations to Tyler's work, by 2010 Tyler's work was receiving nearly 5,000 citations per year and, as of July 2021, Tyler now has more than 117,000 citations to his research on legitimacy and procedural justice (see https://scholar.google.com.au/citations?user=Z_94FToAAAAJ&hl=en&oi=ao). What is remarkable about the topic of police legitimacy is both the breadth and depth of theoretical inquiry by policing scholars and the deep engagement by police policymakers and practitioners. For example, McCluskey and Reisig (2017) used systematic social observations from police encounters with suspects to evaluate the most salient predictors of police officers exercising authority in a procedurally just manner. Madon, Murphy, and Sargeant (2017), using a survey of 1,480 ethnic minority group members, find that procedural justice is more effective for building legitimacy for ethnic minority respondents who report being highly disengaged from police than for those who are already engaged. Building trust and legitimacy is featured prominently as a 'pillar' of policing in the Final Report of the President's Task Force on 21st Century Policing (2015). This type of scholarship in the area of police legitimacy is perhaps one of the greatest translation success stories of the last two decades and featuring prominently in the Final Report of the President's Task Force on 21st Century Policing (2015).

The significance of Tyler's research on police legitimacy (Tyler, 2003) gained prominence in Australia in about 2005 particularly off the back of early work being undertaken by Kristina Murphy on compliance with tax avoiders (2004). Yet the 'tyranny of distance' (Blainey, 1966), a phrase well understood that describes Australia's geographic distance as shaping national identity, challenges Australian scholars to make their mark in the global scientific world. The geographic isolation of the Antipodes often (yet not always) leads to lags in how Australia partakes in global scientific breakthroughs. In the case of applying legitimacy research to policing practice, however, Australian researchers have been at the forefront of scientific discovery and translation research. For example, Mazerolle, Bennett, and colleagues (2013b) conducted a systematic review of legitimacy policing (cited in the 21st Century Policing report, 2015) that identified key tenets of procedural justice that are foundational to police legitimacy (neutrality and trustworthy motives, respectful treatment, and participation), and also that these tenets had not been experimentally operationalized in a policing context.

The fact that the central tenets of procedural justice policing had never been tested under randomized field trial conditions created a unique opportunity to use theory to drive research and translation. The discovery also came at a time when the Australian Research Council had funded a $27 million Centre of Excellence in Policing with Mazerolle as Foundation Director. The Centre of Excellence received federal government research money and police agencies across the country – including the QPS – also contributed significant cash and in-kind resources to conduct applied research that solved policing problems at the time. The establishment of the Centre of Excellence also came at a time when co-author Martin started working with Mazerolle and Bennett in his senior role as an Assistant Commissioner in charge of some 2,000 sworn operational police in the Greater Brisbane City area of Queensland. Martin's police operational role was pivotal in shaping what was to become the QCET. Through the Centre of Excellence, Mazerolle and Bennett sought to test the four key ingredients of procedural justice policing under randomized field trial conditions. Martin suggested that the point of road alcohol tests was an ideal controlled environment to conduct the trial and it also offered the police an opportunity to engage in a different way with members of the general public using a dialogue that could be easily taught to frontline officers. For these reasons, QCET offers a textbook example of how theory-guided practice and how practice interpreted and translated theory.

QCET was a world-first intervention tested under RCT conditions, conducted in the context of Random Breath Testing (RBTs) in Brisbane. The research team based at the University of Queensland (UQ) worked closely with Queensland police to implement the trial with 21,000 drivers. UQ researchers, Mazerolle and Bennett found that drivers who experienced the QCET RBT stops reported significantly increased perceptions of police fairness, respect, trust, and confidence in police, greater satisfaction with the police encounter, and greater willingness to comply with police directives (Mazerolle et al., 2012). Initially, the QPS conducted about three million RBTs each year using a standard 20-second procedure where drivers are directed to the side of the road and asked by police to deliver a specimen of breath into a handheld device that reports indicative blood alcohol levels within seconds. The QCET dialogue is now used in many police regions in Queensland. The dialogue has also been adopted in Victoria and Western Australia (WA), changing the standard operating procedure and outcomes for millions of RBT encounters. Our research also showed that the ratio of RBTs to the number of licensed drivers was also critical to reduce the number of alcohol-related traffic crashes (Ferris et al., 2013). The recommendation to the QPS was to implement the longer QCET dialogue and, at the same time, maintain the 1:1 driver to RBT rate/ratio (Ferris et al., 2013). Other states in Australia at the time, particularly Western Australia, had a 1:3 ratio. WA's alcohol-related crash rate was dramatically higher than Queensland's. As a result of the research dissemination and engaging in media interviews, WA adopted a longer encounter using the QCET dialogue and changed its RBT policies so that it now has a 1:1 ratio, ensuring that police conduct at least one Random Breath Test per licensed driver every year. Significantly, modeling of this action showed that doubling the monthly ratio would almost halve the number of crashes and save more than 10 lives/year with the annual financial cost saving could be four times greater than the cost of conducting RBTs. The results prompted the WA Police Deputy Commissioner, Stephen Brown to state: "Our numerical target in WA is now 1.8M RBTs per annum which we consistently hit. WA has 2.6M people and approximately 1.8M drivers so the ratio is now about 1:1." The QCET structured dialogue and process have been expanded into training programs beyond traffic encounters throughout Australia. For example, Queensland police have embedded the QCET dialogue in recruitment training, for crime scene investigators targeting residential burglaries and encounters targeting drug dealing in hotel rooms (Brisbane City Criminal Investigations Bureau Operation Galley). This demonstrates that the intervention can be adapted and used in different types of police-citizen encounters.

The Value of True Partnerships

The value of collaborative police-academic partnerships is long recognized as a way to improve the operations and practices of police organizations (Hansen, Alpert, & Rojek, 2014) with many books and articles explicating the similarities and differences in collaborations across the world (Rojek, Martin, & Alpert, 2014). In a survey undertaken by Rojek, Smith, and Alpert (2012), 57% of the responding agencies reported participating in formal short-term coordination partnerships and 30% reported participation in long-term and formal collaborative forms of partnership. These partnerships between police and academics are foundational for the success of translation research. In Australia, the Centre of Excellence funded QCET trial was a watershed project that stimulated a long, productive partnership between police and academic researchers in Queensland in particular, and across Australia and New Zealand.

The early experiences of the QCET partnership approach to thinking about, brokering, and then implementing the experimental test led to a proliferation of different evidence-based projects within the QPS between 2013 and the current time. For example, IM-PACT (Identify the problem, Message Development – delivered with Purpose, Acknowledgement, Crime message, Thanks) capitalized on a routine police-community interaction, for real potential to build police legitimacy and to strengthen community relationships for greater community benefit. This sought to inspire community members to share the responsibility of enhancing safety and preventing crime. Ultimately, the strategy sought to engage the community to positively enhance demands on limited policing resources by collaboratively addressing victimization, crime, and safety problems. IM-PACT involved an RCT over a 12-week period in 2018 where officers either delivered a scripted IM-PACT crime message or conduct standard with drivers stopped during a standard RBT. During each encounter, police provided drivers with a copy of a survey and also recorded license plate details in order to measure long-term impact using official records (Bennett, Peel, & Green, 2020). IM-PACT advanced QCET by exploring the impact of the intervention on behavioral outcomes. A total of 94 RBT sites were completed in or near Unlawful Entry Motor Vehicle Hot Spots. These sites were randomly assigned to receive the IM-PACT message or just a business-as-usual RBT requirement. Just over 9,000 drivers were intercepted with IM-PACT encounters, on average, taking an additional 39 seconds. Surveys were handed out to the drivers to identify how the message impacted perceptions of police, awareness of crime problems, and their intent to follow the recommendations put forward by the officers on the RBT line. The number plates of each vehicle were recorded as they went through a site to assess the rate of victimization and offending between the two groups, post intercept. Results from the surveys show that the treatment respondents had an increased likelihood of locking their vehicles and securing their homes to reduce victimization (Bennett, Peel, & Green, 2020).

One of the hallmarks of successful police-academic partnerships that lead to translatable outcomes are those projects where police from different jurisdictions and academics from different institutions come together in cooperative ways. In our experience, police find it very difficult to understand academic turf wars yet, at the same time, find it hard to think about cross-jurisdictional research projects. Some of the projects, therefore, that have been most successful from a translation perspective in Australia have involved cross-institutional and cross-jurisdictional collaboration. One such trial was a hotspots experiment that was conducted by the QPS with Griffith University (with Associate Professor Justin Ready) to bring an innovative Intelligence-Led Policing strategy to persistent crime hot spots in two police jurisdictions (Ready & Thompson, 2021).

One of the fundamental driving forces behind the success of the UQ-QPS partnership has been the long-running EBP Workshops. The EBP workshops are designed to facilitate the adoption of EBP projects across the QPS. The workshops run for around three hours and can cater for up to thirty people at a time. The participants gain a comprehensive understanding of EBP and its relevance to police practice; they were also shown how and where they can access robust evidence and intervention exemplars and given examples of QPS EBP projects; they work in groups with experienced EBP facilitators to identify issues that are relevant to them. The EBP sessions conclude with officers designing their own interventions that can be rigorously evaluated and add to the evidence base. In short, by exposing participants to these initial concepts, these workshops seek to foster the capacity for in-house evaluations into the future.

The EBP workshops run by Mazerolle and Bennett spawned a number of practitioner-led experiments such as the Voice 4 Values (V4V) trial run by Assistant Commissioner Debbie Platz (see Platz, Sargeant, & Strang, 2017) and the Operation Galley trial: an initiative led by Detective Sergeant Paul Morton to reduce production, supply and, use of drugs in hotel rooms. The V4V program was created with the assistance of a not-for-profit organization 'Courage to Care' and was designed to teach participants to recognize and intervene in poor workplace behaviors. Having piloted the program with strong positive evaluations, it was decided to conduct an RCT assessing the effectiveness or otherwise of the program. There were three main drivers behind this trial: first, to reduce poor behaviors within the workplace; second, to ensure the program worked in the way envisaged; and third, due to the expense of the program, to examine whether it was cost-effective. Over three intakes into the police academy in 2015, 260 recruits participated in the RCT. Randomized into experimental and control groups, the experimental group participated in the V4V program. Baseline, post-program and follow-up surveys were conducted to examine recruit's ability to recognize prejudicial, racist, and sexist behavior; acceptance of equality and diversity; enhanced empathy and stated willingness to intervene in racist and sexist incidents. Commissioned officer support to create the program and test it via an RCT created workplace champions to espouse the program and the RCT. Further, previous experience with trusted academics also led to support to co-test the program with the University of Queensland. Together, the analysis showed that the V4V buffered the negative influences of the police academy in such a way that the experimental group's values did not decline to the extent that the control group' values around equality, empathy, discrimination, and intervening in incidents (Platz et al., 2017). The results suggested that V4V acted as a buffer to declining values of recruits. The RCT results led to significant changes in training and policy enhancing safety.

The EBP workshops also led to the creation of Operation Galley which aimed to reduce drug supply by motivating management of these hotels to take more responsibility for preventing and controlling the supply of drugs by offenders tenanting their accommodation. Operation Galley was evaluated under block randomized field trial conditions. In the experimental arm, the police implemented a third-party policing (TPP) approach to the problem where police sent a procedurally just letter that let hotel managers know about the problem of drugs in hotel rooms. The letter was then followed up with a visit where the police sought to motivate management to accept more responsibility by informing them of their liabilities if they fail to take action, in respect to: criminal legislation; workplace health and safety legislation (this is particularly relevant in terms of hazards associated with drug production); and fire legislation and the costs associated with an emergency services response to a related incident. The control arm was business-as-usual and a third arm of the trial involved only a procedurally just letter being sent. The results showed that the Operation Galley treatment produced six and a half times more notifications to detectives about drug problems than the hotels in the Letter group and 4.67 times more drug crime reports than the Letter and business-as-usual groups (Morton, Luengen, & Mazerolle 2018). Leadership of Operation Galley from Detective Sergeant Morton was key to successful translation of the research into routine practice for detectives in the criminal investigations branch.

With the success of QCET and the cluster of experiments emerging from the EBP workshops, the QPS recognized EBP as an important part of contemporary policing. The QPS started to partner with researchers at different universities across Queensland to advance opportunities to improve research partnerships. One initiative that solidified the translational process for the QPS was the establishment of the Police Visiting Fellow program where three inspector-level sworn officers were embedded in the three major universities across South East Queensland. In 2016, co-author Detective Inspector Michael Newman was selected as the inaugural University of Queensland Evidence Based Policing Visiting Fellow (UQVF). This role was embedded within the School of Social Science at UQ, working directly with Mazerolle and Bennett.

As the UQVF Newman was responsible for providing a critical liaison role between the QPS and UQ as a key point of contact for exchange of information, he facilitated the meshing of police practice and research. This involved identifying relevant opportunities for partnerships to further mutually beneficial research programs, including marketing and promoting to the QPS and other law enforcement agencies on the activities undertaken by UQ. As such, he built relationships with researchers and industry and assisted UQ by lecturing and participating in EBP development across a variety of forums including recruit training, management training, and university-based student learning. He also assisted on a range of activities in support of the ANZSEBP including the annual conference, web content, and improving ongoing engagement with members.

The UQVF program stimulated a series of randomized field trials that were true partnerships between police and practitioners. For example, the Mobile Police Community Office (MPCO) Project was run in 2014 and was an approach to improve police-community relations and legitimacy in Queensland's North Brisbane District (Bennett, Newman, & Sydes, 2017). One of the concepts underpinning the development and deployment of the MPCO was the targeting of hotspots whilst using procedural just policing. The MPCO is a fully functioning police counter on wheels – a highly visible police van equipped with all the resources so that officers can conduct most station duties and an interior 'office' where police can meet members of the public. MPCO visitors spent almost 8 minutes with officers and reported overwhelmingly that MPCO officers were approachable, helpful, respectful, professional, and fair. Visitors also thought that the MPCO would decrease crime, fear of crime, and acts of terrorism but not have as much impact on catching offenders. Police assigned to the MPCO similarly viewed the MPCO as having a potential crime deterrent. Interestingly, officers who considered procedural justice an important part of policing were significantly more likely to report that they used procedural justice in their encounters (Bennett, Newman, & Sydes, 2017).

The UQVF role also led to the creation of an experimental test of a blended detective training program (Stevenson, 2021), a Procedural Justice Training of Recruits experiment (Antrobus, Thompson, & Ariel, 2019), and an experiment that triaged non-emergency from emergency calls for service (Newman, 2018). These trials were all formed from partnerships between police and academics, largely brokered by the UQVF, and comprised the following ingredients that fostered the seamless translation of research into policy and practice: first, all of the 'problems' that formed the basis of the trials were problems identified by police; second, the projects all drew from prior research with strong theoretical foundations; third, the projects were all led by police, with academics providing theoretical, technical, and methodological input; and fourth, the projects were endorsed by police leaders and the expectation was that the experimental interventions would become part of business as usual upon completion of the trial, pending successful outcomes.

Off the back of the EBP workshops, the UQVF program, and a number of successful projects, the QPS established a more targeted approach to identifying viable EBP projects called the QLEADS program. The QLEADS program echoed the US National Institute of Justice Law Enforcement Advancing Data and Science (LEADS) program. The US LEADS program seeks to empower law enforcement to integrate research into policies and practices by advancing EBP through supporting the development of mid-career law enforcement personnel who are committed to advancing and integrating science into law enforcement policies and practices (https://nij.ojp.gov/funding/national-institute-justices-law-enforcement-advancing-data-and-science-leads-programs). The QLEADS program now provides small seed funding for up to five Sergeants and Senior Sergeants to provide leadership and professional development opportunities for future and current leaders. It is aimed at increasing the use of EBP processes to shape a culture where decision making is based on evidence and best practice approaches for improved policing outcomes and community confidence in the QPS in relation to one or more of the following: Reduce crime; Reduce disorder (physical and/or social); Policing communities during periods of pandemics (recent events); Improve citizen perceptions of police; Reduce fear of crime; Reduce demands on police resources; Increase clearance rates. The research is being undertaken with collaborative partners, UQ and provides an opportunity for the QLEADS scholar to examine a specific policing problem relevant to their workplace. Academics from UQ provide guidance to participants regarding technical advice, research design and implementation, as well as support for the analysis of results and a final report. There are currently three QLEADS projects underway in the QPS enabling junior police staff to explore crisis first response training (conducted by hostage negotiators) to reduce assaults on police and injury to vulnerable people, forensic search assurance during major crime investigations and crime detections, and reduction targeting railway networks.

Authorizing Environment Support

Ayling, Grabosky, and Shearing (2006) suggest police organizations do not operate in a vacuum but rather they are significantly influenced by their external environments and, like any other organization, they need to adapt to their environments and innovate. In the Australian context, however, police agencies are small in number but generally large and slow to change. Operational decision-making is made at localized levels making strategic and systemic organizational change infrequent and cumbersome. Australian police agencies can be characterized as persistent 'command and control' hierarchical structures with formal processes and procedures (Weisburd, Mastrofski, McNally, Greenspan, & Willis, 2003).

Systemic change in Australian police agencies occurs usually in times of crisis, often in the aftermath of a Royal Commission or Commission of Inquiry, in the lee of corruption scandals or where strong political desire for policy change exists. Otherwise, police agencies in the Antipodes remain large entities that are often difficult and at times (and in some sections) unwilling to change. Yet, we have already highlighted the QCET exception regarding organizational change as it relates to translational research. QCET created a key opportunity for embracing research in police agencies demonstrating how a senior officer (in the QCET case, Martin) who had insight, influence, and the willingness to rally against the *status quo*. Martin's insight came from a desire to move beyond the 'business as usual' conservatism and challenged the department to try something new. Martin also had influence: He occupied a senior commissioned officer rank and had developed significant internal gravitas over years of working within the same police agency. As Neyroud and Weisburd (2014) have argued: Police need to own their own science and take control of their own destiny. This call to police leaders to take control of the science of their occupation resonated loudly in the Antipodes and particularly within the QPS. Martin was, we argue, one of the original 'pracademics' and organizational champions known as EBP champions.

So how did the QPS come to facilitate its very first RCT in 2009? The QPS in 2009 was not necessarily an organization ready to embrace research actively but rather one that could, with evidence, be persuaded on the potential for research to inform a more effective and efficient practice. In Australia, the impetus to test new practices under randomized field trial conditions very much needed to come from within. QCET needed a supportive authorizing environment to facilitate the trial. We argue that QCET could not have happened without the EBP champion in a senior leadership role who had the gravitas to persuade others in the agency to go ahead with the trial and who was willing to create a strong and committed authorizing environment. In shepherding QCET, Martin's role was multi-faceted, complex and came as a project that was in addition to his significant normal operational responsibilities of some 2,000 sworn officers at the time. Martin, however, satisfied and exemplifies our previous contention that for research initiatives such as QCET to be successful there needs to be a senior organizational champion not only sympathetic to research but someone that has significant organization gravitas or influence internally and externally of the police agency.

Martin's role in QCET was critical to success. Not only did he work constructively with university academics to align the procedural justice theory to a practical policing context (RBTs) but his role was fundamentally to execute the research internally. This included 'selling' the motivation for the research with those junior officers who would undertake their new roles consistent with the experimental conditions, but also make the case to the police hierarchy that this was worthy of the organizational investment. His role however, extended beyond facilitation of the research to responding to an array of peripheral challenges and problems presented. These challenges included industrial challenges associated with officers expressing angrily their disdain from departing from historical operating systems and subsequently 'leaking' by officers to the media about their displeasure. Naturally, this caused concerns for the police hierarchy and extended to the political level. Such negative attention on the experiment led to Martin responding organizationally, politically, and directly engaging with the external media. A key learning here is that without the commitment and determination by that 'Research Champion' to see the research through, it is arguably going to be very difficult to complete.

Resourcing and funding research initiatives is also key to translational success. This has led Martin and Mazerolle (2015) to argue for up to 10% of the police discretionary budget in Australia to be allocated for research initiatives as a way to build and accelerate the evidence base of policing. The challenging fiscal environment that western police agencies is something that police departments have been confronting for decades. This has been exacerbated by the post-COVID-19 era where governments are using public funds to stimulate the economy and relying upon government departments to underwrite such activities through savings measures.

It is unlikely that the fiscal environment will change anytime soon. The challenging fiscal environment and particularly the lack of discretionary funding by police agencies to apply to research could be a general disclaimer to stifle any innovation. There are, however, two key dimensions to such thinking: first, there is no better time to invest in research and to innovate, not in spite of the environment but because of the tough fiscal environment; second, much of the research examples in this chapter demonstrate cost-efficiency. In these cases there were very little in the way of fiscal resources applied to these experiments, utilizing instead resources in kind, such as re-engineering or reapplying police activity (again QCET is a relevant example). While acknowledging that it is important for police agencies to allocate finite fiscal resources to research, we identify, however, that without a strong and supportive authorizing environment for research, police agencies are only going to pay lip service to being evidence-based. Police agencies in the Antipodes are arguably well-placed and in a strong position to move to organizational research maturity.

Collaborative Dissemination

In 2016, John Laub and Nicole Frisch remarked that translational criminology is made possible through innovative dissemination strategies. They make a couple of important points that we summarize here: first, policy makers need to be made aware of research findings; second, researchers need to engage policy makers as equal partners where practitioners offer insights about the context in which a program might or might not work (see also Rojek, Martin, & Alpert, 2014); and third, the conversation between academics and policy makers has to be built on mutual trust and respect (Laub & Frisch, 2016). The experimental work around QCET provided the foundation for a collaborative dissemination story that helped to shape and characterize the nature of translational work in the Antipodes. In this section we discuss the weight given to high profile scientific published work, importance of a Centre of Excellence funding, the roles of senior police leaders doing the policy translation, the process of engaging on the international policing stage, and how the ANZSEBP became central to collaborative dissemination.

Our first point about collaborative dissemination is that the integrity and innovative nature of QCET provided ample opportunity for Mazerolle, Bennett, and their colleagues to publish a series of high-profile scientific published work. The first, main results paper published was in the *Journal of Experimental Criminology* (Mazerolle, Bennett, Antrobus, & Eggins, 2012) and has now garnered nearly 300 citations. But it was the follow-up paper where Mazerolle and her colleagues teamed up with the world leader in procedural justice research, Tom Tyler, who put QCET well and truly on the international scientific stage (Mazerolle, Antrobus, Bennett, & Tyler, 2013a). This chapter has now been cited more than 600 times and was in the top ten articles published in criminology and criminal justice based on the number of citations between 2010 and 2015 (Graham, Pratt, Lee, & Cullen, 2019). In the spirit of police-academic collaboration, police practitioners are featured authors in many of the translational research projects conducted between UQ researchers and the QPS (see Bennett, Martin, & Thompson, 2018; Bennett, Peel, & Green, 2020; Martin & Mazerolle, 2015).

Second, the funding, organizational structure, and collaborative nature of the Australian Research Council Centre of Excellence for Policing and Security (CEPS) provided a unique conduit for research to be collaboratively developed, delivered, and disseminated. The significant CEPS funding provided support for a website, a list of email recipients constantly growing and being updated, one-page briefing notes professionally prepared, events to be held, and a variety of outreach and engagement activities to facilitate the translational goals of the Centre. Indeed, the whole Centre of Excellence scheme of the Australian Research Council is well aligned with facilitating translation of research into practice. For example, the scheme supports significant collaborations between universities, publicly funded research organizations, other research bodies, governments, and businesses in Australia and overseas in order to "...undertake highly innovative and potentially transformational research that aims to achieve international standing in the fields of research envisaged and leads to a significant advancement of capabilities and knowledge" (see https://www.arc.gov.au/grants/linkage-program/arc-centres-excellence). In the case of CEPS, police agencies from across Australia were partners in the Centre. The funding along with the partnership nature of the Centre created a unique opportunity in the history of Australian policing-research relations and offered resources to use a range of different pathways to disseminate research findings.

Third, the success of QCET would not have been possible without the efforts of senior police leaders doing the heavy lifting around the policy translation. We have described much of Martin's role in QCET. Since QCET, other senior police within the QPS similarly took on the leadership role of subsequent RCTs. For example, Assistant Commissioner Debbie Platz provided an authorizing environment within the Queensland police training area that saw a number of EBP projects, particularly randomized control trials, led by herself (Voice for Values) and her commissioned officers within that domain (Platz, Sargeant, & Strang, 2017). For example, Inspector Ian Thompson led a trial to establish if procedural justice training for recruits would improve outcomes with their communication skills when dealing with citizens (Antrobus, Thompson, & Ariel, 2019). Detective Inspector Mike Newman identified and led a number of projects within the investigative and intelligence training fields, including a trial examining an alternate method of delivery for detective training modules (Stevenson, 2021), the evaluation of a new sex assault course (Bennett, 2020), an examination of an alternate method of delivery for a basic intelligence course (Newman, 2018), the evaluation of an initial investigative training course delivered to general duties offices (Newman, 2019). Along with encouraging her officers to identify what works, Platz further supported these projects with the funding required to facilitate dissemination and action to implement research findings.

Senior leader support can also be achieved through identifying appropriate mechanisms to highlight the success achieved from a localized trial. For example, the QPS Strategic Tasking and Coordination Committee (S-TAC) provides the forum to table strategic intelligence products on emerging issues likely to impact community safety or policing activity. It assists in the provision of a collective operational response, to state-wide and regional issues which are beyond the resource capabilities of individual districts and regions. S-TAC also provides a forum for the update on Queensland initiatives. S-TAC comprises the senior executive level of the QPS which includes the Commissioner, the Deputy Commissioners, Assistant Commissioners, and Executive Directors. Presentations of EBP projects at this forum have facilitated funding for further research with academic partners, such as ISACURE (Bennett, 2020), and state-wide implementation of local RCT projects, such as IM-PACT (Green, 2021) and the Logan Micro Crime Hotspot trial (Ready & Thompson, 2021).

The fourth key to collaborative dissemination that leads to translation of research into practice is making efforts to engage on the international policing stage. QCET captured the attention of researchers and practitioners across the globe, perhaps because of the simplicity and face value of the intervention. Indeed, UQ researchers in partnership with the QPS developed a world-first structured dialogue to change how police interact with people from different backgrounds. The dialogue, which operationalized the principles of procedural justice, has not only been tested in Queensland but also in the US, England, Scotland, and Turkey to influence greater mutual dignity and respect during encounters. The QCET structured dialogue was replicated in studies in Scotland (MacQueen & Bradford, 2015), England (Langley, 2014), the US (Antrobus, Alpert, & Rojek, 2015) and Turkey (Sahin, Braga, Apel, & Brunson, 2017) between 2012 and 2015 leading to the QCET dialogue being infused in road policing training in Scotland. The West Midlands Police introduced it to training programs for community support officers and for police engagement in a high-risk terrorist context at the Birmingham Airport (UK). Richland County, South Carolina in the US adopted the QCET dialogue for roadblock operations and police responding to residential housebreaks in Prince George's County (Maryland, US) also now use the dialogue. Turkey National Police officials have since used data from the study to improve how they interact with citizens.

Finally, the ANZSEBP has become central to collaborative dissemination of police research by jurisdictions within the Antipodes. The Society is made up of police officers, police staff, and research professionals who aim to make evidence-based police practice part of everyday policing in Australia and New Zealand. The Executive Committee for this body is comprised of senior representatives from every Australasian law enforcement agency with support from academic and business advisors. The Society advocates that all aspects of policing including police patrols, investigations, crime prevention, human resource management, and all other forms of service delivery should be evaluated using sound, scientific methods and used when the evaluation evidence shows that the police practice works to control or prevent crime and disorder or enhance quality of life. One of the key strategies of the Society is to shape and support the production and dissemination of new evidence. The Society encourages and enables researchers and police to produce rigorous and timely research that can then be made available to all police agencies. This is facilitated through an annual conference and the production of a biannual journal, Police Science. Police Science, first published in 2016, is the primary vehicle for the ANZSEBP to disseminate police-led research. ANZSEBP executive members source articles of professional interest from Australasian police officers and police academics. An Editorial Committee has been established to peer review all articles received. Currently, ten editions have been published with authors from around the globe providing insights around "what works" in a wide range of policing settings.

In total, the Society has run six annual conferences since 2015 (2020 was cancelled due to COVID-19) and has been fortunate to secure a range of internationally recognized keynote speakers. These conferences have a focus on police presenting the findings of their police-led initiatives with abstracts received each year from agencies across all jurisdictions involved in the ANZSEBP. The interest from police practitioners has grown each year with the 2021 conference hosting 24 short presentations on a variety of topics including High risk offenders and groups; Investigations; Family violence; and Police legitimacy. The conference also provides police practitioners and academics an opportunity to network and collaborate on areas of mutual interest.

Conclusion

In this chapter, we examined the research translation experience in the Australian and New Zealand context. We did this by focusing on four themes that are characteristic of the experiences in the Antipodes: the importance of theory, the significance of partnerships, the need for an authorizing environment to support EBP, and the role of collaborative dissemination. We covered some of the unique aspects, strategies, and challenges that we as researchers and practitioners faced. In a back-to-basics approach, this chapter argues for translational research in policing to be built on, developed, and sustained through police-researcher partnerships that co-produce and build legitimate translational research collaborations that will last against the "tide of indifference or resistance" (Sherman et al., 2015, p.13).

A critical spark to translational research collaborations in our Australian experience is the convergence of resources to solve a meaningful problem. The QCET trial illustrated a research gap paired with a timely proactive priority in Australian policing to optimize community engagement and cooperation through increased police legitimacy. Evidencing how procedural justice could be systematically operationalized in high volume encounters to shift perceptions of legitimacy had both organizational policing and scholarly benefits. Projects and partnerships without a 'coalition for a common purpose' (Strang, 2012) are likely to involve imbalanced heavy lifting. Modern policing is experiencing significant challenges to achieve more with fewer resources, providing significant impetus to gain evidence to support efficient and effective use of resources. Researchers in particular need to seek genuine input from police about their strategic research priorities and engage police partners actively in research from idea conceptualization through to practice-orientated dissemination such as presentations at briefing events and plain-language research summaries for ease of operationalization. The value of engaged and sustained partnerships is to promote the best in policing practice. Police can also gain by engaging with academic partners to identify areas of mutual interest and to seek out supportive senior leaders who can identify appropriate internal mechanisms for presentations that will encourage translation of the evidence into practice.

Our collective working partnerships in Queensland have grown and matured significantly since Martin championed EBP and QCET. Whilst 'EBP' may not be a buzz term and for some in Australia it is a term that is strenuously avoided, it is clear that the intent of the term is prevalent through the growing appetite for robust research evidence to inform decision making. Imbalanced collaborations in years past have transformed to mutually beneficial and genuine partnerships to produce evidence and advance scholarship on target issues. Perhaps this is a combination of trust as well as the translation of research itself in a way that is distinctly operational-able. These days police expect (in a good way) for their research partnerships to produce outputs that are accessible and applicable to their practice. Furthermore, the academically maligned non-significant result is uniquely interesting in Antipodean policing where such results present opportunities to retire, remove or reset practices in an environment of finite resources alongside significant public demand. A foundational collaboration 'down under' formed to transform police legitimacy has in-tandem legitimized the role of evidence to inform practice in Queensland, providing global benefits of research across diverse policing issues and contexts.

References

Antrobus, E., Alpert, G., & Rojek, J. (2015). Replicating experiments in criminology: lessons learned from Richland. Unpublished short report.

Antrobus, E., Thompson, I., & Ariel, B. (2019). Procedural justice training for police recruits: results of a randomized controlled trial. *Journal of Experimental Criminology, 15*(1), 29–53. https://doi.org/10.1007/s11292-018-9331-9

Australian Government Productivity Commission (2018). Report on Government Services 2018. Chapter 6 Police Services. https://www.pc.gov.au/research/ongoing/report-on-government-services/2018/justice/police-services

Ayling, J. M., Grabosky, P., & Shearing, C. (2006). Harnessing resources for networked policing. In J. Fleming, & Wood, J. (Eds). *Fighting Crime Together: The Challenges of Policing and Security Networks*. Sydney: University of New South Wales Press, 60–86.

Bennett, S. (2020). Transforming sexual assault investigation training: Evidence to inform practice. *Queensland Police Service Strategic Tasking and Coordination Committee*. Brisbane.

Bennett, S., Martin, P., & Thompson, I. (2018). Crafting legitimate police-research partnerships through procedural justice. *European Journal of Policing Studies, 5*(3), 107–124.

Bennett, S., Newman, M., & Sydes, M. (2017). Mobile police community office: a vehicle for reducing crime, crime harm and enhancing police legitimacy?. *Journal of Experimental Criminology, 13*(3), 417–428. https://doi.org/10.1007/s11292-017-9302-6

Bennett, S., Peel, B. & Green, D. (2020). Developing police-public crime prevention partnerships with IM-PACT. *Police Science: Australia and New Zealand Journal of Evidence Based Policing, 4*(2), 39–41. Retrieved from https://www.anzsebp.com/police-science/

Blagg, H., & Wilkie, M. (1997). Young people and policing in Australia: the relevance of the UN Convention on the Rights of the Child. *Australian Journal of Human Rights, 3*(2), 134–156.

Blainey, G. (1966). *The tyranny of distance: how distance shaped Australia's history.* Sun Books.

Bradley, D., & Nixon, C. (2009). Ending the 'dialogue of the deaf': Evidence and policing policies and practices. An Australian case study. *Police Practice and Research: An International Journal, 10*(5-6), 423–435. https://doi.org/10.1080/15614260903378384

Braga, A. A. (2008). Pulling levers focused deterrence strategies and the prevention of gun homicide. *Journal of criminal justice, 36*(4), 332–343. https://doi.org/10.1016/j.jcrimjus.2008.06.009

Broadhurst, R. (1997). Aborigines and crime in Australia. *Crime and Justice, 21,* 407–468.

Brunson, R. K. (2015). Focused deterrence and improved police-community relations: Unpacking the proverbial black box. *Criminology & Public Policy, 14,* 507–514.

Buerger, M. E., & Mazerolle, L. G. (1998). Third-party policing: A theoretical analysis of an emerging trend. *Justice quarterly, 15*(2), 301–327. https://doi.org/10.1080/07418829800093761

Chan, J. (1996a). Changing police culture. *The British Journal of Criminology, 36*(1), 109–134. https://doi.org/10.1093/oxfordjournals.bjc.a014061

Chan, J. (1996b). The future of criminology: an introduction. *Current Issues in Criminal Justice, 8*(1), 7–13.

Cherney, A., Antrobus, E., Bennett, S., Murphy, B., & Newman, M. (2019). *Evidence-based Policing: A Survey of Attitudes in Two Australian Police Agencies.* Australian Institute of Criminology: Canberra, Australia. https://crg.aic.gov.au/reports/CRG-Evidence-based-policing-220719.pdf

Cherney, A., & Chui, W. H. (2009). *Review of the police liaison officer program in Queensland.* University of Queensland.

Cunneen, C. (1990). A study of Aboriginal juveniles and police violence. *Human Rights and Equal Opportunity Commission, Sydney.*

Darvall-Stevens, R. (1994). Police codes of ethics in Australia. *Criminology Australia, 6*(2), 26–31.

Dixon, D. (1999). *A culture of corruption: Changing an Australian police service.* Hawkins Press.

Felege, C., Hahn, E., & Hunter, C. (2016). Bench, Bedside, Curbside, and Home: Translational research to include transformative change using educational research. *Journal of Research Practice, 12*(2).

Ferris, J., Mazerolle, L., King, M., Bates, L., Bennett, S., & Devaney, M. (2013). Random breath testing in Queensland and Western Australia: Examination of how the random breath testing rate influences alcohol related traffic crash rates. *Accident Analysis & Prevention, 60,* 181–188. https://doi.org/10.1016/j.aap.2013.08.018

Finnane, M. (1990). Police corruption and police reform: The Fitzgerald inquiry in Queensland, *Australia. Policing and Society: An International Journal, 1*(2), 159–171. https://doi.org/10.1080/10439463.1990.9964611

Graham, A., Pratt, T. C., Lee, H., & Cullen, F. T. (2019). Contemporary classics? The early onset of influence of articles published in criminology and criminal justice journals, 2010–2015. *Journal of Criminal Justice Education, 30*(3), 348–375.

Green, D., (2021). Saving lives, reducing crime and building legitimacy with IM-PACT. *Queensland Police Service Strategic Tasking and Coordination Committee.* Rockhampton.

Hansen, J. A., Alpert, G. P., & Rojek, J. J. (2014). The benefits of police practitioner–researcher partnerships to participating agencies. *Policing: A Journal of Policy and Practice, 8*(4), 307–320. https://doi.org/10.1093/police/pau035

Hassell, K. D., Zhao, J. S., & Maguire, E. R. (2003). Structural arrangements in large municipal police organizations: Revisiting Wilson's theory of local political culture. *Policing: An International Journal of Police Strategies & Management, 26*(2), 231–250. https://doi.org/10.1108/13639510310475741

Innes, M. 2010. A 'Mirror' and a 'Motor': Researching and reforming policing in an age of austerity, *Policing: A Journal of Policy and Practice, 4*(2), 127–134. https://doi.org/10.1093/police/pap058

King, W. R. (2009). Toward a life-course perspective of police organizations. *Journal of research in crime and delinquency, 46*(2), 213–244. https://doi.org/10.1177/0022427808330874

Langley, B. (2014). *A randomised control trial comparing the effects of procedural justice to experienced utility theories in airport security stops.* Master's thesis, University of Cambridge, UK.

Laub, J. H., & Frisch, N. E. (2016). Translational criminology: A new path forward. In *Advancing Criminology and Criminal Justice Policy* (pp. 78–88). Routledge.

Lewis, C., & Prenzler, T. (1999). Civilian oversight of police in Australia. *Trends and Issues in Crime and Criminal Justice, 141*, 1–6.

Lum, C. M., & Koper, C. S. (2017). *Evidence-based Policing: Translating Research into Practice.* Oxford: Oxford University Press.

Lum, C., Telep, C. W., Koper, C. S., & Grieco, J. (2012). Receptivity to research in policing. *Justice research and policy, 14*(1), 61–95. https://doi.org/10.3818/JRP.14.1.2012.61

MacQueen, S., & Bradford, B. (2015). Procedural justice in practice: findings from the Scottish Community Engagement Trial (ScotCET). *Scottish Justice Matters, 3*(2), 11–12.

Madon, N. S., Murphy, K., & Sargeant, E. (2017). Promoting police legitimacy among disengaged minority groups: does procedural justice matter more? *Criminology & Criminal Justice, 17*(5), 624–642. https://doi.org/10.1177/1748895817692849

Mazerolle, L., Baxter, J., Cobb-Clark, D., Haynes, M., Lawrence, D., & Western, M. (2017). From Bench to Curbside: Considering the Role of Simulations in Scaling-up Justice Interventions. *Criminology & Public Policy, 16*(2), 501–510. https://doi.org/10.1111/1745-9133.12287

Mazerolle, L., Antrobus, E., Bennett, S., & Tyler, T. R. (2013a). Shaping citizen perceptions of police legitimacy: A randomized field trial of procedural justice. *Criminology, 51*(1), 33–63. https://doi.org/10.1111/j.1745-9125.2012.00289.x

Mazerolle, L., Bennett, S., Davis, J., Sargeant, E., & Manning, M. (2013b). Legitimacy in policing: A systematic review. *Campbell systematic reviews, 9*(1), i–147. https://doi.org/10.4073/csr.2013.1

Mazerolle, L., Bennett, S., Antrobus, E., & Eggins, E. (2012). Procedural justice, routine encounters and citizen perceptions of police: Main findings from the Queensland Community Engagement Trial (QCET). *Journal of experimental criminology, 8*(4), 343–367. https://doi.org/10.1007/s11292-012-9160-1

Martin, P., & Mazerolle, L. (2015). Police leadership in fostering evidence-based agency reform. *Policing: A Journal of Policy and Practice, 10*(1), 34–43. https://doi.org/10.1093/police/pav031

McCluskey, J. D., & Reisig, M. (2017). Explaining procedural justice during police-suspect encounters: A systematic social observation study. *Policing: An International Journal, 40*(3), 574–586. https://doi.org/10.1108/PIJPSM-06-2016-0087

McLeod, A., & Herrington, V. (2017). Valuing different shades of blue: From diversity to inclusion and the challenge of harnessing difference. *International Journal of Emergency Services, 6*(3), 177–187. https://doi.org/10.1108/IJES-04-2017-0021

Morton, P. J., Luengen, K., & Mazerolle, L. (2018). Hoteliers as crime control partners. *Policing: An International Journal, 42*(1), 74–88. https://doi.org/10.1108/PIJPSM-08-2018-0126

Murphy, K. (2004). The role of trust in nurturing compliance: A study of accused tax avoiders. *Law and Human Behavior, 28*(2), 187–209. https://doi.org/10.1023/B:LAHU.0000022322.94776.ca

Murphy, K., Murphy, B., & Mearns, M. (2010). *The 2007 Public Safety and Security in Australia Survey: Survey Methodology and Preliminary Findings.* Alfred Deakin Research Institute.

Nagin, D. S., Solow, R. M., & Lum, C. (2015). Deterrence, criminal opportunities, and police. *Criminology, 53*(1), 74–100. https://doi.org/10.1111/1745-9125.12057

Neyroud, P., & Weisburd, D. (2014). Transforming the police through science: The challenge of ownership. *Policing: A Journal of Policy and Practice, 8*(4), 287–293. https://doi.org/10.1093/police/pau048

Newman, M. (2018). *New Evidence from Queensland Police.* Society of Evidence Based Policing Conference: Ten evidence based discoveries that change the way you police. Milton Keynes.

Newman, M. (2019). Investigations Training: An experimental test of the effectiveness of the Introduction to Investigations course for general duties police officers. *Australia & New Zealand Society of Evidence Based Policing 2019 Conference.* Canberra.

Pawson, R., & Tilley, N. (1994). What works in evaluation research?. *The British Journal of Criminology, 34*(3), 291–306.

Pesta, G. B., Blomberg, T. G., Ramos, J., & Ranson, J. A. (2019). Translational criminology: Toward best practice. *American Journal of Criminal Justice, 44*(3), 499–518. https://doi.org/10.1007/s12103-018-9467-1

Platz, D., Sargeant, E., & Strang, H. (2017). Effects of recruit training on police attitudes towards diversity: a randomised controlled trial of a values education Programme. *Cambridge Journal of Evidence-Based Policing, 1*(4), 263–279. https://doi.org/10.1007/s41887-017-0019-6

Prenzler, T., & Mackay, P. (1995). Police gratuities: What the public think. *Criminal Justice Ethics, 14*(1), 15–25. https://doi.org/10.1080/0731129X.1995.9991985

Prenzler, T. (1997). Is there a police culture? *Australian Journal of Public Administration, 56*(4), 47–56. https://doi.org/10.1111/j.1467-8500.1997.tb02488.x

President's Task Force on 21st Century Policing (2015). *Final Report of the President's Task Force on 21st Century Policing.* Washington, DC: Office of Community Oriented Policing Services.

Ready, J., & Thompson, E. (2021). Bringing intelligence-led policing to crime hot spots: The logan experiment. *Queensland Police Service Strategic Tasking and Coordination Committee.* Brisbane.

Rojek, J., Martin, P., & Alpert, G. P. (2014). *Developing and Maintaining Police-Researcher Partnerships to Facilitate Research Use: A Comparative Analysis.* Springer.

Rojek, J., Martin, P., & Alpert, G. P. (2015). The challenges and promise to the future of partnerships. In *Developing and Maintaining Police-Researcher Partnerships to Facilitate Research Use* (pp. 61–75). Springer, New York, NY.

Rojek, J., Smith, H. P., & Alpert, G. P. (2012). The prevalence and characteristics of police practitioner-researcher partnerships. *Police Quarterly, 15*(3), 241–261. https://doi.org/10.1177/1098611112440698

Sahin, N., Braga, A.A., Apel, R., & Brunson, R.K. (2017). The impact of procedurally-just policing on citizen perceptions of police during traffic stops: the Adana randomized controlled trial. *Journal of Quantitative Criminology, 33*(4), 701–26. https://doi.org/10.1007/s10940-016-9308-7

Sampson, R. J., Winship, C., & Knight, C. (2013). Translating causal claims: Principles and strategies for policy-relevant criminology. *Criminology & Public Policy, 12*, 587.

Sherman, L. W., Strang, H., Barnes, G., Woods, D. J., Bennett, S., Inkpen, N., ... & Slothower, M. (2015). Twelve experiments in restorative justice: the Jerry Lee program of randomized trials of restorative justice conferences. *Journal of Experimental Criminology, 11*(4), 501–540. https://doi.org/10.1007/s11292-015-9247-6

Strang, H. (2012). Coalitions for a common purpose: managing relationships in experiments. *Journal of Experimental Criminology, 8*, 211–225. https://doi.org/10.1007/s11292-012-9148-x

Small, M. W., & Watson, R. C. (1999). Police values and police misconduct: the Western Australia Police Service. *The Police Journal, 72*(3), 225–237.

Stevenson, G. (2021). *The Blended Detective Training Program, Educating the digital age detective: Developing high performance police detectives through enhanced self-efficacy.* Doctoral dissertation, University of Queensland, Brisbane, Australia. https:doi.org/10.14264/d7581de

Sullivan, C. J. (2013). Enhancing translational knowledge on developmental crime prevention: The utility of understanding expert decision making. *Criminology & Public Policy, 12*, 343.

Tyler, T. R. (2003). Procedural justice, legitimacy, and the effective rule of law. *Crime and Justice, 30*, 283–357. https://doi.org/10.1086/652233

Weisburd, D. (2015). The law of crime concentration and the criminology of place. *Criminology, 53*(2), 133–157. https://doi.org/10.1111/1745-9125.12070

Weisburd, D., Mastrofski, S. D., McNally, A. M., Greenspan, R., & Willis, J. J. (2003). Reforming to preserve: Compstat and strategic problem solving in American policing. *Criminology & Public Policy*, *2*(3), 421–456. https://doi.org/10.1111/j.1745-9133.2003.tb00006.x

Westling, W. T., & Waye, V. (1998). Videotaping police interrogations: Lessons from Australia. *American Journal of Criminal Law*, *25*(3), 493.

Wilson, J. Q., & Kelling, G. L. (2017). The police and neighborhood safety Broken Windows. In *Social, Ecological and Environmental Theories of Crime* (pp. 169–178). Routledge.

Wortley, R., & Wimshurst, K. (2000). What's in a name? Perceptions of course names for criminal justice professionals. *Journal of Criminal Justice Education*, *11*(2), 267–278. https://doi.org/10.1080/10511250000084911

INDEX

Note: Page numbers in *italics* indicate figures, **bold** indicate tables and page numbers with "n" indicate notes in the text.